DIRTY DEALING

DIRTY DEALING

20 7717

GARY CARTWRIGHT

Atheneum New York 1984

Library of Congress Cataloging in Publication Data

Cartwright, Gary, ———
  Dirty dealing.

    1. Crime and criminals—Texas—El Paso—Case
studies. 2. Smuggling—Texas—El Paso—Case studies.
3. Murder—Texas—El Paso—Case studies. I. Title.
HV6795.E5C37 1984   364.1'523'0976496   81–69130
ISBN 0–689–11243–2

Published simultaneously in Canada by McClelland and Stewart Ltd.
Composition by Heritage Printers, Inc., Charlotte, North Carolina
Manufactured by Fairfield Graphics, Fairfield, Pennsylvania
Designed by Maria Epes
First Edition

FOR MALCOLM MCGREGOR

Contents

Illustrations

PART ONE

Requiem for Robin Hood

1

On the night before he was murdered, Lee Chagra flew home to El Paso flushed with the euphoria a gambler feels when he believes his luck is changing. Lee had been in Tucson trying a case for most of the past two weeks, and the verdict had been sublime: in a highly publicized multicount bank-fraud indictment, Lee had walked his man on every count. It was his most important victory in months—and his most profitable. It was three days before Christmas, 1978; when the Friday-night plane began its approach over the Upper Valley and through the Pass, he caught a glimpse of the lighted Christmas star on the slope of Mount Franklin.

1978 had been the worst year of Lee Chagra's life. Worse than 1973, the year the federal government indicted him on a trumped-up marijuana-trafficking charge in Nashville and nearly destroyed his law practice. Worse even than the chain reaction of disasters in 1977—the year one of his brother Jimmy's planes crashed trying to take off from a makeshift field in Colombia with a load of marijuana, an episode that foreshadowed the doom of the entire Chagra family. The shock waves of the crash and Jimmy's abortive rescue foray hit the front pages of newspapers across the Southwest at the precise time that Lee was making his own headlines, first with his successful defense of an associated ring of smugglers in Oklahoma, and then with his running courtroom battles with federal judge John H. Wood, Jr., and chief prosecutor James Kerr. The judge and the prosecutor were convinced that Lee Chagra was more than a good criminal attorney; they believed that he was in fact a master criminal, the boss of an elaborate gambling and drug-smuggling operation that stretched from El Paso to Miami to Boston. Reports leaked to newspapers by agents of the Drug Enforcement Administration (DEA)

3

hinted that Lee Chagra was a key figure in the Mafia, a Lebanese godfather with ties to such well-known organized crime fighters as Joe Bonanno, Sr., Raymond Patriarca, and Anthony "Tony the Ant" Spilotro. These reports turned out to be false, but by the time they were corrected Lee Chagra was dead, and so was Judge John Wood.

Lee had always lived on the edge of respectability, goading the El Paso establishment by defending hardened criminals, consorting with known drug smugglers, and cultivating his image as the Black Striker, the terror of the casinos of Las Vegas. Through it all, he had somehow clung to the central fact in his life—he *was* a topflight criminal attorney. But the years of fast living were catching up. His practice had foundered, not just because of the rumors but because he had lost his passion for the law, lost his edge. He had run up huge gambling debts and become addicted to cocaine. His life was peopled with shysters, thugs, and killers, and if the truth were known, Lee himself had become little more than a highly paid functionary in Jimmy's inchoate gang of smugglers. That's what really hurt—Lee had become one of Jimmy's drones.

For months Lee had been unable to shake the feeling that something uncontrollable had broken loose. The madness peaked in November, when two men in a van sprayed prosecutor James Kerr's car with buckshot and .30-caliber bullets. Federal agents showed up at Lee's office the following morning to question him about the unsuccessful assassination attempt. They even confiscated Lee's gun collection. Lee was mortified. "If someone had tried to kill me," he asked one FBI agent, "would you be questioning James Kerr?" He already knew the answer—the entire criminal investigative apparatus of the federal government had targeted Lee for extinction, and they wouldn't stop until they got him.

On the plane from Tucson, Lee sat next to a lawyer who worked for one of El Paso's establishment firms in one of the high-rise glass towers that dominated the downtown district of the border city. The lawyer mentioned that he sometimes looked down at the office complex that Lee was remodeling and experienced pangs of envy. "You've got everything I always dreamed of having," the lawyer said. Lee snorted with pride. The other lawyer couldn't appreciate the irony, but until that moment Lee had always envied *him*. The new office was a show of faith, or at least tenacity, and it made Lee feel good to know that someone else appreciated it. His staff had completed the move while he was in Tucson, and in the morning he would officially take possession. It would be his first day there and, as fate decreed, his last.

Jo Annie and two of their five children met Lee at the airport. They had a surprise for him—a new Lincoln limousine with a portable bar, a TV, a stereo, and even a secret compartment to conceal his guns and gambling paraphernalia. It was the perfect vehicle for the Black Striker; Lee hadn't been to Las Vegas more than once or twice since a disastrous fling a year earlier when he lost nearly a half million dollars; but when he returned, he would go in style. Jo Annie had bought the limousine on impulse. "After nineteen years of marriage," she said, "I wanted to do something crazy." She was a slender, attractive woman with the dark features and perfect creamed-coffee complexion shared by nearly all the Syrian women in El Paso. Lee's passions for women, gambling, and general recklessness would have destroyed most marriages, even among the Syrians and Lebanese, whose culture conditioned wives to this code, but Jo Annie's patience and love had forced it to endure.

Lee was so wired on cocaine that he hardly touched his dinner as he talked nonstop about the victory in Tucson. It had been months since anyone had seen him so animated. It was like old times.

Sometime in the middle of the night, after everyone else was asleep, Lee changed clothes and drove to his new office complex. At that hour there was little traffic along Mesa, and he stood on the street admiring the enormous oak door and the white Mediterranean wall that slanted up and away from the second-floor balcony connected to his private office. From the street you could see the palm tree and a corner of the balcony's striped awning. The only sign on the building was a small gold plaque with his name and occupation. The building might have contained a small, elegant restaurant, or a foreign embassy. Lee unlocked the door and walked upstairs to his office. He unlocked the door to his private bath. The money was where he had stashed it, in the canvas tennis bag under the sink. There was a steel floor safe sunk into five feet of concrete, but like the other safes in the complex, it hadn't yet been completely installed. Lee counted out $75,000 from the stash and slipped it into his coat pocket.

As he pulled off the exit ramp above the truck stop on IH 10, Lee could see the Indian's car parked in the shadows behind some eighteen-wheelers that idled in the predawn chill. The Indian brushed a strand of limp hair over his bald spot as he approached Lee's car. He wasn't a man most folks would care to meet in the dark—his face looked like forty miles of bad Mexican highway, and there was a .22 pistol under his stained leather jacket. Nevertheless, Lee trusted him. The Indian was always straight business. His current business included collecting debts for several Las Vegas casinos and doing odd jobs for various Mafia figures, including Joe Bonanno, Sr. Lee offered the Indian a hit of cocaine and joked as he counted off 750 $100 bills. The Indian mumbled something, studying his boots. That was it, the last of the half million the Black Striker had blown in Vegas. Lee drove home and slept like a baby.

Saturday was one of those perfect December days in El Paso when the desert air is so crisp you can hear it and the mountains loom out of blue shadows and change colors before your eyes. Loaves of Syrian bread were baking in the kitchen. From a radio in another part of the house, Sinatra was singing about doing it his way. The song was one of Lee's favorites. He washed his morning cocaine down with strong coffee and remembered the time he had met Sinatra, how genuine he appeared.

Lee had showered and was standing in front of the dresser mirror in his shorts when he heard the door chimes. That would be Vivian, Jimmy's ex-wife. Lee was expecting her. "Back here," he called from the bedroom. Vivian did her best to be cheerful. She knew that Lee had just come through many weeks of hard times, and she hated asking for money, but Jimmy was months behind in child-support payments. She had come to depend almost entirely on Lee—although she suspected that the money Lee gave her came from Jimmy anyway. She suspected that some of the money that was paying off Lee's new office complex and his gambling debts came from Jimmy too. At one time Lee had supported the entire Chagra family, but no longer. Vivian wasn't about to press Lee for details; nothing brought him down faster than the slightest hint that he might be beholden to his brother, even temporarily.

Lee seemed preoccupied, hardly aware that Vivian had entered the bedroom. He looked smaller than life as he stood there, facing the dresser, looking at a picture of his father and seeing his own reflection. Lee held the picture so it caught the morning light. "What's it all for?" he said out loud, and Vivian could see tears in his eyes. "He was up and down all his life . . . struggling . . . just barely making it.

Then he died." Vivian said she didn't know. She had put the same question to herself many times. For six years now she had been divorced from Jimmy, mostly alone, trying to make it with three children; sometimes things looked better and sometimes things looked worse, but they never really changed. All she had ever had was a future somewhat less than promising: Jimmy had given her a couple of kids (the third was from a previous marriage) and a lasting heartache. There was a line from *The Picture of Dorian Gray* that she liked to paraphrase: "I hope that when I die and go to hell, they deduct those four years I spent with Jimmy Chagra." She almost said it now, but the suffering in Lee's eyes cut her short.

"I'm sick and tired of being the fall guy," Lee said. She knew he was talking about Jimmy. Jimmy and his new wife, Liz, were in Las Vegas blowing unbelievable amounts of money. Jimmy had recently returned from Florida, and it wasn't hard to guess that his smuggling operation was thriving just as Lee's law practice crumbled. "Maybe it will get better," Vivian said. Lee kissed her and handed her the money.

By the time Lee finished dressing, Jo Annie had breakfast ready—freshly baked Syrian bread, butter, and a variety of fruit preserves. While Lee ate, Jo Annie puttered with the Christmas decorations. If she realized how pressed he had been for money in recent months, she didn't show it. Jo Annie's own family, the Abrahams, had considerable wealth, and she continued to collect antiques and preserve the family's life-style. The Lincoln limo was no more extravagant than anything else—Lee could lose what that cost in three minutes at a crap table. The gift was the sort of crazy impulse only a man like Lee could appreciate. It was her way of bending under the terrible strain of their marriage. In recent months the marriage had almost broken for good, but Jo Annie had always found a way to save it, some sort of gambit or dodge that prevented, however temporarily, the destruction of a union that neither was fully prepared to abandon. In a few years the children would be grown—the oldest, Terry, was eighteen, and the youngest, Joanna, was almost eleven.

Jo Annie knew about Lee's women—everyone in town knew. And she knew what people were saying about Lee's new office complex with its two fully furnished bedrooms. Almost everyone believed that Lee would be moving out of the family home on Frontera Road and into the master suite at the complex. Lee supervised every detail of the complex, just as he had their home on Frontera, including an almost identical security system of electronic locks and closed-circuit television monitors. Lee had called the home his "fortress," and now the same word applied to his office. Jo Annie thought of the elaborate security devices as another toy, like the new Lincoln, or the ebony walking stick with the satyr's-head gold handle that she'd had especially made for him—his Bat Masterson cane. The toys were part of the role-playing, which was Lee's way of bending.

This morning Jo Annie had another surprise, a block of tickets to the Sun Bowl football game between the University of Maryland and Lee's alma mater, the University of Texas. Lee had $15,000 riding on the outcome. He seemed pleased with the gesture but told Jo Annie there was some work he needed to do at the office—he would try to join the family by halftime. That's when Jo Annie remembered the telephone call.

"A man named David Long phoned before you woke up," she told him. "Something about a will, about some large estate in California? He needs you to look it over before he mails it back."

"David Long?" Lee didn't appear to recognize the name.

"It sounded like a black man," she said. "I told him you'd be in your office until about four o'clock." Jo Annie didn't know why she said four o'clock, except she hadn't really believed Lee would show up for the football game. She knew from experience that when Lee got with his gambling and doping buddies, time got away.

Jo Annie left the Sun Bowl in the middle of the third quarter. It was just after 2:00 P.M.: as she had suspected, Lee never showed. When she stopped by his office a short time later, she found him with a friend and client named Brian "Sailor" Roberts. They had been watching the game on television, and Lee was paying Roberts $15,000 as Jo Annie walked into the office. She had never liked Sailor Roberts, a well-known gambler and bookie, who at the time was under federal indictment for his activities, but Sailor was the sort of free spirit Lee enjoyed. Lee told her that he would be home in an hour or two. That was the last time Jo Annie saw him alive.

At 4:15, Diane Salome and several other old friends arrived unexpectedly at the Chagra home on Frontera Road. They told Jo Annie that Lee was dead, a bullet through his chest and lungs. When she heard the news, Jo Annie collapsed.

Joe Chagra, the youngest brother, who had practiced law with

Lee until the heat became unbearable, was the first to arrive at the office. Jimmy, the middle brother, was flying home from Las Vegas. Patsy, the only sister, heard the bells from St. Patrick's Cathedral two blocks north and thought of their mother, who would be returning from mass any minute, unaware of what had happened. Patsy ran down the stairs and toward the cathedral. An hour later, Jo Annie was at the scene, along with more than a dozen friends and members of the family. No one knew whom to blame, or what to do next.

2

El Paso and its sister city across the Rio Grande, Juárez, Mexico, form the world's largest border town, a valley of sinister warrens and glittering high-rises between two mountain ranges divided by a puny culvert called the Rio Grande. The Great River. From the slopes of Mount Franklin or Mount Cristo Rey it doesn't look so great: it looks as though a child could hop it. As an international boundary, the river is an absurd symbol, though a natural one: it is the reason for this place, and what happened here. You *can* wade it, and for that reason the 1.3 million who live in this poverty-stricken micro city-state have never identified with a common heritage or a negotiated one. They make it up as they go. They appear to go in slow motion, a mile a minute, night and day, creating a smoky delirium in which life is at the same time a bit more precious and a bit less. Some blame a natural tranquilizing agent in the water supply, but others believe it is the attitude of isolation and neglect. There is an almost comic-book somnambulism in the people's indifference to the laws of two nations, and in their attitude to time and place. But there is a chilling reality to this culture's fidelity to its own code.

Outsiders tend to forget the obvious—this is a pass, an *opening*. A collector of lost souls. It's as though nature provided a test rather than a convenience. Lost in a thousand square miles of desolation between the Chihuahuan Desert and the southern tip of the Rockies, the pass orders the terrain and dictates life. At either end are the fertile valleys that sustain the people, but rolling off in every direction are badlands so wild and rough they defy human experience. Even the names have a ring of finality—there is a waterless, trackless stretch between El Paso and Albuquerque that the Spanish called Jornada del Muerto, Journey of the Dead. Spaniards believed that the pass was the entrance to unbelievable riches, and generations have searched and died in this belief. El Paso–Juárez had thrived on mystique, greed, and corruption, but all of its promises were in the eyes of the beholder. You won't find the Seven Cities of Gold on the other side of the pass, you'll just find New Mexico.

The first European to stumble across El Paso del Rio Grande del Norte ("The Pass of the Great River of the North") was lost. The shipwrecked Spaniard Cabeza de Vaca had walked all the way from the Gulf of Mexico. The year was 1536, almost seventy years before the landing of the *Mayflower*. By 1580, Spanish expeditions were crossing the river at the old Frontera ford, close by the spot where Lee Chagra built his home four centuries later. Inspired by earlier successes in Peru and Mexico, and by the blue mountains of the pass, which seemed veined with precious metals, Spanish soldiers, slave traders, and explorers followed the river north, to Santa Fe and beyond. In time this route became known as the King's Highway. In 1659, the Spanish established a mission, Nuestra Señora de Guadalupe, on what is now one corner of the plaza in Juárez, and gradually the settlement of El Paso del Norte (now Ciudad Juárez) evolved on the south bank of the river. It was another two hundred years before anyone settled the north bank, in what is now El Paso, Texas.

Spanish law of the time prohibited foreign trade; then, as now, governments believed that laws could prevent the flow of goods and services across boundaries. In a way, this prohibition was the beginning of the end of Spanish rule in the southwestern part of the United States: merchants from St. Louis had blazed a trade route to Santa Fe, and during the Hidalgo Revolution in Mexico (1810–11) these merchants supported the insurgents, since victory would mean the opening of free trade. As the traders moved south along the river, El Paso fell under Anglo-American influence.

El Paso has always attracted a special breed—bounty hunters, gunslingers, fugitives, adventurers, gamblers, a variety of shady and desperate characters drawn by an ironic prospect of wealth: as history demonstrates, just about the only wealth is what they've been able to take from one another. At the time of the Civil War the population was 428; one-sixth of the Anglos were professional gamblers. Nobody bothered to count the number of smugglers, but since 1846, when the twelve hundred miles of river between El Paso and the Gulf of Mexico became the international boundary, smuggling has been a valid reason for El Paso's existence. Of the legendary tough towns of the old west—Dodge City, Tombstone, Deadwood, Cheyenne—only El Paso's wild reputation persists into the current century, a demonstration of the volatile chemistry in this mixture of races, cultures, and purposes.

Various reformers, almost always followed by and sometimes led by the city's newspapers, have tried to clean up El Paso since the turn of the century. When gambling was outlawed in 1904, the El Paso *Herald* reported that it continued to proliferate: the newspaper counted forty gambling houses and more than six hundred gamblers. A few years later the newspaper reorganized a reform movement, but it wasn't until 1934, when Texas Rangers raided casinos and houses of prostitution, that anything close to reform came to El Paso. The gamblers and hookers simply moved across the river to Juárez, of course. This had a severe impact on the El Paso economy, and inspired the publisher of the *Times* to join forces with the Baptist Association to form the Business Men's Protection Association. This association advocated closing the international bridge at 6:00 P.M. instead of midnight. Anyone caught in Juárez after dark was promised public exposure. The *Times*'s feud with sinners ended abruptly on September 4, 1931, when the First National Bank failed. The Great Depression gave people something else to occupy their attention; and, of course, gambling again proliferated.

Another business that shaped El Paso's character, and that endures in another form today, was scalp hunting—the "hair-and-ears business," they called it at its peak. Forty-niners were passing through, on their way to the gold fields of California, but many never made it any farther than El Paso; scalp hunting by Apaches and Comanches peaked that same year, 1849. In retaliation, the government of the Mexican state of Sonora revived the old Spanish custom of paying for Indian scalps, and that's when the light industry of collecting black hair emerged: a head of black hair was worth 100 pesos, no questions asked. El Paso del Norte became a center for the redemption of scalps, and, as historian C. L. Sonnichsen observed, "The efficiency of the Americans threw many good Mexicans out of work."

Detachments of soldiers, camel caravans, the Overland Mail, and finally the railroad helped El Paso prosper and grow, as did constant immigration. The city is a mosaic of cultures, languages, and ethnic pockets—Jews, Arabs, Germans, Czechs, Americans, Mexicans, Indians, Chinese, Mormons, Mennonites.

In the 1850s, the Army established a permanent post at Fort Bliss, now partly within the El Paso city limits, first to fight off Indians, later to protect American ranching and mining interests, and still later to train artillery crews and test missiles. This vast military complex, which includes Biggs Field, William Beaumont Army Medical Center, the U.S. Army Defense Command, and White Sands Missile Range, gives El Paso much of its present character, and along with the refining of copper and the manufacturing of boots and Western wear, helps support the present economy. Gambling and smuggling do the rest.

It is estimated that one out of every five households in El Paso–Juárez is supported by some type of illegal activity. A former director of El Paso Customs acknowledged: "If we stopped all smuggling activity right now, the economies of two cities would fall flat on their faces."

Millions of dollars' worth of goods are smuggled daily across the three main bridges connecting Juárez and El Paso, and millions more are walked across the hundreds of shallow fords. Drugs are currently in fashion, but over the years whiskey, cigarettes, perfume, Swiss watches, silver, electrical appliances, and, of course, laborers have been staples in the trade of the *fayuqueros* (smugglers). *Fayuqueros* from Mexico usually make two trips a week across the border, carrying about $10,000 worth of goods each way. When the items are small, such as bottles of American perfume or jewelry, the *fayuqueros* hire old women called *chiveras* (shepherds), who tote the merchandise across the bridge and as far as Chihuahua City, 236 miles into the interior. The *chiveras* are paid $45 to $65, depending on the size and value of the haul; out of that money they are expected to bribe the various Mexican customs officials, who survive on bribes, or *la mordida* ("the bite"). "These people used to steal," a Mexican policeman told the Associated Press recently, "but there is more money in contraband. Before, they ate beans and a little meat. Now they eat three meals a day and imported cheese. It's good business for everybody."

American authorities are less benign about these activities, especially when drugs are involved. Before the emergence of this country's drug culture, in the late 1960s, the federal government looked

on El Paso as a distant outpost, a place to send customs officers
who had fouled up somewhere else. "Getting sent to El Paso," said
a former officer of U.S. Customs, "was like getting exiled to Siberia."
Ever since the Nixon administration organized the Drug Enforcement Administration (DEA) and gave it all the responsibility for
shutting down the flow of drugs, El Paso has been the front line of
the war. The interplay of politics, greed, corruption, and well-mean-
ing zealotry, and the temptation of citizens of El Paso to get a piece
of the action, have given rise to an industry as rapacious as the
scalping of the previous century.

As a young attorney just starting his practice, Lee Chagra was
inextricably caught up in this industry, and in time so was every
member of his family.

3

Lee Chagra was the first college graduate in his family, and the first professional. He worked his way through the University of Texas law school, graduating fourth in his class in 1962. Lee Chagra was special, and he went out of his way to prove it: student court, law review, Order of the Coif. Some in the legal community thought he was too outspoken. A major Houston law firm that always invited the top six University of Texas law graduates to a spring gala invited only five in 1962. Some speculated that Lee Chagra was omitted because he was from El Paso and had a Spanish surname. (One old-time university professor referred to Lee as "the smartest Mexican I ever taught.") Most likely the law firm snubbed Lee because, as chief justice of the student court, he had spoken out against segregated dorms and football teams. When Lee was murdered sixteen years later, Charles Alan Wright, one of the country's leading authorities on constitutional law, called him "one of the few students who stand out in my memory."

The Chagras were fiercely proud people, a handsome, hardy, beguiling line of Lebanese military men, merchants, and vendors who migrated near the turn of the century to Mexico and then to El Paso. The family name was originally Busha'ada, but Lee's grandfather, Joseph Busha'ada, Mexicanized it during the revolution. The old man, who was a dead ringer for Pancho Villa, was imprisoned and almost shot before he and his family could escape across the border into El Paso.

Lebanese and Syrian families such as the Chagras, Abrahams, Farahs, Maloolys, and Salomes migrated through Mexico during one of the most turbulent times in modern history, a fact that partially explains their twisted destinies and romantic visions. The jour-

15

ney of the Chagra grandparents, Joseph and Marian Busha'ada, is described in family records and folk tales in terms of a classic love. Marian was to have married another man, a cousin whose family owned a thriving newspaper, but was disgraced on the morning of her wedding day when the bridegroom turned up drunk in the arms of the village harlot. Humiliated, her life in ruin, Marian fled Lebanon, intending to live with an older sister who had recently migrated to Mexico City. But Joseph Busha'ada, a young cavalry officer, followed her and convinced her of his love. They were married in Mexico City, at the chapel of the Shrine of Guadalupe. They could not have known much about the savagery and chaos that was breaking out around them, but when the bloody dictator Porfirio Díaz ordered the slaughter of more than two hundred protesters in front of the National Palace, Joseph and Marian joined the stream of refugees fleeing the capital for the north. There was the province of the revolutionary general and bandit Pancho Villa, a man Joseph Busha'ada apparently admired—the former Lebanese cavalry officer wore a sombrero and droopy mustache like Villa, and even though he was a noncombatant, twin pistols and bandoliers in the fashion of the insurgents of 1911. Marian was pregnant by now, and they traveled by train to Parral in the state of Chihuahua in the company of a ragtag assortment of refugees, peons, and fierce Yaqui Indians—desert rabble bent on joining Villa's Army of the North.

Shortly after their son, Abdou, was born, they moved farther north, arriving just in time for the Battle of Juárez. Joseph was arrested as a suspected *villaista* and taken to jail to await a firing squad. Marian, a resourceful and strong-willed woman who was twelve years older than Joseph, wrapped little Abdou in a blanket and headed for the German embassy, where she somehow secured three German passports. Joseph was released from jail, and that same night, while gunfire echoed from the sand dunes to the south, the Chagra family gathered their few possessions and crossed the unguarded bridge into El Paso. It was years before they got their citizenship straight, but in 1911 such formalities were usually disregarded.

Joseph Chagra worked at odd jobs and in time became a deputy lawman in El Paso County. Old-timers still remember the big man with the oval Mediterranean face, fierce dark eyes, and Villa mustache, sporting a sombrero and pearl-handled pistols. Later, Joseph opened a produce stand in the city market behind the courthouse,

16

and in time became a recognizable though not particularly successful presence in El Paso's growing Arab business community. Joseph gambled and took care of business, but no one doubted that Marian was the strength of the family. Years later, Marian discovered a fading silk handkerchief given her by the cousin who had disgraced her so long ago in Lebanon, and with typical singlemindedness she traced her cousin's family to an address in New York and sent them back the gift. Her aunt wrote in reply that while the family "hated for our little girls to marry outsiders," it appeared that Marian had done all right.

Joseph and Marian found themselves unable to have more children, so they lavished attention on Abdou. (Joseph had wanted to name the boy after himself, but Marian absolutely forbade this, pointing out that naming a first son for his father was bad luck among her people. Joseph gave in, not realizing that there wouldn't be a second son.) Abdou had the dark, brooding good looks that distinguished every member of the Chagra family. He was mild-mannered, passive, and anxious to please, a mediocre student, but a popular one—he stayed over an extra year at El Paso High School in order to serve as president of the student body.

Because of his natural shyness and the strict code that Arab families brought over from the old country, Abdou Chagra did not date until he was almost twenty-three. By then he was working full time in the produce market, gradually assuming responsibilities and preparing for the time when Joseph would retire.

While attending a funeral in 1935, Abdou Chagra ran into a beautiful young woman named Josephine Ayoub and fell madly in love. He had met Josephine some months earlier at the weekly picnic at the farm of Nick Abraham, one of El Paso's resident Arabs, but when he attempted to start a conversation, she turned away. Josephine's family had emigrated from Lebanon about the same time as his own, but Josephine was born in El Paso, not Mexico, which in the social strata of the times made a difference. Her family had prospered, founding the Border Tobacco Company and eventually purchasing an entire block of buildings on South El Paso Street, so near the river a person could throw a rock and hit Mexico.

Joseph Chagra also owned a piece of property on South El Paso Street, but lost it when heavy summer rains turned the lot into an island. While families such as the Ayoubs and Abrahams prospered

17

and prospered more, nature itself seemed to conspire against Joseph Chagra. Some families control their destinies, or appear to, but Joseph Chagra rode his like a wild beast.

Shortly after the accidental meeting at the funeral, Ayoub worked up nerve to ask Josephine for a date. She replied: "I can't go out with you unless you have intentions of marriage." Abdou gave this considerable thought: Josephine was trim and saucy and outspoken, yet remarkably pious; there was an intensity about her, a strength of will that must have reminded him of his own mother. Josephine's mother had been raised in a convent in the old country and had drilled her daughter in absolute obedience to the Roman Catholic Church and tradition. When Abdou told his mother what Josephine said, Marian was ecstatic. "What a good girl you have found!" Marian said. Joseph was equally elated: more than anything else the aging couple wanted grandchildren.

Arrangements for the wedding were made and formalized at an elaborate two-family dinner at which Marian personally placed the ring on Josephine's finger. The Ayoubs wanted a long engagement, at least a year, but Marian was adamant in her resolve that the young people be married soon as possible. "Waiting is bad luck," Marian said.

Five months later, in a ceremony attended by most of the Arabs in El Paso, Abdou and Josephine were married at St. Patrick's Cathedral, where, forty-three years later, last rites would be said for their first son. Ninety-three Lebanese and Syrian families and a large assortment of Mexicans, Jews, and Anglos witnessed the 7:00 A.M. wedding and mass, then stayed around for breakfast, lunch and dinner. It was almost 3:00 A.M. when the party began to break up and the young couple caught a train for Los Angeles. Josephine Chagra still had vivid memories of the honeymoon at the Coconut Grove and at Santa Catalina Island.

It would be impossible to exaggerate the excitement that the birth of Lee Ayoub Chagra caused two years later, or the love and attention lavished on him by the two families. "He was *it*!" Josephine recalled. "The big shot! The brightest, best, smartest. He memorized his nursery-rhyme book before he was three!" Lee was literally the "King of Babies," crowned by the Santa Fe Railroad Conductors Association, at old Joseph's insistence. Years later tinted photographs of Lee in his tiny velvet robe, staff, and cardboard crown stood in prominent places in the homes of the Chagras.

Abdou and Josephine, encouraged by the grandparents, planned to have at least five more children, but the family doctor told her another pregnancy wasn't possible. Still, Josephine prayed for more children. She attended mass every morning and promised that she would climb the cathedral steps on her knees if God allowed her another child. Abdou made his own promise, vowing to walk barefoot to the top of the most prominent peak in the pass, Mount Cristo Rey. Even old Joseph got a touch of religion, swearing that he would offer the church the baby's weight in silver dollars. Then one morning as Josephine was washing dishes, she experienced unaccountable but unmistakable pains of labor—she had discounted symptoms of pregnancy, and hence described the event as "a miracle." Joseph and Abdou rushed her to the hospital, where the pain was diagnosed as a tubular pregnancy. That morning, Patsy, the Chagra's "miracle baby," was born. And that afternoon, Abdou, who had bad feet anyway, stumbled up the peak overlooking Juárez, El Paso, southeastern New Mexico, and northeastern Mexico, and kissed the feet of the statue of the Virgin.

Four years later, following several miscarriages, a second son was born. The Chagras named him Jamiel Alexander, called Jimmy, or sometimes "Little Mischief." Two years after that a third son, Joseph Salim, was born, though old Joseph did not live to see his namesake. Abdou lived to see Lee graduate from law school, and witnessed the marriages of Lee, Patsy, and Jimmy. His final dream was to live long enough to see the youngest, Joe, graduate from law school and share a practice with Lee, but Abdou didn't quite make it.

Josephine lived to see Lee murdered, and Jimmy and Joe serving long prison terms.

4

There was never any doubt that when Lee Chagra passed the state bar examination he would join Sib Abraham, who had finished law school the previous year and already set up his practice in El Paso. The Abrahams had accumulated considerable wealth buying and selling property, and Sib had completed law school without facing the financial struggle that had been such a challenge for Lee. Now he had his own offices in the Cables Building, which was owned by his wife Margaret's family. Some members of the Chagra family resented the Abrahams, resented the fact that they had supported and bankrolled their son, but not their son-in-law, though everyone understood that according to Arabic tradition, when a girl married, she broke all ties with her own family for the first year, symbolizing her obedience to the will of her husband. Lee probably wouldn't have accepted money from his in-laws, even if it had been offered. But starting as Sib Abraham's law partner was another matter.

Jo Annie Abraham grew up in the highly traditional Syrian Orthodox Church. The stern voices of the old priests and cantors still chanted nasal Arabic rituals through the heavy smoke of incense, and marrying outside the church was, until recent times, as unthinkable as divorce. Things had changed since her grandmother's time, when marriages were always arranged by the family, but many of the customs and traditions remained. There was still a strong sense of community and self-preservation for the race. Arab men were expected to be frugal, hard-driven, possessive, and passionately moralistic about their families. They were inclined by tradition to be devilmay-care about almost everything else—wenching and gambling were as much a part of their culture as, say, rodeoing and beer-drinking were for Anglo-Americans. Arab women were strong and assertive in all matters relating to home and family, and learned at an early age to be submissive in other respects: Syrian women were expected to live their lives on pedestals, above common traffic. Jo Annie (the name was pronounced in the Spanish fashion, "Jo Aynay") once told Jimmy's first wife, Vivian, "The secret is to treat your man so well that he doesn't realize he can do without you."

Jo Annie and Lee had been close since they were teenagers, and everyone knew they would marry. When she first met Lee he was a skinny kid with jug ears and a slightly daffy look, working for 50 cents an hour in Abdou's produce market. Even then there was something special about him—those spectacularly dark eyes and a smile so radiant it seemed to fly off his face. Lee founded his own high school gang, called the Gentz, and designed their logo, a skull and crossbones. The other boys called him Batman, because, even then, he operated best after dark. The Gentz wore ducktails and blue suede shoes and bopped as they walked, as though Little Richard were howling "Great Balls of Fire!" down the halls of their brains. They bet on everything—poker, bowling, how many birds might light on a high line. "They excelled," Jo Annie recalled. "They either won big, or got beat bad. None of them seemed to ever have much money, but they'd bowl for two hundred dollars a match. Lee never did anything halfway—he always made things exciting."

Lee's sister, Patsy, remembered that Lee was the defender of the underdog. He loved the streets and the people who took refuge in doorways, and he was ready to fight or give away his last dollar. He defended Patsy from gangs of Mexican toughs, and sometimes from the family itself: Abdou and Josephine were furious when they learned that Patsy was dating a Mexican boy, Rick de la Torre, but Lee supported her, and when Patsy married the boy a few years later Lee made certain that Rick was accepted into the family. "Being Lee's little sister made me feel very special," Patsy said. "When he married Jo Annie, I cried my eyes out. I felt like I'd lost him." Lee used to tell Patsy and Jimmy, and later Joe, "Remember, you're not better than anyone else, but you're sure as hell not worse." High school friends recall how when a bunch of them got arrested after their celebration of a football victory tore up the lobby of the Hotel Cortez, Lee went alone to the police station to protest. Naturally, he got arrested too. "He may have decided right then that he wanted to be a lawyer," Jo Annie said.

After high school Lee and Jo Annie separated for a time. Her family sent her to North Texas State in Denton, seven hundred miles or more from El Paso, while Lee enrolled at Texas Western (now called the University of Texas at El Paso). Texas Western was only a few blocks from the old Chagra home in Sunset Heights, just across the highway from the river. It was a fairly good school, but mainly it was all the Chagras could afford; and it was all Lee could handle. He graduated near the bottom of his class, in 1959. He passed the University of Texas Law School entrance exam by one point. The day after Lee graduated, he and Jo Annie married.

Maybe it was the novelty of marriage, or maybe it was because he was away from home for the first time and appreciated the sacrifice that his family had made; but Lee suddenly settled down after he and Jo Annie moved to Austin. He attacked the problems of law school with the same energy and passion he had once displayed for sports and wagering. They found a small apartment near the law school, and Lee studied constantly. Money was tight, of course. Lee graded papers for extra money, and his parents sold most of their property to support the young couple. For the first—and last—time in his life, Lee Chagra counted pennies. "We saw a movie maybe once a month," Jo Annie recalled. "I learned fifty different things to do with hamburger meat. Every week we'd get a package from home— some Syrian bread and maybe a roast chicken that arrived by bus. I got pregnant and Lee bought a boxer puppy to protect me. The puppy cost twenty-five dollars, which we couldn't afford. Lee named him Regal and trained him. The dog was our entertainment."

Teresa Lynn (Terry) was born in 1960. Christina Maria (Tina) was born two years later, about a month after her father astonished many people by graduating fourth in his law class at the University of Texas. Only after he passed the bar exam did Lee Chagra permit a real celebration, a short trip to Las Vegas. Only once in those years at law school had Lee felt compelled to gamble. "He lost forty dollars—that was two weeks' grocery money—playing golf," Jo Annie said. She hoped her husband was cured of his old addiction, but she made no big deal of it. Lee was going to do what he was going to do.

Back in El Paso, Lee and Jo Annie made a down payment on a house at the base of the foothills, on Santa Anita Street, across the street from where Dad and Mom and the younger Chagras were living. Later, when Abdou died, Patsy and her husband, Rick de la

22

Torre, moved into the family home, and Mom moved into an apartment at the rear of the house. Still later, Jimmy and Joe and their wives bought homes on the same street. Until Lee and Jo Annie finally built their fortress on Frontera Road in the Upper Valley, no member of the family lived more than half a block from the others.

In less than a year the new law partnership of Chagra and Abraham had a reputation as a steadfast defender of El Paso's downtrodden. The partners volunteered for every hardcore criminal case that came along—murder, rape, robbery, burglary. In those days lawyers weren't paid for court-appointed cases; it cost them money to stay in business, but the publicity made it a good investment. Sib Abraham remembered that they were "very *very* successful." The partnership went almost four years before losing a case. That first defeat was a signal case for much that would follow in El Paso. It was also two young lawyers' first encounter with a new type of federal weapon, the use of agents provocateurs, whose job it was to create crime. An unsuspecting El Paso café owner had been conned by two agents into conspiring to buy stolen government weapons. The weapons existed only in the agents' imagination, but at one point the trap got so bizarre that the poor café owner believed he was negotiating for a used submarine. "At first the whole thing seemed ludicrous," Sib Abraham said. "But as soon as we walked into that federal courtroom with all its rigidity and decorum, things got very serious. Fortunately, we had a good judge who saw through it and gave our man probation." But it was a new ball game in El Paso—over the next few years every criminal defense attorney in town encountered cases in which citizens had been lured into crimes by what amounted to federal bounty hunters. Anytime an agent decided to target someone, rules of fair play were suspended; the target, regardless of the facts, was predoomed. As the Drug Enforcement Administration assigned greater numbers of young zealots and motivated them with strict quotas, the game became deadly. Wayne Windell, who graduated in the same law class with Lee Chagra, recalled that when he moved to El Paso, a veteran attorney warned him: "Leave the drug cases alone. When a DEA agent gets in heat, you can find yourself floating face down in an irrigation ditch." Indeed, the night after Windell won an acquittal for two defendants in a heroin case, he got his first of several death threats.

Chagra and Abraham were among the few lawyers in town willing to touch drug cases. Lee took enormous pride in his Robin Hood image. He told prosecutors, "Be good to my client or, come the revolution, we won't spare you." This was a joke, of course, but in Lee's mind there *was* a revolution stirring. Lee adopted a wardrobe suitable to his image—a black cowboy hat, fancy handmade boots, and an assortment of expensive jewelry, including a gold bracelet that spelled the word FREEDOM. He had several of the bracelets made for close friends and family, and the word became his trademark. Jo Annie gave him an ebony cane with a gold satyr's-head handle, modeled after the cane Bat Masterson carried in the television series, and it too became part of his image. Fighting seemingly hopeless causes became his passion. Part of the reason was his honest conviction that even the lowest, meanest, rottenest scum on the face of the earth deserved, and in fact was guaranteed, a fair trial. Part of it was his natural loathing for the enormous power of government agencies. Part of it was the publicity: Lee loved to see his name in headlines, at least until the headlines turned nasty. Part of it was his steadily increasing need for money. "I take from the rich, reward myself handsomely, and give to the poor," he said. Part of it was paranoia, his gut instinct that some malevolent authority was out of control, watching and waiting and preparing his destruction. And part of it was the sort of perverse obstinacy that makes some men walk through a wall rather than open a door.

5

On the way to Las Vegas, Lee had them roll the chartered Learjet just to prove the orange juice wouldn't spill. God, he loved it! They all did. Forty thousand feet above the desert, smooth as the surface of a crap table. By the late 1960s the casino was picking up Lee's expenses—hotel room, meals, drinks, even the Learjet was complimentary for selected high rollers like Lee Chagra. They could already see the blur of lights on the horizon.

"Tell me one more time," Ray Ramos asked. "If we're all so broke, why are we going to Vegas?"

"Because we are all so broke," Lee said, and Ramos laughed so hard he spilled his drink.

If it was a crime to love the fast lane, Lee Chagra was guilty. He had an affinity for cards and dice, for dope dealers and shady politicians and nightclub singers, for dabblers in the black market and exponents of the fast buck. They were *all* scammers, everyone he knew or cared about.

His customary traveling companions on these junkets to Vegas were his oldest friends—Ray Ramos, an ex-cop turned lawyer, Jimmy Salome, a boyhood friend who had prospered in insurance and real estate and owned a fancy house next door to Lee and Jo Annie on Frontera Road, and Clark Hughes, son of a diplomat, a lawyer who eventually tired of the rat race and got himself appointed county judge at law. They were all pretty good gamblers with reputations and lines of credit in most of the big casinos in Vegas, but Lee was more than merely a player: he was what they called a "striker," a gambler literally capable of winning the casino. Money was something else to Lee, a coin of another realm.

They hadn't traveled by chartered jet seventeen years ago—they had made it across the desert in an old junker that wouldn't have sold for four bus tickets. They each had $500, and Lee arranged credit for another $500. When that was gone, Lee found a check-cashing service that charged only 20 percent interest. "Hell, man," Salome had said, "that ain't money management. We give them four hundred dollars to get three-twenty?" Someone else suggested that they pile back in the junker and head for El Paso. "You're all full of shit!" Lee roared indignantly. "We can't go home now." Lee put $300 on the front line at the crap table and rolled a seven. In a few minutes he had run it to $8,000. At that point they decided to split it up. "I pissed mine away," Salome recalled. "Lee ended up winning forty thousand dollars."

They were all struggling in those days, but anytime they got a few bucks they went to Vegas. In some ways they were still struggling—when you had the addiction the way Lee did, there was never enough action. More than once Lee had to borrow money to pay the salaries of his office staff. Sometimes he had to borrow money just to buy lunch. One Thursday, after borrowing $5,000 from another lawyer and writing a bad check for $20,000, which his brother-in-law Rick de la Torre could cover at the bank where he worked until Monday, Lee chartered a plane to Vegas and ran it to $200,000. He won so much the Aladdin couldn't cover it and had to borrow from Caesar's. Lee hadn't just beat the Aladdin, he had humiliated it. But the money was nothing. It was the action Lee loved. He gave Salome ten white chips ($5,000) just to roll the dice for him. When Clark Hughes got a little loaded and dropped $4,500, Lee took it on himself to go to the cage and pay off his friend's marker. He didn't even mention it to Clark.

Lee was always looking for an angle to make money, and his friends were constantly being sucked into his latest brainstorm. They had invested in a racehorse that ended up as dog meat, a pro golfer who never made the cut, a combination lock that served to secure nothing more than a long, bitter lawsuit, and a caper to corner the Colombia coffee market in a year when torrential rains drowned the crop.

"Lee was funny about investing money," Jimmy Salome recalled. "Unless he could foresee a lot of money somewhere down the line, he wasn't interested. He was a terrible businessman, but he had a certain genius for analyzing stock. The trouble was, things never moved at the right time." Salome recalled the time Lee was hot to buy controlling interest in Caesar's World, Inc. Stock was selling at the time for $3 a share. Lee figured that if he could raise $1.5 million, he could take control. He approached Salome, Clark Hughes, and others, but no one was willing to take such a large risk. "It seemed so farfetched at the time," Salome said. "If we had done it, of course, we'd all be multimillionaires by now." Lee confessed once to Clark Hughes that his dream was to stash away $20 million, all taxes paid. Then he would lose it all and start again.

Another old friend, Clarence Moyers, marveled at Lee's frenetic pace, and the tangle of contradictions that snarled everything and everyone in his life. Lee was a fanatic about his family—he could be incredibly extravagant, lavishing gifts on his wife, his children, his mother, his sister—yet he could risk the family's last penny on a roll of the dice. He was a confirmed pacifist, and yet he seemed comfortable around violence. He could be shamelessly sentimental and gentle as a whisper, and yet there was a fury inside that could make him turn on those closest to him. He referred to all his male friends as "brother," and yet there was a time when he couldn't keep his hands off his real brothers' wives and girlfriends. Gambling and women were a sickness with him, and recklessness was a painkilling drug. "He was like a circus performer spinning platters and making them balance on poles," said Clarence Moyers. "He'd have ten platters going at the same time, and while the first one was slowing down and about to fall, he'd be trying to get number eleven started."

Lee didn't usually bring Jo Annie on these junkets to Vegas—gambling was man's work—but the times that he did were indelibly marked on her memory. She thought that one of the pinnacles of their life together was the night at Caesar's when Lee won $260,000. Even in the flash and clamor of the casino, Jo Annie could hear the dice and sense the spell. She could hear blood running through her veins: it was as if this moment were happening in some other place, to some other group of people, as though she were suspended in some warm, ethereal constellation where she alone was privy to the God-given grace of man. Lee kept rolling the dice, one point after another, shuffling the stacks of $500 red chips like a mad magician, faster than the eye could register, rolling and snapping his fingers and carrying on a line of prattle with the pit boss. Terry, their oldest, was at her daddy's right hand, and so was Lee Jr.—the Chagra girls called him Leader. Lee motioned for Jo Annie to light him a fresh cigarette, and Jo Annie could barely comprehend that the jeweled hand reaching for the gold lighter was her own. "I can do this forever!" Lee said in that special manic way. He owned this night; they all did.

When he lost, of course, Lee was a truly pathetic sight, yelling and blaming fate and going half crazy until she put her arms around him and admitted it was her fault from the start—there was very little Jo Annie would not have done to spare Lee this agony. And yet Jo Annie knew when something in their love died. It happened in the summer of 1969, shortly after she gave birth to their fifth and final child, Jo Anna. Doctors discovered lumps in both of Jo Annie's breasts. What should have been a time for rejoicing was instead one of sorrow when Jo Annie was forced to undergo a mastectomy. There was no way to calculate how the mastectomy affected the marriage, but there was no question that it did. Patsy de la Torre remembered that her brother experienced uncontrollable feelings of anxiety and guilt. "Lee kept saying over and over, why *her?* Why not *me?*" Patsy recalled. "He kept saying that he was the one who was no good, the one who should be punished." Jo Annie had to know that the operation impaired the physical strength of their love, even though Lee tried to assess and rationalize what had happened. "If I had lost one of my legs," he asked her, "would you love me any less?" He was at her side almost constantly during those fearful days. He would force a smile and, with his eyes half closed in that comic-romantic way he had of mocking his own feelings, he would sing to her. Lee couldn't carry a tune, but it would break your heart to hear him try.

The last eight years of their marriage consisted of more lows than highs. It wasn't too long after the operation that Jo Annie received a telephone call from one of Lee's former secretaries, who swore that Lee loved her and had promised to take her away. Lee had apparently promised the secretary all sorts of things—a new car, a new home, jewelry, "everything that Jo Annie has." Another secretary who knew about the affair said: "Lee never meant it, of course. You know what he bought her as a going-away gift? A boob job!" Nevertheless, that telephone call brought out a new side of Jo Annie, a rage none of the family had previously seen. "She's gone absolutely crazy," Lee told his youngest brother, Joe. Lee was actually worried that Jo Annie might do him harm, and he disarmed all of his guns and hid them in new places. That summer Lee and Jo Annie packed the children into a station wagon and took a vacation to California, but Lee told his brother Joe the trip was a total nightmare.

6

As drug laws were tightening and enforcement was expanding in the late 1960s, the lawyers in El Paso noticed a seeming contradiction: the drug *business* also expanded. As did their own. It was a phenomenon that sociologists call the "crime tariff syndrome": heat from the law drives up the price, thereby attracting a new and smarter element of criminal. In 1968, it occurred to Lee Chagra and Sib Abraham that they could make a lot more money if they dissolved their partnership and struck out on their own.

Lee had just moved into a new office across from the courthouse when he became acquainted with a personable young marijuana trafficker named Jack Stricklin, Jr. Clark Hughes had warned: "One of the problems with being a criminal attorney is that all your clients are crooks. If you're not careful, your friends become crooks, too." There was no way Chagra could have known it at the time, but his friendship with Stricklin would lead to a string of cases that would make Lee one of the most famous—or most infamous—figures in the state of Texas.

Although still in his twenties, Stricklin was one of the pioneers in local drug-trafficking circles. Strickin grew up in one of the better sections of town and was selling lids when they were still lids—an ounce of marijuana in a Prince Albert tin. Stricklin's father, Jack Sr., was vice-president of El Paso Natural Gas, and Jack Jr. was a typical upper-middle-class boy, pampered, rebellious, and constantly seeking his identity in acts of bravado. The family sent him away to Allen Military Academy, which in those days must have been a good training ground for the marijuana trade: years later when Jack was doing a stretch at La Tuna Federal Correctional Institution, he counted seven other Allen Academy graduates among the prison population.

"There was a progression to the business," Stricklin remembered. "First, you started smoking. Then you'd buy three ounces and sell two. You got educated in economics. You had a solid product, and there was no float involved. You dealt in cash; no books, no checks. It was the greatest experience in free enterprise a kid could have. After a while you started crossing the river with it. The river is what made El Paso special. Without the river waders of El Paso, there would have been no Colombia, no Florida, no Panama. It all started here, on the river."

Stricklin served a few years in the Navy, part of it in the brig for selling grass. His family never knew about the incarceration, and when Jack was discharged his father gave him a new Jeep and money for college. "Somehow I never made it back to school," he said. "Four days later that Jeep was crossing the river. We'd load up in downtown Juárez or out on the highway somewhere. We were muling [transporting other dealers' purchases] for ten percent of the load in those days. We'd lid it and sell it and get new equipment and go back for another load. We didn't even bother hiding it back then. There were no secret compartments. It just took guts."

By the time Lee Chagra met him, Stricklin commanded a small army of smugglers. They used airplanes, trucks, sophisticated two-way radios, night-vision devices, decoy plants, and any other paraphernalia that was useful. Stricklin's group sometimes worked with other groups, not the least of which was the so-called Columbus Air Force, a band of former military pilots who operated from a small airstrip in Columbus, New Mexico. Another group operated from an isolated ranch (sometimes called "the old smuggler's home") in the Gila Wilderness, near the New Mexico–Arizona border. The groups were often interchangeable, as this pilot flew that mission and this contact alerted that distributor; it was a small miracle that the money usually drifted back into the right hands, though sometimes it didn't. There was one group, however, that no self-respecting scammer would touch—an organization headed by teenage badass named Georgie Taylor. Georgie was an Abraham—his mother was Jo Annie's aunt— and he became a local legend by making $1 million before his eighteenth birthday. Georgie Taylor was a heroin addict who sometimes worked with another addict named Tom Pitts, the reputed dope czar of middle Tennessee. By coincidence, Jack Stricklin also worked with Pitts, though he knew nothing about Pitts's connection to Georgie Taylor. Through this convoluted association of gangs, free lancers, rivals, and turncoats, Jack Stricklin was first brought to Lee Chagra's attention. It was also through this association that Lee was brought to the attention of every narcotics agent in the Southwest.

The string of cases started in the fall of 1971 when U.S. Customs agents busted Pitts and two other men who were attempting to bring six hundred pounds of marijuana across the Rio Grande. Pitts called Jack Stricklin to ask the name of a good lawyer. Stricklin knew Lee only by reputation. "I'd grown up in El Paso," Stricklin recalled. "I didn't trust Arabs. But everyone said Lee was the best." Pitts and the two others arrived at Lee's office looking like hippies who had just crawled out of a Goodwill box, but acting like owners of a seat on the New York Stock Exchange. Pitts's case was already set in the court of federal judge Ernest Guinn, who ran the federal system of justice in El Paso in the manner of a feudal lord. A number of attorneys flatly refused to try cases in Guinn's court, and Lee was threatening to refuse. Lee laid out the cold hard facts to Pitts and the others: "I can't save you. You're going to get five years each. You'll do at least eighteen months. And I'm going to charge you ten thousand dollars."

Lee meant $10,000 for all three defendants, but Pitts didn't understand that. Pitts fancied himself a big-timer and concluded that Chagra must be pretty big himself if he was demanding thirty grand. The Tennessee dope dealer rolled down his sock and slapped the cash on Lee's desk. Lee didn't say anything. He just picked up the money and tossed it in a drawer. But his mind was reeling, and his eyes spun like a blur of cherries on a slot machine.

It took Lee less than half a day to discover that the search warrant used to bust the Tennessee smugglers was faulty. Case dismissed. Soon every drug dealer on the border carried one of Lee Chagra's cards. Many of them began depositing large sums in the lawyer's safe, against the inevitable. Chagra and Jack Stricklin became close friends and partners in something they called BHS Enterprises, an "import-export" business that narcotics agents believed was used mainly to launder money from smuggling operations. "I never could prove it," said DEA agent J. T. Robinson, "but I'll always be convinced that Lee became godfather to Stricklin and those young smugglers. He certainly had access to their money." Lee Chagra grossed more than $250,000 in 1972. The next year he paid taxes on $450,000, including $125,000 declared as gambling winnings. That was the year Lee and Jo Annie started building their new home on Frontera Road in the Upper Valley. The fortress was 6,500 square feet, with pool and stables, electronically operated gates, and closed-circuit television monitors. Lee sometimes referred to it as "the fortress that Jack built."

Lee must have thought he had struck gold, but quicksand would be closer to the truth. Fifteen hundred miles from El Paso, the heroin addict, Tom Pitts, had been arrested for another drug transaction and was sweating in a federal isolation cell. Pitts was eager to talk, but so far he hadn't found a subject that interested the agents. When he mentioned the name Lee Chagra, however, he got everyone's attention. Pitts described how he and another dealer had once used Lee's office to negotiate a deal. Yes, Lee had received a commission. As it turned out, this was a lie, but it got Pitts off the hook for a time. Even as Lee and Jo Annie were moving into their new home on Frontera, a grand jury in Nashville was handing down secret indictments charging Lee and forty others with conspiring to import and distribute marijuana.

On the morning of June 20, 1973, a team of narcotics agents appeared at Lee's law office with a warrant for his arrest and hauled him away in irons. Stunned and bewildered, totally in the dark about what the charges were, Lee found himself being shuffled from jail to jail like the criminals he had made a reputation defending. Here he was, thirty-eight years old, one of the brightest and most respected attorneys in Texas, inexplicably handcuffed to his wife's punk nephew, Georgie Taylor. Jack Stricklin and some of his people, such as Mike Halliday and Johnny Milliorn, were also caught in the web, as were a number of others Lee had never met or heard of. It was too ludicrous for words. Late that afternoon, Lee was hauled before U.S. magistrate Jamie Boyd, an acquaintance who sometimes dropped by Lee's office to discuss local politics. Jo Annie appeared at the federal courthouse with $50,000, but Boyd ruled that it was too late in the day to post such a large cash bond: Chagra was forced to endure the night in a jail cell with virtually the entire hierarchy of El Paso drug trafficking. Newspapers across the South billed it as the largest drug bust in the history of Nashville, Tennessee, a city Lee had never even visited.

The indictment was so vague as to make it impossible to respond, much less contemplate a defense. Lee's lawyers, Sib Abraham and Bill Marchiondo of Albuquerque, filed more than 150 motions demanding that the prosecution get specific, but there was little response from the government. The lawyers filed five additional motions demanding that the government either respect the defendants' rights to a speedy trial or drop the charges, and still there was no response. Over the next twelve months prosecutors did dismiss charges against about half of the original defendants, but in the case against Lee Chagra they refused to budge.

The case dragged on for nearly two years. When charges against Lee were finally dropped, the media reported that it was for lack of a speedy trial. In fact, the charges were dismissed because there was no evidence to bring charges in the first place. A scathing memorandum written in March 1975 by Judge Frank Gray, Jr., chief judge of the Middle District of Tennessee, declared the indictment to be "obviously and fatally defective"; that it was "so worded as to be utterly meaningless, and, therefore, the indictment actually charged nothing at all." Judge Gray went out of his way to rebuke DEA agents and federal prosecutors, declaring that the restraints on the defendants' liberty and the "cloud of anxiety, suspicion, and often hostility" under which they were forced to live for two years violated basic principles of justice. Much later, Lee Chagra learned that the single piece of evidence against him was a statement made by the addict, Tom Pitts.

"The publicity almost wrecked Lee's law career," recalled Joe Chagra, the youngest brother, who by this time had joined the law firm. "Hardly anyone wanted a lawyer who was under indictment." Even after the charges were dismissed, there was still the stigma: Lee was just one who got away on a technicality. Thereafter, when the local papers wrote about Lee, the stories invariably started with "Indicted drug trafficker Lee Chagra ... "

Lee never forgot or forgave. His hatred for narcotics cops, particularly agents provocateurs, became a rage that consumed both his private and professional life. He began taping most of his telephone conversations and collecting every scrap of evidence that even hinted of government malfeasance. "It's just me versus the whole

United States of America," he told friends, and the friends knew Lee wasn't joking. He filed a freedom-of-information request demanding that the government furnish him with all documents relating to its investigation of him, and before long the files filled two heavy-duty storage boxes. The documents revealed that hardly a week passed without some agent making inquiries into Lee Chagra's private life. His office and home telephone records from as far back as 1968 had been subpoenaed, and so had his income tax records. Almost all of Chagra's clients who had been sent to prison reported visits from DEA agents who pumped them for information about Chagra and offered deals for incriminating him. From time to time agents provocateurs posing as clients came to his office to discuss a phony case and ended up trying to work a drug deal through him. Lee developed a standard ploy: he secretly taped these conversations, then gave the agent the phone number of "the real Mr. Big." It was the unlisted home number of the local DEA chief.

7

In 1969 the Nixon administration declared war on drugs. The declaration amounted to a lot more than the war, however; and, paradoxically, it amounted to a lot less. The problem Nixon was really addressing wasn't so much drugs as it was the forthcoming congressional elections. Until then, the much-heralded law-and-order administration had done little to reduce crime, for which Nixon and his attorney general, John Mitchell, blamed the courts, the Congress, and the entrenched bureaucracies of government. What they needed to shift the blame was a highly visible issue, a crisis, even an epidemic. G. Gordon Liddy suggested drugs.

Liddy's credentials in this area were based almost entirely on the fact that as a crusading, gun-toting assistant DA in Poughkeepsie, New York, he had led a highly publicized raid on the headquarters of LSD guru Timothy Leary in nearby Millbrook. Freely mixing myths, Liddy compared the raid to "the enraged Transylvanian townfolk storming Dr. Frankenstein's castle." On a local level, Liddy had accumulated considerable mileage by continuing the old themes of killer weed and how foreign devils contaminated American youth with drugs. When Nixon's people asked him to attack the issue on a national level—to attack Nixon's particular drug problem, as it were—Liddy arranged for the administration's inner circle, a group which included John Ehrlichman, Charles Colson, and Egil Krough, to view an old Nazi propaganda film called *Triumph of the Will*. The film demonstrated how a handful of determined men could manufacture a crisis, then use it to manipulate an entire nation. (In Liddy's mind, at least, that's what the war on drugs entailed.) Liddy viewed the drug problem as the perfect vehicle through which the White House could exercise its will and ultimately triumph at the polls.

36

Though the drug crisis didn't require much manufacturing, the Nixon administration took no chances. By juggling and distorting official statistics (numbers of drug addicts, for example, were estimated using a formula for estimating the number of fish in a pond) the administration was able to convince Congress that only the most draconian measures would suffice to control the drug trade.

Liddy, who once bragged that he overcame his fear of rats by cooking and eating one, came up with one scheme after another. He personally flew to El Paso to direct "Operation Intercept"—in one three-week period agents stopped and searched 5 million U.S. citizens, virtually closing 1,200 miles of border. Liddy discussed with the CIA the possibility of "liquidating" all major drug traffickers in the Middle East; he estimated that 150 key assassinations would do the job. Another suggestion was to disrupt the drug market by poisoning the goods. The use of agents provocateurs was one of the least offensive of the proposals—Liddy also drafted plans to use the Internal Revenue Service as an arm of narcotics enforcement, and for a time the IRS filed liens against suspected smugglers. A National Airlines stewardess arrested for a traffic violation and discovered with four pills in her purse was served with a lien demanding $25,549—the amount an IRS inspector estimated she made from sales of narcotics. Her jewelry and savings were confiscated, and although the smuggling charges were dropped for lack of evidence (the pills were prescribed by her doctor) she was unable to have the $25,549 tax assessment dismissed.

In *Agency of Fear,* author Edward Jay Epstein describes the time that Nixon invited Elvis Presley to the White House to discuss the drug problem. Elvis showed up with his shirt open to the waist and a .45 Colt automatic stuffed in his velvet pants. The pistol was a gift for the president, he told the White House guards as they disarmed him. What Nixon had in mind was some songs with anti-drug themes, but Elvis was way ahead of him. As it turned out, Elvis had a plan to assassinate all the drug dealers in Memphis. He also wanted the president to give him a badge—Elvis collected badges. Before leaving, he warned the president that their meeting should be kept a secret. Nixon quickly agreed. Mopping his brow with a handkerchief, the chief executive said: "Absolutely! Don't tell anybody. Preserve your credibility at all cost!"

Although the Democratic-controlled Congress must have realized that the administration's Drug Control Act of 1970 was politics rather than police work, Congress passed it by a lopsided margin. Among other things the new law provided a means for prosecutors to make kingpins out of nickel-and-dime drug dealers and send them away for life. Modeled after a similar law designed to convict Mafia capos, the law created a new crime called "continuing criminal enterprise." It became known as the "kingpin" act. A kingpin was defined, roughly, as the boss of an organization that realized "substantial" profit from the importation and sales of drugs.

Along with the new legislation came plans to appoint get-tough judges and reorganize drug-enforcement apparatus so that it would report directly to the White House rather than the Justice Department. For years Justice and Treasury had been squabbling over jurisdiction of drug enforcement. From 1930 until 1968, Treasury's Bureau of Narcotics (BN) was the major agency, with U.S. Customs and the Border Patrol playing smaller roles. During the Johnson administration, Attorney General Ramsey Clark noted "evidence of significant corruption" in the government's narcotics units—illegal selling and buying of drugs, retaining contraband for personal use or sale, keeping money allocated for informants, perjury, tampering with evidence, bribery, extortion, even murder. Under what came to be called Reorganization Plan No. 1, BN was disbanded and a new agency called the Bureau of Narcotics and Dangerous Drugs (BNDD) was formed and placed under the Department of Justice starting in 1968. According to the Johnson administration's concept, BNDD would specialize in internal enforcement and Customs would concentrate on smuggling and international aspects of the problem. In practice, the agencies bickered among themselves, sometimes to the point of actually sabotaging each other's undercover operations or compromising rival informants. In Washington, there was a constant battle for appropriations as Justice and Treasury struggled for more jurisdiction. Meanwhile, the flow of drugs went largely unchecked.

Early in 1972, Nixon signed an executive order creating a new agency called Office of Drug Abuse Law Enforcement (ODALE). Created without the approval or consideration of Congress, ODALE was conceived as a superagency with extraordinary authority to search, seize, and use electronic surveillance. It reported directly to the White House. Two major events kept ODALE from a full flowering. The first was Watergate, and the second was a revolt of bureaucrats from the ranks of Customs and **BNDD,** the two agencies that were being frozen out of the action. In April 1973, a task force of **ODALE** thugs kicked in the door of a house in Collinsville, Illinois, and spent the night terrorizing an innocent family. Details of the raid were covered up until some disgruntled agents from **BNDD** leaked them. **ODALE** quickly and quietly vanished, and the White House went to work on Plan 2, which created the Drug Enforcement Administration (**DEA**), a division of Justice.

With Watergate coming to a boil, many critics questioned the wisdom of concentrating so much power in Justice. Many believed that the competition between Customs and **BNDD** had been, on the whole, healthy in maintaining checks and balances. A number of congressmen, including Tom Steed of Oklahoma, chairman of the House Appropriations Subcommittee, saw an innate problem in trusting total jurisdiction to Justice. *Wall Street Journal* columnist Alan L. Otten wrote that the plan's approach ran counter to a traditional tenet of American law enforcement: "Strict separation of investigator and prosecutor. This separation has provided a valuable check-and-balance in the past, protecting against poor judgment or excessive zeal in either police or attorneys." Otten also pointed out that the principal architect of Plan 2 was the former director of **ODALE,** an agency viewed by many local police departments as "essentially a Nixon administration public relations device wherein federal manpower was diverted into small-scale arrests so that impressive statistics could be displayed without much effort." Despite the criticism, the administration prevailed and on July 1, 1973, hundreds of former Customs and **BNDD** agents were transferred to the **DEA.** John R. Bartels, former deputy director of **ODALE,** was named administrator. It went without saying that Nixon's people expected quick and dramatic results.

Within a year of its formation, **DEA** was rocked by a major scandal that resulted in a full-blown congressional investigation. Like Watergate, it started with an incident of no great moment when a Washington, D.C., cop noticed a bunch of men in an alley behind a nightclub. The men were trying on suits with no labels, which were being sold from the trunk of a car, in an alley at night. One of the men turned out to be Vincent L. Promuto, a former Redskin football player who had recently been appointed director of public affairs for the **DEA.** Additional investigation revealed that Promuto regularly associated with the gamblers and felons who frequented the night-club, and that on one occasion he had tipped off the nightclub owner that a friend was actually a DEA informant. The Washington police had no evidence that Promuto was involved in any crime, but the fact that he associated with underworld characters while holding down one of the top jobs at DEA had to reflect on the new agency's integrity. Additional investigations revealed that Promuto was having a romance with a $100-a-throw prostitute who was connected to a drug-smuggling operation out of Laredo, Texas. When all of this information was delivered to Andrew Tartaglino, the No. 2 man at DEA, Tartaglino and his chief internal investigator, George Brosan, started their own probe, apparently over the objections of the DEA administrator, John Bartels, a close friend of Promuto's.

By the time the investigation reached the point of hearings before Senator Henry Jackson's government operations subcommittee, the parallels to Watergate were unmistakable. A key figure in the investigation was a mysterious Newark, New Jersey, lawyer named Thomas E. Durkins, Jr., who carried credentials as a "special adviser" to the DEA. Though Durkins had access to sensitive government files and traveled at DEA expense, no one connected to the bureau was able to tell the committee his exact function—he had no experience in drug enforcement or prosecution, nor had he been cleared by a security check. As it turned out, "special adviser" was an "honorary" title granted by former BNDD director John Ingersoll in appreciation for Durkins's work in setting up community relief programs for the widows of agents killed or injured in the line of duty. The new director, John Bartels, had found a more circumspect use for Durkins's talent—Durkins advised Bartels how to respond to subcommittee investigations. Other high-ranking DEA officials phrased it less delicately—they believed Durkins's job was to hinder or "defuse" the investigation, which by now had gone far past the Promuto affair and was including DEA dealings with Robert Vesco and Howard Hughes. Among other things, the subcommittee wanted to know why DEA agents attempting to penetrate a drug ring had gambled at one of Hughes's Las Vegas casinos, using money provided by Hughes and funneled through International Intelligence, Inc. (Intertel), which was suspected by the DEA of having ties with organized crime. Jackson and other senators accused the DEA director of attempting to cover up details of this operation.

Three months into the Promuto probe, Bartels told DEA internal investigators that they were going "too deeply into Mr. Promuto's personal life" and ordered them to wrap it up and have the report on his desk within five days. Bartels's order blew up in his face. In a memo to the Justice Department, Andrew Tartaglino, the agency's No. 2 man, asked to be transferred out of the DEA and requested an immediate investigation into the activities of the administrator, John Bartels. Tartaglino, who had been a senior officer with BNDD, charged that Bartels was indifferent to the "personnel integrity problems" of DEA, that the agency's image within the law enforcement community had been tarnished, and that Bartels had intimidated the DEA's chief internal investigator and impeded the Promuto probe. Tartaglino stopped just short of charging his boss with obstruction of justice, but Senator Henry Jackson felt no such restraint—Jackson requested that the FBI look into that specific charge. Later, the FBI refused to give its report to the subcommittee.

The Promuto affair even had its own Saturday-Night Massacre. A month after Tartaglino's memo to Justice, Bartels unexpectedly relieved Tartaglino and his chief inspector, George Brosan, from their duties. Bartels also leaked the story of a "power struggle" within the DEA to columnist Jack Anderson, who wrote that the charges against Promuto had never been substantiated and didn't amount to much anyway.

Amid charges, countercharges, and the airing of dirty linen, the hearings continued. Bartels's strategy at this point was to undermine the integrity of his No. 2 man, Tartaglino, no matter how much that undermined the integrity of the drug-enforcement community. Bartels testified that as a senior agent with BNDD, Tartaglino had ordered one of his men to "create a crime in order to entice other persons to commit crimes." Then he ordered the agent to lie about it to the grand jury. This was a messy area for everyone involved. Several years earlier, testimony revealed, Tartaglino and the BNDD had assisted the New York City Knapp Commission as part of a much larger investigation of corruption among Queens County cops, lawyers, assistant DAs, and judges who had apparently conspired to fix narcotics cases. One of Tartaglino's men, an international specialist named Sante Bario, was assigned to go undercover, posing as a Mafia hit man. A U.S. attorney in New York arranged for Bario to be arrested on phony gun charges in order to make contact with a certain

41

lawyer suspected of being one of the fixers. The U.S. attorney also ordered Bario to lie to the grand jury. Although Tartaglino had no part in this official misconduct, the fact that Bartels was willing to air the drug agency's dirty laundry was an indication of the core problem in narcotics enforcement. Bario, incidentally, would later be arrested by the DEA and would die under mysterious circumstances while being held prisoner in the county jail in San Antonio.

Eventually, John Bartels was replaced as DEA chief by Peter Bensinger. Promuto and special adviser Durkins also lost their credentials. But the fallout from this long and bitter struggle filtered out to every station in the country. It was particularly intense along the Texas-Mexico border, where large numbers of former Customs agents had been forced to surrender their authority and their network of informants to the DEA. By the summer of 1975 a potential scandal was brewing in the Western District of Texas, a vast federal jurisdiction that stretched over 78,000 square miles of the best smuggling terrain in the country, desert scrabble, mountains, and remote river, from El Paso to Austin to San Antonio, including 650 miles of border. Jamie Boyd, the U.S. magistrate in El Paso, had been conducting his own private investigation into abuses by DEA agents for months. Boyd took his evidence first to the office of U.S. attorney John Clark, in San Antonio, and later, when it appeared that Clark wasn't going to act on the charges, to Peter Bensinger in Washington.

When he had been district attorney of El Paso County, Boyd had developed a close friendship with a number of Customs agents. When the DEA moved in, many of the old-time agents on the border resented the aggressiveness, arrogance, and especially the investigative techniques of this new breed. One of the techniques that Boyd particularly disliked was the DEA's penchant for kicking in doors without benefit of search warrant. As U.S. magistrate, Boyd threw out a number of cases in which this had happened. He also discovered that agents frequently lied under oath, as in the case of an armed DEA raid on an ice cream parlor in which shots were fired at a young couple attempting to flee the scene. According to the DEA, the couple were prime suspects in a conspiracy case. This testimony was totally false; the couple merely fled, as any sane person would do, on observing an armed mob of bearded and disheveled men kicking in the door. "I could have overlooked the agents' incompetence," Boyd said.

"What really galled me was when they misrepresented the facts under oath."

There were other incidents, but the one that finally convinced Boyd to seek assistance from the office of the U.S. attorney was an explosion at a clandestine laboratory where speed (methamphetamine) was being manufactured. It turned out that the lab was owned and stocked by the DEA. It was the agents' answer to a directive from Washington ordering them to bust some clandestine labs. They had found a student chemist at the University of Texas at El Paso, installed him in a mobile home near Chaparral, New Mexico, and even supplied the laboratory equipment and the illegal substance phenyl-2-propanol, the key ingredient in the manufacture of speed. When the lab blew, the agents panicked and kidnapped the student chemist and his girlfriend. They held them for several days while a story was concocted. Boyd was told that the culprits in the lab bust didn't want a lawyer, that they had agreed to cooperate with the government in its efforts to trap other drug traffickers. The magistrate eventually learned the truth from his friend Rick Staton, a former Customs officer who had been transferred to the DEA. Staton and another agent, Herb Hailes, related a number of other illegal activities by DEA agents and agreed to talk to the U.S. attorney. Hailes told an astonishing story about making a case against the notorious teenage dope mogul Georgie Taylor, only to watch his report disappear into his supervisor's desk for almost two years. When Hailes asked the supervisor to return his paperwork, the supervisor supposedly replied, "Don't mess with my people!" Just how Georgie Taylor came to be one of the supervisor's people was never explained. Taylor was eventually indicted, but he skipped the country before he was arrested. He was later gunned down, gangland-style, in the Chihuahuan desert and buried in a shallow ditch, where his body was eventually discovered.

U.S. attorney John Clark and his first assistant, John Pinckney, took depositions from Jamie Boyd, Rick Staton, Herb Hailes, and three other agents who had worked for or with the DEA, but nothing ever came of the investigation. Jamie Boyd still insists that the whole thing was "a gigantic whitewash." Agents Staton and Hailes were threatened with reassignment to Puerto Rico, a station known for the short life expectancy of its agents. Hailes was able to transfer to Customs Air Patrol, though a short time later he took medical leave and never returned to narcotics enforcement. Staton, a veteran of twenty-one years of service in law enforcement, was transferred to Lubbock, Texas, where his job was to assist in burning bales of captured marijuana.

In El Paso, the most significant volley in the war on drugs was the appointment to the federal bench in San Antonio of John H. Wood, Jr., one of the most devout and respected Republicans in Texas. Wood had made his reputation in civil law. San Antonio attorney Gerald Goldstein, whose family had known Wood's family for years, noted that while Wood had no experience in drug cases, he had a vast experience as a hard-nosed defender of insurance companies. "His job was to prevent paraplegics from collecting damages, and he was damn good at it," Goldstein said. "Maybe the job exhausted his compassion." But there was no more ardent law-and-order advocate anywhere. Like Julius Caesar, Wood had several times been offered an appointment to high office, and had several times refused. It was only in 1970, after Senator John Tower and other ranking members of the Republican Party in Texas made personal pleas, that Wood was convinced that it was his *duty* to accept a federal judgeship. The nation was at war, not only in Vietnam but in the streets, alleys, and barrios of America, where the menace of drugs was destroying the will to fight, or to work, or to do almost anything of traditional worth and value. Wood was sworn in as U.S. judge for the Western District of Texas in January 1971, and within a few months the district's chief judge, Adrian Spears, was funneling a disproportionate number of drug cases to Wood's docket. Over the next eight years Wood handed out the maximum sentence in almost every case. He became known across the Southwest, and eventually across the country, as Maximum John.

8

When word reached Lee Chagra's law office in October 1973 that Marty Houltin and members of the Columbus Air Force had been busted by a task force of federal and state narcotics officers, Lee told his youngest brother, Joe: "I don't fucking believe it!" He said it with decidedly mixed emotions; though the event was inevitable, it was also incomprehensible. Nobody in that part of the country had been scamming longer than Marty. He had been a bomber pilot in the Aleutians during World War II and later a bush pilot in Alaska for Standard Oil; then, starting in the 1960s, he flew cargos such as Levis's, TV sets, and Nestlé's cocoa into Mexico, and returned with loads of mercury and silver, sometimes on consignment for the U.S. State Department. For a while he flew chartered flights of swingers from Las Vegas to the whorehouses and cantinas of Mazatlán, then someone offered him two grand to fly a load of marijuana back to the States and Marty got religion. In all that time his only bust had been ten years before in California, a misdemeanor that resulted in a ninety-day summary probation. Marty gave his age as fifty-two, but nobody believed him. Marty came from outer space, where earth years had no meaning. A splendid elfin figure with a shock of palomino hair and a white scarf that flapped in the wind, Marty had been drawn to the tiny town of Columbus, New Mexico, sixty miles due west of El Paso. Columbus is on the Mexican border; it is famous as the village that Pancho Villa raided in 1916. You can hardly get there by car, not that anyone has any reason to. A single two-lane highway runs south from Deming, through Columbus, then crosses into the Mexican village of Las Palomas, and then meanders through the desert to the isolated Mormon community of Nueva Casas Grandes.

Nobody just happens across Columbus, though by plane from El Paso it is only a thirty-minute hop.

Marty bought a private landing strip that he proudly renamed the Columbus Municipal Airport, to distinguish it from the four other landing strips in town. The population of Columbus is three hundred, less than it was when Pancho Villa staged his raid. Marty and his wife, Mary, owned a steakhouse on the Deming highway, a place where scammers from all over the Southwest gathered from time to time to talk business. A sign near the cash register said it all: *Money is just something you got to make in case you don't die.*

"They finally got the Palomino," Lee said to Joe as he hung up. Mixed emotions, yes. Too bad for Marty, but nice for the law practice. Except for their unsuccessful defense of three members of the Bandido motorcycle gang charged with murdering two brothers who sold them talcum powder for speed, the Chagra brothers had hardly seen a client since Lee's indictment three months before. "Who got the collar?" Joe asked. Lee said that he wasn't sure, but he'd bet his last penny it was DEA agent J. T. Robinson. There was just a trace of admiration in Lee's voice when he said the name.

Agent J. T. Robinson had been chasing Marty Houltin for eight years, first for the Border Patrol, then for Customs, and now for the DEA. Robinson was a big man with silver hair and rugged features. He looked like a retired pro football player. He had a sense of humor, but it didn't get in his way. In the reception room outside his office in El Paso, there was a sign that said: *Soft judges make hard criminals.* Robinson had no problem believing this. The law had gone soft. People had started worrying about criminals' rights. "You got to catch 'em fair and clean these days," he explained. "They don't believe in thumping a confession out of 'em anymore."

Sometimes when he was chasing Marty and the CAF, reaching out and grabbing a handful of nothing, his job reminded him of a Tom and Jerry cartoon. It was always something too silly for words. Once when an agent-pilot named Diaz had picked up Marty's trail and followed him undetected right into the Las Vegas, New Mexico, airport, someone in the control tower broke radio silence. Marty instinctively spun his Cessna around and whizzed past Diaz's plane so close their wingtips touched. The last time Diaz saw the smuggler, Marty was shooting him the finger and disappearing in the opposite direction. Another time agents attached a magnetic directional signal under the bumper of a truck that Marty's men were using, but the truck blew a tire and when the bad guys stopped to change it someone found the transmitter. They slapped the transmitter onto a decoy car and went about their dirty business while the agents bumped heads. Agent Robinson and his pilot, Gerry Weatherman, had once actually located a load of manijuana stashed up against the side of a mountain in Mexico waiting for some smuggler to do his trip. They'd found the whole operation—generator, lights, compactor, gasoline cans. Robinson had always regretted he didn't burn the grass on the spot, but the sound of a plane approaching from the south spooked them and the next thing Robinson knew they were airborne, listening to Marty's voice on the radio. Marty apparently assumed they were another smuggling plane that had landed to refuel. "Hey, good buddy," the Palomino said, "where you going?" Another voice answered: "That wasn't *me*!" When they were about sixty miles from the border, the agents heard Marty again, saying: "Be careful—that was the man out here today." Robinson thought of several snappy replies. They were almost out of radio range. It was almost dark and the narc plane was almost out of gas. They would refuel and return at daylight, but Roinson already knew that the ton of grass and all the equipment would be gone, swallowed by the desert. They could hear the smugglers pop-pop-popping their mikes, talking code. Then there was static, then there was silence. Why hadn't he burned that grass when he'd had the opportunity?

In August 1973, J. T. Robinson and a group of federal and New Mexico state narcotics agents met in an Albuquerque hotel room to discuss the problem of the Columbus Air Force. Robinson had some good news: Washington had approved a $2 million budget to finance a new joint effort which would be called Operation Skynight. Washington had assured the narcs that the manpower and technical equipment necessary to catch Marty Houltin would be forthcoming. The radar systems currently in operation were virtually useless against experienced scammers. Marty was a master at terrain flying, "flying the deck," twenty or thirty feet off the ground, to avoid radar.

In addition to the highly sophisticated El Paso Intelligence Center (EPIC) system, which tracked airplanes and ships halfway around the world, new systems had been installed in Albuquerque and Tucson that allowed a single operator to monitor everything moving in three different states. But the scammers knew from their navigational charts where the stations were located, and they knew where the agents' planes were based. It was still like chasing field mice. More and more the scammers were employing decoy flights, a game of hide-and-seek in which three planes would take off at the same time heading in three different directions. This was fairly expensive for the scammers— figure $1,500 for each decoy flight—but three or four decoy flights could deplete the DEA's budget for an entire month.

Now they had an almost unlimited budget, Robinson told the other agents assembled in the hotel room, and they had something else. The government had supplied them with a sophisticated new surveillance plane, the Grumman Mohawk, which had been combat-tested in Vietnam. The Mohawk could fly at speeds anywhere from 45 to 250 mph, and was equipped with a new type of aircraft-detection system, a thermal imaging device called FLIR, for Forward Looking Infra Red. Until now, aerial radar had been considerably more miss than hit. The old aerial radar had a 360-degree range of 25 miles. The narc planes were not permitted to cross the border except with special permission, so they traveled mostly east and west, in a straight line between El Paso and Columbus, flying at 185 miles per hour. The smugglers, of course, were moving north and south. There was only an instant, a minute or two, when anything except empty space appeared on radar. Radar's chances were slim to none. The FLIR, which detected heat from the airplane's fuselage, operated at any altitude, even at ground level, and over great distances.

William Garcia, an agent with the New Mexico State Police, still had reservations. He told Robinson and the other DEA men that what they really needed was a wiretap. Some of the narcs didn't like the sound of it; most of them had experiences in which perfectly good dope cases had been overturned because wiretaps had been improperly authorized. Judges couldn't be trusted. Garcia had already looked into the subject: They only needed to convince one state judge that normal surveillance procedures were not adequate. Certainly the combined records of their various agencies was ample proof of that. Some of the agents still thought wiretapping was overkill, but they reluctantly agreed to try it.

On September 27, 1973, the wiretaps went into operation. The judge balked at allowing the agents to tap the phones of all their suspects, but he approved taps on the telephones at Marty Houltin's home, and at the home of Marty's ace ground support man, Curly

Phillips. The taps monitored and recorded conversations overheard from a house not far from where Marty lived. In addition to the wiretaps, the narcs intensified their surveillance of various airstrips in southern New Mexico, including the much-used Sunland strip just across the state line from El Paso. The operation was directed from a surveillance trailer, called Sector, parked behind the stables at Sunland Racetrack.

Agent Weatherman flew surveillance early every morning and late every afternoon, checking different landing spots and drop zones, and keeping track of the CAF's fleet of Cessna 206 aircraft.

Shortly after the wiretaps went into effect, Agents Robinson and Weatherman spotted Robert Burke and one of the other smugglers heading south. They trailed in their twin-engine Piper Aztec to a pickup area south of Camargo, Chihuahua, where the smugglers landed. The narcs orbited high above the lake bed for almost an hour, but nothing happened.

"They're waiting till dark," Robinson said.

"Maybe not."

"They're waiting. I know it." Robinson hated even to think about it, but he knew that if the scammers waited until dark, the surveillance plane would have to return to base. Their fuel was already low. Then they heard Burke's voice on the radio. Apparently the trucks of marijuana hadn't arrived. Robinson breathed a sigh of relief when he heard Burke abort the mission.

Nothing was happening with the wiretap. They were monitoring Marty Houltin's and Curly Phillips's phones around the clock, but most of the conversation was about babies and dog food and Maytag dealers. Agent Garcia reported that there hadn't been a single mention of drugs in the ten days he'd been on duty.

On October 8, Garcia spotted Burke and Houltin having coffee at the Sheraton in El Paso. He followed them out of the hotel, but lost them in a carwash next door. Operation Skynight was going nowhere fast.

Agent Robinson woke early on the morning of October 12 feeling good, feeling lucky. There was going to be a full moon tonight. Sector reported blowing dust, but nothing bad enough to prevent a chase. When Robinson arrived at Sunland it wasn't yet daylight and Weatherman was already on duty. About 9:00 A.M., Marty Houltin landed at Sunland.

Weatherman followed Marty to downtown El Paso, but lost him in the heavy morning traffic. About noon, Weatherman got word that Marty, Burke, and Morrison had been spotted at the Sheraton, where another agent had unsuccessfully tried to eavesdrop on their conversation.

Weatherman and Robinson were on their way downtown when they got word that the smugglers had left in two cars headed toward Sunland. The agents drove straight to El Paso International, where their twin-engine Piper Aztec was gassed and ready.

Thirty minutes later, at 1:10 P.M., Marty landed at Columbus. Burke and Morrison landed about ten minutes later. Marty telephoned his wife and said: "Call the man. We're running a little late." Mary Houltin telephoned Curly Phillips's wife and relayed the message. That was it. The operation was on. Agent Tommy Holder, who was manning the wiretap, immediately telephoned Sector. Sector alerted Tucson, where the Mohawk was standing by, and Albuquerque, where other planes and helicopters were in readiness. By now forty-five agents, four airplanes, and two helicopters were standing by. The DEA, Customs, Border Patrol, New Mexico State Police, and various sheriff's offices were on alert.

Weatherman and Robinson had flown back to El Paso International to refuel and wait. While Weatherman was refueling, he got a telephone call from Sector. "The guys are going back to their airplanes in Columbus," Sector told the pilot. Weatherman didn't even wait long enough to sign his gas ticket, but grabbed Robinson and they raced for the plane. It usually took half an hour to fly from El Paso to Columbus, but Weatherman cut it by five minutes. A plume of red dust curled out of the Florida Mountains to the north, and far to the south like a glint of light they saw Marty's Cessna taxiing down the runway while the other two planes raced their engines and waited for clearance. Ten miles east of Columbus, flying in a loose formation, the three Cessnas turned south into Mexico.

"Call Sector," Robinson said. "Tell them to get the Hawk and the rest of the airplanes up, that we're heading south. *The Palomino has jumped the fence!*" Within minutes a DEA Duke out of El Paso and the Mohawk out of Tucson had joined the surveillance. After eight years of frustration, Robinson thought, at last we're doing it right. At least it had better be right. They weren't likely to get a second chance.

Robinson knew through an informant that the Columbus Air Force was operating on a radio frequency of 123.4, but guessed that Marty had instructed his men to observe radio silence. He could hear them popping their mikes. Robinson was thinking that they had about three hours of daylight, and he was wondering if Marty was thinking the same thing. Even with three surveillance planes and all that sophisticated radar equipment, even with the full moon, they were dead ducks if Marty decided to wait until after dark.

The smugglers and their chase planes flew southeasterly, over the big dry lake, following the Río Conchos where it ran parallel to the railroad. Twenty miles east of Chihuahua City the smugglers started to descend. They came down over Delicias, then over the edge of the big reservoir. "They're going the same place as before," Weatherman said. "Just south of Camargo." Robinson held his breath. Was it possible?

Marty swooped in from the west and taxied toward an orange-and-white van. He executed a 180 and pointed the nose of his ship back in the direction he'd landed. Morrison and Burke followed. From 15,000 feet above, Robinson trained his binoculars on the three planes. "They've left their engines running," he told Weatherman. "They can't hear us!" He dared not believe that Marty was in a *hurry*. But he kept the glasses on the little commander, and Marty didn't once take time to look up. Twenty minutes later, at 6:05 P.M., Marty was gunning it for a takeoff.

"The Palomino has just made his first mistake," Robinson said with enormous satisfaction.

They returned over the same path, though it looked different at night. The moon scaled the mountains like an angry god, and Marty put it at 10,600 feet crossing the desert. Forty miles shy of the border, Marty popped his mike and all three smuggler planes doused their lights. Weatherman hadn't even thought of turning his on. The Duke had turned back to El Paso for gas, and the Mohawk held back and followed with its FLIR, but Weatherman stalked Marty's tail like a starving hound, flying just below him and a little behind. Robinson listened to them popping their mikes and told Weatherman, "I'd like to get on that mike and say, 'Yoo hoo, Marty, guess where I am?' " Robinson had warned Marty. He'd told him straight: "You can smuggle for as long as you want, but sooner or later you'll make one of three mistakes. You'll get lazy or you'll get greedy, or you'll start fighting among yourselves. One way or another." Marty was a likable guy. One day Robinson ran into Marty at Sunland and Marty told him: "If the circumstances were different, I'd probably invite you to lunch." If the circumstances had been different, Robinson would probably have accepted. The agent breathed deeply as he watched Marty's ship moving blithely along, bathed in the gold October moon. He wondered if Marty realized that today was the first day of antelope season. All those isolated little backroads that the smugglers found so perfect were likely to be swarming with hunters tonight.

They passed over Mount Riley west of Las Cruces, then began to drop down into a long valley between two sections of the Cibola National Forest. They were headed for the big open area southwest of Socorro, the place called the Plains of San Agustín. The Mohawk had closed in now, and the Duke had refueled and rejoined the pursuit: you couldn't tell it with the naked eye, but there were six darkened airplanes descending from 10,000 feet, one almost right on top of another. It was almost 9:30 P.M. when the narcs heard one of the smugglers break radio silence.

"Red Dog Three, Red Dog Three to ground support," the voice said. Robinson looked at Weatherman. For a few minutes there was no sound, then the narcs heard Marty Houltin's distinctive voice saying, "Red Dog One, this is Red Dog One calling ground support."

At first another silence, then a voice said: "This is ground support, go ahead."

"Turn on your flasher so we can identify you," Marty said.

Far below the agents could see the wink of a red light; the light would lead the task force on the ground to the unloading place.

"The Palomino has just made his second mistake," Robinson told Weatherman. The agent adjusted the frequency on a second radio so he could hear the transmissions of the other agents involved in Operation Skynight. Lieutenant William Eddleman of the New Mexico State Police was directing the ground forces from a fourth government plane that had arrived from Socorro. There were two helicopters out there somewhere, but it was hard to tell just where.

One of the smugglers commented that there was an exceptional amount of traffic on Highway 60 which ran east and west between Magdalena and Datil, New Mexico. "Turns out this is the first day of antelope season," ground support said. He suggested they move the drop site four or five miles west to Highway 78, a narrow dirt road that ran toward the Elk Mountains. "This is Red Dog One," Marty said. "Check it out. We'll keep orbiting." Ten minutes later ground support reported that there was hardly any traffic on the dirt road.

"What's it look like?"

"There's a set of high lines and a cattle guard."

"Okay, park at the cattle guard facing south. Turn your lights on. "I'll come in over the top of your car from north to south."

"Okay, you got about a thousand feet."

While the other two smugglers continued orbiting, Marty brought his ship smoothly over the car, turning on his landing lights at the last instant. Weatherman and Robinson discussed waiting until the third plane had landed, then coming in behind them to block their retreat, but within three minutes Marty had unloaded and taken off again. As Burke was landing in the second plane, a white pickup truck turned off the main highway onto the dirt road and headed toward the landing area. Marty's voice barked, "Curly, turn around and blind that truck with your lights. Bobby [Burke], unload and get the hell out." From the transmissions that followed, Robinson gathered that the pickup was just a bunch of locals, probably come back from the hunt. There was some confusion on the ground, though, because the trucks that were supposed to pick up the load hadn't arrived. All three of the smugglers mentioned they were low on fuel. So was the narc plane—Weatherman estimated they were down to fifteen minutes, just the time required to reach Socorro. By now Burke had taken off and Morrison had landed and was unloading the final plane.

"Piece of cake," Marty said, and Robinson heard the trembling in Marty's voice.

"You sound like you're standing on your own tongue," ground control told Marty.

"Let's take it home," Marty said.

It was now 11:29 P.M. Robinson would have loved to follow Marty back to Columbus and make the bust himself, but this wasn't possible. He heard Lieutenant Eddleman order his men on the ground to move in on the trucks, and he knew that Garcia and four other agents were waiting at the air strip in Columbus for the scammers' return. Nothing could go wrong now, Weatherman reminded him. Robinson wondered. Operation Skynight had been a success, but when you figured that the government was spending $2 million on this bust—$1,000 a pound—there was a hollow ring to the victory. Of course, that wasn't the way to think of it. Marty Houltin had made millions smuggling marijuana in his time, and now he was going behind bars. Agent Robinson just hoped they could keep him there.

Lee Chagra had the smugglers back on the streets by noon. As soon as he reviewed the case, Chagra realized that the wiretaps were illegal. New Mexico law, following federal law, required that the attorney general or a district attorney make application for wiretaps. The agents had overlooked this simple requirement—they had persuaded an *assistant* DA to make application.

As Lee anticipated, federal prosecutors in New Mexico declined to prosecute. The case was turned over to the state. A district judge in Socorro agreed to hear the case but he obviously had reservations about the wiretaps. Chagra and the judge worked out most of the details in advance of the trial. Lee wouldn't challenge the validity of the wiretaps, and the judge wouldn't send the Columbus Air Force to prison. The trial itself was a showpiece for the little town of Socorro. The local school dismissed classes early so that the students could crowd the courthouse and watch the famous El Paso attorney in action. Chagra brought along two other well-known attorneys—Malcolm McGregor of El Paso and Billy Ravkind of Dallas. Marty Houltin's friends arranged a series of parties, so the scammers could celebrate even as they paid for their sins. Pretrial lasted several days, but the actual trial was over in a few hours. The lawyers pleaded nolo contendere and the judge sentenced each of the defendants to eighteen months probation and fines ranging from $1,000 to $5,000.

The bust of the Columbus Air Force got a good deal of publicity. National magazines like *High Times*, *Argosy*, even *Popular Mechanics* wrote about Marty and the CAF. The piece in *Popular Mechanics* focused on "a crack team of airborne narcotics agents" using "highly sophisticated equipment" to bring down the Palomino and his "deadly cargo." "That was the end of Houltin and his gang," the magazine concluded. Lee showed the article to Malcolm McGregor and Billy Ravkind and the three lawyers had a good laugh. "Sophisticated equipment, my ass," McGregor said. "They got 'em with a four-bit wiretap, and they couldn't even get that right."

And yet McGregor and the others had an uneasy feeling that the case hadn't ended. They had heard rumors that federal prosecutors in El Paso were furious with the way the case had been handled in New Mexico and might even devise a plan to have the CAF reindicted on federal conspiracy charges in El Paso. Under the concept of dual sovereignty, the trial in Socorro wouldn't prevent the feds from trying the defendants again, and besides, the feds were talking about a conspiracy case. They could claim that the conspiracy originated in El Paso. McGregor learned that the feds had already subpoenaed hotel records, and there was no question that Marty and the others had bought their airplanes in El Paso, even though the date of purchase was months before the alleged conspiracy. Every lawyer who practiced in the federal courts knew that conspiracy laws were vague enough to allow almost anything prosecutors cared to argue and the judge cared to receive. Much stranger things had happened in El Paso when Judge Ernest Guinn was alive. Guinn had died just a few weeks earlier—prisoners in the El Paso County Jail cheered when they heard the news—and now the entire El Paso federal docket was in the hands of Judge John Wood, Jr.

Although none of the three lawyers for the Columbus Air Force knew much about Judge Wood at that point, what they did know was bad. Wood had come to town some months before to assist Guinn with the overcrowded docket, and the men had apparently become close friends. Wood looked to Guinn as his mentor. For years Guinn had been far and away the most reversed judge in the district, and this didn't bother Guinn a bit. "I can sentence 'em faster than they can reverse 'em," he was frequently heard to say. When Wood heard how prisoners had cheered at the news of his beloved mentor's death, he had vowed that "they will rue the day." That's the kind of man Wood was. He was *proud* to be called Maximum John. In three and a half years on the bench, Wood had never once granted probation in a heroin case. He bragged about this. But it wasn't just hard-drug cases; Wood appeared to make no distinction among drugs. He once sentenced a dope dealer to thirty-five years for contempt of court. The bonds that he set in marijuana cases averaged $200,000, three times the average of any other judge in the district. His harsh, unbending policy of sentencing and his blatant pro-prosecution posture astonished lawyers and embarrassed other judges, including those who sat on the Fifth Circuit Court of Appeals, who used some of the more punitive language in memory in reversing Wood. Wood seemed to enjoy putting people away for serious time. El Paso attorney Ray Caballero, who was a federal prosecutor before entering private practice, told of the old Mexican who stood before Wood, hat in hand, listening as the judge gave him sixty years. "But judge," the old man said, "I don't think I can do sixty years," and Wood looked down with a cynical smile and said: "Try!"

Within months of Wood's appointment to the bench, his reputation had spread well beyond the district. Prosecutors as far away as California connived to have their drug cases transferred to Wood's jurisdiction: the simple fact that a drug-smuggling plane flew over San Antonio or El Paso on its way from Florida to Los Angeles was sufficient grounds for Wood to hear the case.

Almost every defense attorney in the district had a scare story about Wood, but few realized that Wood had his own deep-seated fears and guilts. They could be traced to a case in 1972. Mike Apollo was a small fish caught in the government's big net, a Milwaukee pot dealer who bought his goods from a Chicago distributor who in turn purchased them from a delivery service operated by a major association of smugglers who worked the river between El Paso and Del Rio. The smugglers were a band of trust-fund hippies who called themselves "the Company." CBS Television used the Company as a subject of a documentary called "The Mexican Connection," but at the time of his trial Mike Apollo had never heard of them. All he knew was he'd been busted in Milwaukee and had somehow ended up in the badlands of West Texas being hauled before a judge everyone called Maximum John. Most of the evidence against Apollo was hearsay testimony from other members of the conspiracy who had already pleaded guilty or were trying to cut a deal against future prosecution.

Apollo's only hope was that the judge would bungle the case, which he did. In its reversal more than a year later, the Fifth Circuit noted that "from beginning to end, the record . . . is replete with instances in which government witnesses recited extra-judicial statements. . . ." Ironically, the appeals court went on to note that there was sufficient evidence to convict Apollo without the use of hearsay. Wood's real mistake was not instructing the jury on the limits of hearsay. As legal scholars studied the ruling, they realized that it supplied a dramatic new weapon for prosecutors—hearsay was permissible among people charged in the same conspiracy, as long as the trial judge so instructed the jury. One can imagine the jubilation in the U.S. attorney's office when the Apollo decision came down.

Judge Wood was far from pleased with the reversal, especially in light of what happened next. Before Apollo could be brought back for retrial, three witnesses in three separate parts of the country were murdered in unusually brutal fashion. A fourth witness developed amnesia. Wood blamed himself. He cited Apollo many times in future cases and noted: "Every time I give a light sentence, they turn it around on me. They return to trafficking and someone gets killed." After the CBS-TV documentary was shown, the judge started referring to Apollo as "my Mexican connection case" or sometimes "my Midwestern connection case." Many lawyers got the impression that the judge never really understood why he'd been reversed in Apollo, only that three people who should have been in jail were dead.

On July 10, 1974, one month before Richard Nixon resigned in disgrace, an El Paso grand jury indicted Marty Houltin and five others on two counts of conspiracy and bound them over to judge John Wood for trial. Lee Chagra filed a motion to suppress evidence based on the illegal wiretap, but the judge refused. "The government has the burden to prove beyond a reasonable doubt that the wiretap had nothing to do with the arrests," Wood said. But determining the truth of this matter was the jury's job. The case was set for trial on October 15.

Chagra and the other attorneys didn't waste any time trying to shake the basic story of what had happened on that moonlit night one year before. Though Wood obviously didn't agree, the only issue was the wiretap. Could they or couldn't they? A dozen different official reports made it clear that without the wiretaps, the narcs would never have known when Marty and the others took off. The prosecutors had no doubt anticipated this line of defense, because most of the agents now told different stories. Some said they'd never even heard of the wiretaps, and almost all of them attempted to give the impression that they could have grabbed the Columbus Air Force anytime, anytime at all.

In cross-examination, Lee Chagra began to shake Agent Weatherman's recollection of that key telephone call from Sector.

Q. Had Sector not called you, you wouldn't have left [El Paso International Airport] so soon, would you?

A. No, sir.

Q. So that had Sector *not* called you, the [smugglers'] planes would have left for Mexico unobserved by you?

A. If they left, yes.

Q. Pardon me?

A. If they had left [for Mexico] on that day, yes, sir.

Q. I didn't hear you.

A. If their aircraft had departed that day and I didn't take off, yes. They would have left . . .

Q. Well, what I'm trying to say is, had Sector not called you, you wouldn't have left El Paso at the time you did.

A. No, sir.

Q. And you *barely* got there in time to observe them taking off, did you not?

Weatherman continued to maintain that he had no prior knowledge that the smuggling operation was set for that afternoon, but Chagra pointed out that his official report filed months earlier indicated otherwise. At the time the report was written, Chagra pointed out, the wiretap was not an *issue*. Now that it was an issue, Weatherman seemed to be changing his story.

As soon as the government closed its case, Chagra approached the bench and argued for an instructed verdict of acquittal. First, the government had failed to prove that any overt act relating to the conspiracy took place in Texas. They had clearly failed to prove beyond a reasonable doubt that the wiretaps had no relationship to the bust. And the mere fact that government reports written immediately after the arrests were now being repudiated raised a reasonable doubt.

It didn't in Judge Wood's mind. He said: "I can't see where those wiretaps . . . would have given anybody a clue as to what to do. They didn't tell you anything. This conversation between Houltin and Mrs. Houltin and the other defendant's wife . . . that wouldn't tell me where to go." Wood acknowledged that the narcs had a number of conflicts in their testimony, but told Chagra: "That's something to be resolved by the jury."

"But, your honor, these are conflicts among the government's *primary* witnesses," Chagra argued. "That's what motions of acquittal are all about!"

"The jury must reconcile their testimony," Wood said and recessed for lunch.

The defense attorneys were convinced that Wood had already made several reversible errors, but that didn't solve the immediate problem: like his mentor, Judge Guinn, Wood could sentence 'em faster than they could reverse 'em. The government was attempting to claim that an agent overheard Marty and two others talking about the conspiracy that day in the Sheraton coffee shop, and that's how the narcs knew it was about to come down. In fact, Marty and the others were talking about a Maytag salesman and a water-purification system. Until this trial, none of the reports had even mentioned the agents overhearing this suddenly important conversation at the coffee shop. The defense lawyers decided to take a calculated risk—they decided to call as their first witness the government's main man, Agent J. T. Robinson. Chagra didn't believe that Robinson would perjure himself to help the government's case. Otherwise, why hadn't the government called him as a primary witness?

Chagra started his examination of Robinson by referring to the official report.

Q. Okay, in this report you say at approximately 2:30 P.M. Agent Weatherman received information that Houltin and the others would attempt to smuggle a load of marijuana later in the afternoon. At this time, Agent Weatherman proceeded back to El Paso to refuel. Is that what the report says?

A. That's what it says.

Q. Were you with Mr. Weatherman when you received this information?

A. I would have to go along with Mr. Weatherman on that. I don't recall the information. I sure don't.

Q. Do you agree that you and Mr. Weatherman left [El Paso] International *because* of a telephone call from Sector?

A. Yes.

Robinson told the court that Weatherman actually took the call from Sector, but he agreed with Chagra that they left in a big hurry and that they would not have left that quickly without the phone call. The agent also acknowledged that Weatherman's original notes used in the official report had mysteriously disappeared. He stopped just short of accusing someone of stealing the notes.

Billy Ravkind questioned Robinson about the government's latest contention that one of their agents overheard the whole plot in the Sheraton coffee shop. Wasn't it true that until today, neither Weatherman nor Robinson had heard this amazing piece of intelligence? Robinson admitted it was true.

Q. Let me ask you, if the government knew of any agent who could testify that he sat next to [the defendants] and overheard them use words to indicate they were about to run a dope deal, there is no question in your mind whatsoever that that man would be on the stand testifying to that jury, is there?

A. Yes, he would be here.

Q. Whatever force it took to get him here?

A. Yes, sir.

There was no way the defense could make it more clear. Without the wiretaps, there would have been no bust. This wasn't an issue for the jury, it was an issue for the judge. It was Wood's sworn duty to instruct the jury on the law. Instead, Wood told the jury: "I personally fail to see anything in that wiretap that's relevant."

So that was it. There was nothing left for the defense except to cut its losses. Otherwise, Wood could send each of them away for ten years. Chagra was about to make his argument for mercy when Judge Wood suddenly got off on the Apollo case. He started a long tirade about dope and violence, and how every time he was lenient in one of these cases the defendants went back to smuggling and got killed. "It just so happens that this is the second largest [marijuana case] ... that I've been involved with," Wood said, second only to his "Mexican connection" case. Wood seemed to be under the impression that Marty and his people were somehow connected to the smugglers who were murdered in the Apollo case. Chagra argued vehemently that there was no connection and asked Wood to call Agent J. T. Robinson or any of the other narcs to swear that there was no history of violence among members of the Columbus Air Force. Nor were they likely to become fugitives. He pointed out that all of the defendants were currently on probation in New Mexico and had had perfect records for the ten months since the bust.

Wood didn't appear to hear the argument. He told the lawyers,

"I've had a pretty bad track record in the sense that I have a large number of people at large that are fugitives. I have the worst track record in America on this." Then he sentenced all five defendants to the maximum.

As they were leading Marty off to jail, he caught J. T. Robinson's eye. The agent shook his head as though to say he was sorry it had to end. Marty laughed and said: "I just got careless."

One of the aftereffects of Operation Skynight was that other scammers began to avoid Marty's mistakes. "They'll wait until dark now to take off," Agent Robinson noted later. "They'll make air drops now instead of landing. In Florida, sixty pounds of coke hit a man on the head last week." Robinson had heard that smugglers were experimenting with heavy nylon bags and vulcanized boxes to protect the dope during air drops. Operation Skynight had taught them a lesson, all right.

Chagra and the other defense attorneys were correct about Judge Wood. He'd bungled the wiretap ruling. All of the smugglers went to prison after the trial, but some months later the Fifth Circuit overturned Marty Houltin's and Curly Phillips's convictions. Since theirs were the only phones tapped, the Fifth Circuit ruled, the other smugglers had no standing under the appeal. Marty was returned to Judge Wood's court for a new trial. This time Chagra took a calculated risk and waived the right to jury trial. He wanted Wood to try it himself. He was certain the judge would blow the wiretap issue again. But the prosecution came up with a new tactic. Instead of using evidence from the wiretaps, they found a method that would force the other members of the Columbus Air Force to testify against Marty. Judge Wood couldn't actually *force* them to testify, of course, but he could refuse to reduce the sentences they were now serving, and he could also find them in contempt of court and add many years to their current sentences. It was a time of great soul searching for all the scammers. Chagra saved them from the embarrassment of actually testifying against their leader by conceding to the court that their testimony would support what the narcs said in the first trial. The judge found Marty guilty and returned him to prison. Chagra was certain that the case would again be reversed, but this time he was wrong.

It would be a long time before Marty got his wings again.

9

Taking care of the middle brother, Jimmy, had become a preoccupation with Lee and everyone else in the Chagra family. Little Mischief, as Mom Chagra had called him as a child, was now Big Mischief. He spoiled everything he touched. He ruined his marriage to Vivian, left her and the children without a penny or even an explanation. Dad and Mom invested their savings in a carpet store so as to give Jimmy something to occupy his restless nature, but Jimmy forgot to manage it and the business went bankrupt. Some even blamed Jimmy for Dad's fatal heart attack. He ran a floating blackjack game sometimes, and sometimes peddled dope. He gambled in Vegas and wrote bad checks and was constantly calling Lee to bail him out. Lee was always there.

Jimmy could be selfish and cruel. The family joked about the time a relative who had cured a serious drinking problem was visiting, how Jimmy walked through the room and asked as if it were the most casual question, "Hey, you back on the juice yet?" Or the time they were out in the middle of the lake in Joe's speedboat. His sister Patsy weighed 180 pounds back then. She had finally worked up nerve to wear a swimming suit in public, but had hedged the bet by also wearing a pair of panty hose. Jimmy called everyone's attention to this bizarre outfit and ripped her panty hose along one thigh. "A big blob of fat came pouring out," Patsy remembered. "It was something Lee never would have done, but Jimmy couldn't stop talking about it." And yet all of them loved Jimmy and endured his pouting and complaining as though he were the family birthright.

People said that Jimmy had no ambition, that there was nothing in this world that he wanted to be, but this wasn't entirely true—more than anything else, Jimmy wanted to be *Lee*. He wanted to dress the way Lee dressed, in fine clothes and jewelry, and he wanted to sense respect when he walked into a room and attention when he told a story. Sometimes Jimmy pretended he *was* Lee, signing Lee's name or repeating Lee's stories as though they had happened to him. There was a rivalry between the two brothers, a fierce and unyielding competition that only the two of them completely understood. Lee protected Jimmy, but he also contributed to Jimmy's sense of inadequacy. Paradoxically, Lee was secretly jealous of Jimmy. Lee fought like hell for everything he had, but things came easy for Jimmy. In some twisted way, Jimmy seemed better able to laugh off the competition, to have his cake and eat it too. Once Vivian and Jimmy went to Vegas with Jo Annie and Lee. Lee had lost heavily in the first few hours, but on this particular night Jimmy was on a roll and stayed in the casino until daylight. Lee did not react well to the role reversal; Vivian and Jo Annie had to spend most of the night in the hotel room consoling him, pampering and coddling him as though he were a baby with colic.

Vivian was a nineteen-year-old divorcée working the switchboard at the El Paso Sheraton Hotel when she first met Lee Chagra. Lee was just starting his law practice, and he and his friends came by the hotel almost every night to play cards. Vivian had been in El Paso only a few months, and the fact that this rakishly handsome young attorney with his classic Mediterranean features, dark reassuring eyes, and air of mystery even bothered to find out her name was a compliment outside Vivian's narrow experience. "I'm already taken," Lee told her, "but I got two brothers."

Vivian was unusually handsome, though she didn't think of herself that way. She had flowing auburn hair and the fine, sharp features of people who migrated to Texas from northern England in the last century. Her eyes changed colors with her mood, from subtle green to dusty brown, and she was tall. There was a hardness about her, too, a will to do more than just survive. She had grown up on a hardscrabble farm in North-central Texas, one of eight children born to a family that had known generations of poverty and hopelessness. One of her mother's few pleasures in life was thinking of cute hick names for her daughters—Darlene, Myrlene, Irene, Gracine, Charlene. Gracine got pregnant when she was fifteen, and not long after that took her baby, Cindy, and caught a bus for El Paso, where one of her sisters had moved. Somewhere along the road to El Paso, Gracine

decided to change her name to Vivian. She hated El Paso on sight—
the naked mountains, the ore refinery puffing orange smoke, the sprawl
of international slums—and yet El Paso was a gut thrill, like taking
part in a secret ceremony. When she met Lee Chagra several months
later, she knew she had made the right decision.

As promised, Lee introduced her to his brothers. At first she
dated Joe. He was handsome, polite, and strikingly well mannered,
but he was too young. Jimmy was almost terminally immature and
trivial, but in some ways he was almost a carbon copy of Lee, the
brother she would have preferred. Lee used to tell her: "Jimmy's got
the looks, but I've got the balls." It was true: Lee was rugged, handsome, proudly self-sufficient, but Jimmy had the larger-than-life coun-
tenance of a matinee idol, smooth coal-black hair and sleepy eyes like
Valentino. Even as she dated Jimmy, Vivian became Lee's confidante,
an attentive addition to the harem who seemed to constantly make
themselves available to the Chagra brothers. In December 1967, Vivian
and Jamiel Alexander Chagra were married. Dad and Mom Chagra
were not exactly delighted by the match, but as usual Lee intervened.
"I want to keep you in the family," he told Vivian.

Jimmy was working at the time for Saad Shaheen's Imported
Rug Company, but he didn't let work interfere with his true calling,
gambling. Jimmy had a little college—a cup of coffee, as they say—
but Jimmy was no more interested in formal education than he was
in formal employment. "He'd either bowl or shoot pool all night,"
Vivian said. "I'd watch and keep track of their bets. The gambling
money scared me. We were always broke, but Jimmy thought nothing
of betting five thousand dollars. At the same time, there was a thrill
I couldn't explain. Jimmy had so much guts; he wasn't timid or afraid
to ride a streak all the way." Six months after the wedding Vivian
got pregnant. For a few days Jimmy appeared elated over the prospect of fatherhood, and like Arabs throughout history talked about
his family and its lifeline to immortality. Then the emotion vanished
and Vivian saw very little of her husband. "I couldn't go out with
him [at night] and he wouldn't stay home," she said. "He'd go for
days without coming home."

Two months before the baby, Cathy, was born, Jimmy moved out,
but later he returned and things were good again. Abdou and Josephine Chagra mortgaged some property on Sunset Heights and
bought Jimmy his own carpet store, with the hope that he would

finally settle down. Jimmy loved the trappings of the new business, just as he loved his family, but both responsibilities were more than he could handle. "He had no discipline, no patience," Vivian remembered. "Mom would call from the store and tell me to get Jimmy out of bed after he'd been up all night gambling. I tried to protect him. I just wanted him to conform enough so that we could survive." When Vivian got pregnant again, Jimmy moved out. "I just can't go through that again," he told her. "I can't fit that role." Vivian moved back to her family's farm, but a few weeks before the baby was due Jimmy showed up unexpectedly, demanding that his wife return with him to El Paso. Though Vivian's doctor advised against travel, Jimmy was determined that the baby be born in El Paso, where every Chagra for half a century had been born. Vivian's mother asked, "Is it gonna work?" and Vivian said she would *make* it work. "The children were Chagras," she said. "I felt I had an obligation to the family. I knew that's the way Lee wanted it. For better or worse, I was a Chagra woman. That meant something."

Lee was extremely protective of Vivian and her children, and for a change Jimmy seemed to respond to responsibility. When the baby was born, Jimmy bought Vivian a $300 gold watch, the first piece of jewelry she had ever owned. Vivian got the impression that some of the Chagras resented her having the gift, but she wore it anyway. "I thought of it as services rendered," she said. Things were going badly at the carpet store. The store was still in Jimmy's name, but Dad and Mom Chagra had taken control of the money. Jimmy continued to gamble with his part of the income, and Mom slipped Vivian money from time to time. As always, Lee filled in the gaps. Shortly before Christmas 1971, Jimmy split for California, leaving Lee to cover his trail of bad debts, and his parents to manage the business. Lee was furious. Dad was in poor health and the business was tottering on bankruptcy. Nevertheless, when Jimmy telephoned in the spring and asked Vivian for "one more chance," Lee encouraged her to go. She gathered her children and some furniture and drove to California, but she already knew the marriage was doomed. The last straw was when she caught Jimmy with another woman. "I called Lee and told him I was renting a U-Haul and heading home," she said. "He begged me to at least stay until Mom could fly out to the coast. She arrived with three hundred dollars, which she gave to Jimmy. I had thirty-six dollars in the bank. She told me, 'I'm sure that when the thirty-six dollars runs out you'll come back. I've been through the same thing with Abdou for years.' " This time Vivian defied the family code. She returned to El Paso and filed for divorce.

"I was numb from what the Chagra men had done to me," she remembered. "I was still a Chagra woman but I couldn't play the part anymore. I couldn't gush and hang on to every word the way the other women did. I know it hurt Jimmy, but it hurt Lee even more. I stayed close to the family because of the children and because that's what Lee wanted, but I knew I had had it. Jimmy made some attempts to support me and Lee did the rest. With Lee's help, I gradually got well. I'm very loyal to the family but I can't hide the fact it was a horrible marriage."

While the divorce was running its course, Abdou suffered a heart attack. Before Jimmy could fly home from California, Dad Chagra was dead. Now Lee was truly the patriarch. Vivian couldn't bring herself to attend her father-in-law's funeral, and some members of the family wanted to cut off her financial support, but Lee wouldn't hear of it. "She's the mother of Jimmy's children," Lee reminded them. With the help of both Lee and Jimmy, Vivian bought a home in Anthony, New Mexico, just across the state line in the Upper Valley. She worked for a while as a stable girl for a ranch that raised racehorses. Later, Lee helped Vivian borrow enough money to open her own bar, a place called the Fox on North Mesa, near the Sheraton. She dated other men, but the Chagras let it be known that they disapproved, and her suitors quickly got the message. Lee never completely abandoned hope that Vivian and Jimmy would get back together, even though Jimmy didn't show the slightest interest in Vivian except when she showed interest in other men. Vivian knew Jimmy was running a floating blackjack game full-time now, and she had heard, though she did not believe, rumors that Jimmy was involved in drug trafficking. She knew for a fact that Jimmy *disapproved* of all drugs, including alcohol; he'd lectured her on the subject enough times.

But something was happening: the Chagras were spending enormous sums of money on new Lincolns and gold and trips to Vegas. Somebody had made a score. That summer, the summer of 1975, Jimmy telephoned his sister, Patsy, from Boston and asked her to meet Mike Halliday at the airport. He sounded very mysterious, but Jimmy

66

could sound mysterious ordering an ice cream cone. All Lee had told her was that Jimmy, Jack Stricklin, Mike Halliday, and some others had been doing something on the East Coast. When Halliday deplaned he was carrying a small suitcase and cackling like an escaped lunatic. He grabbed Patsy's hand and sprinted her toward the front entrance of the terminal; obviously, the only piece of luggage that interested him was the one in his hand. A few feet from the door he stumbled, taking Patsy with him to the floor. The suitcase flew open and for a few seconds Patsy was staring at more cash than she had ever seen before—$120,000.

It was four years before anyone recognized the achievement, but the operation that Jimmy had helped put together that summer was a landmark in marijuana trafficking. It was the first time anyone from El Paso had thought of using a tramp steamer. Instead of flying the customary small planeload of two thousand pounds from Mexico, they imported fifty-four thousand pounds from Colombia. El Paso's smugglers were for the first time working on a world-class scale. Although the taste of dope smokers in the Southwest hadn't yet reached the point where customers were demanding more exotic weed than the no-nonsense stuff grown in the mountains of Mexico, Jimmy recognized that the market was ready: exotic weeds from South America were already selling for $400 to $500 a pound in the East, compared to the $80 to $100 that Mexican grass brought in Texas. Jimmy had also learned that there were some families in Colombia willing to front both the marijuana and the ship. This was a new ball game; they were talking about millions rather than hundreds of thousands of dollars.

The idea of shipping the load to an isolated cove on the northwestern point of Massachusetts Bay above Boston came from Jimmy's new partner, Peter Krutschewski, a highly decorated former Army helicopter pilot who had been stationed in El Paso. Krutschewski, also known as Peter Blake, was rumored to have Mafia connections in Boston. They took as their third partner Jack Stricklin, an expert at distribution and logistical problems. Stricklin's own business, which Lee Chagra had incorporated under the name BHS Enterprises, had suffered several recent setbacks. He had narrowly escaped a setup bust at the Desert Inn Motel in El Paso, only to suffer the ignominy of being busted by a roving patrol of officers from the New Mexico Game and Fish Department who stopped him on a desolate pipeline road near Roswell and found not illegal game but 2,250 pounds of marijuana. If Lee couldn't beat that rap on an illegal search, Stricklin would do his first prison stretch since his days in the Navy brig. Meanwhile, there was the consolation of a multimillion-dollar score in Boston.

While Jimmy Chagra and Peter Blake flew to Barranquilla, Colombia, to arrange for the load and the ship, Stricklin and his ace technician, Mike Halliday, conducted an on-site inspection of Foley's Cove. It was perfect—remote and inaccessible except by sea. There was no beach at all, only granite cliffs tall as three-story buildings. The mouth of the cove was deep enough that a mothership could anchor under the protective shadows of the cliffs, a perfect shelter for the off-loading operation. Halliday supervised construction of a plywood dock anchored to the wall of a cliff where the current was weakest, and from the top of the cliffs he rigged a pulley apparatus anchored to two apple trees and attached to a giant fisherman's net in which the hundred-pound bales would ride. Stricklin rented a stash house nearby and spent time charting the currents and making practice runs with small boats.

Ninety-nine out of a hundred dope operations turn out to be a series of slapstick misadventures that would offend the sensibilities of the Three Stooges, but this one seemed to have been blessed by the gods. Jimmy Chagra and Peter Blake had been in Barranquilla less than a week when they met a dope dealer named Juaco who introduced them to his boss, an impresario named Lionel Gomez, with whom Chagra would do business for the next several years. A few weeks later an old freighter steamed into Foley's Cove. It took three days to unload the bales and hoist them to the top of the cliffs, and trucks began arriving as the first load was deposited in the stash house. Within a week every kilo, every leaf, stem, and seed, was on its way to market. The distributors advanced the smugglers about $500,000, which was used to cover immediate expenses and pay off the crews. Then Jimmy Chagra went home to wait for the profits to filter back.

The old black sheep, the family goof-up, had just made more money in two weeks than Lee had made his entire life. Jimmy didn't tell the family how. But they heard him say over and over: "We're all rich!"

10

That next summer the Chagra brothers hit Las Vegas like a blizzard of kamikaze locusts. The money from the big score in Massachusetts was pouring in, and Lee and Jimmy were racing to see who could lose it first. Folks in Vegas can be terribly blasé, assuming, as they do, that they have seen it all: Kentucky colonels, Arab sheiks, Latin American dictators, Houston oilmen, French industrialists, even the legendary head-to-head poker game between Nick the Greek Dandolos and Dallas gambler Johnny Moss that lasted five months. Hunter Thompson once described how they shot a three-hundred-pound bear out of a cannon right in the middle of one casino and no one bothered to look up. But Vegas had never seen anything that surpassed the performance of Lee and Jimmy Chagra in the summer of 1976.

Lee drew a crowd simply by walking through the front door at Caesar's Palace, passing out money, and asking how much they loved him. "Do you love me, do you *love* me?" He knew the answer, but he had to hear it again. Everything was on the house. On five minutes' notice, Caesar's would dispatch a Learjet to fetch one or both of the Chagra brothers. People in the Chagras' party didn't bother to register; they just walked up to the desk and someone handed them a key to a six-room suite. Jimmy preferred the Sinatra duplex penthouse with its white baby grand piano and spiral staircase. Food, drinks, girls—anything anyone fancied was there in a whisk.

On the casino floor, special sections were roped off for the Chagras. Security guards kept the riffraff away. Only a few select friends or celebrities like Rosey Grier or Gabe Kaplan were allowed in. When an average high-stakes player sits down at one of the seven places around a blackjack table, his limit might be as high as $1,000 a hand. Lee's limit was $3,000, and he would have played for $10,000 had Caesar's Palace allowed it. He had $250,000 credit at Caesar's, and an equal amount at two other casinos. Eventually, Jimmy's limit *was* $10,000 a hand and his credit virtually unlimited anywhere in town. When either of the Chagras sat at the blackjack table, he took all seven spots. Lee loved being at the middle of the table, flanked by armed guards and at least one beautiful "broad" who lit his cigarettes and served as his lucky piece. They couldn't deal fast enough for Lee . . . all the spots covered with white chips, $21,000 riding on every deal.

Time came when both Chagras got bored with blackjack—it was too slow. The real action was at the crap table. A friend described a typical roll of dice for Jimmy Chagra. Jimmy would put $10,000 on the pass line and roll his point. Say it was a four. Then he'd put another $10,000 behind the pass line on the odds, and another $10,000 on the come. His second dice roll was a five. He put another $10,000 odds on the five and another $10,000 on the come. By now he had thrown the dice twice and there was $50,000 on the table. Pretty soon there was $120,000 on the numbers, $10,000 on the come, $10,000 on the line, and $10,00 behind the line—what gamblers call "loading the boat." At this point the only roll that would hurt him was a seven. "It doesn't take long to throw a pair of dice," the friend said. "In five minutes he might bet a million dollars."

Curiously, this kind of heavy action seemed to bring out the best in Jimmy and the worst in Lee. When Lee hit a losing streak, he could fly into a snit, blaming anyone handy, especially Jo Annie, who more than once hurried off the casino floor in tears. Clark Hughes recalled Lee throwing a tantrum because Clark had forgotten to wear his freedom bracelet. Jimmy, on the other hand, had a true gambler's instinct, a fatalistic kill-or-be-killed attitude. "For pure gambling," said Jimmy Salome, "Jimmy may have been the strongest anyone in Vegas ever saw. There have been people who gambled higher in one sitting, but week after week, month after month, nobody kept coming, kept flat *firing* at 'em like Jimmy Chagra."

No one except Lee and Jimmy knew how much they lost that summer; the family wasn't even sure that Jimmy knew. But Lee did. Although he seemed at times incorrigibly reckless, Lee kept detailed records of his gambling activities. That previous football season Lee had bet and won at least $100,000, and when it came time for Super Bowl X, he bet everything he had on the game. In fact, he bet everything that every member of his family had. The bet was so enormous that his regular bookie laid it off on a group of hoods from Chicago. He won the bet by a single point when Dallas Cowboys quarterback Roger Staubach threw one of his miracle passes in the final seconds; the Cowboys didn't win the game, but they beat the points, saving the Chagra family from ruin. Clark Hughes recalled making a trip with Lee to Las Vegas where the Chicago mobsters were waiting to pay off. "We knocked on the door of a suite at Caesar's and were admitted to a room full of some very big and sinister-looking men who looked as though they ought to be in some alley waiting for Elliot Ness," Clark said. They had $300,000 stuffed into plastic garbage bags. Lee thanked them, and he and Clark left without another word. Lee blew the $300,000 and a lot more that summer. Joe Chagra guessed that together Jimmy and Lee went through $3 million or more.

Joe Chagra hardly saw his brothers for four months. On one occasion they flew home from Las Vegas and Lee deposited $500,000 in the law firm's account, but that was just about Lee's sole contribution to the practice, such as it was. Joe had married his secretary, Patty Malooly, the previous January, but because Lee was away so frequently the couple didn't have time for a honeymoon. Most of the work was old or holdover business—Marty Houltin's appeal, Jack Stricklin's indictment in the New Mexico game-warden bust, cases of that nature. Until Lee deposited the half million, the firm was almost broke. Patty's sister, Sandy Messer, also went to work for the law firm that summer, ostensibly as Lee's secretary, though she hardly ever saw him. One night in August, Lee called Sandy and said, "I blew it . . . I blew it all." Sandy didn't have any idea what Lee was talking about. "Don't you *understand?*" he yelled. "I just blew my guts out!" There were gestures to the family, of course: Lee bought one of his children a new car, and gave out some expensive gifts of jewelry; he even arranged for Joe and Patty to take a belated honeymoon to Sun Valley, where a friend of Lee's from Caesar's Palace loaned them his condominium. The family didn't realize it at the time, but this was also the summer that Lee started using cocaine. Jimmy and his girlfriend, Liz Nichols, and even the youngest Chagra, Joe, had used drugs for some time, but until the summer of 1976, Lee refused to touch any kind of dope, though he made his money representing dealers.

By early autumn the money was gone and Lee was back in El Paso "pumping money," as he called his practice by now. He hustled personal injury cases, divorces, wills—he was practically chasing ambulances. "He didn't seem at all depressed," said Donna Johnson, the law firm's bookkeeper. "He was really happy that all the money was gone and he had to work again. Lee was always much more lovable when he was broke and hustling for a living."

In the weeks that followed the binge in Vegas, the law practice flourished as it had not since Lee's indictment in Nashville more than three years earlier. Two highly publicized cases in particular created the momentum—one involving a twenty-seven-year-old former El Paso medical student named Teddy Mapula charged with capital murder in the shooting of an Anthony, New Mexico, cop, and the other a bizarre case involving a veteran narcotics agent named George Hough, who claimed that he had been framed by a superior in a cocaine bust.

Mapula, who came from an upper-middle-class Syrian family, had apparently fried his brains on drugs and was wandering along the highway between El Paso and Anthony, New Mexico, carrying a bag of plums, a Hank Williams, Jr., record album, and a small vial of marijuana. When Anthony policeman Ernesto Rascon stopped him and asked where he was headed, Mapula answered, "West." The cop drew a pistol, a struggle ensued, and Rascon was killed with his own weapon. El Paso district attorney Steve Simmons was asking the death penalty. In their own investigation, Lee and Joe Chagra discovered that the cop had been fired from the El Paso police department two years earlier, following an incident in which he allegedly took three juvenile runaway girls to his apartment and engaged in sexual intercourse with one of them. There were other allegations against Rascon, including the testimony of a Fort Bliss soldier who claimed to have been beaten by the cop. Lee convinced the jury that the encounter on the highway was a tragic meeting between two people who could not possibly understand each other—a bad cop and a young man of "simple pleasures." Even the small vial of marijuana worked in favor of the defendant: testimony demonstrated that after the fatal shot, Mapula did not flee but sat down to eat his plums and smoke a joint. Instead of capital murder, Mapula was found guilty of voluntary manslaughter and given five years' probation. After the verdict, Judge Sam Callan delivered a lecture on "an endless parade of moral zombies [who] pass before me" and spoke of his strong feelings that because of drugs the country was sinking "into an abyss of totalitarian hell." Hardly anyone realized it at the time, but there was another incident during the course of the trial that illustrated even more clearly the consequences of drug abuse. During jury selection, Joe Chagra suffered a mysterious seizure and passed out. The young attorney was just overworked, most people said; the Mapula case had been a pressure cooker. What hardly anyone except the family realized was that Joe had got himself strung out on diet pills and cocaine.

As many predicted when the Nixon administration declared war on drugs, the country was embarking on a nebulous pursuit wherein the hunters could frequently be mistaken for the hunted: The case against Customs Patrol officer George Hough demonstrated that he was less a victim of the culture than of the war. When the DEA assumed responsibility for drug enforcement, Customs lost the manpower to conduct investigations and maintain networks of intelligence, but still had the duty to interdict narcotics along the border. Customs reacted by establishing a new unit called the Customs Patrol Office (CPO) and transferred a number of former sky marshals and dock patrolmen from the East and Midwest to the Texas-Mexico border. The new recruits had no training in narcotics and knew nothing of the traditions and methods of people along the river. Many former Customs officers who had been transferred to DEA applied for a second transfer to CPO, among them George Hough. According to Hough, the CPO and the DEA were now in a race to see which agency could commit the most vile transgressions—illegal wiretaps, breaking and entering, kidnapping, planting evidence, attempted assassination, no method was too strong for the warring enemies of drugs. Hough admitted taking part in all of these crimes. He ran afoul of the system, however, when his supervisor planted a stash of cocaine near the airport and videotaped Hough trying to carry the drug home. It was the cocaine charge that brought Hough to the office of the famous drug attorney Lee Chagra.

Fascinated by the possibilities, Lee and Joe Chagra tape-recorded Hough's recollections of life in the narcotics service. Hough described in detail how he and his prize informant burglarized the homes of two local dope dealers and stole documents and other valuables, how he tried to kidnap another dope dealer and turn him over to the Mexican *federales* for a reward of 50,000 pesos, how agents satisfied "quotas" by falsifying evidence and sometimes stealing loads of marijuana in Mexico and then suddenly "discovering" them on the American side of the river, about attempts to trade government weapons for narcotics, how rival agencies "torpedoed" each other's operations by tipping off suspected smugglers, and how he and another CPO trapped a West Texas businessman by blackmailing him with a phony Internal Revenue Service file. "We made him a simple offer," Hough said. "We'd destroy the IRS file if he would rat off a few of his friends. He told us he didn't have any friends who were smugglers, and we told him he better make up some." Hough named names and gave dates; he even had some official documents supporting his stories.

The most grisly part of the taped account was when Hough described how he and his partner, a young agent recently reassigned from the sky-marshal program, were ordered by their superior to assassinate a well-known New Mexico scammer named Jim French. "The Frenchman is a psycho," one of Hough's bosses told him, always armed and dangerous. "If you see him, blow his shit away." One morning after locating 800 pounds of grass beside a smugglers' landing strip in the Chihuahuan desert and waiting there in ambush with an automatic rifle, Hough saw the Frenchman's yellow-and-white Piper Aztec approaching from the north. Then he saw a second plane: it was possible the Frenchman had someone flying cover. Hough had his own surveillance plane circling somewhere in the area. According to Hough, his orders were to waste French but spare his plane, which would be flown across the border and conveniently discovered at some later date; so he waited until French landed and got out of the Piper Aztec. Several times Hough had French in the sights of his automatic rifle, but each time he was ready to squeeze the trigger, the Frenchman moved behind his airplane. As Hough once more trained his sights on French's head, his radio squawked and his surveillance pilot reported: "He's got someone flying cover. Don't take him off!" Hough and his partner watched helplessly as French refueled and took off. Apparently the 800 pounds belonged to another smuggler, because the Frenchman went nowhere near the stash. Hough flew the stash back to El Paso and stored it in his locker near the Bridge of the Americas. A few days after that he found French's plane parked at the Truth or Consequences, New Mexico, airport. While other agents poured sand in the plane's gas tank, Hough and his partner sprinkled marijuana sweepings on the carpet. Then they seized the plane as a suspected carrier of contraband. Lee Chagra remembered the case well; in fact, Lee's work on behalf of the Frenchman had forced the government to return the plane.

Now that George Hough was caught in the dirty web he'd helped to spin, he was angry, frustrated, and ready to rat off every narc in town; but as Lee played back the four hours of tape, it became apparent that the only one Hough was really incriminating was himself. Lee knew about the investigation into DEA that U.S. magistrate Jamie Boyd had initiated, and he arranged for Hough to testify before the grand jury. Not that he believed Hough's allegations would serve any purpose. Lee agreed with Boyd's assessment that the whole affair would be whitewashed. U.S. attorney John Clark did agree to grant Hough immunity for the burglaries, illegal wiretaps, and other admitted transgressions, but Hough would have to stand trial on the cocaine charge.

The case was set in the court of Judge John Wood. While Lee realized that his client's chances were not good, he regarded the trial as a showcase for his own passionate hatred of narcotics enforcement. There was at least a chance the jury would be sympathetic. On the day of the trial, as they were walking to the federal courthouse, Hough told the lawyers that he had changed his mind, that he had decided to waive trial and plead guilty. The lawyers were stunned: it was suddenly apparent that Hough had not been honest with them. Lee reminded the agent that admission of even one count of cocaine possession could get him fifteen years, but Hough said that some "promises" had been made. What promises? By whom? Hough wouldn't say, except that someone in authority had promised that his sentence would be light, and that even if he had to do time, it would be in a place where he could be protected from other inmates, some of whom Hough had helped send to prison. "We couldn't figure it out," Joe Chagra said. "Hough was scared to death of prison. Yet he was trusting some unnamed authority with nothing in writing. We strongly advised him to change his mind before it was too late. Lee even put it in the record that Hough was pleading against advice of his attorneys." Whoever promised Hough a sweet deal wasn't there on the day of sentencing. Hough received twelve years and no guarantee of special treatment. The Chagras filed a motion to withdraw the guilty plea, but Judge Wood refused. While Joe Chagra was filing a motion for a rehearing, George Hough disappeared. He hasn't been seen since.

In contrast to the Mapula and Hough cases, another case that occupied a good deal of Lee Chagra's attention during the autumn of 1976 went almost unnoticed, at least at the time. The client was Jerry Edwin Johnson, a local con man and admitted drug smuggler who had tried to defraud the IRS of $250,000. Johnson was doing time on the fraud charge at La Tuna federal correctional institution, which was on the New Mexico state line not far from El Paso. Now the government was trying to prove that Johnson had helped smuggle a pound of heroin out of Mexico.

Lee didn't know at the time that Johnson had, as they say, "gone over." He'd become a government snitch, albeit a not very reliable one. Without Lee's knowledge, a group of DEA agents and prosecutors took Johnson from La Tuna to a secret meeting at a motel. Ostensibly, the purpose of this unorthodox and legally questionable meeting was to gather information in a case against another of Lee Chagra's clients, Tommy Hiett. Johnson told the agents and prosecutors that he and Hiett had once smuggled a pound of heroin from Mexico. But the interviewers quickly moved away from Hiett and directed the informant's attention to a lost list of other names. Johnson implicated at least sixty El Paso citizens as major drug traffickers. There wasn't any Mr. Big, Johnson said, but if the narcs preferred to look at it that way, Lee Chagra's was as good a name as any. The interview was patently leading; most of the questions were of the when-did-you-stop-beating-your-wife-variety. A sample:

Q. What about Lee Chagra? Is he connected with Tommy Hiett or is his [dope smuggling] operation separate?

A. I think now it's a separate deal. . . . I'm not sure. At one time when Tommy was doing anything Lee got an override on everything. He got so much a pound for his weed or so much an ounce if there was something else.

Q. Are you in close enough to Lee that he would trust you in introducing somebody back east or something like that?

A. Lee is like Tommy . . . he's a cagey son of a gun. I've got a boy from back east, he buys about $25,000-$50,000 a month, and he's bought off of Lee's outfit now three times and he's yet ever to meet Lee,

Jack Stricklin, or anybody. They strictly use me as the buffer and the nut, you know? If anything would come down, that's as far as it could go . . . back to me. No, I don't think Lee would ever let himself be involved with a direct buy.

The agents thought so little of the information gleaned in the interview that they didn't even bother to place Jerry Edwin Johnson under oath. "I think he just told us whatever he thought we wanted to hear," DEA agent J. T. Robinson later admitted. The fifty-page text of the interview was used as supplemental material by the grand jury in Tommy Hiett's tax-fraud case, but was never given the slightest weight as courtroom evidence. By law, the interview was to remain secret, known to only a handful of agents and prosecutors who read the transcript as part of their official duties. Instead, this flimsy, highly prejudicial document eventually became public knowledge and it dogged both Lee Chagra and his nemesis, Judge John Wood, to their graves.

11

In his eleven years in the El Paso politics scene, Jamie Boyd had been elected to public office only one time, to fill out the unexpired term of district attorney in 1970. Yet no politician in town had a better feel for the bureaucracy or for subtle shifts of power and opinion. Jamie knew how to pick a winner, how to recognize a loser, and when to jump ship. Once a staunch supporter of liberal Senator Ralph Yarborough, who had helped him get appointed assistant U.S. attorney in 1960, Jamie read the mood of the state ten years later and backed Lloyd Bentsen's successful challenge for Yarborough's seat in the Senate. When Nixon came to power in 1968, Jamie could have stayed in his job as an assistant U.S. attorney, but his political senses told him to look for work elsewhere, and this loyalty to the Democratic Party eventually paid dividends. By maintaining close ties to Travis Johnson, El Paso's Democratic Party kingmaker, Boyd had run the gamut of offices: assistant county attorney, assistant U.S. attorney, district attorney, U.S. magistrate.

It was during his tenure as magistrate, and especially during the grand jury investigation into the DEA, that Jamie Boyd and Lee Chagra became friends, though they were never close friends. Boyd parked his car in the lot next to Lee's office across from the courthouse and fell into the habit of stopping by after work. Chagra understood how things were at the federal courthouse: if Jamie set high bonds, it was because Judge Ernest Guinn demanded high bonds. Jamie was just a good soldier. Lee, Sib Abraham, and a number of other criminal lawyers came to look on Jamie Boyd as a bright, ambitious politician whose interests ran more or less parallel to their own. When the Democrats regained control of the White House in the elections of November 1976, state senator Tati Santiesteban telephoned several old friends, including Lee, Sib, and bail bondsman Vic Apodaca, and convinced them that Jamie Boyd would be a good candidate for the job of U.S. attorney. There had never before been a U.S. attorney from El Paso; the pass was always the outlands of the Western District. A few weeks after the elections, Santiesteban, Chagra, Abraham, and Apodaca called on Travis Johnson and recommended Jamie Boyd for the job. Jamie was sworn in two months later. In the year that followed, the new U.S. attorney launched investigations and attempted to indict three of these four men.

With one major exception, Boyd had never been a crusader. That exception was his views on gambling—he had developed a passionate hatred for all gamblers after the shotgun murder of an Oklahoma gambler in El Paso while Boyd was district attorney. Though Lee Chagra got the killer, another gambler, acquitted by convincing the jury it was self-defense, Boyd became convinced that the "Dixie Mafia" was making a power play on the city and instigated a controversial grand jury investigation. "I wasn't a crusader but gambling was so open and obvious it appeared the DA was either stupid or on the take," Boyd recalled. "I didn't care for either title." From the grand jury room leaked some prominent names from the business and sports world. Lee and Jimmy Chagra were among the many citizens called to testify. One of the more sensational aspects of the investigation was a raid in which men from the DA's office kicked in the door of a private club in downtown El Paso.

With drugs turning in an even higher profit than gambling, Boyd was more convinced than ever that a Mafia had taken control: the Dixie Mafia, the Mexican Mafia, the Syrian Mafia—whichever name it was called, Boyd believed it was his job to bring it down. What he needed was a tough and relentless prosecutor to take over the El Paso docket. He decided on James Kerr, one of the assistant U.S. attorneys he had inherited from the Republican regime.

A graduate of SMU's law school, Kerr had worked for the Justice Department and helped draft the 1970 Drug Control Act. Later he built a reputation as a hard-driving prosecutor in charge of the docket in Del Rio, where he and Judge John Wood became fast friends. This friendship, the fact that the prosecutor and the judge were seen socializing so often, caused many lawyers to question Wood's impartiality. "Kerr exercised enormous power in that small Texas town," said another assistant prosecutor. "Every lawyer who practiced in Wood's court had to kiss Jim Kerr's ass." Together, the judge and the prosecutor formed a judicial juggernaut, sometimes disposing of two, three, or even four cases in a single marathon session. In 1975, Wood established a record by handling eighty cases in two days. Because of this unique relationship, Kerr was eventually transferred out of Del Rio. "A judge can't associate with a prosecutor the way Wood did with Kerr and still call 'em correctly," said John Pinckney III, who was chief assistant U.S. attorney at the time. "John H. [as the judge's close friends called him] was pro-prosecution and it showed."

Boyd had his reasons for uniting Kerr and Wood. Kerr's long association with FBI, IRS, and DEA agents—clients, he called them—had convinced him of the same sort of monolithic conspiracy theory that fascinated Jamie Boyd. Narcotics and gambling were crimes that grew from a common stem, composed of the worst elements of society. Composed of, and by, and for organized crime. The Mafia. "The El Paso office was in bad shape," Boyd said. "Frankly, I was concerned that some of the prosecutors were making it too easy for Sib Abraham's clients to plea-bargain. Also, Kerr was single, so moving to El Paso wouldn't cause a hardship on his family. But the primary reason was this—Kerr was an empire builder. Everywhere he went he was inclined to organize things to his own type of operation. I knew that he would take a hard look at narcotics and organized crime."

Though Boyd did not, at least for the moment, spell it out, he regarded Lee Chagra as the boss of bosses, the godfather of organized crime in El Paso. So along with the proven chemistry of Kerr and Wood, Boyd must have understood the volatile possibilities of mixing Kerr with Lee Chagra. It was hard to imagine two men more different. Kerr was frail and sallow-faced and talked in a high-pitched voice that suggested he was about to shatter. Chagra had little use for public servants, especially prosecutors, and Kerr was a classic bureaucrat, squeaking with authority and wedded to the book. Chagra's idea of a good time was slapping a Willie Nelson album on the stereo, snorting cocaine, and getting naked in a pile of aromatic bodies. Kerr preferred playing Bach fugues in the dim light of the First Presbyterian Church and going to the symphony. In a short time Lee Chagra despised James Kerr, and Kerr had every reason to despise Chagra. Kerr thought Chagra was vulgar and common, and Chagra enjoyed enhancing this image by slipping up behind Kerr and whispering things that made the prosecutor blush. Chagra could win or lose more in a single roll of the dice than Kerr made in a year. Kerr claimed that the money didn't matter, that his mission was "vigorously and, I hope, successfully" prosecuting all offenders that his clients could provide, but the mere fact that his adversary put such emphasis on money and the trappings of wealth must have touched some deep reserve of resentment in him.

In no time at all, James Kerr was on Lee Chagra like a mongoose on a snake.

12

The summer of 1977 was a time of great exhilaration in the life of Jimmy Chagra, but it was the beginning of the end for Lee. Still flush from the big score in Massachusetts, using the same connections in Colombia, Jimmy seemed to be jumping from one disaster to another, but he invariably landed on his feet. Lee, on the other hand, was sliding off the edge. Sparring with judges like Wood and prosecutors like Kerr had once been fun, but now it was drudgery. It seemed like dirty, degrading work, and more than that, it seemed agonizingly commonplace, compared to the high times Jimmy was enjoying. "I don't know what I was trying to prove," Lee told friends. He felt like junking his whole career. Until the Massachusetts scam, Lee had been inclined to look down his nose at his brother's smuggling operation, but now he felt like joining it.

But in the summer of 1977 two dramatic events half a world apart signed a new, exciting, and tragically final phase in the life of Lee Chagra. The first was a highly publicized bust in Ardmore, Oklahoma, in which some of Jimmy's smuggling crew, including pilot Jerry Wilson, were caught red-handed with 17,000 pounds of top-grade Colombian marijuana. The second, seven months later, was the crash of a DC-6 in Colombia. Jerry Wilson and several others survived, but the copilot Jimmy Chagra had hired for the mission died from burns.

Jerry Wilson was an old friend of the Chagras, a professional pilot who had worked for Jet Avia charter service out of Las Vegas and had flown Lee and Jimmy and almost everyone else in the Chagra family from El Paso to Las Vegas and back many times. In recent months he'd begun moonlighting for Jimmy Chagra. Wilson, who was a dead ringer for TV star Gabe Kaplan, same brush mustache, same dry wit and ironic personality, had four kids and an ambition to do something more than jockey gamblers to and from Vegas. Jimmy Chagra gave him the opportunity. The narcs had been watching the operation at least as far back as July 1976, when a U.S. Customs aircraft spotted Wilson's twin Beech D-18 crossing the Mexican border near Antelope Wells, New Mexico. Customs radar lost him, but agents located the twin Beech a short time later at the airport in Cochise County, Arizona. Customs agents claimed that they detected "a strong odor" of marijuana in the aircraft's interior, which had been stripped of its seats and modified by installing a heavy cargo floor of Plexiglas. Wilson was arrested on a technicality—failure to clear Customs—and the aircraft was seized, but there wasn't enough evidence to file dope-smuggling charges.

All during the summer and fall of 1976, the narcs kept an eye on Jerry Wilson and on another pilot who frequently worked with him, a man from Kansas City named Dick Joyce. The trail always led to Jimmy Chagra. The narcs also suspected Jack Stricklin of being one of the leaders in the smuggling operation, even though Stricklin was doing time at La Tuna. Jimmy Chagra, Jerry Wilson, and some others who had been part of Stricklin's old group spent a lot of time talking behind closed doors in Lee Chagra's law office. The narcs must have sensed that this time they were on to the big guys. It was common to spot Jimmy Chagra hurrying out of his brother's law office to the pay phone on the corner near the courthouse. Jimmy always carried a canvas bag of quarters. In November, Customs agents convinced a judge to allow them to attach a beeper transmitter to Dick Joyce's twin-engine Lockheed Lodestar. Right after Thanksgiving, agents arrested both Dick Joyce and Jerry Wilson at the airport in Cochise County, Arizona, again on the technicality that they had violated navigational regulations. Some marijuana debris was discovered on the floorboard of the Lodestar, but not enough to make a case.

In December 1976, the narcs got their break. An informant told them that the smugglers were now using an abandoned airstrip outside of Ardmore, Oklahoma. The narcs learned that both pilots were flying new aircraft. Jerry Wilson had acquired a Douglas DC-4 and Joyce was flying a yellow-and-white Cessna 310. The net was prepared and an alert went out to every agency that might possibly offer assistance—the DEA, Customs, narcotics agents in Louisiana, Texas, Oklahoma, and New Mexico, the FAA, and air traffic controllers in four states.

On the cold, clear night of December 30, 1976, the task force of agents got the first alarm when Dick Joyce's Cessna 310 landed at New Orleans and routinely cleared Customs. Joyce told Customs officers that he had flown from Grand Cayman Island in the Caribbean, a good 1,500 miles from New Orleans. He said that he was headed for Oklahoma City, and the officers observed that the Cessna flew off toward the northwest.

About three hours later the air traffic controller in the small East Texas community of Longview had an interesting experience that almost went unnoticed. A transmission from a DC-4 that identified itself as Ross 109 radioed the Longview tower and asked if the facility had twenty-four-hour fuel service. Ross 109 appeared momentarily lost. The pilot knew that he was somewhere over East Texas but he wasn't sure where. He could see some lights off in the distance but he couldn't determine if the town was Tyler, Kilgore, Marshall, or Longview. The pilot was obviously a stranger to these parts. The air traffic controller contacted his counterpart in Marshall and by blinking the tower lights in different sequences, they were able to guide the pilot to a safe landing in Longview, where fuel was available. Ross 109 thanked the Longview tower and added, "Don't tell my boss I did this!" The voice in the tower replied: "If you won't tell mine!"

This camaraderie was exactly what Jerry Wilson had hoped for, and he slipped into his best Gabe Kaplan voice and told the tower: "Uh, we're flying for the Atomic Energy Commission and we have some, uh, contaminated waste material and, uh, we'll need to park off the ramp, uh, at least five hundred feet."

"Roger," the tower said. "No problem. Where you headed tonight?"

"We're going up to Tonopah, Nevada," Ross 109 replied. Jerry Wilson was familiar with the small, isolated landing places in the Nevada desert sometimes used by the Atomic Energy Commission aircraft, and he knew the names of the air taxi services that worked them. That's why he had used the name Ross. The man in the tower directed Ross 109 to the south end of the field, a thousand feet from the ramp, well away from the lights. As soon as Jerry Wilson had stopped the aircraft, he shut down everything. The air controller could barely distinguish the DC-4 in the beam of headlights from the fuel truck, but there was no reason at all to question the action. The man in the tower knew that Ross Air Taxi frequently flew nuclear waste for the AEC, and parking far from the ramp was standard procedure. Ross normally flew De Havilland Twin Otters, but this didn't occur to the air traffic controller at the moment.

Minutes after the DC-4 had refueled and taken off, there was a radio transmission from the chief of air traffic control in Fort Worth. They were looking for Dick Joyce's Cessna.

"The only aircraft that I've got is a DC-4 that just took off," the Longview told Fort Worth. He could see the flickering lights from Ross 109 heading west. Then he saw another, smaller plane. It had apparently been circling overhead all the time. He tried calling Ross 109 on several different frequencies, but there was no response. Fort Worth instructed Longview to monitor frequency 122.9. For a few seconds Longview overheard the two pilots chattering. He heard the name Jerry, then a voice said: "We'd better go to another frequency," and the tower lost them. A few minutes later the radar in Fort Worth spotted two blips side by side in a parallel heading, moving north.

"Isn't that strange!" Longview observed. "You don't suppose the other plane was waiting for him to get off, do you?"

"That's what it looks like," Fort Worth answered. While the air controller in the Longview was repeating the story that the DC-4 was a Ross Air Taxi flying nuclear waste, it occurred to him that Ross didn't *fly* DC-4s.

By now air traffic radar units in Fort Worth, Houston, New Orleans, and Baton Rouge had joined the attempt to track the two planes, and so had the pilot of a Continental Airlines DC-10 who happened to be monitoring the transmissions. A DEA aircraft from Oklahoma City was scrambled to join the search. Customs agents in New Orleans reported that the DC-4 was the plane with the payload of marijuana, but radar operators couldn't tell which plane was which. "We're having trouble following him," Fort Worth reported. "He's only painted about every other sweep. We don't know if he's changing altitude or what."

New Orleans Customs had alerted Agent James Birdsong of the Oklahoma Bureau of Narcotics, and Birdsong had assembled a small army of law officers who were waiting in Ardmore for instructions. Of course, there was no guarantee that the smugglers were headed for Ardmore, though they were headed in that direction. It was obvious by now that they were using the old piggyback scam, two aircraft flying in tight formation so that they appear as a single blip on radar.

Sooner or later the plane with the payload would land, the decoy would continue, and radar wouldn't detect a thing.

"We're having a rough time," Fort Worth reported, confirming the obvious. "These people aren't dumb. They're two and a half miles apart now, and I can't tell which is which. They're side by side, going northwest."

Somewhere between Longview and Ardmore, the DC-4 lost one of its engines, and only the superb piloting of Jerry Wilson enabled them to land safely. Dick Joyce's Cessna was supposed to continue north and land near Oklahoma City, but for reasons that were never explained, Joyce decided to land at Ardmore. When the blips dropped off the radar screen near Ardmore, the final alarm was sounded and Agent Birdsong's army raced toward the airport in the hills seven miles southeast of town.

By the time Birdsong and his men reached the site, 276 burlap bags of pot had been transferred out of the DC-4, and four U-Haul trucks were motoring down the highway. All except ten of the smugglers had vanished. Highway patrolmen stopped the trucks and searched them. Two rented cars carrying the pilots and some of the ground crew were also stopped and the occupants arrested. When the narcs finally sorted out the pieces, they realized they had blown it: they had the pot and they had ten mules, but the man they wanted, Jimmy Chagra, was nowhere to be found. They couldn't even prove when and how the 17,000 pounds had been delivered. Even if the search of the trucks proved to be legal, all the authorities could really establish was that four drivers of U-Hauls were arrested in possession of a commercial quantity of weed.

News of the Ardmore bust hit El Paso like a sonic boom. By the following afternoon it was the leading story in town. Jack Stricklin heard the news on the radio in his cell at La Tuna. Though Jimmy Chagra's name wasn't mentioned in any official way, five of the ten defendants gave El Paso addresses, and the city claimed the bust as its own. In a short time it would be described as the biggest bust in El Paso history. School kids were already speaking of them as heroes. Someone printed up T-shirts that said: FREE THE EL PASO 10! The narcs didn't help stem this flow of reverse publicity: one of them told a reporter that "80 million people have been disappointed" by the seizure in Ardmore. The hyperbole didn't seem all that exaggerated on the streets of El Paso. Two of the defendants, Daniel and Mike Ren-

LEE CHAGRA
Student Council
R.O.T.C.
Sr. Follies

Lee Chagra's high-school yearbook photograph

Lee walking out of the Federal Courthouse in El Paso

Federal judge John H.
Wood, Jr., "Maximum John"

U.S. magistrate Jamie Boyd (left)
and his assistant, prosecutor James
Kerr. In 1978, would-be assassins
sprayed Kerr's car with buckshot
and bullets.

Above: *San Antonio medics load Judge Wood's body into an ambulance.* Left: *Kathryn Wood and a friend leave her apartment for the hospital where Wood's body was taken.*

Jimmy Chagra, ringside at a fight in Las Vegas a few days before a Midland, Texas, grand jury indicted him on drug charges

Vivian Chagra, Jimmy's first wife

Liz Nichols Chagra, Jimmy's second wife, manacled following her arrest in connection with Judge Wood's murder

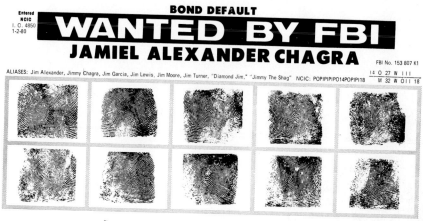

Jimmy defaulted on his bond in August 1979 and went on the lam.

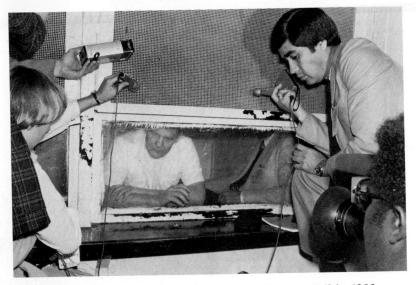

Charles Harrelson talking to reporters from a Houston jail in 1980

Harrelson and his wife Jo Ann in court in Houston, where he was tried on gun charges

Conviction: Above: Jo Ann Harrelson and Liz Chagra after their convictions in the Wood murder trial. Right: Harrelson squints in the sunlight as he is taken away after his conviction.

Acquittal: Jimmy on his way to the Jacksonville, Florida, courtroom where he was tried in connection with Wood's murder. After his acquittal, he and his lawyer, Oscar Goodman, talked to reporters.

Joe Chagra after taking a lie-detector test that, the examiner said, indicated he was innocent in Wood's death. Below: A year later, he was arrested in the case.

teria, were cousins of Joe Renteria, a young nightclub singer and television actor who had become Lee Chagra's protégé, and that in itself heightened the glamour. The mere fact that Chagra was the lead attorney made the case big-time.

The trial date was set for July 7, 1977, but before that something else happened that jarred El Paso's public imagination and put the media in a dither. Jimmy Chagra and the crew of a Jet Avia Learjet were arrested in Santa Marta, Colombia. Details were sketchy at first, but there was something about the crash of a DC-6 followed by a mercy mission that was supposed to rescue the badly burned pilot, identified as Jerry Wilson. No charges had been filed, but Chagra and five other Americans were being held by Colombia authorities.

For the first few days the Chagra family was as much in the dark as the media. Lee telephoned Clark Hughes, who had some connections in Mexico who, in turn, might have some connections in Colombia ; then he telephoned Chris Karamonos, one of the owners of Jet Avia. Karamonos was one of Las Vegas's leading businessmen and a member of the University of Nevada board of regents. He'd known Lee for a number of years and they were good friends, but he knew Jimmy only by reputation. Jet Avia owned three jets and leased six others, and had contracts with Caesar's Palace and with an air emergency service called Mercy Ambulance. The FBI and other federal agencies were reportedly investigating Jet Avia, having heard that it was backed financially by Las Vegas businessman Allan Glick, who was allegedly associated with Mafia figure Anthony "Tony the Ant" Spilotro. (Karamonos himself was not implicated in the investigation.)

Karamonos told Lee that Jimmy had called him from Atlanta on June 14, asking for help. According to Jimmy, there had been a car wreck in Santa Marta a couple of days earlier and Jerry Wilson had suffered first-degree burns over 70 percent of his body. Jimmy wanted Jet Avia to fly two paramedics from Mercy Ambulance to the scene. Karamonos knew and liked Jerry Wilson—Wilson had flown for him until recently. The pilot had told Karamonos he was quitting to help Lee Chagra market some sort of exercising device. In fact, as Lee knew, Jimmy and Jerry Wilson and several others had flown to Colombia in a newly purchased DC-6 with the intention of smuggling a load of marijuana which would offset the loss of the load seized in Ardmore. Jimmy still owed his Colombia supplier, Lionel Gomez, for the ill-fated Ardmore load. It was entirely possible that Jerry Wilson had been burned in a car wreck, of course, but it was more likely that they had overloaded the DC-6 and crashed on takeoff. Jerry Wilson was the most skilled pilot Lee had ever seen, but under the circumstances it wasn't difficult to imagine someone getting greedy and overloading the aircraft. If this was indeed the case, and it turned out it was, Jimmy Chagra was in a real bind this time. He was a prisoner of the authorities in Colombia, and now he owed Gomez for *two* loads.

The priority, of course, was saving Jerry Wilson's life. The jet that Chris Karamonos dispatched made three stops before departing for Colombia. It stopped in El Paso to pick up Jimmy Chagra's passport, it stopped again in Atlanta to pick up Jimmy, and it laid over one night in Miami, where the two paramedics aboard the flight bought a special burn ointment suggested to them by doctors at Brooks Army Hospital burn treatment center. Karamonos had cleared the rescue flight with the FAA and the State Department, and arranged for the victim to be flown directly to the burn treatment center in San Antonio.

Just before the jet landed in Santa Marta, Jimmy Chagra made a curious request to the two pilots and two paramedics. He instructed them to tell the authorities that Jerry Wilson had been aboard the flight from Las Vegas. This didn't make a lot of sense to chief paramedic Jeff Ellis—after all, the purpose of the flight was to treat Jerry Wilson—but within an hour after they landed, Ellis began to realize that Chagra had been less than straightforward.

Chagra immediately disappeared, leaving Ellis and the others at airport Customs. A short time later an ambulance pulled up in front of the Customs headquarters. By now the place was swarming with cops from the Colombia Department of Administrative Security (DAS). Ellis and the other paramedic were permitted to examine the victim on the cot in the rear of the ambulance for only about thirty seconds, but they weren't permitted to remove or even treat him. The burns were more severe than Ellis imagined. The victim was experiencing great pain and probably dying. While the paramedics were doing what they could for the man in the ambulance, DAS officials searched the jet. Then they arrested the pilots and paramedics and hustled them downtown to DAS headquarters. A short time later, Jimmy Chagra and the real Jerry Wilson arrived. It turned out that the victim was the copilot, Bruce Allen, who had just made his first and last dope run. Wilson and some others had somehow jumped from the DC-6 before it exploded, but Allen caught the full force of the blast. The cover story was apparently designed to allow Wilson to accompany them back to the United States. It soon became clear, however, that nobody was going anywhere.

During their confinement, Jimmy Chagra arranged to make the prisoners as comfortable as possible. Since Chagra himself was a prisoner, it wasn't easy, but he bribed guards to bring food and blankets and scored a small quantity of Santa Marta Gold for himself. He even paid a DAS officer to deliver painkillers to Bruce Allen, who died five days later.

The following morning the six Americans were transferred to Bogotá and put in individual isolation cells. For the next seven days they were interrogated. Then they were returned to Santa Marta and confined without charges for another two weeks. From the scraps of information that reached El Paso, it was deduced that the arrests had something to do with dope trafficking, and the media reported that Jimmy Chagra was being held on "drug-related" charges. American DEA agents in Santa Marta joined DAS in the investigation, but nobody ever located the wreckage of the DC-6 or discovered any drugs except the painkillers and burn cream brought aboard the chartered jet. The American embassy was contacted by both Chris Karamonos and the Chagra family, but nobody in the embassy made much effort to help. Lee and Joe Chagra hired a lawyer in Santa Marta and wired $10,000 to Jimmy, but they learned later that Jimmy already had the situation well in hand. With the help of his Colombia contacts, he arranged freedom for himself and Wilson. The others were released after Karamonos paid someone $150,000. Jeff Ellis, the paramedic, recalled that Chagra's lawyer met them at the jail entrance and drove them to the Porta Galleon, a hotel on the outskirts of Santa Marta. Two apparently disgruntled Colombians took Chagra to a room in the rear of the suite, and sometime later four more Colombians joined them. The paramedic couldn't overhear the conversation, but he gathered that they weren't back there toasting Jimmy Chagra's recent success. The following morning the Americans were driven to Barranquilla and put aboard an Avianca jet to Miami.

It was almost two years before the Colombian government returned the jet owned by Jet Avia, by which time the corporation had declared bankruptcy. About three months after Karamonos paid the ransom for his employees, a Jet Avia plane crashed near Palm Springs, killing

Frank Sinatra's mother. Exactly four minutes later, another Jet Avia plane crashed in a snowstorm in Minnesota. The loss of three aircraft in three months finished the corporation.

The public fascination with the Colombia adventure didn't wane until the start of the Ardmore trial, July 7. Clark Hughes and several of the other lawyers who had been hired to help defend the "El Paso 10" wondered how the sensational headlines would affect their clients in Ardmore. Jerry Wilson, the only one linked to both adventures, did his best to play down the Colombia affair, but Jimmy Chagra found the spotlight irresistible. Someone would mention the weather, and Jimmy would be reminded of that time that he bribed a prison guard in Santa Marta. Jimmy didn't waste a lot of time mourning the death of Bruce Allen. He and Jerry Wilson visited Allen's widow, expressing sorrow and giving her some money, but Jimmy Chagra's net feeling about the experience in Colombia was one of exhilaration.

Jimmy's exhilaration had the effect of deepening Lee's depression. For weeks Lee had seemed moody and out of sorts, irritated by little things that should have made him laugh and laughing at things he'd never thought funny before. Part of it was the constant shadow of the new prosecutor, James Kerr. Kerr had definitely turned the heat up in El Paso. There was talk of a new racket-busting grand jury. "Witch hunt" would have been a better description, Lee believed. Kerr was so prim and prissy in his little blue blazer and gray flannel trousers, like a fraternity captain rousing out the pledges, but he was smart, and, more than that, wily—the worst kind of adversary because he knew how to get an opponent's emotional mercury soaring. Lee believed Judge Wood to be dumb and dangerous, the way an unexploded bomb is dangerous, but the prosecutor was another kind of threat.

Much of Lee's depression could be traced to family problems, which were accumulating faster than he could catalog. Jo Annie was talking about divorce. Joe was talking about resigning his partnership in the law firm, and Jimmy was just talking. Even as Lee was struggling to salvage what he could from the ruins of Jimmy's last deal, Jimmy was plotting new ones. Lee was aware that Jimmy had been involved in some smuggling before Boston, but only aware. He knew that his brother had done business with Jack Stricklin and with some of the scammers in New Mexico such as Marty Houltin and Jim French, and Lee had heard there were bad feelings—bruised egos, missing money, reckless talk. He'd heard that Jim French refused to work in any op-

eration in which Jimmy was a party. Lee placed no moral judgment
on the act of smuggling, but he put great importance on a man's word
and honor. And yet these were not subjects he felt comfortable addressing to Jimmy. On the contrary, it was Jimmy who sometimes lectured Lee on abstractions like codes of honor, codes of the West, codes
of brotherhood, mimicking the phrases as a child does when he repeats
words he has heard but not really understood. There was more than a
touch of irony in the fact that the narcs believed that Lee was Mr. Big.
Lee resented this accusation, but of course so did Jimmy. Jimmy
wanted nothing more than to be recognized as Mr. Big.

Lee was using a lot of cocaine, more than anyone needed. It fed
his ego and made him feel invulnerable, but he must have recognized,
too, that the feeling was an illusion. Just below the illusion he felt the
doldrums of stagnation, felt them taking over. He had talked to Vivian
and others about dying. "I don't know how much longer I can do this,"
he said. "Every time I gain a foot, I lose three." He wasn't just talking about the cocaine ; his whole life seemed to be sliding out of control.

The trial in Ardmore, as it turned out, was the perfect tonic for
Lee. Clark Hughes called Lee's courtroom performance "the best piece
of bullshit advocacy I ever saw." The trial was almost a remake of the
showpiece in Socorro, New Mexico, where the local population had
turned out three years earlier to adore the Columbus Air Force and
its elegant, dynamic defender, Lee Chagra. As he hurried up the steps
of the old courthouse in Ardmore with his gold-tipped cane and cowboy
hat, waving to giggling flocks of schoolgirls who had cut classes to see
him, Lee Chagra was the personification of self-confidence. There were
four other defense lawyers in the convoy, but Lee was clearly the star.
The defense knew that the prosecution's case was hurting : they had
already turned down a deal that would have freed six of the defendants
in return for a guilty plea by the four drivers. Chagra and Clark
Hughes had talked about it the night before—they were fairly certain
that some of the law-enforcement people would swear that they actually *saw* the smugglers unloading the DC-4 and packing the goods into
the trucks. They might even claim they discovered some spills of marijuana on the ground beneath the DC-4's cargo door, but the lawyers
were certain they wouldn't go so far as to actually introduce samples
of the spill into evidence. There hadn't been any spills.

Clark Hughes believed that for all practical purposes Lee won the
case when he made his opening remarks to members of the jury panel.

It was a lesson in the presumption of innocence. Chagra used one of his trademarks, his solid-gold retractable pointer, to demonstrate. With the pointer retracted in its minimum position, Lee approached the jury box, smiling. He touched the tip of the pointer and said: "This small tip represents innocence. The defendants didn't do a thing. This other end represents guilty beyond a reasonable doubt. The government proved its case. They did the crime, the government proved they did, and you, the jury, are convinced beyond a moral certainty." Lee held the members of the panel with his eyes, taking a few seconds so that everything could register, then he expanded the pointer a inch at a time. Again he paused to allow time for reflection. "The rest of it," he said, his voice as sure and unwavering as Walter Cronkite delivering the evening news, "represents *not guilty*!" As he said the magic words, Lee extended the pointer to its full projection.

"Before there was ever a word of evidence," Clark Hughes recalled, "every member of that panel was thinking not guilty."

As expected, several of the lawmen testified that they arrived at the airport in time to be eyewitnesses to the off-loading of the DC-4. When Lee pinned them down on the exact location from which they watched, several jurors started snickering: not only was the position almost a mile from the scene, there was a massive hill blocking the view. Lee turned so that he could enjoy the joke with members of the jury, his eyes twinkling as though he expected to see tiny okra plants sprouting from the witness's nose. When one of Agent Birdsong's men told of finding marijuana debris scattered beneath the DC-4's cargo door, Lee asked the painfully obvious: why hadn't the lawmen bothered to sweep it up as evidence? An old farmer on the jury laughed so hard he nearly fell out of the box. Throughout the testimony an attractive woman juror kept making eye contact with Jerry Wilson.

It was obvious that the best the prosecution could hope for was a draw. If they had focused on the four drivers, someone could have gone to prison, but they elected instead to put it on all ten defendants; by going for the whole bundle, they were going to lose the whole bundle. After two days of deliberation, the jury reported itself hopelessly deadlocked, eight to four for acquittal. The judge had no choice but to declare a mistrial. Several of the jurors, including the woman who had her eye on Jerry Wilson, attended the victory party that night. "I know they did everything they said they did," she told Lee Chagra, "but damn it, they didn't *prove* it!"

There had been cases in which he worked harder and longer, cases in which he was more brilliant, but considering the facts, the enormous publicity, and the outcome, there had never been a victory quite like this one. Of course, it wasn't exactly a victory: the prosecution was certain to try again to convict the El Paso 10. But Lee was already certain about the outcome of the rematch. He had them now, had them on record. Someone passed a bottle of champagne, but Lee waved it off. He didn't need it. Later, Jimmy telephoned congratulations. By request, Jimmy had stayed far away from Ardmore. Jimmy wanted to speak to his ace pilot, Jerry Wilson, but Wilson had disappeared with his juror.

In the second trial two months later, the prosecution made the same mistakes and added a few twists. Chagra was on them like a cat. In closing arguments the district attorney admitted that the investigators were "cotton-picking sloppy," but appealed to the jurors' sense of value and civic duty. "Just because the officers are sloppy in doing their work is no reason for you to say . . . not guilty," the DA told the the jury. It wasn't going to work: this jury was with the defendants all the way. The cops weren't the only ones who had bungled it—the prosecution blew it back when they were picking the jury, though the DA didn't seem to understand this. Somehow the prosecution had overlooked an old-time bootlegger, and he was just sitting there in the jury box waiting to strike back for years of torment. Another juror was an obvious hippy: who did the prosecutors think *smoked* all that marijuana? Still another juror was the mother of a young girl who had recently been prosecuted in that very courtroom for possessing a small amount of pot.

"That trial was a defense lawyer's dream," said Richard Esper, who had replaced Clark Hughes on the defense team for the retrial. (Hughes had just been named to a judgeship.) "Those jurors were infatuated with the whole scenario [of the drug scam]. It was like they were extras in a movie and the defendants were the stars."

For weeks after the acquittal, authorities argued among themselves, trying to fix the blame. Prosecutors and DEA agents back in El Paso wrote it off as a typical performance by a bunch of provincial bumpkins in Oklahoma, but that didn't alter the fact that they had lost. Lee Chagra had beat all of them.

That's when Jamie Boyd and James Kerr came up with a new game plan.

13

Judge Wood was distressed to learn that some people were calling him a racist. Mexican-American groups, of which there were a number in the largely Hispanic district, had looked on Wood as anathema since shortly after his appointment to the bench. His ruling that there was no evidence of segregation in the Uvalde School District outraged Chicanos and surprised even white moderates. Wood handed down the stiffest Medicare fraud sentence in a five-state region—five years and $5,000—to Dr. Raul Ganoa, a Chicano physician from San Antonio who had pleaded nolo contendere in the belief that the judge would give him probation. After the League of United Citizens and other groups protested, another federal judge in Louisiana permitted Dr. Ganoa to withdraw his plea. A jury ultimately cleared Ganoa of all charges. Wood seemed genuinely perplexed by the charge of racism, and pointed out that a few months after sentencing Ganoa, he gave an Anglo-German physician eight years on an almost identical charge.

Wood couldn't help playing the aristocrat, any more than he could help championing law and order. His great-great-grandfather, John Howland Wood, was descended through his mother, Maria DeCantillion, from the Van Stoutenburghs, who were among New York's original Dutch settlers. Hyde Park on the Hudson was originally known as DeCantillion's Landing. John Howland Wood came with members of the New York Battalion to help Texas fight its war of independence with Mexico. For his part in the war John Howland Wood was awarded a herd of cattle. In 1849, he bought a tract at Black Point on the marshy grasslands of Capano Bay, and more than 130 years later the Wood family still controlled land between the small coastal resort of Rockport and the eastern banks of Corpus Christi Bay. Though the judge and his wife lived in San Antonio, they spent weekends and vacations at their exclusive resort near Rockport, called Key Allegro.

Wood thought of himself as a Republican's Republican and a lawyer's lawyer. He bragged that his grandfather had once been iron-fisted sheriff of Bexar County (San Antonio), and that as an attorney himself he had tried more than three thousand jury cases to a conclusion. Wood was a member of every exclusive club in the city—Sons of the Republic of Texas, Sons of the American Revolution, Texas Cavaliers, Argyle Club, San Antonio Club, Order of the Alamo, San Antonio Gun Club, the list went on and on. San Antonio has been called "the most Texas city," mainly because of the Alamo and the old missions, but also because it has managed to maintain the old Spanish *patrón* mentality. A certain part of San Antonio still thinks of the minimum wage as a handout. As late as the 1960s a mayor of the city characterized the Mexican-American majority as a pack of childlike manual laborers "who just like to sing and dance and have a good time."

The Chagras weren't the only lawyers who had problems with Wood. For the last four years there had been bad blood between Wood and El Paso attorney Ray Caballero, and in the summer of 1977, at about the same time the Chagras were making headlines in Ardmore and Colombia, the blood was threatening to spill over.

Caballero, who had served in Washington with the Department of Justice and later as an assistant U.S. attorney in the Western District, had irrefutable evidence that Judge Wood was a racist, though he had never made it public. Caballero and his wife, Dorothy (who, incidentally, was the sister of future Reagan cabinet member Ann Gorsuch Burford), attempted to buy a lot at Key Allegro. When Caballero put down his $2,000 deposit, he did not know that John Wood was a charter member of the Key Allegro Canal Owners Association, nor would that have made any difference. Caballero also came from a pioneer family—his people had lived in El Paso since his grandfather came down from the mountains of northern Mexico at the time of the Mexican Revolution, and for more than fifty years they had been prominent in the city's business community. Caballero was stunned when his application to become a property owner at Key

Allegro was turned down. He found out why a few months later when he read this section of the Key Allegro bylaws:

"No portion of said premises, nor any interest therein, shall be conveyed by deed, lease or otherwise to any person other than a person belonging to the Caucasian race, nor shall any person other than one belonging to the Caucasian race occupy any portion of said premises, except only domestic servants, domiciled upon premises where they are actually employed."

That such a prohibition should be in effect in the Year of our Lord 1977 seemed outrageous, and that a federal judge should be a party to it unconscionable.

Caballero had tried a number of cases before the late Ernest Guinn and was no stranger to judicial arrogance, but his first experience in the courtroom of John Wood was a shock he hadn't forgotten. He had been appointed to defend a twenty-one-year-old student caught crossing the bridge with a small amount of marijuana stashed in his boot. Although it was a relatively minor offense, prosecutors carved it into three separate indictments, each carrying a possible sentence of five years. The jury found Caballero's client guilty on all counts. Caballero assumed that Wood would run the sentences concurrently, maybe even grant probation. Instead, the judge gave the student fifteen years. "I thought I misunderstood," Caballero remembered. "I said, 'Judge, did you say fifteen?' and Wood told me: 'I would have given him a lot more if I could.'" In his years of practice, both as a prosecutor and a defense attorney, Caballero couldn't remember any judge appearing so gratuitously cruel.

Caballero's second face-to-face confrontation with Judge Wood was in December 1974. Guinn had died and Wood was working frantically to keep ahead of the docket. On the morning of December 6, 1974, Caballero had two separate cases set in Judge Wood's court. The first involved a defendant named James Gordy accused of stashing twenty-two hundred pounds of marijuana in a storage locker in El Paso. The manager of the locker noticed something fishy, picked the lock, and discovered the grass. She telephoned police, who ordered a stakeout. After five days no one had claimed the stash, so they removed the evidence and placed a new lock on the locker. Gordy was arrested the following day snipping off the police lock with a pair of bolt cutters. Gordy was charged with two counts—possession *and* conspiracy. It was a strange combination, considering that there was no marijuana in the locker, but Wood allowed it and a jury was duly sworn.

The second case set for trial that same day involved a defendant named Diharce-Estrada caught crossing the bridge with a hundred pounds of grass in a suitcase with a false compartment. The Diharce jury and the Gordy jury were both sworn in at 9:00 A.M. that same morning, even though the Diharce case couldn't be heard until testimony concluded in the Gordy trial.

Judge Wood was in an exceptionally foul mood, and everyone around the courthouse knew it. The judge appeared on verge of exhaustion as he hurried through the long docket. The current session had almost ended—it was Thursday and it was common knowledge that come hell or high water Wood was dead set on catching the last plane to San Antonio Friday afternoon. From there the judge and his wife would drive to Key Allegro for a well-deserved rest. It was common prayer that he would make that plane.

The Gordy case was ticklish, and Caballero tried to avoid taking the judge into gray, awkward areas. Caballero was a recognized expert in rules of evidence. Like Judge Wood, he had published on the subject, but his expertise, unlike the judge's, was universally recognized by his peers. Wood's boast that in thirty years of private practice he had tried three thousand jury cases to a conclusion was a joke among lawyers in the district; that would be an average of almost two cases every week. Most lawyers regarded Wood as a judge with no concept of his limitations, and Caballero concurred with this opinion. But the popular wisdom didn't make much difference to Caballero as he stood before Wood trying to convey a very tricky point to the jury. Conspiracy was one thing, but Caballero wanted the jury to concentrate on the second charge—he wanted them to think about the absurdity of being in possession of something that wasn't there. Then he could pose the other question: If it wasn't there, how could someone be guilty of conspiring to distribute it?

Wood cut him no slack, and by 7:00 P.M. the jury had heard final arguments and been dismissed for the night. They would report back in the morning to begin deliberation. Lawyers on both sides were exhusted after ten hours in the courtroom. As the lawyers were stuffing papers into their briefcases and no doubt contemplating a couple of stiff drinks, Judge Wood rapped his gavel and announced a *ten-minute recess*. Then the court would start hearing testimony in the Diharce case. Caballero couldn't believe it, and neither could the Diharce jury, which had been cooling its heels since early morning.

From the judge's opening remarks to the jury, the Diharce case was fraught with error. Wood repeatedly rebuked Caballero in front of the jury and allowed prosecutors to make highly improper remarks. At 10:00 P.M., as Caballero was attempting to make a point of law, Wood interrupted and said: "You can't ask that question unless you have an expert witness!" Caballero noted the time and told the judge that his expert witness would be there bright and early the following morning. The witness could have gotten there at daybreak and it wouldn't have mattered, because Judge Wood called for final arguments *right now*.

In reversing the Diharce verdict more than a year later, the Fifth Circuit noted, among many other errors: "In addition to denying the request [to call an expert witness], the judge, in the jury's presence, accused the defense council of trying to take advantage of the court and very plainly intimated that he was to be punished by being required to complete closing arguments before recess."

On Friday morning, Ray Caballero was sweating two juries simultaneously. The Gordy jury was sending in notes wanting to know the definition of *"possession,"* which Wood refused to clarify, and the Diharce jury was ominously silent. Around noon the Diharce jury returned a verdict of guilty on both counts.

Everyone in the federal courthouse was watching the clock. Around 3:00 P.M., five hours after the Gordy jury began its deliberation, Wood called Caballero to his chambers. The judge was unusually friendly and told the lawyer, "It looks like the jury is hopelessly deadlocked." Caballero thought this was strange. There hadn't been a note or any other indication of what was happening in the jury room. Nevertheless, Wood called the jury back into the courtroom. The transcript tells what happened next:

JUDGE WOOD: Members of the jury, you may be seated. Mr. Foreman, if I interpret what you say right, you all have a hung jury, is that right? You cannot agree?

FOREMAN: On the second count, sir.

JUDGE WOOD: (obviously surprised by this response): Have you reached a verdict on one count?

FOREMAN: Yes, sir.

JUDGE WOOD: You *did* reach a verdict on one count?

FOREMAN: On one.

JUDGE WOOD: All right. All right, hand the verdict to Mr. . . . is that a *unanimous* verdict on that one count? All twelve of you did agree on it?

FOREMAN: Yes, sir.

At this point, the judge asked the lawyers and the jury foreman, Mr. Yanez, to approach the bench. Yanez explained that the jury had voted not guilty on the conspiracy charge and were still deliberating on the possession charge. The vote stood at six-six. Wood sent Yanez back to the jury box. He accepted the verdict of the first count and began thanking the jury, obviously in preparation for dismissing them. Caballero felt a cold rush of panic as he realized Wood was about to declare a *mistrial* on the possession charge. It seemed obvious that the jury was still in the process of deliberation: They were having trouble with the exact point Caballero had to tried to convey, the ambiguity of possessing something that wasn't there. The law seemed clear: It said that the jury must find that Gordy had possession of the locker at some time when it *actually contained* the contraband, but the prosecution hadn't bothered proving this highly significant point, and the judge refused to enlighten the jury on the language of the law. Caballero asked permission to approach the bench.

CABALLERO: For the purpose of the record, your honor, as I stated before to the court when I believe the second question [from the jury] came back on possession . . .

JUDGE WOOD: Oh, let's don't go into that right now. I'm going to discharge this jury. I can make my plane if you will just get off my back long enough for me to do it. I can make my plane if you'll let me. Can't you make a motion?

CABALLERO: Well, your honor . . .

JUDGE WOOD (to the jury): Members of the jury, you are excused. Thank you very much. Bear in mind your deliberations are secret. Do not discuss this case with anyone. You are excused.

After the jury had gone, Caballero argued frantically that the jury had never declared itself deadlocked, that the judge had no right to declare a mistrial and subject Gordy to the jeopardy of a second trial, particularly in view of the court's refusal to properly instruct the jury on the law.

"Overruled!" Wood snapped and hurried off the bench.

Before Gordy was tried a second time the government was allowed to amend the indictment, a procedure rarely allowed except in cases of clerical error. This time—Caballero unsuccessfully argued that his client had been placed in double jeopardy—the jury found Gordy guilty of possession.

This was probably the low point in Ray Caballero's career. "I've never been treated the way Wood treated me," he told his wife, Dorothy. There was no doubt in Caballero's mind he was right, but there was also no doubt that Wood would give his man the maximum when the case came up for sentencing. What happened next was so unexpected that the lawyer was momentarily dumbstruck: Ray and Dorothy attended a party after a UTEP basketball game and Dorothy accidentally overheard a woman she had never met tell about her experiences as a member of the Gordy jury. The woman recalled that the bailiff kept knocking on the jury-room door reminding them that the judge was in a hurry to leave town. "Holy shit!" Ray Caballero said once he had found his voice. "That's exactly what we need."

Although the revelation was dynamite, almost certain grounds for a reversal of the verdict, there remained the very delicate matter of how to approach Judge Wood. Judge Wood didn't like being told that he made mistakes, however blatant they were. All lawyers who practice in the Western District of Texas are familiar with a local rule, Rule 20, which prohibits anyone from discussing a case with a member of the jury. The purpose of the rule was to prevent lawyers or members of the media from hounding jurors after a trial, though its absolute administration seemed to violate several amendments to a much higher law, the Constitution. The matter at hand seemed an exception to the rule: Dorothy Caballero hadn't solicited information, she'd merely overheard it. The information implied serious judicial misconduct. Caballero had an obligation to the court, and he also had an obligation to his client. But Caballero knew that the judge would use Rule 20 to attack him and Dorothy. He warned his wife that both of them might end up in jail.

Caballero filed a carefully worded motion asking the judge to waive Rule 20 and interview members of the Gordy jury. He attached an affidavit from his wife telling of the accidentally overheard conversation, and he pointed out that in allegations of jury misconduct the burden to prove otherwise is on the court.

On March 17, Judge John Wood took the initiative from the start. He pointed out that it had come to the attention of chief judge Adrian Spears that Caballero and his wife had violated Rule 20. The scowl on Wood's face told Caballero that the judge considered this violation nasty business indeed.

"Now, obviously, I was under no compulsion or deadline to catch a plane," the judge said mildly. On the contrary, the judge continued, he had *missed* the last flight to San Antonio that night. As for the mistrial, he was well within his rights because the jury reported that it was "hopelessly deadlocked." What did concern the court, Wood declared, was the cavalier attitude that the attorney and his wife had demonstrated toward Rule 20.

Caballero picked his words very carefully. He repeated the wording in his motion that nobody was accusing the judge of an impropriety—perish the thought!—but that a number of people around the courthouse were aware that the judge was in a hurry to leave El Paso, and from the conversation that Dorothy overheard it seemed apparent that the jury was also aware of this.

"I know nothing to do except report these things to the court and ask for a hearing," Caballero said. "All I know is what the court told me when the jury was sitting in this box, that if I would get off your back you could catch a plane."

Caballero wondered if the judge had even bothered to read his own words in the transcript. From the cloud that seemed to be crossing Wood's face, Caballero guessed that he had. Either that, or his memory was starting to feed it back.

"Actually," Wood admitted, "I said something to that effect. But what I wanted to do was get out of the courtroom and start calling to try to get away that night if I possibly could. But that wouldn't have anything to do with the jury because they had already come in and said they were deadlocked."

Wood finally permitted Dorothy Caballero to take the witness stand and repeat what she had heard, but since she couldn't remember the name of the woman at the party, Judge Wood refused to pursue the allegation. "That would be unidentified hearsay," the judge informed her.

At the conclusion of the hearing, Wood asked Dorothy Caballero if she had ever read Rule 20. She told him she'd never even heard of it. Wood read it to her, then asked: "If you had known about this rule, would you have talked to that juror?"

MRS. CABALLERO: In all sincerity, your honor, I don't see how that applies to me.

JUDGE WOOD: In other words, you can do indirectly for your husband what he can't do himself, is that what you are telling the court?

MRS. CABALLERO: No, your honor, because I wasn't interviewing this witness.

JUDGE WOOD: She was talking to you about a case in which your husband acted as defense counsel. And you were readily talking to her about this case in spite of the prohibition prescribed by Rule 20 because you thought it applied to your husband and not to you, is that what you are telling the court?

MRS. CABALLERO: No, your honor, because I didn't know...

JUDGE WOOD: That's all. You may be excused.

Wood overruled the motion to interview members of the jury, then sentenced Gordy to five years followed by five years special probation, the maximum. Bond was denied.

On January 29, 1976, the Fifth Circuit reversed the decision and Gordy was released. But, of course, no appeals court could give him back those seven months he had spent behind bars. The really appalling part of all this was that John Wood didn't appear to care. In reversal after reversal, the appeals court took note of the judge's gross improprieties, his lack of fairness, and his apparently uncontrollable penchant for prejudicing juries by his open criticism of or hostility toward the defense counsel.

The bad blood between Caballero and Wood finally spilled over in the summer of 1977. Caballero had about decided that he would refuse cases headed for federal court, but in this case a federal judge appointed him and he couldn't refuse. His client was initially charged with three counts: possession of marijuana, possession of cocaine, and possession of a deadly weapon. Since there was only a tiny amount of coke involved, the government offered a deal: it would drop two counts in return for a plea of guilty in the pot case. Caballero agreed.

But by the time it came to trial the case had been transferred to Judge Wood's court. According to Jamie Boyd, who had just been appointed U.S. attorney, Wood personally requested that James Kerr be assigned to prosecute.

"When we tried to plead, Kerr said the deal was off," Caballero recalled. "He wouldn't honor a deal made by another prosecutor. And damned if I would get down on my hands and knees and beg mercy from James Kerr."

But Caballero was severely limited in what he could do at this late stage of the game. Kerr was threatening to reindict on the coke charge. Caballero's man was facing thirty years. In Maximum John's courtroom, that sentence was almost preordained.

Caballero felt he had no choice. "I told Kerr that we'd go to trial and fight him all the way."

The trial was postponed until October. In the meantime, Caballero learned a number of unsavory facts about the government's star witness, an agent provocateur. He learned that the witness had once been fired for embezzlement and that he had lied in a sworn deposition.

Early in the trial, Wood asked Caballero to remind the court to read the deposition in which the informant lied under oath. But as Caballero was attempting to cross-examine, Wood wouldn't allow the attorney to ask where the informant had worked or why he had left his job.

"Can't we get on with the case?" Wood said. "Let's move on."

"I'm not trying to impeach him on prior misconduct," Caballero reminded Wood. "But this man has lied under oath! I can establish that he has made inconsistent statements . . . "

Kerr interrupted: "Your honor, I don't like Mr. Caballero testifying."

"I don't either," the judge said.

When Caballero reminded the judge to read the deposition to the jury, as Wood had instructed, the judge again cut him short and ordered him to move on. Caballero was losing his temper, but he couldn't help it. He blurted out, "Judge, this court has appointed me to represent my client and that's what I'm going to do!" Wood hurried the jury out of the room and harshly rebuked the lawyer for telling the jury that he was court-appointed.

"Mr. Caballero," the judge said, "you know very well that's against the rules!"

103

Against what rule? There was no such rule, and Wood had to know it. Caballero felt that Wood had been abusing him in front of the jury throughout the trial, and the temptation to lash back was becoming irresistible.

JUDGE WOOD: I want to know why you did that.

CABALLERO: Are you asking me a question you want me to answer?

WOOD: Yes, I do.

CABALLERO: All right, and don't interrupt me.

WOOD: Mr. Caballero, as an officer of this court, I'm going to warn you now you are very close to contempt of this court.

Caballero took his time. He knew what was coming, and he was powerless to prevent it. Nothing on earth would stop him from speaking his mind. He just wanted to speak it right:

"Judge, I can't be in contempt of this court. It's impossible to be in contempt of this court. You don't *know* how to give a man a fair trial. You don't *know* how to act like a judge. I'm telling you that right now outside the presence of this jury. I was appointed to represent this man. My duty is to him and not to you. And you tell me that I can't impeach the credibility of a man I know to be a liar and that I can prove him to be a liar and you want me to stand here under my oath and take that from you and take abuse from you in front of the jury, the kind of abuse I don't take in front of *any* man? No judge anywhere has ever treated anybody like that, and I don't care if you stick me away in jail forever, I'm telling you, you are no judge!"

Wood was too startled to interrupt. When Caballero had said his piece, the judge struggled with his composure, then announced in a voice on the verge of breaking: "All right, you are fined five hundred dollars."

Caballero's client was acquitted on the coke charge but found guilty on the marijuana and gun counts. U.S. attorney Jamie Boyd and several other officers of the court pleaded with Wood to suspend the $500 fine, but instead the judge filed a motion ordering Caballero to show cause why his license to practice law should not be revoked. Caballero sent copies of the transcript to every judge in the district and filed his own motion protesting that his client had not received a fair trial. Wood lashed back, alleging that Caballero had a long record of being disrespectful of the court and was a proven trouble-maker. Caballero refused to pay the fine or apologize. Wood refused

104

to drop the contempt charges. The name-calling and document-filing might have gone on indefinitely but for the good offices of Jamie Boyd, who acted as peacemaker. Dozens of lawyers in and outside the Western District offered to pay the fine, but Caballero paid it himself. Caballero's friends wondered if he could put his bitterness aside and carry on. The answer was that he could and did. Wood's friends wondered if the judge was coming apart. John Pinckney III, who had been chief assistant U.S. attorney before returning to private practice in San Antonio, warned Wood that his attitude was endangering the system and possibly his life.

14

In April 1977, James Kerr made an unpublicized trip to Nashville to review the files of the 1973 indictment against Lee Chagra and Jack Stricklin. True, the case had been dead for years, but Kerr and Jamie Boyd planned to force Stricklin to turn on Lee Chagra by threatening to reindict him under an obscure section of the 1970 Drug Control Act that spelled out the crime of "continuing criminal enterprise," popularly known as the kingpin act. Boyd was more convinced than ever that Chagra was their kingpin.

In the seven years or so that it had been on the books, few had bothered to read that section of the drug law. But Kerr, who had worked on the original bill, knew it by heart. The language was vague, but essentially it said that a person was a kingpin if he (1) committed a continuing series of violations of the drug act, in concert with "five or more other persons with respect to whom such person occupies a position of organizer, a supervisory position, or any other position of management," and (2) obtained "substantial income or resources" from those violations. The law was wide open to interpretation— tailor-made for a crusading lawman, an empire builder, like James Kerr.

Part of the law required banks to report all cash transactions of $10,000 or more to the IRS. Prosecutors knew that certain bankers were on the payroll of smugglers to do nothing more than see that records of large transactions never got to the IRS, but the main complaint of narcs was that the IRS wouldn't cooperate with the DEA. Pressure in high places was put on the IRS, and soon cooperation was forthcoming. A second part of the law allowed the government to seize property bought with drug profits. Of course, the government had to prove that the profits were specifically ill-gotten, but common sense told prosecutors that lawyers such as Lee Chagra didn't command the sort of fees to support Chagra's life-style. But the real bite of the law, the element that made it harsher than any other federal law on the books—harsher even than penalties for rape, murder, or kidnapping—was its inordinate range of sentences. Minimum sentence was ten years, maximum was life. And that wasn't all. Defendants convicted on a kingpin rap were not eligible for parole, period. In a critical history of the provision published in the *U.S. Congressional Code and Administrative News*, the authors observed: "There can be no doubt that the Justice Department . . . has shown little sensitivity either toward constitutional rights or toward modern concepts of penology and rehabilitation." This criticism perhaps explained why the kingpin section had seldom been used. Be that as it may, it was on the books and the prosecutors of the Western District of Texas intended to use it.

As Kerr reviewed the 1973 conspiracy charges in the dead files of the Middle District of Tennessee, he must have felt sympathy for the prosecutor, Irvin Kilcrease. There were at least twenty lawyers for the defense, but apparently the entire burden of prosecution fell on poor Kilcrease. It was obvious that the prosecution and the DEA had problems coordinating their investigation. In fact, many aspects of the conspiracy were *never* investigated. Kerr had the advantage of new information from interviews with a number of dealers who had been arrested since 1973, including the con artist, Jerry Edwin Johnson, who was Lee's client when federal agents took him out of La Tuna for that clandestine interrogation almost a year earlier. Another recent informant claimed he had personally paid Stricklin $500,000. Still, there was one nagging question: why hadn't Kilcrease filed charges under the kingpin act? "I just didn't consider it," Kilcrease told Kerr. "We were interested in the conspiracy angle of this particular case." Well, Kerr was interested in something more. He concluded that all the elements needed to satisfy the kingpin law were amply present—many separate transactions and many people, most of whom worked for Stricklin. *Or for Lee Chagra.* If you scratched Stricklin deep enough, Kerr reasoned, you would find Chagra.

Agent Ken Bloemker, who had made the trip to Nashville with Kerr, believed that when threatened with life without parole, Stricklin would rat off his best friend, but not all the narcs agreed. Agent

J. T. Robinson agreed that Lee Chagra was the "godfather" of Stricklin's group—the group had even commissioned a painting of Lee posing as the godfather—but that alone said something for them. "They're very loyal," he said. "They would take the fall for him." But the prosecutors wanted to see for themselves.

Shortly after the Ardmore trial, Bloemker and another agent visited Jack Stricklin at La Tuna. "You help us and we'll help you," Bloemker told Stricklin. They wanted information on the real kingpin of dope trafficking in El Paso. They mentioned four names—Lee Chagra, Jimmy Chagra, Sib Abraham, and bail bondsman Vic Apodaca. If Stricklin cooperated, they would work for his early release. If he refused, they would see that he was reindicted under the kingpin act. They showed him a Xerox copy of that section of the 1970 Drug Control Act.

"Do yourself a favor," one of the agents said. "One way or another, we're gonna get Lee Chagra."

Stricklin looked at the copy of the law for a few seconds, then returned it to the agents. "Fold this five ways and stick it where the elves don't play," he said. A month later, Jack Stricklin was standing before Maximum John Wood, contemplating life without parole.

At first Lee wasn't terribly worried about the new charges against Stricklin. "Kerr's just working the tailings," he said. The case appeared to be nothing more than a rehash of the long-discredited Tennessee indictment mushed together with evidence from the deal for which Stricklin was now serving time. The only thing new was an allegation involving the setup bust of the Desert Inn Motel in July 1972; the statute of limitations was about to expire on that one. That bust involved a group of amateurs from California, a coterie of straight-arrow businessmen who, as one of them later termed it, tried to do a "get-rich-quick, one-shot deal" with one of Stricklin's friends. Stricklin had smelled the setup and was long gone before the bust. Maybe they could prove that the marijuana came from Stricklin, but it was a long shot at best. Except for the Desert Inn case, the other allegations in the kingpin charge were so vague as to be meaningless. If there was a single piece of new evidence, it wasn't mentioned, or even hinted at, in the indictment. The government seemed to know it didn't have a case, but it was determined to see how far it could travel. In the court of John Wood, Chagra realized, that could be some distance.

15

Jimmy was the only member of the Chagra family who didn't notice the heat in the summer of 1977. Joe and his wife, Patty, and especially Lee, were advising Jimmy to get out of El Paso for a while. The Internal Revenue Service was on Jimmy's back, and so were some of his creditors. He'd never paid his Colombia connection for the tons of marijuana lost at Ardmore and in the DC-6 crash that killed Bruce Allen. Up until the time that the two agents visited Jack Stricklin at La Tuna, there wasn't any hard evidence that the DEA was on Jimmy's trail, but now there could be no doubt. Jimmy kept the details from his family, but they knew that he had hooked up with a borderwise ex-con named Henry Wallace, who worked out of New Mexico and in recent years had done business with Marty Houltin, Jim French, and the other old-time scammers.

In July, Joe and Patty persuaded Jimmy to move to Canada. Since Lee told the family Jimmy was dead broke, Joe sold some of his furniture and gave Jimmy some money and his Blazer. They learned later that Jimmy left town with about $50,000. Jimmy and his girlfriend, Liz Nichols, left town, but they didn't head for Canada—instead they made a whirlwind sweep of California, Lake Tahoe, and New York: "Liz came back to El Paso one time because they needed more money," Patty Chagra remembered, "then we didn't hear from them again until October or November. Jimmy called and said they were living in Florida."

A short time later, Lee flew to Fort Lauderdale and set up a dummy corporation for Jimmy. It was called Capital Acquisition, and its purpose was to channel funds through several banks in Mexico and then into Jimmy's new smuggling operation. No one alive knows for certain when Lee Chagra crossed the line to the dark side of the law, but by this time all the Chagras knew that Lee's arrangement with his brother and his relationship with Jack Stricklin were more than traditional lawyer-client dealings. And yet federal agents still had no proof: for all the loose talk, there was not a shred of hard evidence that Lee had committed any crime. Lee had never let his name be linked to an illegal enterprise before the fact. Until now. The Florida operation had the potential to make millions, but it also had the potential for disaster. If the feds could compromise even a single member of the conspiracy, the whole organization might crumble—and Lee with it. By setting up the corporation for Jimmy, Lee had, for the first time, made himself vulnerable.

Joe Chagra told Lee he was a fool.

"You've got it wrong," Lee replied. "I've *been* a fool."

There was no bitterness or rancor, but by the end of August, Joe Chagra realized that he had had all he could take. Joe was quieter and more introspective than his brothers. Gambling bored him. His idea of a good time was going home to his wife and newborn son, Joseph, maybe tinkering with his stereo or waxing his speedboat, swimming or lifting weights. Since his cocaine seizure in the courtroom a few months earlier, Joe had stayed clean from drugs, throwing himself into his work. He was a good, sound, all-around lawyer, but he didn't have Lee's appetite for controversy. When Joe and Lee first drew up their partnership, the arrangement was that they would share all revenues and losses, but Joe hadn't counted on sharing Lee's gambling losses. "Every morning when I drive down to the office, I get sick at my stomach," Joe told Patty. "I never know if we have fifty thousand dollars in our account or fifty cents." He'd fought a lot of tough battles at Lee's side, and he'd loved them because they were something that he and Lee did together. But lately Lee was taking new directions. Joe announced plans to open his own law firm.

At almost exactly the same time, Jo Annie filed for divorce. As always with the many mysterious activities of the Chagras, there were many theories around the courthouse about the divorce. It was entirely possible that it was a legal ploy to block the IRS from seizing communal property. Donna Johnson, the bookkeeper who handled much of the paperwork for the divorce, was certain this was the case: she knew that the divorce agreement placed the deeds to all property in Jo Annie's name. Friends refused to believe Lee would agree to a divorce as long as the children were still living at home. But others wondered. Lee was openly attracted to his new secretary, Patty's sister, Sandy Messer. Like Patty, Sandy was a stunningly beautiful blonde with dancing eyes. Whatever the truth of the matter, Jo Annie believed that her husband and Sandy were having an affair. Considering Lee's record with his secretaries, this could have been taken as a last straw. A few months after the divorce was filed, Sib Abraham telephoned district judge Henry Pena and asked if the judge would preside over the divorce in the privacy of his chambers. The attorney told Pena that no property was involved, that both sides agreed on all issues, and that all they wanted was a simple ruling granting divorce. Pena agreed and scheduled a hearing for that same afternoon, but neither party showed up. The judge learned later that Lee and Jo Annie spent the afternoon in the courthouse parking lot, talking about something. He wasn't surprised. "I knew damn well that as soon as they got to my office, Jo Annie would start talking about what a wonderful husband and father Lee had been. I knew they would never go through with it," Judge Pena said.

Maybe the marriage would continue, maybe it wouldn't. No one could say. Something else seemed clear, though: The Chagra family was breaking apart.

16

On August 31, 1977, Lee Chagra appeared in Judge Wood's court to file a motion of discovery, asking that the judge require the government to turn over DEA reports, Customs reports, grand jury probes, any material that would reveal when Stricklin was supposed to have engaged in continuing criminal activity. Chagra argued that the indictment smacked of double jeopardy, but there was no way he could prove it until the government got specific.

Kerr responded that it was the government's position that Stricklin was involved in "a myriad of conspiracies" and it would not be in the public interest to turn over government files of an ongoing investigation. Chagra argued that in cases where the defendant claimed jeopardy, the Supreme Court had ruled that the appeal had to be settled *before* the actual trial. As Chagra talked, he studied Wood's face: the judge didn't seem to have a clue what the attorneys were talking about. For the first time in memory, Wood confessed that he was ignorant of the law, at least that section governing continuing criminal activity. He pointed out that "my three thousand contested cases were all civil cases, and while I have, of course, heard of the continuing criminal activity statute, I do not think I have ever tried such a case."

"Few judges have," Chagra told him. "It's never been filed in a marijuana case before."

"I don't think it's ever been filed in a controlled substance case," the judge said.

"Except heroin, your honor."

"Not in my court."

"It's never been filed in this district, never," Chagra said.

Wood was having trouble comprehending. "What I don't see," he said, "if the alleged conspiracy existed as far back as Tennessee, how would that preclude the bringing of conspiracy in Texas, in California, in . . . "

"It wouldn't, a *conspiracy*," Chagra interrupted. "But we're not talking about a conspiracy."

"Has the government brought a conspiracy here or is this a continuing criminal activity case?" the judge asked, turning from one lawyer to the other. Both lawyers assured the judge that the case before him was being prosecuted under the kingpin statute. Kerr admitted that this section of the law had not been widely used: "The Department of Justice has apparently reserved the utilization . . . until it gets appropriate offenders." Kerr also admitted there was no clear procedure: "I think we're in an area where this case may be one which develops it," Kerr said. This seemed to please Wood. Chagra could see that his worst fears were coming to pass—Kerr was intent on exploring how far he could take it, and Wood was letting him do it.

In a written response to Chagra's motion the following week, Kerr reminded the court that although Lee Chagra was not named in the present indictment, he had been indicted in the Tennessee affair. Then Kerr observed that "the request for reports . . . is an overt act on the part of the defense attorney . . . to obtain government reports and documents concerning him." That is, concerning *Lee Chagra*. "The government questions the good faith of this request," Kerr concluded.

Borrowing heavily from Kerr's own wording, Wood totally agreed: "This request appears to be primarily an effort by the defense attorney to obtain reports of an investigation pertaining to him. This conduct suggests to the court that the defendant is not making a good faith claim concerning former jeopardy, but that he is more interested in determining the extent of the government's evidence against him."

When he read copies of Kerr's motion and Wood's reply, Chagra was flabbergasted and then outraged. *What* investigation against him? It was Stricklin who was on trial, not Chagra. Lee had been accused of a lot of things, but this was the first time anyone had ever accused him of representing himself instead of his client. Until now the media had treated the charges against Stricklin as routine news, but Wood's ruling added a bizarre new twist. Reporters flocked the federal courthouse to get a look at what was happening to Lee Chagra.

On October 21, as Chagra stood before the bench objecting to

113

Judge Wood's personal attack, arguing that it was totally without evidence or cause and that the resulting publicity had done great damage not only to Stricklin but to Lee himself, the judge interrupted and dropped his bomb.

"I imagine everyone in this area knows that you've been the subject of a grand jury investigation since the Tennessee indictment," Wood announced. "Is there any secret about that?"

"Well, *I* didn't know it," Lee said, dumbstruck. He had known that the DEA was watching him, but a *grand jury*? And even if it was true, for Wood to reveal it in open court was outrageous.

The judge said he had spent "eight or ten hours" reading Jerry Edwin Johnson's 1976 grand jury testimony. Wood was apparently confusing the fifty-page transcript of the secret interview with actual grand jury testimony. Technically and legally, the unsworn interview shouldn't even have been a part of the grand jury report. Not a word of it had ever been admitted as evidence in open court. And what did any of this have to do with the Jack Stricklin case? Wood pressed on, however, announcing that the grand jury investigation concerned not only Lee Chagra and Stricklin; it also involved Sib Abraham. Out of the corner of his eye Lee could see the reporters scribbling furiously. Visions of the 1973 fiasco in Nashville that had almost ruined his law career danced through his hot brain. What was happening here?

"Your honor, I have never *seen* this testimony," Lee told the court. "And the remarks that the court is making now I'm sure are going to appear in the afternoon paper and there is going to be another inference that there is some other investigation going on. I have never been told by Jerry Johnson or anyone else that my name was ever mentioned. . . . "

Wood looked at Kerr. Kerr didn't seem eager to jump in just yet. The judge told Chagra: "I think maybe in view of the circumstances I had better make it available to you. I may be under a misapprehension. I thought that you did realize that you were the subject to a certain degree of this investigation."

"Your honor, this is incredible! This is the first time . . . and you mentioned Mr. *Abraham*?"

"Wasn't he under investigation?"

"I have no idea."

Incredible was too mild a word. A first-year law student would have known better than to be spouting details of a secret grand jury investigation in open court, and Wood wasn't even talking about a grand jury, he was talking about an unsworn interview with a known con artist being held against his will by federal agents. Chagra made a lame effort to turn the proceedings back to the reason they were here—to discuss charges against Jack Stricklin—but the judge had something else on his mind. Wood noticed that Chagra seemed to be laboring under the impression that the judge was bending to the will of James Kerr, that perhaps Kerr had come through the back door and exercised improper influence on the court.

"I want that dispelled," Wood said firmly. "My reputation on that, Mr. Chagra, is pretty well known."

Lee continued to object. He made a motion for Judge Wood to recuse (disqualify) himself in the Stricklin case. "I can't practice in front of you, and I don't think you can honestly say that you can treat me or my client fairly in any court," Chagra told Wood.

Now it was the judge who was having difficulty with his composure. Wood began to crawfish. "You didn't let me finish," he said pleasantly. "I have never found anything in any of these grand jury investigations. That's the reason I'm going to release it to you. . . . That's what I've been trying to tell you. I have not seen anything that would actually disqualify me from trying this case." The judge added that he thought he was doing Chagra a favor. After all, he was granting them an opportunity to appeal on the jeopardy question instead of forcing them to try the case immediately, as he had originally planned.

The affair of Jerry Edwin Johnson didn't end there, however. Johnson, who was now out on parole, contacted Kerr the following morning and said that Lee Chagra had threatened his life. Kerr filed a new batch of motions arguing that Jerry Johnson, "a government witness," was in danger of bodily injury, maybe even death, from Lee Chagra, and requesting that Johnson be placed on the federal witness protection program. Chagra had not threatened Johnson, but he had telephoned the snitch and asked what he had told the agents. Johnson replied that he had told them nothing. Anticipating that Johnson would probably call Kerr, Chagra had taped the conversation. In a hearing in mid-December, Chagra offered to play these tapes. Even better, Chagra argued, would be to call Johnson to the witness stand. "If the government has chosen to use his name and his statements," Chagra told Wood, "then I ask that he be requested to swear [in court]

115

to what he says." Even at this late date, Chagra didn't know what Johnson had told the agents, but he was certain it was a pack of lies. Wood denied the motion, but announced that Chagra would be allowed to read the transcript of the interview, after which it would be sealed and kept from the prying eyes of the news media.

Wood must have recognized that his order to seal the transcript was too little, too late. News reports already overflowed with speculation. In short order, Sib Abraham appeared in court and asked Wood to disqualify himself in a separate drug case involving two of Sib's clients. Chief judge Adrian Spears denied the request, noting that while Judge Wood had mentioned a "Mr. Abraham" in open court, there was no proof that this was the same Mr. Sib Abraham who was attorney of record in the case at hand. At the same time, Wood assured Abraham that the disputed records were locked inside the vault of the U.S. district clerk's office:

" . . . It will be in the vaults and that's where it shall remain just as though it were in a cemetery vault . . . it will remain in the rigor mortis of the vaults. It will be dead . . . so everybody—if I die or you die or whatever happens when none of us are here, the record will be straight. . . . "

Despite the gravity of Judge Wood's funereal rhetoric, the rigor mortis did not take. In a matter of months most reporters in town owned a copy. Most of the material was too ludicrous, not to say libelous, to release to the public. But the innuendo that the report contained some sort of master list of organized crime in El Paso was far worse than anything the report actually contained. Sixty names were mentioned in the document. One El Paso newsman thereafter referred to the list as "sixty El Paso low lifes." A writer for the San Diego *Union* was slapped with a libel suit for quoting a paragraph in which Jerry Johnson told how an attorney tried to hire him to kill an informant.

There was no way to calculate how all the damning publicity affected the careers of Sib Abraham and others, but there was no doubt that Wood's blunder landed a crippling, perhaps fatal, blow to Lee Chagra's already battered reputation. Lee's law practice never recovered. The tragedy was that it was all unnecessary: before the Fifth Circuit had a chance to rule on the question of jeopardy, Jamie Boyd decided to drop the continuing criminal enterprise charges against Jack Stricklin.

17

One weekend after the fiasco in Judge Wood's Courtroom, Lee Chagra did what he always did when he felt the world collapsing around him—he telephoned Clark Hughes and suggested a trip to Las Vegas. Hughes knew these had been hard times for his friend. Chagra and Wood were on a collision course that was bound to end in catastrophe.

Jimmy and his new business partner, Henry Wallace, were in Florida awaiting their first freighterload of Colombia marijuana, and from what Lee had heard, the operation had all the earmarks of a disaster. Lee's finances were in shambles, but he had borrowed $25,000 "seed money" and still had plenty of credit in Las Vegas. No force on earth could stop him. "This is gonna be one they'll write a book about," he told Hughes. "I'm gonna take the joint apart."

Caesar's Palace dispatched a Learjet and in less than two hours a limousine deposited them at the casino door. Lee handed out $200 in tips before they got to the suite. He always got excited the moment he felt the clamor and hysteria of Caesar's, but this time he was practically dancing up the walls. "For sheer élan," Hughes recalled, "I don't think I'd ever seen him any higher." Hughes knew that it would be several hours before Lee worked himself into the proper frenzy. There was a ritual that he always observed before going downstairs to the casino. First, he made at least a dozen telephone calls. Clark Hughes never knew whom his friend called, or why—Chagra's life was like a hornet's nest with thousands of isolated cells, and no one person, however close, ever saw more than a single cell—but the mere act of talking on the telephone seemed to boost his confidence. After the phone calls, Lee would take a long time, maybe two hours, maybe longer, to bathe, groom, and dress himself in the black wardrobe that he reserved for these occasions. Standing in front of the mirror, he

117

would snap the pearl buttons of his red checkered cowboy shirt, then climb into the black Western-cut leisure suit. He would attach his belt to the giant solid-gold buckle with the thick crust of diamonds, and draw on his black alligator cowboy boots. Checking himself again in the mirror, he would fuss with the black cowboy hat with LEE CHAGRA and FREEDOM embossed in gold on the brim until he achieved the proper tilt and slope. Finally, he would pose with the ebony cane with its gold satyr's-head handle, squinting and turning until he was satisfied. It was an incredible sight. Right before your eyes Lee Chagra became the Black Striker.

Clark Hughes went ahead to the casino "to lose my piddling three or four hundred." He never knew why Lee liked to bring him along, but he seldom refused. Lee was Clark's friend, maybe the best friend Clark had, but in some strange, almost unthinkable way he felt the friendship slipping away. He had known about Lee's cocaine habit, but since Clark had been appointed a judge, Lee hadn't flaunted it. It wasn't the cocaine so much as the life-style it symbolized. It was as if their friendship had come to a fork in the road, and Lee had wandered off in another direction.

It was almost midnight when the Black Striker made his appearance on the casino floor. He marched straight to a crap table on one side of the casino and told the pit boss to clear the table. The pit boss snapped his fingers and motioned for guards to bring the velvet ropes. "Gentlemen," he told the other players, "this table is now reserved for a private game. Please feel free to use any other table in the casino." Like so many sheep, the nickel-and-dime players started backing away. At the same time a swell of excitement seemed to rumble from the floor and people started shoving to get a look at the action. As Lee reached for the dice, he recited a spiel that was also part of his ritual. "Look at 'em," he said to the pit boss, grinning. "You ought to pay me fifteen hundred dollars an hour to entertain the customers. Where do you get off? Who do you think you are?" The pit boss had heard the spiel many times and smiled patronizingly as he counted out the stacks of $500 chips. In the first minutes of Lee's run, a little old lady burst through the crowd just as Lee released the dice. "Any craps!" she shouted, throwing a $5 chip on the table.

After about an hour Lee had lost $90,000. He didn't appear disturbed. He and Clark went back to the suite for a while. A short time later there was a knock, and Lee admitted two hookers to the room.

It looked as though he was set for the night. Clark excused himself and went to his own room, alone.

Shortly after noon the next day, Lee telephoned and said: "Ninety thousand is nothing for a stepper. Let's go downstairs and give them one they can write home about." Clark said he would dress and meet Lee in the casino.

The casino was almost deserted. It was that strange hour when the golfers are on their morning rounds and the drunks are still asleep, that time when they clean the sand in the ashtrays and empty the slots and put fresh ice in the urinals. By the time Clark arrived, Lee had already lost another $80,000 and was yelling at the floor manager because he was threatening to cut off his credit. "How come when I'm winning you let me do anything I goddam please, but when I lose you won't let me out of the trap?" he shouted in a voice that could be heard in the coffee shop on the opposite side of the casino.

That night as he was dressing, Lee announced intentions to change his luck. He was going to play baccarat instead of craps. Clark didn't say a word. He was painfully aware that all serious gamblers harbored deep and irrational superstitions: once he'd seen Lee go berserk because a *Chinaman* approached the table. "I thought maybe *I* was the Jonah," he said. "I decided to disappear over to the Hilton for a while." When Clark Hughes returned to Caesar's about nine that evening, Lee had almost exhausted his credit line. In the twenty-four hours since their arrival, he had signed markers totaling $240,000.

They checked out of the hotel that same night and moved to the Aladdin, where Lee had a $250,000 line of credit. Once again Lee went first to his suite and carried out the ritual. When he arrived several hours later in his Black Striker ensemble, a woman asked Clark Hughes if his friend was a movie star. The pit boss shooed the sheep away from the table that Lee selected for his private performance. Unlike many casinos, the Aladdin allowed a player to lay double odds; thus it was possible to win or lose twice as fast. In less than fifteen minutes, he won $90,000. Clark assumed that Lee would go straight back to Caesar's and claim some of his markers, but that wasn't Lee's intention. He did quit for the night, though. Some people thought Lee Chagra didn't know how to quit, but that wasn't quite true. He knew how to quit when he was *winning*. Clark was dog tired and went straight to bed. He didn't know what Lee did for the remainder of the night, only that he didn't gamble.

The following afternoon at the Aladdin, Lee took the worst beating Clark had even seen him take. In a single short sitting he lost almost $190,000. He still had $150,000 credit, but that night he went through another $70,000.

They were scheduled to fly back to El Paso Monday morning. When Clark arrived downstairs with his luggage, he saw Lee at one of the blackjack tables, arguing with a Teamster guy who was apparently in charge of credit for the casino. Lee had seated himself at a table and ordered $5,000 in chips, but the dealer refused. "Lee," the man was saying, "I'm not gonna say this again . . . *no more credit!*"

Lee didn't protest as Clark led him out of the casino to the waiting limousine. He looked as though he hadn't slept for three nights. The silence was monumental. Lee stared out the limo window at the blur of cold neon. His cowboy hat was pushed forward until the brim almost touched his nose, and shaggy locks of graying hair spilled over his collar. Though neither knew it, this was the last time the two old friends would ever go to Vegas together.

After a while Clark said, "You must have dropped close to half a million back there. You sonuvabitch, how are you gonna pay off those markers?"

"I don't know," Lee said.

There was another silence, then Lee took a deep draw on his cigarette and pressed Clark's shoulder. "It's like Teddy Roosevelt always said," Lee told him, and now his smile was back in place. "It's better to *try*. It's better to bust your ass trying and get kicked all over tomorrow than live all your life like those little gray fuckers out there."

A few weeks after the Vegas trip, Lee was hospitalized for a long-overdue hemorrhoidectomy. He was not very good at suffering alone, and friends and family visited him almost constantly. One day while Vivian was there, they delivered a dozen red roses to the room. Lee read the card and laughed. "It's from some friends in Vegas," he said, handing her the card. The card read: "I hope your ass feels like what you did to us."

18

The long slide that had begun in 1976 and hit high speed in 1977 rumbled and shook like a freight train out of control as it passed into the final year of Lee Chagra's life. Except for a few faithful clients like Jack Stricklin, Lee's practice was at rock bottom; and yet nearly everyone else in the family was planning and buying as though money were just another seed that would blow in with the spring winds.

Joe was still talking about investing $100,000 in a franchise discotheque, even though Lee had already vetoed the idea. Lee's idea for producing and marketing a hotshot television antenna that was supposed to pick up stations as far away as New Zealand had gone down the tube, along with thousands of dollars. Mom was off on another trip, and Patsy was buying jewelry even though she already had enough to ballast a battleship. Only a few years ago the Chagra women dressed modestly, if not conservatively, reflecting the family's natural grace and beauty and fidelity to their culture. Lately, they had come on like new money at a charity ball. A woman attorney in El Paso told of seeing one of them in a sequined dress and clear plastic high heels with live goldfish swimming inside. Another Chagra woman was observed wearing legwarmers and a mink jacket on a day when the temperature hovered near ninety degrees. Patsy's husband, Rick de la Torre, still worked as vice-president of the First State Bank, where he had started as a messenger boy nine years before, but Lee knew he was involved in a half-baked drug scam with Mike Halliday and Joe Renteria, the local nightclub singer whose career Lee had been promoting for several years. Jimmy and his pal Henry Wallace were still doing their number in Fort Lauderdale, and Jimmy was throwing money around even though the Coast Guard had seized one of his dope ships just a few weeks earlier. Jimmy had telephoned to say that everything was cool, they couldn't trace the ship to his organization, and, anyway, they had managed to offload 24,000 pounds before the Coast Guard discovered the old freighter. Jimmy was expecting another freighter in six weeks, and in the meantime Henry Wallace would be flying to El Paso with a bag of money that Jimmy wanted Mom to have.

In January 1978, all the family except Joe and Patty, who had to stay in El Paso to file some legal briefs, flew to Florida for Jimmy's wedding. Jimmy and his girlfriend, Liz Nichols, were expecting a baby. If Jimmy seemed self-destructive at times, Liz was an animated time bomb. The daughter of a career Army man, Liz had been running with a fast and considerably older crowd since she was fourteen. Her friends were mostly businessmen and theater people. One afternoon while attending a bullfight in Juárez, she announced intentions of becoming a bullfighter and for several months traveled through Mexico, studying the ancient art and fighting in small rings throughout the country. When she was sixteen, Liz hooked up with a fifty-three-year-old writer, actor, and businessman named Charles Chauvet, whose family had been instrumental in building Peyton Meat Packing Company into a major El Paso concern. "At that point in my life," Liz remembered, "Charles was the most intelligent, sophisticated person I'd ever known." Chauvet aspired to be a Hollywood actor and producer and persuaded Liz to run off with him to California, but the closest he got to being famous was selling cocaine to a bit player who turned out to be a narc. Liz did some time in juvenile detention. Lee represented both Liz and her lover. Indirectly, that's how Liz became a member of the Chagra family. Jimmy fell for her right away. Liz may or may not have been one of Lee's lovers, but there was an unspoken feeling that this image was what attracted Jimmy. Liz and Jimmy lived together for several years before their marriage in January. A temperamental girl with a sharp tongue, Liz could be terribly dramatic, even suicidal. Not long before they moved to Florida, she dressed herself in a silk lavender gown, dimmed the lights, arranged soft music, and swallowed enough pills to kill four or five people. This would-be Hollywood suicide was prevented by a chance telephone call from a dope dealer looking for Jimmy.

Wedding guests were amazed to see firsthand the large house that Jimmy and Liz purchased in Fort Lauderdale. It was set well back on the property, just like Lee's house on Frontera Road in El Paso, and like Lee's house it was surrounded by a high wall and an elaborate security system of electronically controlled locks and closed-circuit television cameras. The house had horses and a stable and a swimming pool every bit as large as Lee's. After another big score, Jimmy told Lee, he planned to move to Las Vegas and build a house that would make this one look like a shelter for stray dogs.

Early on the morning of March 2, a task force of heavily armed agents from the DEA and the Bureau of Alcohol, Tobacco and Firearms busted three members of Joe Renteria's dope conspiracy at El Paso International Airport. Renteria himself was in Mexico City at the time; when he heard about the bust, he vanished. Lee's brother-in-law, Rick de la Torre, wasn't arrested at the airport, but some weeks later Rick and a friend from Los Angeles, Ben Garcia, were indicted along with other members of the alleged conspiracy. No drugs were seized. In fact, no drugs were smuggled or even in danger of being smuggled. The conspiracy was a government trap from the start. The agent provocateur was former El Paso hustler named Richard Gross, who operated a weight-control clinic near San Jose, California, and got his thrills doing his patriotic duty for the DEA.

Although Renteria, Halliday, and some others had been talking about a marijuana-smuggling operation for several months, the talk had gone nowhere. They didn't have a pilot or an airplane or even a drug contact. Rick de la Torre recalled, "It all seemed pretty harmless at the time." Then two weeks after Christmas, Ben Garcia, an old friend who had become sports publicity director at Loyola University in Los Angeles, had a chance encounter with Richard Gross, a character from their past. Gross started talking about his adventures flying cocaine and marijuana from Peru to Mexico, and within five minutes a conspiracy was formed. Garcia called Joe Renteria, and Renteria called the others. In the weeks that followed, Renteria met a number of times with Gross, and with another pilot named Mike Moran, who was actually an agent with the DEA. It started out with a plan to smuggle eighteen thousand pounds of grass from Colombia: Renteria had once done a nightclub tour of Colombia, and he bragged that he had connections there, though in fact the connections existed mostly in his imagination. Gross convinced him that as long as they were going to smuggle marijuana, they might as well smuggle some

123

cocaine, too. Each time the would-be smugglers encountered a problem—a pilot, a plane, a place to refuel, a landing strip in Colombia, or in Mexico, or in Texas—each time the conspiracy seemed about to collapse under the weight of its amateurishness, the bounty hunter and the DEA agent found a solution. Renteria made several trips to Mexico and Colombia, leaving a trail of airline and hotel records, logs of long-distance calls, everything the narcs needed to substantiate their case. The nightclub singer even invented codes for the scam—name codes, telephone codes, radio codes—which he was thoughtful enough to put in his own handwriting for Gross, who gave them to Agent Moran, who sealed them as evidence. At one point Renteria got so carried away with his own potential that he bragged that he had masterminded the famous Ardmore operation. When the DEA thought it had played the hand far enough, it moved in for the bust. Unfortunately, Joe Renteria got away and became a fugitive, as did Mike Halliday. For the moment, all the narcs really had was the small fry—de la Torre, Garcia, and an ex-con named Fred Bella.

As Lee and Joe Chagra reviewed the case against their brother-in-law, it appeared that the DEA had very little solid evidence. True, Rick de la Torre had attended one or two "meetings" in which Gross and the undercover agent were present, and Renteria had used Rick and Patsy's Blazer during his trips to El Paso. Renteria had also introduced Rick as his "banker," which was technically true, though not in the way it was being interpreted by the DEA. Lee guessed that the worst Rick would get was five years, with the sentence probably suspended.

When the indictments came down, the Chagras were shocked and outraged. James Kerr had managed to cut the so-called conspiracy into four counts—conspiracy to import and to possess marijuana, and conspiracy to import and possess cocaine. The prosecutor had high hopes of sending Rick away for forty years. Kerr had become an expert in multiplying conspiracies. The various appeals courts were divided on the constitutionality of this technique. Two circuits had ruled that when the government "punishes two aspects of the same conspiracy" it is double jeopardy. Two other circuits disagreed. By coincidence, the Fifth Circuit in New Orleans was looking into that exact subject now in its review of Marty Houltin's conviction. In a recent opinion the court had written: "Were we free to consider that problem anew, we would conclude . . . that the double jeopardy clause prohibits the punishment of a single conspiracy by more than one penalty." In the meantime, however, James Kerr was ready to prosecute, and Judge John Wood was ready to preside. It was Lee's first confrontation with Kerr and Wood since the affair with Jack Stricklin, and also his last.

Since neither Rick de la Torre nor Ben Garcia had any previous record, it was agreed to try them together. Fred Bella, the other member of the conspiracy who was in custody, had an impressive rap sheet going back many years and would therefore stand trial separately. The defense that Lee and Joe Chagra designed was basically simple—de la Torre and Garcia denied intentional and knowing and willful involvement. Garcia's only involvement was his one conversation with Richard Gross and a couple of telephone calls. Rick admitted that he was in the car with the agents during an eight-minute ride to the airport and that Joe Renteria introduced him as his "banker," but he denied there was any talk about smuggling marijuana and he particularly denied Richard Gross's astonishing testimony that de la Torre had taken credit for the Ardmore scam. Perhaps Gross was confusing him with Joe Renteria.

The jury acquitted de la Torre and Garcia on the first three charges and, in what appeared to be an act of compromise, found them guilty of one count of conspiracy to import marijuana. Wood gave each the maximum—five years, followed by ten years special probation, and fines of $15,000. Though the verdict seemed reasonable, Kerr took it hard. Joe Chagra noticed tears in the prosecutor's eyes as he listened to the three not-guilties. Later, Kerr insisted that the jury had proved him correct. "The jury said he [de la Torre] was a major narcotics smuggler. That means I won." Others got the impression that the prosecutor took the verdict as a personal defeat, his first ever in Judge Wood's El Paso courtroom. Maybe Kerr resented losing to the Chagras, or maybe he really believed that the Chagras' brother-in-law deserved to do forty years in prison. Whatever his motive, Kerr's next move shocked nearly everyone, including Kerr's boss, Jamie Boyd. He compiled a list of de la Torre's responses under oath and prepared a new indictment charging the defendant with multiple counts of perjury, each carrying a five-year sentence.

Kerr's charges of perjury were eventually cut to five by the Justice Department. De la Torre was convicted and served time for one of the perjury charges, though, ironically, he never served time for the conspiracy conviction. Fourteen months after the conspiracy trial, both Garcia's and de la Torre's convictions were overturned by the Fifth Circuit. Judge Wood had rushed the trial through three and a half long, arduous days, denying motions for recess and abusing Lee Chagra on several occasions. However, the Fifth Circuit reversed on a small technicality that occurred after Wood had left the courthouse to go fishing. Both sides had agreed that magistrate Harry Lee Hudspeth could receive the verdict in Wood's place. When the jury sent in a note asking the judge to reread a portion of the charge dealing with conspiracy, Hudspeth had called Wood in San Antonio and gotten permission. But the magistrate had overruled the defense's motion to also read the definitions of "specific intent," "knowingly" and "willfully" when Kerr objected. This turned out to be the reversible error. In a footnote apparently directed at Wood, the Fifth Circuit pointed out that there was no way to say for certain if this small error affected the jury's verdict, then quoted this yeasty remark by a former chairman of the Texas House of Representatives judiciary committee: "We all know that just being a lawyer doesn't make a man a magician or give him supernatural powers. Only an appointment to the federal judiciary can do that."

At the beginning of the summer, Lee and Joe Chagra visited their brother, Jimmy, in Fort Lauderdale. The biggest shipload of the whole operation had unloaded a few months early, and Jimmy was awash in cash and high spirits; there had been a number of drug busts in recent weeks, however, and Jimmy was ready to wrap up his operation and move to Las Vegas. Jimmy and his friend, Peter Krutschewski (aka Peter Blake), had made a trip to Boston, where Jimmy was introduced to some high-rolling East Coast crime figures, among them a handsome and dashing young man named Salvatore Michael Caruana, who was said to be linked with New England crime boss Raymond Patriarca. Jimmy and Caruana had become friends and business associates; in fact, Jimmy's stepdaughter, Cindy, was spending the summer with Caruana and his wife. There was a rumor that Peter Krutschewski was about to be indicted under the kingpin statute, and Jimmy was clearly impressed. Krutschewski owned half of a Boston nightspot called the Black Friars Club, which had been the scene of a sensational gangland murder—five men, including Krutschewski's partner, Vincent Solomente, were cut down in the assault. In Boston, Jimmy had also met and retained the law firm of

126

Oteri and Weinberg, which represented some of the megastars of the underworld. He boasted to his brothers that he had deposited $100,000 with the firm, just to prove his credentials.

One night as the Chagra brothers bragged and gossiped beneath the Florida sky, Lee went into a long, almost incoherent harangue about Judge Wood and James Kerr. Until that night the judge and the prosecutor had been just names to Jimmy, villains out of some melodrama in some faraway place; he hadn't realized what harm Wood and Kerr had done to his family and friends, or with what intensity Lee hated them. Joe Chagra talked about what they had done to Rick de la Torre, and what they were getting ready to do to Renteria. There were hardly words to describe what both Lee and Joe regarded as the mean-spirited arrogance and foul tactics of the federal establishment in El Paso. Jimmy listened to this conversation without comment, but for a change they had his attention.

In August, Lee and Joe traveled to Boston to meet with lawyers Joseph Oteri and Martin Weinberg. Lee wanted to sue James Kerr and the DEA, and he set out a long list of incidents in which he believed the DEA solicited false and perjurious testimony. It was decided that investigators for Oteri and Weinberg would interview and take affidavits from Jack Stricklin, Jerry Johnson, and a number of others who had claimed to have received promises and threats from DEA agents.

Twelve days after the trip to Boston, the Chagras learned that police in Palm Springs, California, had arrested Joe Renteria and were squeezing him to give information about Lee and Jimmy. One agent told Renteria that his mother was dying, and threatened to throw her in jail on charges of harboring a fugitive. Renteria confessed to his part in his own drug conspiracy, but insisted he knew nothing incriminating about the Chagras. Joe Chagra flew to California to talk to Renteria and learned that the singer had made a secret tape of his first conversation with Richard Gross. When Lee listened to the tape, he told his brother: "That's the best proof of entrapment I've ever heard."

News of Joe Renteria's arrest was cause for celebration in the offices of the U.S. attorney in San Antonio. Jamie Boyd had known Renteria for years. When Renteria was voted Boy of the Year by the Boys Club of El Paso, Jamie and his wife had chaperoned him to a state conclave in Austin. In the late 1960s and early 1970s,

Renteria was a regular entertainer at the Rodeway Inn in El Paso, where Lee Chagra heard him and made him his protégé. For starters, Lee got Renteria's teeth straightened and capped, and then bought him a new wardrobe to replace the ratty threadbare tuxedo with the wide lapels. A contract was drawn up specifying that Lee would guarantee Renteria $250 a week plus expenses for a term of fifteen years, or until the boy became a Hollywood star. Renteria and his band toured the Southwest and West Coast and played gigs in Mexico and South America; he even landed single-episode parts in such TV shows as *Mod Squad* and *Baretta*, but after ten years Renteria was no closer to being a star than he had been at the start. At one point Lee had personally raised money so that Renteria could produce and direct his own movie, loosely based on his own semitragic love affair with one of the Chagras' cousins, Jo Ann Wardy. Jo Ann Wardy was a cultured, self-assured, somewhat worldly beauty whom Renteria dated for seven years. They might have married except for the old-world customs that still gripped both of their families: she was Lebanese, he was Mexican. "We felt like Romeo and Juliet," Jo Ann Wardy admitted. "Only in the wrong time and place." Several times they talked of eloping, as Jo Ann's cousin, Patsy Chagra, had some years earlier when she married Rick de la Torre. But somehow they never found the right moment. Renteria's screenplay was a crude attempt to tell the story of his star-crossed love, but somehow the plot got twisted into a giant drug caper: Renteria ended up filming his own prophecy. The movie was called *Toke*, and except for a few private screenings, one of them in a suite at the Waldorf-Astoria arranged by Frank Sinatra's chief gofer, Jilly Rizzo, the film died in the can.

Over the years, Joe Renteria had become like a member of the Chagra family, and Jamie Boyd was not at all surprised to find the onetime Boy of the Year in his present fix. The U.S. attorney believed that as soon as Renteria realized the seriousness of his problem—he faced forty years in prison—he would rat on Lee Chagra. But Boyd was wrong. Renteria stuck to his story, which was basically that he had been framed by Richard Gross and made trips to Colombia only to work a deal to import coffee beans. Jamie Boyd and James Kerr both prosecuted the case. The tape that the defense believed would prove entrapment was stolen before the trial, and Renteria was found guilty on all counts. Right up until the day of sentencing, Jamie Boyd held out hope that Renteria would change his mind and name Lee Chagra as the kingpin. The night before Judge Wood was scheduled to pass sentence, something happened that sealed Joe Renteria's fate. Renteria agreed to a television interview from his cell at La Tuna (he was being held under $1 million bond), and during the course of the interview Renteria made a melodramatic little speech advising all the youngsters out there in TV land not to get involved in big-time smuggling activities as he had. Rather than being pleased by this rather touching performance, Jamie Boyd was outraged. "Renteria had told this ridiculous story about importing coffee on the witness stand," Boyd said, "and then he goes on TV and gives them a clear admission of guilt! If I was the sentencing judge, this would certainly influence me." Boyd subpoenaed the TV footage and showed it to Judge Wood, who then sentenced Renteria to thirty years, followed by another thirty years special parole. Even Jamie Boyd was surprised by the harshness of the sentence. Boyd said later: "I think Judge Wood was just trying to shock him into talking, that at some later time he intended to reduce the sentence." There was no way to say for sure: before that could happen, Judge Wood was murdered.

Few realized it at the time, but even without Renteria's cooperation the U.S. attorney still had an ace in the hole. Jimmy Chagra's partner, Henry Wallace, had been busted in New Orleans and again in Denver, and now that the DEA was turning up the heat, Wallace was singing like a drunken angel. Wallace had no information incriminating Lee Chagra, although he confirmed that Lee had set up dummy corporations to launder money, but he was willing to finger Jimmy as the kingpin. Boyd's strategy was to indict Jimmy on multiple counts and wait for him to break. Boyd believed that one way or another Jimmy would take him to Lee. At least he'd better. Boyd, Kerr, and the DEA had worked so hard selling the media on the contention that El Paso was the hub of dope trafficking in the Southwest that everyone took it as gospel. Now the feds had a yard of hot real estate on their hands; they desperately needed someone to buy it.

Although Kerr's racket-busting grand jury was still active, it had produced very little hard news. An attorney from the Organized Crime Division of the Justice Department was assisting the prosecutor in preparing cases, but there had been very few cases prepared. Except for a few minor gambling indictments, the only indication that the racket busters were getting anywhere was a probe directed toward topless dancers who worked at a joint called the Lamplighter Club, which was allegedly owned by some people who were associated with a Mafia figure in Seattle. Most of the dancers were girlfriends of Bandido Motorcycle Club hoodlums, who were suspected of being major dealers in cocaine and amphetamines.

A number of Lee Chagra's friends were called to testify in the gambling probe, including Jimmy Salome, Ray Ramos, and Clark Hughes. Salome was later indicted on gambling charges and paid a fine. "I think they would have left me alone, except they thought Lee was involved," Salome said. "They offered me all kinds of deals if I would nail Lee." The government had also tried to get two well-known gamblers, Thomas "Amarillo Slim" Preston and Bryan "Sailor" Roberts, to implicate Lee but both refused. Sailor Roberts was later indicted and convicted, but he was far and away the biggest name uncovered by the probe into organized gambling.

As for the Mafia, there were plenty of big names bandied about, but not a single indictment. A secret eleven-page memorandum compiled by the Federal Strike Force in Las Vegas was leaked to the media, disclosing that Kerr's El Paso grand jury was inquiring into "the relationship" between Lee Chagra, Anthony Spilotro, reputed Mafia chief in Chicago, and Ted Binion, son of the owner of the Horseshoe Casino in Las Vegas. Spilotro, also known as Tony the Ant, was alleged to be the hidden owner of Argent Corp., whose Vegas holdings including the Stardust and Fremont hotels and casinos. Argent's holdings were bought principally with $93 million in loans from the Teamsters Union Central States Pension Fund, according to documents from the Chicago Crime Commission. About that same time, the Associated Press quoted an unidentified federal authority as saying they were "a hair's breadth away" from linking "high-level organized crime to the racketeering probe centered in El Paso." Joe Bonanno, Sr., who had lived in Tucson since his expulsion by warring underworld families in New York, and Raymond Patriarca, reputed czar of the New England Mafia, were said to be "under intensive scrutiny." The unnamed souce told the Associated Press: "It's a growing Southwestern organization. We know [Joe] Bonanno has a big hand in it." It was also revealed that since 1975 agents of the Arizona Narcotics Strike Force had been rummaging through Joe Bonanno's trash, and had discovered handwritten notes and correspondence from Mafia crime figures implicating "a multimillion-dollar criminal empire stretching from Sicily to the United States, South America and the Middle East." According to a story syndicated by *Newsday*, a high council of Sicilian-born dons would soon meet somewhere in the United States and pass judgment on Joe Bonanno for allowing his garbage to fall into government hands. Four years later Bonanno had published his memoirs and was alive and well in Tucson, members of the El Paso grand jury had long since returned to normal lives, and nobody ever mentioned high-level organized crime except when they remembered the Chagras.

Whether or not he knew the details, Lee surely sensed the magnitude of the disaster that was bearing down on him. As 1978 progressed, so did his paranoia, his insistence that someone was out to get him. Even the jokes about how it was just him versus the government of the United States were wearing painfully thin. Clark Hughes found a cartoon of a mouse shooting the finger at an eagle—it was titled "The Last Great Act of Defiance"—and Lee's secretary, Sandy Messer, was having it made into a wall plaque. On the cartoon, Clark had written "Wood" below the eagle and "Chagra" below the mouse. "No, you got it backward," Lee said when he saw it. "*I'm* the eagle!" But Sandy noticed there were tears in his eyes.

The only evidence that Lee expected things to improve was his new office complex on Mesa, at the edge of the downtown district between Interstate 10 and St. Patrick's Cathedral, where all the Chagra men had once been altar boys. While the complex was being renovated, Lee occupied an office in a building on Montana owned by another lawyer friend, Mickey Esper, who was related to Lee's wife, Jo Annie. It was during this period that Lee was introduced to Mickey's black-sheep uncle, Lou Esper, a pale, seedy, rat-faced Syrian hoodlum, who had spent about half his fifty years in various prisons. Uncle Lou, who had recently been paroled in California, supported his drug habit by means of a small-time burglary-robbery ring composed mostly of young black soldiers from Fort Bliss. Lou Esper liked to mainline speed and spent most of his afternoons in the company of hookers and gamblers shooting up in the small apartment he rented just north of Lee's new office. When he learned that Lee was a cocaine user, Esper found a good supply and usually delivered the goods in person. On several occasions he watched Lee remove one of his boots and count out the cash. Esper sometimes hung around as Lee made large cash payoffs to various collectors. None of Lee's friends, and especially Jo Annie, could understand why Lee tolerated the old hood, but that's how Lee was.

Almost every day Jimmy telephoned his brothers from his new home in Las Vegas. The family was worried about Lee. Lee cried a lot these days—he cried when he thought of Jimmy, especially. He didn't advertise the fact, but Jimmy was helping pay the huge cost overrun on the new office. Jimmy was also taking care of Lee's half-million-dollar marker at Caesar's. Then, in a fashion that was typical of his relationship with Lee, Jimmy decided to take it a step farther. He went to the big guys at Caesar's and told them that, by God, the next time his brother walked in that joint he wanted him treated like *a goddam celebrity*! That was it, Lee's ultimate humiliation. He would never go back to Vegas. Jimmy had ruined it. Lee always suffered shamelessly when he was down and Jimmy was up, but this was different. He'd never *cried* about it before. Sandy and the others began to realize that this was something truly personal; it was as though Lee were mourning his own impending death. He talked obsessively about death and dying. His sister, Patsy, recalled, "It scared me to hear Lee talk that way. Lee had always been our strength."

Throughout the months of October and November, Lee couldn't shake the feeling that something or someone was stalking him. He told Jimmy Salome that he was taking out a new insurance policy. He asked Bobby Yoseph, a young law school graduate who had recently started work as a clerk in the firm, what he would do if he came in and found the office had been robbed. Before Yoseph could think of a reply, Lee asked an even stranger question: "*What would you do if you came in and found I'd been murdered?*"

This preoccupation wasn't totally without foundation. Early in the fall someone had broken into Mickey Esper's law offices and attempted to haul off a safe. Not long after that, someone attempted to rob a high-stakes poker game at Jimmy Salome's house. Lee and the other players heard the crash of metal against the patio door. Fortunately, the glass was shatterproof. Lee grabbed an old musket, the only gun in the house, and chased two black men across the field before losing them along the river. Lee speculated that the attempt was an inside job, that someone was supposed to have opened the door from the inside. "I thought it was just an isolated thing," one player said. "But Lee kept brooding about it. As it turned out, he was right."

By mid-November, rumors of Jimmy Chagra's imminent indictment were rampant. Few people outside the office of the U.S. attorney knew that Henry Wallace was spilling out details of the Florida scam, or that several other members of the conspiracy had been arrested on unrelated charges and were jockeying for deals with the government. But hardly a day in El Paso went by without some report linking the Chagras and the grand jury investigation. Early on the morning of November 21, James Kerr turned his Lincoln Continental out of his driveway on a well-shaded street in the silk-stocking section of San Antonio called Alamo Heights and headed for the federal courthouse. At the intersection of Broadway a mint-green van blocked his route. Kerr was maneuvering around the obstacle when the rear doors of the van opened and two gunmen started firing. A blast of double-ought buckshot and a volley of .30-caliber slugs ripped across the hood, left fender, and windshield of the Lincoln; police later counted nineteen bullet holes.

For some unexplained reason, the three assailants (there was a third behind the wheel) raced from the scene without bothering to walk five or six feet to make sure Kerr was dead. If they had, they would have seen the small, trembling figure of the prosecutor crouched below the dashboard. The big engine block of the Lincoln had stopped the bullets from reaching Kerr. The prosecutor was dazed and bleeding from the shards of splintered glass, but otherwise unharmed. Kerr was able to give a description of the van; as it turned out, it had been stolen in Austin just hours before, and was found the following day abandoned not far from the scene. Kerr also picked out mug shots of several members of the Bandidos as suspects, but nearly five years later nobody had been arrested for the assassination attempt, despite one of the most massive investigations in the history of the FBI.

When Lee and Joe Chagra heard what had happened in San Antonio, they looked at each other in wonderment. Neither was prepared to speak the unspeakable, but Joe thought of that night the previous summer in Florida, and he imagined that Lee did, too.

19

When Donna Johnson arrived at the office the day before Christmas, the day Lee was murdered, Lee was already there. Donna was the law firm's bookkeeper and one of the few women Lee had ever hired without sex aforethought. Not that Donna was unattractive, but her relationship with Lee went much deeper than simple physical attraction. In a way, Lee had saved her life. Some years earlier, Donna had got involved in a long-distance flirtation with a man she believed to be an East Coast "gangster." The man turned out to be an agent provocateur on the payroll of the DEA, and within a few weeks he had talked Donna into delivering some cocaine, for which she was arrested and threatened with forty-five years in prison. Donna had never even heard of Lee Chagra when friends hired him to defend her. A DEA agent told her that Chagra was "a lawyer mixed up with organized crime" and promised she would do the full forty-five years if she even talked to Chagra; Donna swore she wouldn't. The agents also promised she would be released on bond and the arrest would be kept secret, but that morning in the courtroom of U.S. magistrate Jamie Boyd she was stunned to hear the agents tell Boyd she was a big-time cocaine merchant from Alaska. "I was on the verge of freaking out," she recalled. "I had spent three nights in jail listening to the proposition of these agents: they wanted me to hang out in bars and convince men to buy or sell drugs. They knew I had never had any dealings with drugs, and now here we were in court and they were telling the magistrate I was a big-time cocaine dealer from Alaska. I was ready to kill myself. That's when Lee walked over and put his arm around me. He said, 'Can you stick it out one more night?' And I said I thought I could." Her case was assigned to the court of Judge John Wood, and Lee leveled with her: she would probably have to do five years. But Lee beat the rap by playing for the jury a tape of the agent provocateur bragging about the setup and admitting he had worked the same scam with young women all over the country. Lee looked her up a few weeks later and hired her as his bookkeeper. She had been his most trusted and loyal employee ever since.

That old watch-me-carry-the-world smile was back on Lee's face this final morning, his first and last in the new office. He was bubbling over with tales of the previous day's Tucson victory: Donna hadn't seen him this happy in months. He came to town early and bought corsages for all the women on the staff. He was wearing his boots and jeans and enough jewelry to sink a deep-sea diver, and Donna knew there wouldn't be much work done today.

The office was a maelstrom of activity, none of it having anything to do with the practice of law. Friends, relatives, and people Donna had never seen before paraded through as though the place were a museum. The complex included not only a maze of well-appointed offices but also a fully equipped kitchen, a law library, and a completely furnished two-bedroom suite. Lee had never discussed with his staff the purpose of the apartment at the rear of the complex, but they knew the rumors. They knew, too, that he was having a regular evening affair with a stripper from the Lamplighter Club. Most afternoons as Donna and Sandy were crossing the parking lot after work, they saw her, and sometimes two or three other strippers from the Lamplighter, hurrying toward Lee's office. It was apparent from the manner in which the furniture was rearranged and toppled about that the orgies were quite vigorous. Still, few people believed that Lee would go so far as to leave Jo Annie and the children.

Donna made fresh coffee and explained the new telephone system to Lee. He sparkled like a kid with a new toy as he showed Donna and Sandy Messer where the various safes were concealed. They knew about the safe in the floor of the bathroom, but there were others— one beneath the carpet near the fireplace in the living room of the private suite, and another in the master bedroom.

As was his custom when he was in one of these expansive moods, Lee sat in his new office with his feet on his desk, telling war stories and handing out money. There was plenty of cocaine to guarantee the holiday mood; at least five ounces had been delivered a few days earlier. Lee gave Jack Stricklin $1,000 and passed out other amounts to other friends. During the morning a man they called the Cowboy appeared at the television camera mounted over the alley entranceway. Donna had never seen him before, but Lee buzzed him in and gave him $10,000; the others guessed that the Cowboy was a collector for some bookie.

Lee kept detailed records of gambling transactions, but no one else had any concept of how much he bet or with how many different bookies. He had telephoned Sandy from Tucson on Friday and told her that a woman named Butch would stop by the office later in the day. Sandy was to count out $20,000 from the stash under the bathroom sink and have it ready. This wasn't an unusual request: just a week before, Lee had given Sandy $50,000 to carry around in her tote bag, ostensibly for safekeeping. Donna helped Sandy count the $20,000. They didn't count all the bundles of cash in the bathroom hiding place, but there was more money than either of them had ever seen in one place, something like $450,000, maybe more. Jimmy Chagra and his friend Peter Blake had delivered it earlier in the week. While they were counting, the new law clerk, Bobby Yoseph, appeared at the door and tried to shove his way inside. "I blocked the door with my body," Donna recalled, "but he opened it enough to see the money."

Neither Donna nor Sandy trusted Yoseph. Nobody knew much about his background. He had graduated from the University of Washington law school and moved straight to El Paso, where his uncle was a prominent Syrian real estate dealer. The uncle had sent Yoseph to Sib Abraham, and Sib had sent him to Lee, who hired him without references; Yoseph's uncle was a business acquaintance and a friend. Lately, Yoseph had become a minor dictator around the office, assuming authority when Lee was away. He started aping Lee's style, picking up Lee's hippy-jivey way of talking, outfitting himself in jeans, boots, and even a touch of body jewelry. When he started sitting at Lee's desk and barking orders, the secretaries threatened to resign.

Soon after noon the staff and hangers-on had finished the Christmas party and gone. Jo Annie telephoned her husband from the Sun Bowl at halftime, but Lee said he still had a pile of work on his desk. What she didn't know was that Lee was in his private apartment, watching the game on television with his friend Sailor Roberts, the bookie who had been busted in James Kerr's recent organized-crime probe. Sailor Roberts was a minor legend among local gamblers, having won the annual World Championship of Poker at Binion's Horseshoe Casino three years earlier. Jo Annie didn't like Sailor Roberts.

She thought of him as a *user*—he used Lee, he used anyone he could, and the only thing he gave in return was trouble. She had heard from Jimmy Salome's wife, who heard it from one of the regular poker players, Doug Holt, that Sailor was hanging out with Lou Esper.

Jo Annie left the football game early, and when she stopped by the office Roberts was just leaving. "I waited around to wish you and the kids Merry Christmas," the gambler told her. She dismissed the greeting as typical Sailor Roberts bullshit: she didn't believe for a second that he'd gone out of his way to wish her anything.

Lee seemed restless and preoccupied, as though he were late for an appointment and couldn't wait for Jo Annie to leave. He said that he would meet her at home in a couple of hours. At 2:30 P.M., Lee telephoned his brother Joe and said he would stop by Joe's house on his way home. Joe got the impression that Lee was expecting someone, and when he thought about it later, it occurred to him that the stripper from the Lamplighter was probably dropping by.

Jo Annie telephoned one final time, from her mother's house on Rim Road. It must have been nearly 3:30 P.M. Again, Lee sounded as though he had something else on his mind. It was the way he sounded when he was counting money or totaling figures, an abstract, business-first attitude.

"I've got to go," he told her. "There's a client buzzing at the door." Jo Annie tried to picture the man who had called that morning waiting outside the door.

Lee turned the channel-selector knob to the camera over the alley entrance. On the monitor he saw a tall, muscular black man in his early twenties. A second man stood behind him, out of camera range. "It's David Long," the first man said. An electric current unbolted the door. Lee left the money spread across the bed and closed the bedroom door behind him. He crossed the living room and closed the apartment door behind him. He walked to the top of the stairs and looked down at two black men and the guns in their hands.

About 4:00 P.M., Bobby Yoseph returned to the office from a shopping trip in Juárez. Yoseph let himself in the front entrance with a key that Lee had given him that morning. He walked upstairs to his own office. He'd never seen it so quiet there.

The first thing he noticed was his filing cabinet. All the drawers were open and papers were scattered on the floor. He left his hat and keys on the couch and walked down the hall to Lee's office. The door was partially open, but the office appeared empty. Yoseph's gaze moved around the room. A chill ran up his back as he realized that someone had also ransacked Lee's files. Two overstuffed easy chairs were pushed together against the front of Lee's desk, blocking the path across the room. Lee's vial of cocaine was open on the corner of his desk. It was not the kind of clutter Lee Chagra would leave. Yoseph walked behind the desk and dialed Lee's home number.

While the phone was ringing, Yoseph allowed his eyes to run along the wall to the left of the desk. First he saw Lee's boots standing in one corner by the door to the balcony, then he saw the blotch of blood on the wall. As one of Lee's daughters answered the phone, Yoseph saw Lee's body. He hung up without speaking. Lee was lying face up on on the floor, blood trickling from his mouth. His eyes were open, but he was obviously dying.

20

Joe Chagra remembered later that at first he hadn't felt a thing. He didn't notice the December chill or the heat from the lights or the cup that someone pushed into his hands. He kept thinking: "It'll be okay. Lee will be here in a minute and fix everything." Then he would look again at the body on the floor: he couldn't connect this body with anything or anyone in his experience.

He had known something awful was happening as soon as he turned down the alley and saw the ambulance. Six or seven cop cars were jammed in random array, some with their doors still open. A cop blocked the door and said he'd have to wait outside. He asked another cop if Lee was hurt, and the cop nodded. "Then why the hell don't you get him in that ambulance?" Joe yelled. The cop didn't answer. Joe ran to the pay phone at the corner across from the hospital and telephoned Jimmy in Las Vegas. "Something's wrong," Joe told his brother. "I think Lee's dead." There was a silence, then Jimmy said he was on his way.

Joe spotted an old friend, a detective, Jerry Lattimer, who took him inside and upstairs to Lee's office. Lee was stretched on the floor on the opposite side of his desk, staring at the ceiling as though he were lost in thought. There was a trickle of blood from his mouth and another from his nose. Joe's first thought was that his brother had suffered a hemorrhage. He couldn't yet see the small entrance wound under Lee's right arm, or the gush of blood from his lungs that had splattered the wall. The motive of robbery had not yet occurred to anyone. All of Lee's jewelry was in place. Joe knew that Lee usually carried money in his boots, but the fact that his boots were off his feet still didn't suggest what had happened. Then Joe remembered the

139

canvas bag of money in Lee's bathroom. He unlocked the bathroom door. The bag was gone.

Jimmy had chartered a jet and arrived about two hours later. Jack Stricklin met him at the airport and drove him to the office. Sib Abraham and some other old friends and members of the family were there by now. Someone had gone after Jo Annie, who collapsed when she first heard but now wanted to be there with the family. Patsy heard the bells from St. Patrick's in the next block and remembered Mom Chagra. Mom would be returning from mass just about now, walking toward Lee's office, unaware anything had happened. Patsy ran out the back entrance and toward the cathedral. Jimmy knelt beside the bag that now contained the remains of his brother and started bawling. Joe thought they were so much alike it scared him; they could have been twins. The numbness was draining away, and Joe felt the ache bouncing down his back and legs and tasted the tears that ran down his face.

When Jo Annie arrived, Joe offered to drive Lee's car home. Lee had driven his Continental, not the new limo, and as Joe opened the door on the driver's side he saw a canvas bag in the back seat. He froze, thinking of the missing money, thinking what would happen if the cops got it. Using his body as a shield, he hugged the bag against his chest and hurried to his own car. Detective George Drennan spotted Joe opening the trunk. The detective wanted to know what was in the bag. Joe told Drennan that the bag contained privileged information, documents from the Tucson trial. He could tell that Drennan didn't believe him, but the bluff worked. When Joe got home and looked inside, he realized that the bag really did contain the Tucson papers. Then what had happened to the money? What had happened to $450,000?

Wakes are not for the dead but for the living. As they tried to piece it together throughout that interminably long night, grief turned to anger, then to frustration, then to that special kind of irrational hatred born of frustration. They didn't know whom to hate. In those first unreal hours, with fear and rage running head and head, they believed that they were all trapped in a conspiracy, that they were all victims, that the killer or killers were nearby, waiting, and would appear to them when they were least prepared. All the men had guns. All the women were terrified and clutched together. Jimmy was ranting and waving his gun, almost out of control. Jack Stricklin thought the DEA had done it. So did Jimmy. That thought must have crossed everyone's mind. But why? Someone mentioned the name of Lou Esper, the rat-faced ex-con who had been hanging around. Uncle Lou was definitely a suspect in the attempted burglary of Mickey Esper's office a few months before. Jo Annie thought of another relative, an aunt who had turned on Lee when he refused to advance her more money on a personal injury suit. And what about the law clerk, Bobby Yoseph? Yoseph had told the emergency squad that he didn't have a key to the front door, that he'd meet them at the rear. Had Yoseph forgotten that he had just let himself in through the front door? When the emergency squad arrived, Yoseph somehow took a wrong turn and found himself locked inside the garage next to the alley. Firemen had to chop down the garage door to gain entrance.

And what about the mysterious phone call from David Long? Was it possible that on Christmas Eve Lee entertained a black client who had come to talk about an estate he might inherit? Would Lee have allowed such a man inside his inner sanctum, his fortress? Lee did strange things. Lee couldn't say no. Sib Abraham, who knew Lee's legal mind better than any of them, pointed out that estates in probate can be big scores for lawyers. If the man convinced Lee that he had a claim on $1 million, Lee might have invited him home for Christmas dinner.

Lee had been shot once with a small-caliber pistol, probably a .22. The bullet was most likely a hollow-point, filed across the top so that once it entered a body it would shatter and shred the vital organs. From the angle it appeared that Lee had been holding his hands up. They found a lighter near his body, and a bloody cigarette. Lee wouldn't have resisted a holdup attempt, but maybe the killer mistook the gesture. Maybe when Lee turned to light the cigarette, the killer thought he was reaching for a gun. The .38 that Lee kept in his upper left-hand drawer was missing, and so was the .22 that he carried in his tote bag. Lee wouldn't have been carrying a gun; if he had expected trouble, he wouldn't have opened the door. It was possible that the killer had panicked during the course of a robbery, panicked and fired. One lucky shot. Or a very unlucky one.

There was another possibility: the gunman had planned to kill Lee all along. It was beginning to dawn on them that whoever did the killing had been sent there by someone else, someone who knew the money was there, someone Lee trusted—someone who wanted Lee dead or didn't care if he lived. But who? Why? Patsy was thinking: "Why *Lee*? Lee helped everyone. Lee would have given them the money. Who would want to kill Lee? Jimmy, maybe, but Lee . . . why?" It could have been a gambling debt, but Lee had lived with gambling debts for years. As far as anyone knew, he was clear. Besides, gamblers are not interested in a man's morals, only his money. Lee always paid. Nobody was crass enough to mention the possibility of a jealous husband. There, too, they were stymied by the clear voice of reason: Why *now*?

The media, and therefore a large segment of the public, took it for granted that the murder was "drug-related" and probably connected to the Mafia. Within minutes after the shootings, the El Paso *Times* reported a barrage of telephone inquiries. One call was from a "prominent doctor." The city editor confirmed that Lee Chagra was dead and asked if the doctor knew him well. "No, not well," the doctor was quoted replying. "We were on different ends of the drug scene. I'm trying to get people *off* narcotics."

Another call reported by the *Times*:

Woman's voice: "Is it true? Is he dead?

City editor: "Yes."

"Oh my God!" Click.

The *Times* reported: "The specter of organized crime, wherever its tentacles may reach, takes on new dimensions with Chagra's murder, if for no other reason than the speculation it fuels." Most of the speculation, of course, started with the media and spread to the street. No doubt certain federal agents helped it along. Some of it had to come from the grand jury room. There was speculation about an El Paso bank suspected of laundering drug money, speculation about Lee's 1973 indictment and Jimmy's arrest in Colombia after the DC-6 crash, speculation about the huge gambling debt Lee had incurred in Vegas. By and large, the public preferred complex conspiratorial theories, such as one advanced by one local journalist that went like this: the mob had wrestled control of a ring of loan sharks, whores, thieves, and drug merchants from high military officials at Fort Bliss, and Lee Chagra's murder could be traced back to the mysterious crash of an Air Force jet in the desert, details of which were covered up by both the military and the mob. What a conspiratorial triangle—jets, drugs, and Mafia!

It was speculated, too, that Lee Chagra's murder was connected to the attempt on James Kerr. Drugs again. A writer for *High Times*

142

even hinted that there was a connection to a mysterious revolutionary movement called Aztlan, a mercurial coalition of Mexicans, Spaniards, Aztecs, mestizos, Lebanese, Assyrians [sic] and renegade Marxist priests who were said to headquarter in the Chihuahuan desert, trading drugs for guns and living for the day when a third nation would emerge from El Paso–Juárez.

Some FBI agents speculated the Bandidos were involved. (Members of the motorcycle gang were the usual suspects in almost any unsolved crime.) O. Leon Dobbs, agent-in-charge of the El Paso FBI office, told reporters that his sources informed him that the Bandidos had once threatened Lee Chagra. This piece of FBI intelligence was badly dated. The rumor had started five years earlier, after three Bandidos, including the club founder, were found guilty of murdering two brothers from Houston. After the trial, Lee had written a letter confessing he had given the Bandidos an inadequate defense, hoping that the letter would result in a new trial, which it did not. Dobbs was forthright about one aspect of Lee's death: the FBI wasn't looking for the killer—murder was the city's jurisdiction. The feds were looking for the missing money.

There was speculation about everything except the possibility that Lee was murdered in a straight-out, walk-in robbery. That possibility was absurd. It was like believing that Robin Hood had got himself mugged in Sherwood Forest.

21

The night before Lee's funeral, Jimmy and Joe Chagra ran across what appeared to be a red-hot lead—they learned that just before Lee's killing, a collector of debts known as the Indian had been looking for Lee. The Chagras dispatched two brothers with exceptionally tough reputations, Johnny and Jimmy Milliorn, to find the Indian. When they located him, the Indian was carrying a .22 pistol and there was blood on his leather jacket. The Milliorns delivered him to the Chagras, who took him to the garage for interrogation. The Indian swore he had nothing to do with Lee's murder and offered to help find the real killer. The blood, he told them, was from a fight weeks earlier. As for the .22, there were tens of thousands just like it in El Paso. The Chagras were inclined to believe him, but they turned the weapon and the bloodstained jacket over to the FBI anyway. Both clues proved negative. The Chagras learned later that U.S. attorney Jamie Boyd had contemplated filing kidnapping charges against them, but backed off when he learned that the Indian wouldn't testify.

Lee Chagra's funeral was a microcosm of all the extremes in his life. The Most Rev. Sidney Metzger, bishop emeritus of El Paso, came out of retirement to say mass. The bishop was a folk hero in his own right, having led the long and bitter boycott against the Farah Manufacturing Company. While federal agents snapped photographs from the parking lot across the street, hundreds of mourners jammed and overflowed St. Patrick's Cathedral.

State senator Tati Santiesteban, who had known Lee Chagra most of his life, led the procession of pallbearers. The district attorney, several district judges, and a former mayor stood elbow to elbow with Sailor Roberts, Amarillo Slim, and at least a dozen convicted dope dealers. There was no way to count the number of ex-lovers who crowded the cathedral to say a last farewell, but they were discreetly scattered and only occasionally exchanged glances. If Jo Annie was conscious of this, she moved among them without rancor, beautifully composed and self-possessed. Those near the front leaned forward to hear the final words she whispered in Lee's ear, but no one heard.

Finally, Lee's four daughters, Teresa Lynn, Tina Maria, Leslie Anne, and Joanna Leigh, and his son, Lee Ayoub, Jr., stood in front of the casket and sang, "I Would Give Everything I Own Just to Have You Back Again." Tina clutched her father's black cowboy hat, and Leader carried his father's trademark, the gold-tipped walking stick. The dark, brooding faces of the Ayoubs, Abouds, and Salomes wept for the Chagras and Abrahams. It took the funeral procession twenty minutes to pass.

A block from the cathedral, on North Mesa at the edge of the downtown business district, Lee Chagra's new office building was closed for good. A black banner was stretched across the entire front of the building. In broken white letters like shards of milk glass on velvet it said FREEDOM. The family posted a $25,000 reward and announced that the freedom banner would hang until the killers were caught and the case was closed. A year later it was still there.

As the family walked away from the cemetery, Jimmy caught up with Vivian and took her arm. "I'll drive you home," he said in a low voice. "I want to talk to you." Vivian was startled to see how much Jimmy looked like Lee, how he had grown out his mustache, how his hair was full and shaggy and touched now with streaks of gray. But more than anything it was his clothes: Jimmy showed up at the funeral wearing an outfit exactly like Lee's Black Striker costume. The gesture was unmistakable: he'd come to replace his brother.

They drove in silence, headed west out the freeway toward the Mesilla Valley. With Lee and Jimmy's help, Vivian had bought and was remodeling an old adobe farmhouse near the river, in an area that 125 years ago was the eastern boundary of the Gadsden Purchase, and 250 years before that the route of the Oñate expedition. Vivian studied the granite face of the Organ Mountains and waited for Jimmy to say what was on his mind.

"Did you fuck Lee?" he asked suddenly.

"What?"

145

"The morning he was killed. I heard you came to the house. I heard that the two of you were in the bedroom with the door closed."

Vivian thought of a lot of things before she answered. In all of her years with the Chagras, the paradoxical love of the Chagra brothers never ceased to amaze her. Each would have given the others anything he had, unless he thought the other really wanted it. Jimmy might have gone to the grave for Lee; and it was possible Lee had gone for Jimmy. And yet the priority of the moment was that one egomaniacal question: had she jumped in the sack with Lee on that last morning? A simple lie, a word, could carry the forces of a lifetime of revenge. Off to the left of the freeway, snuggled in the rich valley, they could see La Tuna, the federal correctional institution where Jack Stricklin and a lot of other family friends had done time. The mission towers and high cloistered walls made it look like a monastery. Jimmy had to be thinking of La Tuna: his situation was not good, and with Lee gone it might be hopeless. Jimmy looked at her, his eyes hard and begging. He had to know.

"No," she said. "No, I didn't. We just talked and he gave me some money."

Jimmy relaxed his grip on the wheel and shifted his weight. After a while he said, "Damn him anyway! I told him . . . I told him those things can happen. He got what was coming to him. If he'd just listened to me . . ." All of a sudden Jimmy was bawling like a baby and fighting to keep the car on the road. Like everyone else, Jimmy didn't have the slightest idea what had happened.

PART TWO

The Crime of the Century

22

Jimmy Chagra was embarrassed to admit it later, but in the summer of 1977—eighteen months before his brother Lee was murdered—he was just a glorified mule in a smuggling operation headed by Southwest dope czar Henry Wallace. Those were hard times for Jimmy. He had blown all the money from the big score in Boston, most of it in Las Vegas, but his losing streak hadn't stopped at the casino tables. First there had been the bust in Ardmore, with its loss of two planes and seventeen thousand pounds of marijuana, then the DC-6 crash in Colombia, and his subsequent arrest during the ill-fated rescue mission. No charges were filed, but the loss of the aircraft and cargo, combined with the massive publicity, put a killing frost on Jimmy Chagra's budding career as a dope entrepreneur. That was why he went to work for Henry Wallace.

Wallace operated out of Berino, New Mexico, a tiny farming community in the Upper Valley, just across the state line from El Paso. Jimmy had known the Fat Man, as Wallace was sometimes called, for more than a year, and they had become good friends—gambling, doping, shooting pool, comparing notes. Jimmy swallowed considerable quantities of pride when he had to ask the Fat Man for a job, but that was the only way he could get himself back into action.

Wallace was half Mexican and half Irish, a deceptively simple mixture of cunning and old-fashioned bluster. As the brains behind an exceptionally well-conceived operation, the Fat Man was a smuggler's smuggler. He had his own unlimited source of marijuana, supplied by friends in the *federales* in northern Mexico. The *federales* patrolled and maintained the landing strips that Wallace used, supplied the grass, and even loaded it. Wallace subcontracted with a number of experienced pilots, including Marty Houltin, commander of the Co-

149

lumbus Air Force, and Jim French, an aging scammer who lived in semiretirement on the old smuggler's ranch in the Gila Wilderness. Wallace ran his operation the way the Red Brigades and the CIA ran theirs, with each section ignorant of the doings of the others. Richard Young, a San Francisco musician who worked for Wallace in the winter of 1977 and later became a full partner in other scams, recalled his first very narrow glimpse of the big picture. Young was paid $2,000 a trip to truck marijuana from New Mexico to Indiana. He never saw the people who delivered the truck in New Mexico, and he never saw the people who received it in Indiana. His job was to drive, period. Just in case he got any big ideas, a "chase car" followed him all the way.

In the summer of 1977, Jimmy's friendship with Wallace was severely strained when Wallace was unable to pay Jimmy $150,000 for his part in a marijuana shipment out of Mexico. Wallace called a summit meeting at the home of one Leslie Harris in the Upper Valley to discuss what had happened to the missing funds. It was a decidedly acrimonious meeting: almost everyone carried a gun, and at one point two former Bandidos who worked for Jimmy Chagra threatened to pour gasoline over Leslie Harris's dog and light a match. Acting as peacemaker, Wallace suggested privately to Chagra that the two of them form a new partnership. Wallace needed Chagra's connections in Colombia—it was becoming increasingly difficult to peddle low-quality Mexican weed, which partly accounted for the missing money—and Chagra, dead broke, needed a grubstake. This was Wallace's plan: they would first smuggle fifty kilos of cocaine, then use the profits to buy a freighterload of prime Santa Marta Gold, the choice of discriminating smokers, who would pay four or five times the price of Mexican grass. Chagra agreed, and they sealed the partnership with a snort of coke.

Wallace borrowed $15,000 seed money from Richard Young, promising Young a piece of the deal, and another $60,000 from friends in Florida. At one meeting Wallace fronted Chagra six ounces of cocaine, and at another he gave Chagra $50,000 of his own money. Jimmy cadged more money from his family by complaining that his notoriety made it impossible for him to continue living in El Paso. He said he wanted to make a new life in Canada, but that was a lie. He intended to move to Fort Lauderdale, Florida, where he would set up an off-loading operation for the eventual shipment of marijuana.

He knew a man who had several large fishing boats suitable for the task.

The immediate problem was finding a pilot (Jimmy didn't want to use Jerry Wilson after the crash in Colombia) and an airplane of sufficient range to fly from Florida to Colombia and return with the cocaine. Wallace suggested Jim French, but Chagra was hesitant: Jimmy had stiffed the Frenchman on several deals, and he was sure French hadn't forgiven him. Wallace told Chagra that he would take care of French. Meanwhile, Wallace set about lining up more financial support. He was introduced to an El Paso travel agent named Dudley Connell, who expressed interest in some cut-rate, high-quality cocaine. Wallace promised Connell at least one kilo of coke for the amazingly low price of $10,000. Connell didn't have the cash on hand, but he promised to contact a friend in Denver, Paul Taylor; he was sure Taylor could raise some money.

Shortly after Jimmy and his girlfriend, Liz Nichols, left El Paso for Florida (via the casinos of Nevada), the Fat Man took a trip to the Gila Wilderness to call on Jim French. French had announced his retirement from scamming, but he did that whenever he was flush. Only a year earlier, Wallace had paid Marty Houltin a $5,000 finder's fee to lure French back to action. The lure would work again if Wallace was careful. Of course, the Fat Man had no intention of telling French that Jimmy Chagra was part of the operation. All French needed to know was that he, Wallace, and Richard Young were equal partners in a cocaine scam.

There wasn't much about smuggling Jim French didn't know. He had been scamming since he brought his first burros across the river in 1946. He used the World War II GI bill to take flying lessons— he'd fought with General Patton's Third Army, been taken prisoner by the Germans, and escaped. He was from the old school of scammers, one of the time-tested pros who disdained big planes and big operations, who preferred to work as an independent contractor, nickel-and-diming it with his single-engine plane, one or two or maybe three trips a week, never greedy, never talkative, never bold—just a good man for the long haul. There weren't many left like him.

French still got a lump in his throat when he remembered a night two or three years earlier in a steakhouse near Silver City. Some of the old-timers were having dinner—Ralph Hansen, Vic Newman, Marty, and a couple of others—when a waitress appeared at their table with a round of complimentary drinks. "Those two men who just come in sent yawl these," the waitress said.

"Well, kiss my ass!" Ralph Hansen said, and they all started laughing. "Honey," Ralph told his wife, "see those two pigs over there? They been chasing our ass for ten years. All they got is a little older and a little balder."

"Narcotics agents?" Ralph's wife asked.

"Two of the best. Ol' Charley there has sent three kids through college, and Howard, the tall one scratching his ear, built a lake cottage at Elephant Butte. Them were ten good years."

There was an almost tender moment as the smugglers lifted their glasses and toasted the narcotics agents. Not long after that Vic Newman topped off the tanks of his vintage B-26 and took off from Las Vegas. He hadn't been airborne more than twenty minutes when an engine exploded. The B-26 was a ball of fire before it hit the highway.

Ralph Hansen got his in Mexico. "He had no business trying to fly that old twin Beech," French said. "It was a lot more plane than the one he was used to flying." On takeoff Ralph hit the flap switch instead of the gear retractor, causing the plane to go nose down instead of nose up. Both topped-off fuel tanks exploded, and Ralph died on the way to the hospital in Torreón. They buried him beside the road.

Not long after that French's Navajo blew an engine on takeoff and he was trapped for more than eight hours in the wreckage with a broken collarbone and a side of cracked ribs. French knew that it wasn't the narcs a man had to worry about. It was fate. It was the nature of the business. It was zooming along at 225 mph, fifty feet above zagged outcroppings of rock, wings nearly clipping the rims of dark ravines, whistling under your breath and trying to spot the truck lights that guided you to safety. It was a bolt of lightning, or a wild pig that darts across the landing strip in the dead of night while you're at full throttle. It was bad equipment, bad judgment, and bad luck. It was trusting bad people. The Frenchman was on the ragged side of fifty, nearing sixty. He was married to his eighth wife, and there were a lot more miles behind than there were ahead. There was no way at this stage of life that Jim French would have worked an operation that included a loudmouth hot dog like Jimmy Chagra, but then he had no idea that Chagra was part of the deal when he accepted the Fat Man's offer of a one-third share. When he found out a month later, it was too late to stop.

By October, Chagra and the other smugglers were ready. French and Richard Young had delivered a newly purchased twin-engine Aerocommander to Florida, and Wallace had gone to Santa Marta to arrange to have the cocaine fronted. Now came the first major hitch. Chagra's longtime supplier, Lionel Gomez, refused additional credit: he had never been paid for the marijuana confiscated in Ardmore or the load burned in the plane crash. The resourceful Wallace found another supplier, who agreed to front six kilos (they had planned on *fifty*) at a price six times higher than expected. Wallace had no choice but to accept the offer, but in the meantime he would stay in Santa Marta as human collateral. There could be no doubting what would happen to the Fat Man if his friend Jimmy Chagra didn't come up with the money.

Wallace was broke, frightened, and increasingly messed up from sampling the cocaine. He telephoned the El Paso travel agent, Dudley Connell, pleading for money, which Connell claimed not to have. Connell's partner, Denver businessman Paul Taylor, did fly to Colombia to look at the operation, but Taylor had only a couple hundred dollars to loan Wallace. The best Connell and Taylor could offer was to help sell the cocaine and put the profits back into the boatload of marijuana. Back in Florida, meanwhile, the other investors in the scam were screaming for their money, and tropical storms were creating havoc with the timetable.

It was late October before they got a break in the weather. Chagra telephoned the Frenchman's motel room about dawn on October 21 and said: "Let's go. The Fat Man will be waiting with the goods." At the last minute Richard Young decided to go along for the ride. They were about four hours into the flight when Young was awakened by fierce clattering and clanging from the left engine. Over French's shoulder he could see that the tachometer was on the red line, indicating maximum revolutions. The Frenchman's face was so hard you could roller-skate on it as he shut down and feathered the engine. They were losing it fast. The Aerocommander was over the Windward Passage, between Cuba and Haiti, and French estimated he could keep it in the air for another ten minutes, about enough time to circle back and land at Great Inagua. Chagra began shoving wooden boxes of pistols out of the airplane, and Young started tearing up passports and lists of telephone numbers. Before landing, they invented a cover story: they would claim to be on their way to the gambling casinos of Puerto Rico. Young had about $5,000, which he distributed among them. A thousand miles away, the Fat Man and a dozen Colombia federal cops who had come along to guard the cocaine and protect the supplier's interests waited on the beach for a plane that wouldn't arrive.

It was another two weeks before Chagra located a new airplane and the six kilos were finally delivered to Florida. Meanwhile, Wallace remained hostage in Colombia. The cocaine turned out to be of poor quality, and none of the money ever found its way back to Wallace or his Colombia connections. Connell and Taylor took a kilo on consignment but never bothered to pay. Again, Wallace saved the day. He convinced the Colombians that the money would be forthcoming and worked a deal whereby a second supplier, José Barros, agreed to front thirty thousand pounds of marijuana and provide a ship if Chagra would make a down payment of $100,000, which would be used to bribe Colombian officials. Chagra sent $80,000 by courier and agreed to have another $20,000 delivered to Barros's wife, who was vacationing in Mexico City. Wallace remained hostage, but Chagra arranged for his wife and young daughter to join him in Santa Marta.

Wallace didn't know it, but Chagra was working a side deal with huge profit potential. While waiting for their shipment, Chagra began making daily reconnaissance flights over the shallows of the Great Bahama Banks, looking for ships that had missed their rendezvous points and were anchored there like sitting ducks. This was extremely dangerous business, elbowing in, as it were, on someone else's operation, but Jimmy reasoned—or so he said— that once the marijuana was off-loaded and headed for market, he could locate the real owners and work out the financial details.

Jimmy was lucky enough to have arrived in Florida at the crest of the marijuana boom. By late 1977, marijuana trafficking was far and away Florida's leading industry, almost doubling the amount brought in by tourism. In Dade County alone, marijuana generated an estimated $7 billion. Colombia's gross income from marijuana and cocaine was $8 billion, five times the national budget. Two million tons of grass were being shipped each week to the United States, most of it undetected. The thirty-five-ton coastal or island freighter had replaced the airplane as the preferred conveyance. In most cases, the Colombians were willing to front both the dope and the ship. A government report estimated that at least 160 coastal freighters made regular runs from Colombia. The U.S. government's best shot was to nab one of these freighters under an old Prohibition statute that referred to "hovering vessels"; the law permitted the Coast Guard to seize illegal cargo on the high seas, but did not provide for the arrest of the crews. They were shipped home at government expense, and the freighters were sold at auction, frequently to brokers representing the original owners. Most motherships, of course, escaped detection. Once the marijuana had been off-loaded into one of the thousands of deep-sea fishing boats that plied the waters, the contraband was almost impossible to detect. If the fishing boats made rendezvous with one of the countless high-speed cigar-shaped boats which transported the goods through the maze of intercoastal canals, detection was a lost cause; the cigar boats could outrun anything the government had.

Two days before Christmas, 1977, as Wallace, in Colombia, supervised the loading of a coastal freighter called the *Doña Petra* in a cove on La Guajira Peninsula, Jimmy Chagra was busy free-lancing the cargo of two other ships. He had spotted the *Miss Connie* and the *Eco Pesca IV*, two freighters of questionable registration, anchored in the shallows of Orange Cay. The pilot of a Coast Guard spotter plane had noticed the same two ships: they were anchored thirty miles from the nearest shipping lane, a dead giveaway that they carried illegal cargo. Chagra's crews had barely departed with 24,000 pounds when the crews of two Coast Guard cutters boarded the vessels and seized the remaining 106,000 pounds. (Though the captains of the *Miss Connie* and the *Eco Pesca IV* named Jimmy Chagra as their contact, this was not sufficient evidence to warrant filing charges against Chagra.)

Once the *Doña Petra* sailed, Wallace was able to leave Colombia. When Wallace returned to Florida and learned that his partner had branched out into the free-lance business, he was furious. He considered it unprofessional, especially since Chagra didn't seem willing to cut him in. Wallace was accompanied on the trip from Colombia to Florida by the operation's cocaine supplier, who was anxious to settle up. Chagra stalled him with a payment of $40,000 and a promise that Wallace would deliver the remainder of the money within a week, which he did, along with some very expensive radio and navigational equipment for the next freighter.

Jimmy had been so busy free-lancing that he had done a slapdash job setting up the off-loading operation for Wallace. Four days after Christmas, a Coast Guard cutter spotted the *Doña Petra* anchored fifty-five miles east of Miami. By New Year's Day, the *Doña Petra*, still fully loaded, was moored at the U.S. Customs Service dock in Miami.

By this time Wallace and the others had had a bellyful of Jimmy Chagra. No one, not even the Colombians, had been paid. A lot of money was unaccounted for, and if the paranoia weren't already so stiff you could stand it against the wall, Jimmy's blithe dismissal of the fate of the *Doña Petra* was reason enough for mutiny. Several of the conspiracy's army ants were talking, including Jud Myers, Jimmy's "command boat" pilot, who tried to sell some of the cocaine Jimmy gave him to a narc. Wallace had the uncomfortable feeling that Chagra was leaving him to explain things to the Colombians: Jimmy already had a new supplier in Miami, another Colombian named Theodoro, and he demonstrated little interest in settling old debts. Chagra's greed and stupidity had compromised the entire scam.

In early January, Wallace flew to El Paso for a secret meeting in Juárez with José Barros and another Colombian named Mejias. He gave Barros $50,000 as partial payment for the loss of the *Doña Petra*, and gave Mejias another $50,000 as insurance for a future deal. Wallace also carried with him three kilos of cocaine that the Colombians had advanced the smugglers as a show of good faith. According to Wallace, he gave away some of the coke, but used most of it himself. A week later he returned to Florida for Chagra's wedding. No one realized it at the time, but Wallace was formulating a plan to cut Jimmy Chagra out of the operation.

In late February, Wallace called a secret conference in New Orleans, inviting Jim French, Richard Young, and most of the others, but pointedly neglecting to tell Jimmy Chagra, who was to be the main topic of conversation. The group convened in a suite at the Hilton Inn near New Orleans International Airport. Wallace, a prodigious user of alcohol and cocaine, provided refreshments—he still had part of the three kilos of coke—and did most of the talking. He told the others that the next shipment of marijuana would arrive in New Orleans, not Florida as Chagra anticipated. Chagra was out of the deal, period. Nobody objected. "Everyone there was mad at Chagra," recalled Young, who had been sent ahead to set up a headquarters and rent some stash houses. "We had used him in Florida because we had no one else to off-load the boats. That was his only job, and he'd screwed it up royally." Wallace had detailed plans, including a new off-loading operation using boats owned by a friend who had helped finance the Florida scam. Wallace still had $114,000 in his pocket, and a promise of more from some of the original backers.

It was nearly dusk when Wallace, swacked on power and on assorted chemicals, staggered out of the Hilton Inn parking lot to his rental car. Seconds later he rammed the car into the side of an airport limousine. He was attempting to *buy* the limo when the cops arrived. That was the beginning of the end of the conspiracy, past, present, and future.

The police turned Wallace over to the DEA. Agents found only a trace of cocaine, but the $114,000 and his reputation as a major cocaine dealer were taken as evidence that he wasn't in town for Mardi Gras. During interrogation, Wallace admitted that he knew Jimmy Chagra and Jim French and agreed to cooperate with the DEA, if the agents returned his $114,000. The agents quickly agreed. When Wallace returned to Florida a few days later, he told the others that he had been charged with drunken driving, but didn't mention his chat with the DEA. Wallace realized that sooner or later the narcs would call in their note, but in the meantime he saw no reason to jeopardize the new shipment of marijuana. A few days before Easter, Wallace was astonished to learn that the captain had missed signals and was about to land the cargo in Florida, as originally planned. Wallace never told the DEA about this score; instead, he informed agents that a Colombian named Raul Ruíz was in Miami. Wallace still owed Ruíz more than $2 million and perhaps saw this as an opportunity to take care of the debt. (If Ruíz was in prison, Wallace reasoned, there would be no pressure to pay up. Ruíz eluded the agents, however, and returned to Colombia, where he was reportedly killed in a gun battle unrelated to his dealings with Wallace and Chagra.) As far as Jimmy Chagra knew, the operation worked perfectly. More than 50,000 pounds of marijuana was on its way to market by March 1978.

Jimmy and his new wife were so busy making plans to move to Las Vegas that Jimmy didn't bother to keep track of what happened to members of the old conspiracy. One by one they were getting busted.

PART TWO

Richard Young tumbled a day after Easter, when his van, loaded with marijuana, broke down in Ocala, Florida; he happened to take it for repairs to a garage frequented by the highway patrol. Dudley Connell and Paul Taylor were popped in unrelated drug busts. In June, Wallace was busted again, this time in Denver. With the exception of Jim French, every major member of the gang was talking to the feds. Talking about Jimmy Chagra.

23

Jimmy Chagra's co-conspirators were being busted from coast to coast, but money from the Florida score had filled Jimmy's pockets, and he was having the time of his life. Nearly every gambler, hustler, con man, and federal agent in the western half of the United States heard about Jimmy's exploits in Las Vegas in the summer and fall of 1978. Dope traffickers and successful entrepreneurs of other illicit enterprises had used the casinos to launder dirty money in years past, but this was something new: Jimmy wasn't washing his money, he was burning it.

Jimmy was no stranger to Caesar's Palace, of course, but this time the hotel and casino treated him in a style that would have benumbed King Farouk. Everything was on the house—including a new Lincoln Continental that the casino had delivered to Liz. While Jimmy and Liz were house-hunting they quartered in the Sinatra suite with its grand piano and spiral staircase, surrounded by round-the-clock bodyguards, private secretaries, and a steady stream of couriers delivering money. On one occasion Jimmy chartered a Learjet just to pick up a package of cash that had arrived back in Fort Lauderdale.

Jimmy had possessed a Caesar's credit card since 1969, and his credit limit had steadily increased over the years—from $500, to $50,000, to $100,000, and finally to $200,000. In the fall of 1978 his credit line doubled again, to $400,000. In addition, Jimmy was also allowed to hold Caesar's credit cards under several aliases, including Jim Garcia and Jim Lewis. Each of these bogus-name cards had limits of $200,000. Considering that he also had lines of credit at other casinos, Jimmy Chagra was more than merely a "preferred" customer, he was probably the biggest player in town. When gamblers talked about "going off on some big numbers," they reserved a special cate-

159

gory for Jimmy Chagra. "He was probably the most dangerous player Las Vegas had ever seen," Joe Chagra said, "because he didn't care how much he lost." Records at Caesar's Palace reflect that in the period between September 28, 1978, and December 21, 1978, Jimmy won $2,568,800 and lost $4,761.300. IRS records show that he declared $1.8 million in gambling earnings for the year. These records reflected only a small portion of the action.

Despite his virtually unlimited credit, Jimmy usually played for cash. Gerald Gengler, dice-pit boss for the graveyard shift at Caesar's, remembered Chagra as "one of the more serious players" in the last decade. Gengler had watched him win in excess of $50,000 on a number of occasions, and recalled one night when Chagra took his shift for $300,000. Gengler also remembered the night in October when Chagra hit a major losing streak—he dropped $915,000 in less than four hours. The pit boss wasn't sure how to handle this situation. "When he left the table I went with him to sign a marker," Gengler said. "But instead he decided to pay in cash. We went up to his suite. There were a bunch of security men standing around, and he brought out this footlocker and dumped money out on the floor. There were packs of bills—ones, fives, tens, twenties, hundreds—packs of five thousand dollars, tied with rubber bands or with Caesar's wrappers." Chagra counted the money, but it wasn't enough. He walked into another room and reappeared with an armload of cash. It still wasn't enough. After a second trip to the back room, the $915,000 was paid in full.

Jimmy was at the casinos every night, but not always in public view. Sometimes he was in the back rooms, engaged in private games of gin rummy, at which he was very good, and poker, at which he was mediocre to poor. Most afternoons he took to the fresh air of the Dunes golf course, playing for major stakes. Las Vegas regulars talked about Chagra in tones normally reserved for particularly memorable pieces of cheesecake; and cardplayers and golfers from out of town paid finder's fees for an introduction. Jimmy fancied himself a good and clever golfer, a real hustler, and this fantasy cost him millions in the autumn of 1978. A Hollywood producer told friends that he took $400,000 off Jimmy in a golf match. "The crazy bastard was trying to *hustle* me," the producer said with pride. But the money didn't matter to Jimmy: as long as he had it, he wanted to flaunt it. He urged Liz to buy jewelry whenever she saw something she liked, and ordered her to always carry at least $10,000 in her purse. One night he tipped a cocktail waitress $10,000 (two packets of fifty $100 bills) for bringing him a bottle of spring water.

Except for a couple of business trips, Lee avoided Las Vegas during the autumn of Jimmy's extravaganza. Lee had never recovered from his own disastrous fling the previous year, not to mention the humiliation of learning that Jimmy had gone to the bosses at Caesar's Palace and told them he wanted his brother treated like a celebrity in the future. In late September, Lee arrived to look at some houses that real estate agent Mary Brodeur was showing Jimmy and Liz. He could have spared himself the trip: Jimmy had already decided on a sprawling Spanish stucco place in Paradise Valley a few miles from the Strip. It was listed for $245,000, and Jimmy was in no mood to dicker. "This is the one I want," he told Lee. "Give her the money." Lee pulled his brother aside and told him that wasn't the way it was done; he thought they could buy it for much less. "I don't want to go through all that credit and employment application crap," Jimmy said, reminding Lee that it was his money they were spending. A few days later Mary Brodeur met Jimmy at the cashier's cage at Caesar's and collected the down payment, $75,000.

Over the next several months Jimmy and Liz spent $500,000 on additions and changes to the property. Jimmy wanted a swimming pool as large as or larger than the one Lee had in El Paso. A garage and parking area were expanded to accommodate at least a dozen vehicles. The yard was walled and transformed into something resembling a child's garden, complete with a babbling brook, ornamental iron benches, and little bridges and waterfalls. Every room in the house was reworked—Jimmy wanted a bar like the one in the Sinatra suite, and gold fixtures for the plumbing and even for the air-conditioning vents. But it was the master bedroom, which they built from scratch, that truly capsuled the man and woman for whom it was intended.

The bedroom was as big as three normal rooms and completely paneled with mirrors. The walls, the ceiling, even the *floors* were polished panels of mirror: a single person crossing the room constituted a crowd. All the closets, cabinets, and drawers were mirrors built into mirrors, and the single piece of furniture, a canopied four-poster bed in the exact center of the room, was completely structured of mirrors and thin strips of polished chrome. The bed was the width of two king-size mattresses. In a compartment concealed in the headboard was a console of buttons and switches that controlled all the gadgets in the room. Flip a switch and a six-foot TV screen appeared from behind a panel of mirrors. Another switch activated a fireplace that burned not wood but red lights, reflected many times from a backdrop of mirrors. The bath of the master bedroom was as large as a handball court, with a sunken granite tub that could accommodate a chorus line. Tucked in the corner of the dressing room was a sauna-like Four Seasons environment chamber—at a whim, a body could select tropic rain, Baja sun, jungle steam, spring showers, or Chinook winds. The only color to the bedroom decor was the plush lavender curtains; they were Liz's idea.

By late 1978 the remodeling was virtually complete. By this time Jimmy was doing most of his gambling at Binion's Horseshoe Casino: aware of rumors that he might be indicted on federal drug-smuggling charges, Caesar's Palace had scratched Jimmy from its comp list. Jimmy's staff, including his "girl Friday," Gloria Stroupe, and his chief bodyguard, a former karate instructor named Ron Disecco—as well as Disecco's girlfriend, Cindy Cote, who became Liz Chagra's private secretary—occupied their own quarters in the new house. Part of Gloria Stroupe's job was to pay all household bills—in cash. Jimmy also ordered almost a dozen telephones installed, though he usually used a coin phone in the neighborhood. "He believed the others were tapped," Ms. Stroupe recalled.

Jimmy lived for the day when he could show off his dream house to Lee, but that day never came. Lee was murdered before he had a chance to see it.

24

For five days and nights after the murder of Lee Chagra, police sealed off his law office and helped themselves to his confidential files. During 119 hours of "continuous investigation," the El Paso police, investigators from the district attorney's office, and FBI, DEA, and IRS agents pored over the lawyer's documents. Lee Chagra's files contained what one officer called "a gold mine of intelligence." There was a howl of protest from the legal community, of course, but agents in El Paso were used to howling lawyers. A number of files that should have been kept secret because of the attorney-client privilege were copied on Lee's own Xerox machine, and others were carried off and never seen again. Lee's meticulous gambling records disappeared, and so did tape cassettes containing conversations with clients and with people Lee suspected of being agents provocateurs. Files pertaining to the Joe Renteria case were moved and presumably copied, and the tape that Renteria made of his first conversation with the agents, the tape that Lee was certain would prove entrapment, disappeared and was never located. Although Renteria had already been convicted and sentenced, Joe Chagra had hoped that the tape would be grounds for a new trial. Now that hope was dashed.

Police claimed that every document in the files was potential evidence in the murder case, but few believed the police were all that intent on finding Lee's killer. The killer had apparently removed Lee's boots looking for money, but the cops didn't bother to dust the boots for fingerprints. They did think to bring in drug-sniffing dogs, however. The dogs didn't find a thing.

A court of inquiry presided over by district judge Woodrow Bean II ruled that the cops committed two criminal violations by searching the lawyer's confidential files. The case was turned over to county at-

163

torney George Rodriguez, Jr., who refused to prosecute. As it turned out, the cops had a loophole: they thought the search was covered by a written policy from the district attorney. "It was one of those rare cases where ignorance of the law *was* a defense," Judge Bean explained.

Two months after Lee's murder, El Paso police acknowledged that they didn't have a single lead. "When you have a man mixed up in as many things as Lee Chagra was, the possibilities seem endless," said Lieutenant John Lanahan. "It could have been vengeance, a disgruntled client or customer, or somebody who didn't like the way his case was handled. We're not discounting the possibility he was surprised by a burglar, but the fact the office was ransacked doesn't prove anything. It could be an attempt to make it look like the work of a burglar." There had been hundreds of telephone calls to the police, and to the Chagra family, from parties interested in collecting the $25,000 reward, but not a single worthwhile lead had developed. Federal agents had devoted thousands of hours to investigating every aspect of Lee Chagra's life, but they didn't have a clue to who killed him, or why. The fact that the killer had left behind thousands of dollars' worth of gold jewelry was a puzzle that weakened the motive of robbery. There were rumors of the bag of money, of course, but only the family, and the killer, knew for sure. There were rumors, too, that police had found stacks of $100 bills alongside envelopes addressed to people whom, for whatever reason, Lee Chagra was "paying off." Another rumor put the total amount of cash in excess of $2 million, and hinted that it was mob money. The autopsy report revealed a small amount of cocaine in the victim's blood, and this sparked speculation that the murder was the result of a drug deal gone bad.

It was as though a curse had been put on the Chagra family, some demonic force that pulverized the spirit, that turned even ordinary gestures into portents of evil. No one outside the family and immediate friends seemed to place much importance on the murder of Lee Chagra. The police seemed less interested in solving the crime than in investigating the victim. No one wanted to listen to the Chagras' side of the story. Joe Chagra contacted someone associated with CBS-TV's "60 Minutes," but the network wasn't interested. A reporter and camera crew from ABC-TV's "20/20" did do a feature on the family, but it made the Chagras look like a family of Lebanese criminals who had somehow managed to evade justice. It was Jimmy Chagra's idea to bring his friend Michael Caruana to El Paso to conduct a private investigation, and, as frequently happened with Jimmy's ideas, it backfired. Caruana was supposed to have conducted some voice-stress tests on several people, including Bobby Yoseph and Sailor Roberts, but the tests established nothing, and after a while the only thing people remembered was that some Mafia tough guy was in town on the Chagras' payroll. The family had also contacted several psychics and fortune tellers in an effort to learn the identity of the killer, and had contacted former pro football star Roosevelt Grier, a friend of Lee's who had some political clout in Washington. Grier got in touch with Senator Edward Kennedy, who asked the Justice Department to investigate possible civil-rights violations during the search of Chagra's office.

There were times when Patsy de la Torre thought she couldn't take it one more day. She dreamed about her brother, heard him talking to her. Joe Chagra felt the numbing paranoia dividing and conquering his family. Jo Annie hardly spoke to other members of the family. Nobody ever saw or heard from Sib Abraham. Some old and trusted friends with legitimate fears for their own well-being found excuses to drift away. Jimmy and Liz went back to Las Vegas. Life, such as it was, was on hold.

Indeed, police and federal agents had much more on their minds than finding Lee's killer. They still had no idea who had tried to assassinate prosecutor James Kerr, for one thing. For another, the growth of the smuggling business needed tending. For a third, the time the feds spent reading Lee's files had given them whole new subjects for investigation.

Headquarters for these efforts was the federal building near Hemisfair Plaza in downtown San Antonio. The modern drum-shaped building, which had housed the American exhibition at the 1968 World's Fair, contained the office of the U.S. attorney and housed the various federal courts and grand juries. Although the FBI, DEA, and most other federal agencies had headquarters in other nearby buildings, the federal courthouse was the center of activity.

You couldn't live in San Antonio in the winter or spring of 1979 without being aware of an alarming acceleration of violence. There had been a rash of cop killings, and drug dealers were slaughtering one another with an openness not seen since Prohibition. In April, as the city celebrated Fiesta Week with a series of balls and parades, a sniper opened fire into a crowd of onlookers watching the Battle of

Flowers parade near Alamo Plaza. Underneath the city's lazy, lovable, amiably corrupt exterior of old buildings, landscaped riverwalks, street musicians, and Spanish missions seethed a cultural and spiritual malignancy that no one understood, much less controlled. San Antonio was one of the fastest-growing cities in the country, outstripping even Houston; in less than a decade San Antonio had grown 20 percent, jumping from the fifteenth to the tenth largest city in America. It was also one of the poorest cities in the country: One of six residents lived below the poverty line, and one in four occupied substandard housing. It was home to almost half a million Mexican-Americans, the largest concentration of persons of Mexican descent outside of Mexico City and Los Angeles, and yet until very recently the Mexican-American majority had almost no political power. Its rate of heroin addiction ranked in the country's top seven, and yet its official crime rate was ordinary to the point of being suspect: one index listed San Antonio eighteenth in the *state*. The official crime rate reflected the reluctance of the people to involve themselves in the reality of life, though reality seemed to be tightening its grip. It reflected, too, a contradiction in priorities, at least so far as the office of the U.S. attorney was concerned: even while a massive effort was being directed to the federal district's western outpost in El Paso, few prosecutors seemed anxious to stir up trouble close to home. One federal prosecutor noted that the number of criminal cases filed in El Paso that year was roughly triple the number filed in the much larger city of San Antonio. "The San Antonio office is a joke," the prosecutor said. The reason for the inordinate amount of attention directed to the outpost of El Paso could be explained in a word: Chagra.

The voltage of events in San Antonio seemed even more extraordinary, if that was possible, because of the local media's longstanding adoration of sensationalism. San Antonio newspapers usually featured such headlines (often in two-inch blood-red type) as GIRL ATE DAD TO SURVIVE! or GARBAGE BABY BORN ALIVE! TV news shows habitually led with zoom-in shots of pools of fresh blood or firemen carrying charred and lifeless bodies of children out of ravaged tenant houses. Against such beyond-shock reports mere accounts of drug trafficking and organized crime were likely to end up next to the dog-food commercials or crossword puzzles. But in the winter and spring of 1979, that changed.

Since the attempted assassination of prosecutor James Kerr the previous November, U.S. attorney Jamie Boyd had personally taken command of the grand jury probe into racketeering, gambling, narcotics trafficking, and now, of course, hired murder. Not one but three grand jury investigations (two in El Paso, one in San Antonio) were operating simultaneously, and the show was being closely monitored by a U.S. Justice Department strike force in Las Vegas and the federal prosecutor's office in Seattle. Kerr had been transferred from the criminal to the civil staff following the assassination attempt, but he continued to work behind the scenes, as did several other assistant U.S. attorneys, and a horde of federal agents.

Although the murder of Lee Chagra was ostensibly a problem for the El Paso police department, the racket-busting federal grand jury in San Antonio was also at work. Few, if any, knew what was going on behind the heavily guarded doors of the grand jury room, but what was going on outside was damn good theater. Witnesses with coats pulled over their heads, and in some cases hoods, ran the gauntlet of reporters who stalked the courthouse hallways. No one in authority was talking. No one in authority made eye contact, even with other authorities. Rumors swarmed like flies around sweet wine, and the air crackled with apocalypse.

"For a long time I've been getting reports that things were out of hand in El Paso," U.S. attorney Jamie Boyd explained. "I've been planning to do something about it. The Chagra thing came about the same time, and we were obligated to look into it. A large amount of money has disappeared and we want to know where it came from and where it went."

Boyd was not unaware that events under his jurisdiction were attracting national attention. In late January, an article in the Washington *Post* summarized the situation in tones as critical of authorities as it was of the criminals. Writer Lou Cannon mentioned the feds' long-running crusade against the Chagra family, and pointed out that the search of Lee Chagra's private files was likely to have "a chilling effect" on activities of Chagra's clients. A few days after this article appeared, El Paso FBI agent-in-charge O. Leon Dobbs announced that the bureau had decided to enter the case.

In his press conference, Dobbs took an opportunity to slam the media, particularly the Washington *Post* story by Lou Cannon. "I hope that our local media will try to be more factual and professional than that story is," he said. "It contained several editorial comments

such as saying the El Paso Police Department is incompetent ["El
Paso police, whom many in these parts think couldn't find a bend in a
pretzel . . ."]. . . . It also states that assistant U.S. attorney Jim Kerr
has been frequently bested by Lee Chagra in court. I can tell you very
truthfully, Chagra has never beaten any case that Mr. Kerr prosecuted. . . ."

Shortly after his announcement that the FBI was moving to the
front of the investigation, Dobbs startled members of an El Paso civic
club by proclaiming that he had evidence that a number of people
right there in the room were involved in the rackets. Dobbs left little
doubt that he would pursue this evidence, and advised the citizens to
turn themselves in while there was still time. "You have about six
weeks to get on the boat," Dobbs told his audience. "Otherwise, the
boat leaves without you." A few months later, Dobbs inexplicably announced his early retirement and faded from the scene without another word. There were rumors about some kind of impropriety at a
convention of lawmen in Amarillo, but no one in authority was willing
to discuss the incident.

Naturally, members of the Bandidos Motorcycle Club were swept
into the vortex of this massive investigation. The Bandidos were always easy targets—in the words of one South Texas deputy sheriff,
"a bunch of crazy bastards who'd do anything for money." Since the
abortive attempt on James Kerr, agents of the FBI, DEA, and U.S.
Bureau of Alcohol, Tobacco and Firearms had "hit the Bandidos
hard wherever we can find them." Two of the bikers were arrested in
a van outside the sheriff's office in Corpus Christi. Authorities couldn't
prove the Bandidos were up to mischief, but inside the van they found
binoculars, a shotgun, and a Russian-made semiautomatic AK15 with
three hundred rounds of ammunition.

Even before the arrests in Corpus Christi, agents had raided two
Bandidos hangouts in El Paso, looking for the weapons used in the
Kerr job. The most publicized raid occurred on February 12 when
local, state, and federal cops surrounded a house in the Lower Valley
where El Paso chapter president James "Shakey" Maio and a number of other members resided. After first using a bullhorn to identify
themselves, the raiding party kicked in the front door and stormed
the dwelling. One officer pushed open a bedroom door and reported
that Shakey Maio, who was in bed with his "old lady," pointed a .357
magnum in his direction. The cops didn't find any of the weapons

specified in the search warrant, but they found some other guns and a pound of marijuana. Four club members were charged with possession of marijuana with intent to distribute, and Maio was additionally charged with assault on a federal officer. "They're just trying to make us look bad for this grand jury," Maio shouted to reporters as cops hustled him to jail.

In San Antonio, where the main thrust of the investigation was the Kerr attempt and the alleged racketeering activities of the motorcycle gang, many of the same witnesses who had been called the previous September were called again. Kerr himself was participating in this aspect of the investigation, assisted by special prosecutor Ron Sim of Seattle. Sooner or later almost every Bandido leader in the state was called before the grand jury, including club founder Don "Mutha" Chambers, who was hauled from the prison where he had been serving a sentence for murder since Lee and Joe Chagra's unsuccessful defense of his case six years earlier.

It wasn't clear at the time, but one reason the feds still believed that Lee Chagra had been tied to the motorcycle gang was a secret thirty-six-page document used to secure a wiretap of the Bandido headquarters in El Paso. The document was strikingly similar to the Jerry Johnson interview transcript which had caused so much grief for the Chagra family. That is to say, it was mostly innuendoes, hearsay, and slander. *Source A told a federal agent that Source B told him that Source C said* . . . One source, who turned out to be Jimmy Hicks, a Bandido charged with murder and robbery in another jurisdiction, told three FBI men that he personally attended a meeting in San Antonio in which other Bandidos discussed killing James Kerr. Some months later, when they put Hicks under oath in a grand jury room, he denied the whole story, and was never indicted.

According to the affidavit, Hicks told the feds about amphetamine labs that the motorcycle club operated in Houston and San Antonio, and about several murders committed by gang members. He also told about numerous drug deals involving fellow Bandidos, including a shipment of cocaine that "belonged to the Milliorn brothers of El Paso and the Jimmy Chagra group."

Jimmy, of course, had been a target of drug agents for years, but only in recent months—starting with the arrest of Henry Wallace in New Orleans a year earlier—had solid evidence began piling up. Documents examined in the search of Lee's office apparently added nothing to the government's file on Jimmy's smuggling activities—or on Lee's either, for that matter. But the murder had focused attention on Jimmy. The feds felt they were ready to move.

In late February, two days before Judge Wood sentenced Joe Renteria to thirty years, a federal grand jury in the West Texas oil town of Midland indicted Jimmy Chagra on five counts of conspiracy to possess and distribute drugs. Although Chagra volunteered to turn himself in, Jamie Boyd preferred a more dramatic arrest: on the same day Renteria was sentenced, there was a front-page picture in the El Paso *Times* of a disheveled and manacled Chagra being led into El Paso County Jail by a posse of armed agents. There was no discernible reason why the feds selected Midland to seek the indictments, except that Judge John Wood had sole jurisdiction over the Midland docket. If Chagra had been indicted in El Paso, the chances were only one out of four that the case would have ended up in Wood's court. The judge set bond at $1 million, which the Chagra family was not able to post.

Several weeks earlier, Jimmy had retained a well-known Las Vegas criminal attorney, Oscar Goodman. Immediately after the arrest, Goodman and Joe Chagra filed a motion to reduce bond, and a hearing was set a few days after that in Midland. At this point neither of Jimmy's lawyers had any idea of the extent of the government's evidence: they didn't yet know that Henry Wallace had become Jamie Boyd's star witness.

On the night before the bond hearing, Boyd, his wife, Suzy, and three DEA agents were riding around in Boyd's old Chevy, feeling very good about things. Henry Wallace was in the back seat, on the lap of one of the agents. Boyd was personally prepping Wallace for the ordeal of the trial, and the Fat Man had been a model student. There was a lot of whooping and laughter when Wallace said: "Just think, a year ago I was a filthy dope smuggler, and here I am riding around with the DEA and the U.S. attorney, drinking their whiskey." Jamie Boyd couldn't help himself; he was starting to like ol' Henry.

At the hearing the following morning, the U.S. attorney dropped his first hint that there was more to this case than just the five-count indictment. The government had not used the biggest gun in its arsenal, the kingpin charge, but that didn't mean it wasn't in the works. Boyd was prepared to make a deal—fifteen years for a plea of guilty. If Jimmy didn't grab it, and Jamie thought that he would not, the

government could always reindict under the kingpin law. In the meantime, the prosecution wanted to show that Jimmy was indeed a big
fish who swam in a very big pond. During the course of the bond hearing, the prosecution alleged that Jimmy was an associate of Salvatore
Michael Caruana, who was identified as an associate of Raymond
L. S. Patriarca, reputed head of organized crime in New England.
Despite objections from defense attorneys Joe Chagra and Oscar
Goodman, the names of several alleged organized-crime figures were
introduced into the record, and although the government produced no
evidence that directly connected Jimmy Chagra to the Mafia, the
publicity obviously shadowed Chagra's chances for a fair trial. At the
conclusion of the bond hearing, James Kerr agreed with the defense
that the $1 million bond was not suitable for the case at hand: Kerr
asked the court to raise it to $1.5 million. Magistrate Harry Lee
Hudspeth recommended, however, that the bond be reduced to $400,-
000, provided Jimmy Chagra surrendered his passport and checked
in weekly to his probation officer. By March 12, Jimmy was free on
bond. The trial date was set for April 2.

25

The break in Lee Chagra's murder case came at almost exactly the same time that Jimmy was trying to post bond. It came suddenly and without warning. It was months before most people in El Paso, including members of the Chagra family, were able to accept the truth.

Until the first week in March 1979, the only useful piece of information was a tip from Doug Holt, one of the regulars in the poker games at Jimmy Salome's house. Holt heard that Lou Esper had masterminded both the attempted safe burglary at Mickey Esper's office and the attempted robbery of the poker game. More than anything else, these two attempts convinced Lee that he was being stalked. And there was something else, something that only a few members of the Chagra family knew: Lou Esper had become Lee's cocaine supplier in the weeks just prior to the murder. Esper couldn't have known about the bag of money, but he knew that Lee usually carried large amounts of cash. For a short time the Chagras had the Milliorn brothers staking out Esper's apartment, but the police arrested them for carrying guns, and for a while they forgot about Esper. In late February, however, they heard that Esper had bought a new Cadillac and was making the rounds of gambling casinos. "We kept that news from Jimmy," Patsy recalled. "We were worried Jimmy would run into him in Vegas and kill him." Around March 2, Joe Chagra received a telephone call from a soldier at Fort Bliss, who asked about the reward and claimed he had information about the murder.

"He told me to meet him at a parking lot on Dyer Street out by Fort Bliss," Joe said. "He said for me to come alone. I was pretty frightened—I think I took a gun along—but something that he said on the phone made me believe he might know something. When I got there, he told me about this other black guy in his barracks, a soldier named White, how he'd come in one night around Christmas with this bag full of money. When he described the bag, I knew it was the one from Lee's office. He said he'd never seen so much money in his life, that it was tied with rubber bands. I almost freaked out—that was it!'"

The soldier who called Joe Chagra also called the police. That same morning they arrested PFC Don White, a twenty-one-year-old black from Richmond, California, who was scheduled to be discharged in less than a month. White confessed to the robbery (though not the murder) and implicated Lou Esper and another soldier, Spec. 4 David Leon Wallace. The next day Wallace was arrested in his hometown of Compton, California, and Esper was nabbed at a motel in Las Vegas. Don White and David Leon Wallace signed separate confessions, naming Esper as the man who set up the job and admitting their part in the robbery. The confessions were almost identical, except that each accused the other of actually pulling the trigger. Both were charged with capital murder. The nature of the charges against Esper hadn't yet been determined, though it was clear that Esper had planned the heist, supplied the getaway car and the two pistols, and got off with the bulk of the money. The pistols, a cheap nickel-plated .22-caliber and an even cheaper .32 with a cylinder that kept falling out, were traced to an El Paso pawnshop whose owner identified Esper. Interestingly enough, both White and Wallace agreed that White was carrying the .22, the murder weapon.

The two confessions also made it clear that Don White was a late entry to the conspiracy. White had never met Esper until the day of the robbery and murder. Wallace, on the other hand, had known Esper since August and had been involved in several burglary and robbery schemes with the ex-con. According to Wallace, he had met Esper at a downtown bar called the Playmate, a dive across from the El Paso Plaza identified by police as a hangout for prostitutes and assorted lowlife who might find mutual interests with the likes of Lou Esper. Esper once suggested that Wallace break into the home of Lee Chagra on Frontera and rob the family at gunpoint. This never came off, but Wallace admitted taking part in the abortive robbery attempt of the poker game at the Salome house next door. Shortly after the poker-game episode, Esper hatched another plan in which Wallace and others would rob Lee Chagra's office on Montana. This plan also came to nothing.

On December 22, 1978, Wallace said, Esper telephoned him at the Playmate. They went to Esper's apartment, the Warren House on North Mesa, where Esper outlined his plan to rob Lee Chagra the following day. Sailor Roberts, who lived in the same apartment complex, had told Esper that Chagra was holding a substantial amount of money for him.

"He told me that Lee Chagra was going to be in the office by himself . . . after one o'clock, but did not tell me how he knew this," Wallace told police. "Lou Esper either made arrangements for us to get into the building or had somebody else make the arrangements. He said that Mr. Sailor [Roberts] . . . was going to go to Mr. Chagra's office and pick up some money that Lee Chagra was holding for him and there would be something like seventy thousand dollars in the office."

Esper told Wallace to use the name David Long. He gave him the cover story about a will in probate, and told Wallace to telephone Chagra's home that morning to make certain the lawyer still planned to be at his office. According to Wallace, Lou Esper loaded the two pistols and gave them to him. He also handed the keys to an old Oldsmobile Delta 88 that had been purchased recently from a used-car lot in New Mexico, and told him where to leave the car after the job was finished. Esper tried to persuade Wallace to do the job alone, but Wallace had already decided to include his friend Don White.

On Saturday afternoon, David Wallace picked up White at his barracks and the two black soldiers drove along the foothills to Montana Street, and then headed downtown. Wallace parked the yellow Olds directly behind Lee Chagra's office. Wallace recalled that he gave White the .22 and kept the .32 with the bad cylinder for himself. Wallace rang the buzzer and the voice on the intercom asked if he was David Long. They entered and followed Lee Chagra to his office.

At this point their stories began to conflict.

Wallace told police:

"We both pulled out the weapons and told Lee Chagra . . . freeze, that we did not want to hurt him, that we just wanted the money. Lee Chagra then slowly raised his hands and told us that he would give us what we wanted, just don't shoot. White told him something like hurry up, motherfucker, and he was slowly bringing his hands down and I told him to get his hands up but he kept bringing them down and at this time I heard one gunshot and possibly two and this shot or shots were fired by Don White, who had the .22-caliber pistol. There is no doubt in my mind that it was Don White who shot and killed Lee Chagra.

"Lee Chagra fell to the floor and I went to [him] and kept calling him by name and even told him I was sorry, but he was still alive and was looking at me. Don White said, 'Fuck him, man, he's just another dude.' . . ."

Don White's version was this:

"David Wallace asked Lee Chagra where the money was and by this time [we] had our pistols out and Lee Chagra said, 'You can have anything you want.' Lee Chagra then walked towards two windows . . . and when he turned around [he] came out with a pistol in his hand, and David Wallace fired one shot . . . and Lee Chagra fell to the floor by the windows and . . . I saw blood was coming out of his mouth.

"I looked at Lee Chagra and to me he was dead then. David Wallace started going through his pockets. . . ."

Only the two killers knew for certain if Chagra really did pull a pistol, but a reconstruction of events makes it highly unlikely. Chagra was wearing Levi's and a sport shirt tucked in his pants. If he was armed when the two black men entered the office, they would certainly have *seen* the pistol. It seemed inconceivable that under these circumstances they would not have disarmed him first.

Wallace and White pretty much agreed on what happened next. They searched Chagra's pockets, then removed his boots. Wallace recalled that Lou Esper told him, "Seven days a week [Chagra] would have at least ten grand in his boots." They didn't find any money, but they found a ring of keys and began a hurried search of the office. Within ten minutes they had worked their way to the apartment in the rear, where they discovered the brown tennis bag stuffed with twenties and hundreds. Other stacks of bills were spread across the bed.

"We threw most of the money inside the suitcase," Wallace said. "I know I dropped two twenty-dollar bills on the floor and White wanted to pick them up but I told him, fuck it, man, let's get the hell out of here."

On their way out White grabbed two pistols that were in Chagra's desk drawer, a pair of handcuffs, and a tape recorder. Esper had instructed Wallace not to touch Chagra's personal jewelry, because it would be too easily traced.

The plan was for the two soldiers to meet Esper at his apartment, but on the hunch that they might be falling into a trap they checked instead into a motel on North Mesa and telephoned Esper. According to Wallace, Esper didn't appear particularly upset that Lee Chagra had been murdered in the bargain. "Don't worry about it," Wallace said Esper told him. Many believed that the murder of Lee Chagra was part of the plan, that Esper never intended to leave his victim to retaliate.

Lou Esper arrived at the motel a short time later and they began counting the money. Apparently Esper did most of the counting, because neither Wallace nor White ever knew how much was inside the bag. Esper told them it was $150,000. It wasn't clear from the statements to police how much Esper gave the two soldiers. Wallace guessed that their take was $20,000 each. White thought the figure was $7,000. Esper took the rest. By the next day both of the soldiers were headed for Christmas leave in California, and Esper had vanished. None of the money was ever seen again.

Don White pleaded guilty to a reduced charge of murder and was sentenced to sixty years. Wallace refused to plead and stood trial for capital murder. His lawyer, Mike Gibson, tried to convince the jury of the possibility that White and Wallace were delivering ten pounds of cocaine to Lee Chagra, that the shooting took place during an argument over drugs, and therefore it was not a crime punishable by death. The jury didn't buy the story and Wallace was given the death sentence, although it was later modified to life in prison by the state Court of Criminal Appeals. Lou Esper was convicted of criminal conspiracy to commit aggravated robbery and was sentenced to fifteen years. All three men are currently serving their sentences in the Texas Department of Corrections.

26

The arrests and confessions of Lee's killers, coupled with his own indictment and arrest, had shaken Jimmy to the core. For one thing, Jimmy was convinced that the confessions were a cover-up: he still believed that federal agents were responsible for his brother's murder, and in some way that he couldn't articulate, he believed that Judge Wood had masterminded the whole plot. While Lee was alive, Jimmy had managed to hide the depths of his love; but he had worshiped Lee, not only as a brother, but as a genuine hero. The shock of Lee's death was made worse by the ramifications of Jimmy's own legal problems.

In Wood's court, a conviction and a long prison sentence were almost a foregone conclusion. A few months earlier when the rumors of Jimmy's indictment first began, when the Caesar's Palace management ordered him out of the Sinatra suite and told him they didn't want his business anymore, Jimmy was cocky and defiant. Lee had practically assured him that Judge Wood would blow the case, that he would get a reversal. Now Lee was gone, and so was Jimmy's cockiness. He told his wife's secretary, Cindy Cote, "I heard that Wood gave a man seven years for killing an eagle. Imagine what he'll do to me."

After Jimmy was released on bond and returned to his new home in Las Vegas, Joe and his wife, Patty, visited several times. Joe tried to convince himself that Jimmy was adjusting to the reality of his situation, but he didn't always believe it. Jimmy operated in another dimension. Jimmy had installed a gigantic walk-in safe; Joe recalled that it was usually overflowing with bundles of cash. Now that Caesar's had kicked him out, the only casino willing to gamble for the insane sums that pacified Jimmy was Binion's Horseshoe.

Jimmy was there every night, usually with a couple of million on the table. The Binion family was not easily impressed—Benny Binion, a legendary Texas gambler and former bootlegger who settled in Las Vegas in the early 1950s after doing a stretch in the federal penitentiary at Leavenworth for income-tax evasion, had arranged the famous five-month poker game between Johnny Moss and Nick the Greek Dandolos, which later inspired the casino's World Series of Poker. His son, Jack Binion, who ran the operation now, acknowledged that Jimmy Chagra had brought a new meaning to the casino's no-limit policy. In the short time that Chagra played at the Horseshoe before his trial, Binion guessed that he took the casino for more than $2 million. Binion recalled that early one morning, after losing heavily at the poker table, Jimmy walked to one of the blackjack tables and slapped $100,000 on the green baize. He wanted to play it all on a single hand. Binion approved it and the dealer laid out the cards—a nine and a six for Chagra, a six showing for the house. Playing the old Syrian rules, Chagra stayed with what he had. The dealer had a king in the hole: under the house rules, he was obliged to hit. He took a seven, which bust him. "Jimmy was amazing," Binion said. "He had icewater for blood."

Whatever flowed in Jimmy Chagra's veins, whatever it was that gave him courage, he was going to need all he could muster. "The Colombian connection," as Judge Wood inadvertently styled Jimmy Chagra's indictment one day in open court, was destined to dominate the headlines in Texas for many months. The judge's remark, acknowledged as a blunder by both sides, was unfortunately typical of the war of words, recalling the acrimony of the past and preordaining the bitterness of the future. Jimmy Chagra may have even biased his own case in his selection of defense attorney—Oscar Goodman, the man Jimmy selected to head up his defense team, was one of Las Vegas's top criminal attorneys and had made a sizable reputation defending such Mafia notables as Meyer Lansky and Kansas City crime boss Nick Civella. Goodman was considered one of the country's leading experts on wiretap law, mainly because he had defended nineteen of the twenty-six defendants arrested in a massive federal raid on bookmakers: most of the cases were dismissed when Goodman established that the wiretaps used to make the cases had not been properly authorized. "That's how I got the reputation for being a mob lawyer," Goodman explained. "Most of the gamblers were high-profile figures whose last names ended in vowels."

Even without Oscar Goodman, the Chagra trial was bound to be one of the most sensational and controversial in years. It was front-page all over Texas. The Dallas *Morning News*, a highly conservative newspaper that had supported the harsh drug laws of 1970, published a series of articles by investigative reporter Howard Swindle that all but agreed with Lee Chagra's contentions that a longtime "federal conspiracy" had tabbed him as "Mr. Big, the man behind massive amounts of Colombian cocaine and marijauana." Judge Wood took particular offense at two quotes in the series and wrote letters on the subject to other judges in the district, denying that he was playing "footsie" with prosecutor James Kerr, as both Sib Abraham and Joe Chagra had charged.

"If Mr. [Joe] Chagra has any such basis for recusal, as he is alleged to have charged in this article," Wood wrote, "the proper procedure, of course, is for him to file a sworn motion on behalf of his client charging with particularity his basis therefor. To publicly criticize the court and prosecution in this media fashion is not only a violation of his legal Code of Ethics, but of our own court rules as well." In a second letter written four days later to his fellow judges, Wood referred to Joe Chagra's "media releases" and added: "Both defense and government lawyers appear to be overreacting to pressures engendered by recent developments. I have received complaints (however, fortunately, not in the media) from United States prosecutors and government agents that members of my staff have been overly sympathetic to the defendant and counsel, and particularly to the Chagra family."

Joe Chagra did not feel compelled to respond to Wood's references to his "media releases" (did the judge really believe the quotes in Swindle's story came from media releases?), or the absurd notion that the judge's staff had been overly sympathetic to his family. As to the charge that the Chagras were using the media instead of proper judicial procedure, Joe Chagra read this as one of Wood's more ironic exercises in hypocrisy: shielded by the extraordinary powers of the federal bench, Wood had virtually made a career out of the media leak. Joe Chagra drafted a tersely worded motion asking Wood to excuse himself from hearing the case against Jimmy Chagra, citing the judge's gratuitous and highly unethical remarks about the Colombian connection, and working back to the day in 1977 when Wood told Lee Chagra in open court: "I imagine everyone in this area knows that you've been the subject of a grand jury investigation ever since the Tennessee indictment." The motion requested that the hearing on its merits be heard by some judge other than John Wood.

There were other motions, thirty-one in all, including requests for a change of venue. The defense attorneys did not really believe that Wood would grant any of their motions— they were made mostly for the record—but neither did they anticipate that the judge would take this moment to unseal the 1974 grand jury material in which Jerry Johnson made his wild and uncorroborated accusations. In the five years since Johnson poured out his story, not a single person had been arrested or indicted on this information. Wood himself had sworn that these documents would remain sealed and "in the rigor mortis of the vaults." Why had Wood suddenly found it necessary to make them public?

Joe Chagra speculated that this was "just another attempt by Judge Wood to prejudice the public against the Chagra family." The timing did appear suspect: actually, Wood didn't so much release the document as call attention to it. Every reporter in town (and every reporter who came to town) knew of the document's existence. In fact, the El Paso *Times* had found a transcript in the public records as far back as May 22, 1978. The most charitable explanation was that someone had made a clerical error, though this didn't explain why Judge Wood brought it to public attention a week before Jimmy's trial was scheduled to start. Even while Wood was making this document public, he ordered sealed subpoenas for the witnesses in the current case against Jimmy Chagra. The defense couldn't interview the prosecution's witnesses, and the indictments were so vague that preparation of the defense was little more than a shot in the dark. It appeared that the prosecution had offered immunity or reduced sentences to every dealer and smuggler who had ever worked with Jimmy Chagra. The April court date in Midland was supposed to be an evidentiary hearing, but Jimmy was afraid that the judge would insist on picking a jury and starting the trial the next morning. Joe Chagra called it "trial by ambush," a term apparently borrowed from Wood himself. Instead, Wood reset the trial date for May 14.

Jamie Boyd had reviewed and revised his position a number of times since the Renteria trial. In Jamie's mind, Joe Renteria was inexorably tangled with the Chagras, which made him both a victim and a perpetrator of evil. It was Lee, not Jimmy: *Lee* should be doing those thirty years. Boyd remembered Renteria now as "a gentle, decent, sensitive young man who had pulled himself up." Boyd admired that. In Boyd's mind, Joe Renteria was a tragic living model of what drugs could do. "I saw Renteria, lured by the promise of easy riches," Boyd said. "I saw him taken into that phony world that robs people of the rights to enjoy certain things in life. Work is fun. It gives most of us the will to keep living. If it robbed Joe Renteria of that right, it is evil." And yet, Boyd couldn't help but reflect that Joe Renteria had testified favorably for Jimmy Chagra at the bond hearing, and would no doubt testify again at the trial. Had the Chagras sucked the final drop of decency from this young man? Since Lee Chagra's murder, Boyd had avoided asking tough questions about Lee's activities—that would have been in poor taste, and of no prosecutorial value—but Boyd may have believed that death had cheated justice.

The time had come to make some hard choices. Once the defense officially filed its motion to recuse Judge Wood, Boyd decided to pull James Kerr off the case for good. Kerr didn't comment, but Boyd believed he was relieved. Within a few weeks, Kerr had moved out of San Antonio to a place where he remained incognito for many months, appearing only when needed. The next step was to reindict Jimmy Chagra, this time in El Paso, adding the kingpin rap to the other five charges. This could have been a problem, at least with semanticists: If Lee was the kingpin, how could Jimmy be the kingpin, too? It could be argued that there was more than one kingpin, but having them both from the same family, accused of the same crimes, was, to say the least, not very neat. A case could have been made that Jamie Boyd's star witness, Henry Wallace, was in fact the kingpin. Wallace, not Jimmy Chagra, thought up most of the details of the scam and hired or contacted most of the other co-conspirators.

It boiled down to one very pertinent, very practical point: Henry

Wallace was willing to make a deal. Jamie Boyd needed evidence, and Wallace had it. Boyd acknowledged that it was a high price to pay: Wallace was as canny and capable as any drug smuggler the prosecutor had known, and once Wallace was granted immunity he would almost certainly go right back to his old trade. "But, frankly, I felt Chagra and his cohorts were worth it," Boyd said. Boyd did not spell out what "cohorts" he had in mind: With the exception of pilot Jim French, who, for reasons that were not immediately apparent, had not been named as co-conspirator, every single one of Jimmy Chagra's cohorts in this deal was now a government witness, under grant of immunity. Boyd was trading virtually the entire conspiracy for a single man, who, if all those years of investigation were to be believed, was not even the boss. This required some rationalization. At one point the prosecution even offered Jimmy Chagra a deal—they would forget about the kingpin charge if he would plead guilty to one fifteen-year cocaine count. Jimmy's lawyers proposed a counteroffer: he would plead to two five-year marijuana charges. Now, at last, the prosecution was off the hook. "Our clients, the DEA and the public, would have felt cheated, and rightly so, if we had let a major narcotics trafficker off with five years," Boyd said. That's when Boyd decided to file the kingpin charge. By May 1979, Jimmy Chagra was facing life without parole, in John Wood's court.

A month before the assassination of Judge Wood, downtown Las Vegas was in high fever as Binion's Horseshoe prepared for its annual World Series of Poker. For this one event, downtown Vegas, or Glitter Gulch, as they called it (somewhat ruefully, it is supposed), surpassed the more famous Strip, if not for glamour and luxury then certainly for old-time audaciousness. The hotels along Fremont Street didn't have tennis courts or golf courses or gyms, and the few that had swimming pools had located them on the roofs. Glitter Gulch was a world of serious gamblers, whether they were little old ladies with Dixie cups of small change or stout used-car dealers with bundles that would choke a hippopotamus, and once a year they mingled with students, garishly dressed tourists, punters, and punks to watch an event that, in their world, was the Super Bowl, the World Series, and the Kentucky Derby rolled into one.

Throngs of women in halters and men in cowboy hats pushed along

Fremont Street, past the pawnshops, the stores that peddled cheap clothes, souvenirs, and pornography, past the Mint and the Golden Nugget, nudging aside the transients and pensioners who normally congregated here. They collected like debris at the open door of the Horseshoe, pushing to get past the Binion's seven-foot gold-tinted $1 million horseshoe with a hundred real $10,000 bills enclosed in shatterproof glass, straining to get a glimpse of the players behind the rails. By Binion's standards, the *stakes* weren't all that high, but this was a special breed of *player*, the hall-of-famers who made fabulous livings playing cards and calculating odds, legendary figures like Treetop Jack Strauss, Amarillo Slim Preston, Bobby Baldwin and Doyle Brunson. In this league, a gambler like Jimmy Chagra was bush. Chagra gambled as though there were no tomorrow—these men could tell you precisely when tomorrow would come, tell you in their sleep, and quote odds on the solar index the following Tuesday.

Amid the tangles of television cable, reporters, officials, and hangers-on, Jimmy Chagra was much in evidence, as were any number of con men who had made the trip just to meet him. The World Series of Poker had become like old home week for Las Vegas regulars, and Chagra's presence gave it added meaning.

One evening as Chagra pushed through the crowd on his way to the craps table he recognized a face from the past, a onetime Las Vegas blackjack dealer he remembered as Jo Ann Starr. Some years earlier Jo Ann and her boyfriend, Pete Kay, had gambled with Jimmy in El Paso. Pete Kay, a portly man with a graying beard, had once pulled a pistol on Chagra over a gambling debt, and that had ended their relationship. Jimmy was well acquainted with Kay's reputation, having watched his brother, Lee, successfully defend Kay on murder charges in Oklahoma. Jo Ann was with Ron Coller, a gambler and car salesman, who had recently delivered a complimentary Lincoln to Liz Chagra on behalf of a casino, and a sandy-haired man Jimmy had never met, whom she introduced as her new husband, Charles Harrelson. Although he claimed to be something of a gambler himself, Harrelson said he hadn't been around Las Vegas for a while. That was because he was in Leavenworth doing time for murder, Harrelson said, grinning as though he had just confessed to being captain of the polo team at Princeton. Despite the prison pallor, Harrelson was impressive, sturdy, and cocksure, like a good middleweight boxer. Jo Ann told Jimmy how sorry she was to read about the murder of his brother, and Harrelson made a vague inquiry into what Chagra intended to do about it. (Lee's killers, White, Wallace, and Esper, were still awaiting trial, though Esper was in the process of plea bargaining, and White was considering the same option.) Jimmy said that he had problems with his own upcoming trial: Lee's murder would have to take care of itself.

Harrelson and a friend, Hampton Robinson III, followed Chagra to the craps table. Robinson, son of a wealthy Houston doctor, recalled that at one point Jimmy had Harrelson roll the dice. He lost $50,000 on the throw, but wound up winning $350,000 in a short time.

Several days later as Chagra, Ron Coller, and some others were having lunch in the Sombrero Room at Binion's Horseshoe, Charles Harrelson walked over to the table. Harrelson was still wearing his hard crooked grin; Coller recalled that he said he was broke and on his way back to Texas.

"If I can be of any help to you if you get sentenced to prison, I will," Harrelson told Chagra.

"Will they let me have a television set," Chagra asked, "if I go to Leavenworth?"

"No, you can't."

"What if I buy one for everyone in the joint?" Jimmy seemed mildly surprised when everyone laughed, but his line became a joke around the casino for months. After Harrelson left, Chagra asked Ron Coller what he thought of the man. Coller didn't know much about Harrelson, other than what Harrelson himself had told them, but he thought it unusual that a man with the sort of background Harrelson was claiming would be advertising it so openly.

Not long after that Chagra telephoned Pete Kay in Texas and made additional inquiries about Charles Harrelson. Kay knew Harrelson as well as anyone. They had grown up together in Huntsville, where both of their fathers worked for the state prison. Kay knew that Harrelson had been tried as a hired killer on two separate occasions, and he knew Harrelson's feelings regarding the taking of human life. "A person's head is just a watermelon with hair on it," Harrelson believed. Harrelson had once bragged to Hampton Robinson that getting away with murder was his long suit. You heard a lot of big talk in Pete Kay's social circle, but there were few men around more capable or determined than Charles Harrelson.

"Is this guy Harrelson okay?" Jimmy asked in his cryptic fashion. Kay wasn't sure how to answer that question. He didn't know what had happened between Chagra and Harrelson in the last few days, but he knew that when Harrelson and Hampton Robinson left Texas their plan was to lure Chagra into a card game and "cold-deck" him. Harrelson was a cardshark of the first rank, having practiced his art of arranging the deck during many months in solitary confinement. As an added precaution, Harrelson had borrowed Kay's "holdout" table, a specially constructed card table designed to conceal extra cards in a hidden compartment. Harrelson had not been able to lure Chagra into a game, but Kay had no way of knowing this at the moment.

"I mean is he really okay?" Chagra repeated his question.

"Yeah, sure," Kay told him. What else could he say?

About the same time Harrelson was in town, some of Harrelson's old friends were executing a scam to take Jimmy Chagra to the cleaners. Most of them were high rollers from San Antonio or Houston, who regularly made the scene in Las Vegas. One Texan, who called himself Sluggo, challenged Jimmy to a high-stakes golf game. Jimmy didn't know it, but Sluggo's accomplices (they had nicknamed Chagra "Mr. Bill") were dressed as groundskeepers and had two-way radios. Every time Jimmy hit a ball, they arranged for it to end up behind a tree, while Sluggo's ball was habitually discovered a few feet from the pin. "Mr. Bill" dropped $580,000 that afternoon. Everyone around the casino heard him bitching and moaning that his luck had never been so bad. When Jimmy asked for an opportunity to recoup his losses, the gamblers invited him to play cards, and then dice. Both games were rigged, of course. They ended up taking better than $1 million.

27

Thunderheads stacked up along the Edwards Plateau west of San Antonio, but there was an abundance of sunshine and a harmless scattering of high, thin clouds to the southeast as John and Kathryn Wood drove toward their Gulf Coast retreat at Key Allegro. Brushy plains, occasionally broken by the Nueces River and its tributaries, gave way to black waxy fields topped with spring wheat and corn. Tidy settlements of Germans and Czechs lay off in the distance like backgrounds in a painting. Gradually, the horizon seemed to blur in the vastness of the coastal grasslands where Wood's great-great-grandfather had started his cattle empire 150 years earlier. It was Thursday, May 24, the start of a long Memorial Day weekend. It had been almost nine months since the judge had had time to take his fishing boat out beyond the bay, and he was looking forward to testing his new motor. If the fish weren't hitting, or even if they were, he might get in a few sets of tennis, too. Wood had once been captain of his tennis team at the University of Texas, and at sixty-three he could still wear out men half his age.

John Wood loved it here on the Texas coast. San Antonio was his city, but this was his home, his birthplace, here among the salt marshes and tidal flats, the constantly shifting dunes and wind-sculpted trees, where the only sounds were the wind and surf and the gossip of sea birds. Wood was a big man, almost six foot three, and he felt comfortable with the shrimpers who gathered to talk shop on the trawler decks beside the miniature harbor. Jimmy Chagra and El Paso and drug traffickers seemed, and literally were, a thousand miles away. The trial had been repeatedly postponed, first to May 14, then to May 29, and then again just a week ago to July 24. In a surprise move, Wood had agreed to move it to Austin. He had issued a gag order, prohibiting anyone from discussing the case, but Jimmy Chagra, highly visible at the annual World Series of Poker, ignored it. When a reporter asked about his chances for an acquittal, Chagra answered with a question of his own:

"With Judge Wood on the case? Oh, about fifty-fifty."

"And without Wood?'"

"Much, much better."

One El Paso newspaper reported that a letter threatening Wood and his family had arrived at the judge's office in San Antonio that week; it was also reported that a second letter using "almost exactly the same wording" was mailed to another federal officer in El Paso. Since the assassination attempt on James Kerr, Wood and the other federal judges in the district had been under constant protection from teams of federal marshals; Jamie Boyd and some of the prosecutors were also being guarded. Wood was steadfastly fatalistic about such threats, however, and some days earlier had dismissed his own marshals: he considered this around-the-clock surveillance a waste of time and money, and an invasion of his privacy. Frankly, he doubted it was doing much good. "I was shot at during World War II and I didn't like it, but there was nothing I could do about it," Wood told his law clerk. "If they're going to kill you, they're going to kill you. We've got a job to do, so let's do it." There was even a measure of pride in the threats. Wood told a fishing companion, "I must be making a dent in their ranks or they wouldn't be so dead set on trying to do away with me." Out of long habit, the judge had written numerous letters to fellow judges and politicians regarding the seriousness of the situation. In a letter to Representative Henry Gonzalez following one of the congressman's speeches on "King Crime," Wood wrote: "Words cannot express the depth of my feeling of outrage at the attempt to intimidate the prosecution of criminal cases by such threats on the lives of the members of the federal prosecutors and the courts." According to attorney Oscar Goodman, who had made his complaint a part of the record, Wood also wrote a letter to another federal judge claiming that the Chagras were "responsible" for the attempt on Kerr. Wood denied this, and again refused to recuse himself from Jimmy Chagra's trial. There had been another accusation that Wood was biased, this one surprising. By a curious coincidence, Wood's friend and former law partner Seagal Wheatley, himself a former U.S. attorney, had found himself in John Wood's court two days earlier, arguing for a reduction of sentence in the three-year-old tax evasion case against Tommy Hiett, Lee Chagra's onetime client, who had been implicated of trafficking drugs with the infamous snitch Jerry Johnson. Wheatley argued that "the prosecution nearly got a hernia" trying to prove Hiett made his money on drug deals. Wheatley's main gripe was the same one that caused Lee Chagra so much agony—that Wood had prejudiced himself by reading the 1974 grand jury transcript and particularly the tainted interview with Jerry Johnson. While the confrontation between the judge and his old friend Seagal Wheatley was casual and friendly, Wood went on record as declaring his total lack of bias. "I'm not brainwashed to that extent, am I?" he asked Wheatley, before denying his request to reduce sentence.

The weekend at Key Allegro was pleasant and, except for some minor annoyances, blessedly uneventful. Early Saturday, Wood took his boat across the bay toward Aransas Pass, but the new motor was malfunctioning and after a while it conked out. While he tinkered with the motor, the boat drifted, rocking gently in the smoky gray water of the Gulf. After a time Wood hailed another boat and got a tow back to the Key Allegro marina. Monday morning, Wood ran into an old friend, stockbroker John O. Dix, Sr., at the general store on the highway into Rockport. They talked about fishing: Wood caught a few, Dix didn't. Some sports fishermen claimed that the shortage of redfish and saltwater spotted trout was due to overfishing by commercial fishermen. Others blamed the exceptionally dry weather, or the problems of upstream damming, industrial pollution, and the increasing practice of cutting channels through tidal flats. John Wood thought it was because of the increased traffic of pleasure boats. The bay was starting to look like Houston at rush hour.

Driving back to San Antonio later that morning, Wood noticed that the family station wagon needed maintenance. The muffler was about gone, the brakes needed checking, and the wheels were out of line. It was midafternoon when Wood parked the station wagon in the parking area of his brownstone townhouse in the luxury apartment complex called the Chateaux Dijon. The condominiums were in Alamo Heights, in a grove of giant oaks and pecan trees just off

Broadway, less than a mile from the site of the attack on James Kerr. The U.S. courthouse located on the Plaza of Americas on the Hemisphere grounds was only about a fifteen-minute drive from Wood's townhouse.

As usual, the judge woke early on the morning of Tuesday, May 29. Though the Chagra case had been postponed, Wood had several other cases set for jury selection. At 8:20 A.M., Kathryn Wood telephoned A&B Axle, their regular auto-repair garage. She told manager Gene Pilgram that she would "be by in a little bit" to drop off the station wagon. The judge would follow in his sedan and give her a ride downtown. But when Kathryn Wood tried to back the station wagon out of the carport, she realized one of the rear tires was flat.

It wasn't quite 8:30 A.M. when Wood left the apartment and walked to his own car. The judge usually parked around the corner, in the parking area where the station wagon sat, but for some reason his sedan on this particular day was parked right in front of the townhouse. Wood tossed his briefcase in the front seat and opened the door on the driver's side.

In the apartment directly across the driveway from where Wood's car was parked, James Spears, a twenty-eight-year-old stockbroker, sat drinking coffee with his brother, Monroe, his sister, Carol, his mother, and a family friend. This was the family of U.S. judge Adrian Spears, chief judge of the Western District; the judge and his wife were divorced, and he didn't live at the Chateaux Dijon. Judge Spears was near retirement age. In a few months Judge John Wood was scheduled to replace him as chief judge of the district.

James Spears and his sister, Carol, who live in Dallas and didn't know John Wood except by reputation, both happened to glance out of the breakfast-room window just as Wood started to climb into his car. That's when they heard the noise. "It sounded like a loud backfire," James Spears recalled. "A *loud* backfire." Carol Spears said: "I saw the man who was leaning into his car . . . step backward. I didn't know he was shot. There was no blood or anything. Then he sort of twisted around and fell on his back." At this point Carol Spears realized the noise was gunfire and screamed for everyone to get away from the window.

James Spears telephoned the police emergency number, then ran downstairs and across the driveway to where the judge lay, next to the open door of his sedan. "There was no one in the area, no one at all," Spears said. "No moving cars, no people, no more noise after the shot." Wood's eyes were open, but he didn't speak or move. Spears couldn't see any blood, nor could he see the small entrance wound of the high-velocity rifle bullet that had slammed into Wood's lower back and shattered into dozens of fragments. He pressed a finger against an artery in the judge's neck, but there was no apparent pulse.

Kathryn Wood was talking on the telephone to her daughter when she heard the shot. Some instinctive dread must have overwhelmed her, because she dropped the telephone and ran out the front door to where her husband lay dying. She cradled his head in her arms, not really knowing if he was alive or dead, and said: "Who shot you, John W.?" She untied his tie and loosened his belt, praying that he was still alive, then ran back to the telephone and told her daughter, "Get off the phone. I have to call EMS [Emergency Medical Service]. Daddy has been shot." When she returned to the judge, Mrs. Wood had a pillow and a cold compress. In the five or six minutes before the ambulance arrived, Kathryn Wood and James Spears attempted to make the judge comfortable, but they must have known it was too late. John Wood was dead on arrival at Northeast Baptist Hospital.

The killer had disappeared into the heavy flow of morning traffic along Broadway. It had been a clean, perfect shot. He'd watched Wood quiver for a fraction of a second, then twist and drop in his tracks. Then the killer was gone.

Within minutes one of the most intensive and costly investigations in history was underway. City police and FBI agents cordoned off the Chateaux Dijon and began questioning residents. Elizabeth Sudron, whose apartment was about fifty yards from where Wood was shot, told police that she heard someone running across the roof seconds after she heard the shot, but when police climbed onto the roof they found nothing. Police broadcast an alert for two cars seen in the area, but again nothing came of it. There wasn't a single clue. Police speculated that the assassin was responsible for the flat tire on the station wagon. Whatever else one might speculate, the killer's method was precise, professional, and deadly. "It could have been anyone," said San Antonio detective Marion Talbert, who handled the preliminary investigation before relinquishing control to the FBI. "A relative of someone the judge sent up for a long stretch, organized crime, a motorcycle gang. Most drug peddlers would have better sense. I would suspect more of an intimidation thing, or revenge. This will be a long, drawn-out investigation."

Seldom had an assassination shocked and outraged so many people in high places. The nation had survived the murders of presidents, politicians, religious leaders, men whose death had disenfranchised millions, or tested the fundamental tenets of their faith. But no one could remember a federal judge being assassinated; there certainly hadn't been one in this century. Some rote impulse, some high-blown catch phrase about the sanctity and invulnerability of the federal judiciary, told politicians that a new type of criminal was out there, wiping his boots across the system. It was true that nobody had elected John Wood. He had been appointed by an administration that was now in disgrace. But they did not react for Wood the man, or even Wood the judge; the reacted primarily for themselves.

John Connally, himself the victim of an assassin's bullet, called it "terrorist behavior." Representative Henry B. Gonzalez, whose congressional speeches on "King Crime" had got him some headlines, labeled the murder "the crime of the century," a phrase that was later picked up by FBI agents. Former president Nixon expressed "outrage" and called for quick arrest and punishment. President Carter called it "An assault on our very system of justice" and assured reporters, "All Americans join me in condemning this heinous crime." Attorney General Griffin Bell, himself a former federal judge, talked about "a dark time" in our nation's history, and vowed that the FBI would "leave no stone unturned" in its search for the killer.

Most stunned and shocked of all were the politicians and lawyers who had known and worked with Wood. "Unbelievable" was the phrase most used. Former Republican state committeewoman Glenda Sutton said: "He truly died in the line of duty for his country. He died as surely as if he had been at war, because it is war!"

John Pinckney, the former federal prosecutor and Republican loyalist, ruffled some feathers by admitting to several reporters, including one from the *Wall Street Journal*: "After the initial shock, I wasn't surprised." Pinckney had personally warned Wood about his open bias for the prosecution. "I think he enjoyed the reputation of being known as Maximum John. But there was always the feeling, at least on my part, that some of the defendants he sentenced must

191

have been very bitter." Attorneys Richard Keene and Seagal Wheatley, two of Wood's former law partners, insisted that the stiff sentences were the result of Wood's deep indignation with those who broke the law, but another federal judge who requested that his name not be used said: "It wasn't so much the harsh sentences. It had more to do with demeanor than substance. I may sentence somebody to thirty years, but I try to explain to them why I did it. If anything, I sympathize with them rather than chastise them, because thirty years is thirty years any way you dish it out. But Judge Wood seemed to sentence with relish." Another former federal prosecutor noted the obvious: "If you want to find the killer, you'll have to check the case file for the past nine years."

The morning that John Wood was killed, Jimmy Chagra had been up most of the night playing cards. They say he turned deathly pale when he heard the news. "I nearly puked," he said later. "It wasn't supposed to be that way."

About a month after the murder, a pretty young woman with long blond hair played a slot machine near a bank of telephones at the Fremont Casino. Though the casino was quiet and nearly deserted that time of day, she appeared nervous and uncomfortable. The ring of a pay phone startled her, then she glanced around and answered. She listened, mumbled something, and hung up. Taking a cab back to her room at the Jockey Club, she packed and waited. Half an hour later there was a knock on the door. It was a woman with long brown hair, carrying a briefcase. The woman appeared to be about six months pregnant. She walked to the sofa, dropped the briefcase, and left without speaking a word. The pretty blonde opened the briefcase. There was a box wrapped in brown paper inside. She shook the box but didn't open it. It was what she had come for. A few hours later she was on a plane back to Corpus Christi, Texas.

28

Judge William S. Sessions sat ramrod-straight, impervious to the August heat that wilted everyone else in the Austin courtroom. A tall, thin-lipped, humorless man with the bearing of a nineteenth-century British headmaster, Sessions seemed so stiff and correct that he might have been wearing a whalebone corset under his black robe. More likely, he was wearing a flak jacket. Most of the judges and prosecutors in the district adopted that as a standard item of clothing after Wood was gunned down.

Sessions, who would soon turn fifty, was a former U.S. attorney who had been appointed to the federal bench by Gerald Ford in 1974. He was next in line to become the district's chief judge (an honor that would have gone to Wood) and was arguably the best-qualified judge to hear the Chagra case. Though he had been a pallbearer at Wood's funeral and delivered the eulogy at a memorial service, Sessions had never had many dealings with any of the Chagra family, and the few that he had had demonstrated compassion: when Joe Chagra collapsed in the courtroom several years earlier, Sessions had personally telephoned to ask about the young lawyer's condition.

Under the best circumstances—and these were just about the worst —Jimmy Chagra's trial promised to be delicate and difficult. The three-month-old investigation into Wood's murder, said to be the most intensive since the assassination of John Kennedy, had cost the government at least $1 million and produced hardly any clues. The media attention to the Chagra family, dope smuggling, and organized crime; the necessarily elaborate courtroom security; and the FBI's description of Judge Wood's murder as "the crime of the century"—all of these things overshadowed the trial, as did the cynical suspicion among some members of the press that there was less to the investigation than met the eye.

Some of the cynicism was the result of another trial in Sessions's court a week before Wood's murder. A jury in Austin had found Rudolph James "Shakey" Maio, president of the El Paso chapter of the Bandidos Motorcycle Club, guilty of the felony assault on a federal officer during a raid on Maio's home the previous February. FBI agent Jim Beck testified that when he and a team of armed officers, shouting that they were from the FBI, broke down Maio's door and discovered him in a back bedroom with his girlfriend, Maio pointed a .357 Magnum in his direction. This was the "assault." Although Beck and other agents claimed to have shouted "FBI . . . search warrant!" as many as twenty times, a next-door neighbor who was in her front yard at the time told the jury she didn't hear any shouting or yelling. A week after the jury had returned a verdict of guilty in the assault, defense attorneys Sib Abraham and Charles Roberts filed a motion for a new trial, attaching an affidavit from a juror named Marilyn Stabeno, who claimed she was coerced into changing her not-guilty vote. A number of people in the courtroom had noticed the woman crying when the verdict was read and had suspected intimidation by other jurors. Sessions threatened the lawyers with contempt of court for violating Rule 20, prohibiting discussion of jury deliberations, and though he convened a hearing he refused to permit the lawyers to question the juror or even inquire whether the jurors had discussed Maio's membership in the motorcycle gang. Though this case had no direct link to the case against Jimmy Chagra, other than the fact both men were indicted by the same racket-busting grand jury (two of only three indictments returned in fifteen months of the investigation), the fact that Maio's conviction was tainted by controversy reflected poorly on the government. The same prosecutors and judge would now be trying Jimmy Chagra before an Austin jury very similar to the one that convicted the motorcycle club's chapter president.

Even without the gusher of publicity, there were intrinsic legal problems in Chagra's case. No one seemed sure how to proceed under the kingpin law. The statute itself was hopelessly vague. There seemed to be two burdens on the government: (1) to prove the defendant was the boss of the smuggling ring, as opposed to merely another hand, and (2) to demonstrate that Chagra made a "substantial" amount of money from drug trafficking, as opposed, say, to gambling, which he listed as his profession. To support its contention, the government had granted immunity to almost all of the other members of the conspiracy.

The case for the defense rested on the jury's believing that Jimmy Chagra was a "two-fisted professional gambler" victimized by the "purchased testimony of government witnesses." Chagra maintained that the feds had an ongoing vendetta against his family. Lee was the man they had really wanted; Jimmy was just a consolation prize. One witness for the defense, in fact, was U.S. attorney Jamie Boyd, who had once testified that DEA agents lie, tamper with evidence, and commit other crimes in pursuit of their trade. Boyd had said these things six years before, in defense of a friend in U.S. Customs, who had been mauled in an interagency political battle with the DEA, but having said them, he was on record. Boyd, of course, was now heading up the Wood murder investigation, and though both sides agreed to avoid any mention of the murder during the course of this trial, the jury's knowledge of Boyd's present crusade would not necessarily hurt the defense: It would be consistent with their theory of a vendetta.

There was no way around it; Wood's murder had to hurt Chagra's chances in Austin. Joe Chagra, who along with Las Vegas attorney Oscar Goodman was handling the defense, told reporters: "I'm not going to pretend that I liked Judge Wood, but I hate to see anyone murdered. I've just gone through it with my brother Lee. But the one I'm really feeling sorry for is Jimmy. His trial was supposed to start the very day Wood was murdered. It was postponed just a week before, but a lot of people didn't know that. A lot of people are bound to assume Jimmy was involved, even though it was the worst possible thing that could have happened to Jimmy. There is no way any judge or jury can blot this out of their minds."

Judge Sessions himself found it necessary to make repeated references to Wood's murder as he questioned prospective jurors. The judge had to be aware of the barrage of publicity. At least one television network (ABC) had featured a story on the Chagra-Wood feud the previous day. There had been numerous other national and even international news reports in recent weeks. ABC's "20/20," which had already featured the Chagra family in an unfavorable light, had more recently turned its cameras on the Bandidos, which entailed a review of Kerr, Wood, the Chagras, and the whole sordid entanglement. Six weeks before the start of the trial, DEA chief Peter Bensinger delivered a widely reported, highly inflammatory speech to a group of narcotics officers meeting in Dallas, pointing out what he perceived as the growing arrogance of the criminal community. "The criminal element is at the stage where values on human life and the prospect of a massive manhunt is an insufficient deterrent," Bensinger said.

A survey commissioned by the defense revealed that "a very significant percentage" of eligible jurors in Austin had knowledge and attitudes that affected the case. Among other things the survey showed that 28 percent of the potential jurors "recall mention of Chagra's name in connection with Judge Wood's murder"; 22 percent believed that Chagra was probably guilty of whatever it was the grand jury accused him of doing; and 56 percent believed that Wood's murder had to do with "a narcotics case." The report concluded: ". . . It would be extremely difficult or impossible to empanel a jury of twelve unbiased jurors." The defense included a copy of the survey as it filed a motion asking Judge Sessions to move the trial somewhere outside the western district. Sessions denied the motion without comment. He also denied a motion asking that the attorneys be allowed to question members of the jury panel individually to determine not only their exposure to media reports, but attitudes on drugs and gambling. Sessions was determined that this trial would start on schedule.

Working with no more information than names, addresses, occupations, and names and occupations of spouses, the attorneys picked a jury as oblique and shapeless as a column of obituaries. Eight were women. The jurors were predominantly low-level bureaucrats, people accustomed to taking orders from higher authority in government. Four either worked for the state or had retired from state jobs, two were married to city employees, one was an accountant at the University of Texas, and another was a part-time examiner for the IRS. Three lived in small, rural communities twenty-five miles or more outside of Austin. Although not an exemplar of the city's hedonistic, egalitarian reputation, the jury was probably a good cross section of the community. Austin was a government town. Law and higher education were its principal products.

In the city that made the laws, crimes were everyday occurrences, not just in the ghettos of east Austin but among the brightest, wealthiest, and most powerful. Not long before the trial, several district attorneys from North Texas had been nabbed in an after-hours joint, and a DA from East Texas was nailed while performing a homosexual act in the back room of a peep show. Frank Erwin, the chairman of

196

the board of regents of the University of Texas, had been nabbed several times driving his orange-and-white Cadillac while pickled to the gills, and a number of state legislators who had also been popped for DWI sympathized with the chairman's plight and rallied to retain lax laws for drunk drivers. Two recent house speakers had been indicted for bribery, and one was convicted. A former governor and a former lieutenant governor barely escaped the same charges. A legislator from West Texas was convicted of stealing several thousand dollars worth of postage stamps to pay for a new pickup truck. A state senator caught snorting cocaine with some lobbyist, quoted Tallulah Bankhead: "I know this stuff ain't habit-forming, 'cause I been doing it every day for six months." The game in Austin was to fit the crimes into neat, symmetrical packages—victimless, white-collar, organized, heinous, crimes of passion, crimes of ignorance, crimes of class, crimes of piety, crimes that hardly anybody believed were crimes. There was a saying among politicians: You're okay as long as you don't get caught in bed with a dead woman or a live man. But getting caught, that was a crime everyone in town understood.

Wednesday, August 1, the day the Chagra trial opened, was one of those relentless, wilting hot days that characterized Austin in the summer. The temperature hovered near a hundred, and the humidity was about the same. The austere 1940-ish federal courthouse was supposed to be air-conditioned, but you couldn't tell it: the atmosphere in Judge Sessions's courtroom was thick enough to melt boot leather. Members of the jury panel fanned themselves with their questionnaire forms and tried their best to stay awake. The only person in the room who didn't seem on the verge of fainting was Judge Sessions, who, for some unexplained reason, required all the men in the courtroom to wear coats.

Jimmy Chagra had been especially groomed for the occasion. His Zapata mustache had disappeared, and so had a good part of his shaggy black hair. He wore a minimum of body jewelry, and a dark business suit cut at least a size too large. He looked younger, smaller, and relatively harmless; he looked like someone Ricky Ricardo might bring home to meet Lucy. His lead attorney, Oscar Goodman, wore a plaid sports jacket: he might have been mistaken for the master of ceremonies of a quiz show. Though few members of the jury knew that Goodman had made his sizable reputation defending suspected Mafia dons, Goodman was not the best choice in this particular case. His fast-paced Philadelphia delivery wouldn't elicit much sympathy from this jury of low-ranking government workers. By contrast, Joe Chagra was resplendent in his lightweight summer suit and carefully styled hair. Joe's image was not unintentional—he was handsome, clean-cut, and appealingly wholesome, all the qualities that the defense wanted the jury to see in Jimmy. Playing second chair to Oscar Goodman, Joe Chagra would hardly open his mouth during the trial, but the fact that he was seated at the defense table was at least of cosmetic assistance, particularly since some of the Chagra women in the audience dripped with jewelry and designer dresses.

The fact that Jamie Boyd was on call as a defense witness precluded his active participation in the prosecution, for which he was secretly relieved. The U.S. attorney preferred to orchestrate from the wings. No matter how it looked to outsiders, this was Jamie Boyd's show. He had waited a long time to poleax a Chagra, and getting a kingpin in the deal was a bonus without parallel. For days now, Boyd had personally prepped his star witness, Henry Wallace. Wallace had beguiled the prosecutors, and when he started beguiling the jury with his tales of life in the big-time dope trade, the jury would understand what Jamie Boyd understood: that whatever Henry had done he wasn't nearly as bad as Jimmy Chagra.

By the end of the first day of testimony, Wallace had set the stage for everything the prosecution hoped to prove. He was like a big teddy bear with a singsong Frito Bandito voice, and as he talked on tons of dope and millions of dollars and how Jimmy Chagra, the boss, had cheated them all, the jury hung on every word. Jimmy smiled and sometimes laughed at Wallace's testimony. Judge Sessions had to warn the defendant several times that these proceedings were in no way humorous. Wallace told the jury that he had first met the defendant, Jamiel Alexander Chagra, in the summer of 1977 at the home of Leslie Harris, where a group of smugglers and dealers had gathered to discuss what had happened to the money from a shipment of marijuana.

Carl Pierce, the prosecutor Jamie Boyd had tapped to lead the government's case, wasted no time in establishing the thesis.

PIERCE: When you first met Mr. Chagra . . . what did you say to him?

WALLACE: My first words to Mr. Chagra were: "Are you the boss? Is your name Jimmy Chagra?"

PIERCE: What did he reply?

WALLACE: "Yes."

Carl Pierce had become knowledgeable about the kingpin law, much as had the man he replaced, James Kerr. When the prosecution decided to add the kingpin rap to the other charges, it was Pierce who convinced Judge Sessions to allow the superseding indictment. Pierce had assured the judge that the reason the prosecution hadn't filed continuing criminal enterprise charges in the first place was that the government had lacked a key witness, who had since been located. Sessions overruled a defense motion to force the government to reveal the name of this new witness. Even at the close of the trial, the name of this new witness was not apparent, if, in fact, there was one.

Like ducks in a line, the co-conspirators told their sordid stories and named Jimmy Chagra as the boss. Several witnesses got their stories crossed, but the weight of the testimony had an obvious effect on the jurors, none of whom had ever heard the confessions of big-time dope traffickers. The defense was able to establish some salient points —all of the government witnesses were testifying under grants of immunity, and even if all the stories were true, much of the evidence suggested that rather than making a substantial amount of money, Jimmy Chagra was losing it hand over fist. For example, the only people who apparently profited from the cocaine shipment were the witnesses Henry Wallace, Dudley Connell, and Paul Taylor. Of course, there was evidence that Chagra had a great deal of money by the time that he moved to Las Vegas, but this was consistent with the defense's theory that Chagra was a two-fisted professional gambler. What the jury didn't understand was that even now, even as they testified under immunity, the government witnesses were still under the government's hammer. At one point in direct examination, Richard Young sputtered: "I'm lost!" At the next recess, the prosecutors and a DEA agent took Young aside and apparently explained the consequences if he got lost again.

For several days the prosecution paraded an array of government officials, U.S. Coast Guard officers, and records keepers to support the many contentions of the other witnesses. Officers of the cutter *Steadfast* told of boarding and seizing contraband from the *Miss Connie* and the *Eco Pesca IV*, and the commanding officer of the *Cape Shoalwater* described nabbing the *Doña Petra*. None of the officers had direct evidence connecting Jimmy Chagra to the three freighters—the crew had long since vanished—but the jury had Henry Wallace's word that it was so. The total haul, something like twenty-four hundred fifty-pound bales, was impressive. The prosecution wanted to bring several of the bales into the courtroom, but the combination of the heat and the pungency doubtless would have paralyzed everyone. Sessions denied the request. Telephone logs, reports from U.S. and Bahamian Customs, motel and airlines records, and dozens of other documents were introduced to substantiate that the smugglers did the things that the government contended, on the dates that the government contended.

While Oscar Goodman was cross-examining the last of the government witnesses, Joe Chagra kept wondering about Jim French. Where *was* French? Why hadn't he been indicted with the others? Not long before the trial, Joe Chagra had located French in Ruidosa, New Mexico, and asked him point-blank about his deal with the government. French said there wasn't any deal. The government hadn't even questioned him. It was no secret that the Frenchman was a longtime, ongoing target of the DEA. Maybe the government wanted to indict and try French separately, rather than granting immunity: they had a fairly solid case without him. The defense had considered calling French as its own witness but decided it was too risky. As it turned out, this was one of its fatal mistakes. It was almost exactly one year later, during his own smuggling trial in August 1980, that French, corroborated by Richard Young, made it clear that Henry Wallace was the boss. It was Wallace, not Chagra, who located French and convinced him to join the conspiracy. It was Wallace who hired Richard Young and convinced Young to put up fifteen grand for the purchase of a new airplane: in his testimony at Jimmy Chagra's trial, Wallace had failed to mention that Young was *already* working in his organization. It was Wallace who arranged to have the Aerocommander registered in Young's name, Wallace who had the plane refitted with new fuel tanks, Wallace who floated a loan of $60,000 from a man in Florida, a man with whom he had had previous financial dealings.

"It was basically Wallace's deal," French said. "He got the money, put the deal together, and went to Colombia. The only reason Jimmy was even there was because he knew some people to off-load the marijuana. Wallace definitely called the shots—not Jimmy. Nobody in their right mind would work for Chagra. He was a liar and a cheat and a thief. *Nobody* in our business trusted him." Young testified that he never regarded Chagra as anything except a flunky. Why hadn't

Young said this at Jimmy's trial? "Nobody ever asked me," he replied. One reason Oscar Goodman and Joe Chagra worked at such a disadvantage in Jimmy's trial was that the would-be kingpin knew so little about Henry Wallace's end of the operation.

The defense's second big mistake was not properly analyzing its own case. Regardless of the government's evidence, it was still possible to take the low road: it was still possible to maintain that while the defendant had smuggled some marijuana for Henry Wallace, he had never been involved in the more serious crime of cocaine smuggling. The DEA had conceded that "not one iota of cocaine" had been traced to Jimmy Chagra. The problem was, Jimmy seemed to want it both ways: he wanted to be found not guilty, but he also wanted people to believe that he was the boss. He insisted that his lawyers continue to pound at the theme that the real criminals were the unscrupulous agents of the DEA and their hired stooges, the co-conspirators. Against the better judgment of his lawyers, Jimmy Chagra took the witness stand. "We wanted to believe he could do it," Joe Chagra said later. "We knew there were a lot of questions he couldn't answer, but at the time it seemed like the only thing to do."

From start to finish, Jimmy Chagra's testimony was a disaster. Even under the friendly guidance of Oscar Goodman, he came across as arrogant and petulant, and when the prosecution started working him over, his responses were so bellicose that even his friends in the gallery felt a sense of resentment. Jimmy denied that he had ever been involved in drug smuggling. *Ever*! He had made all that money gambling. He didn't even know that his friend Henry Wallace was a drug smuggler. He thought Wallace was a farmer. He barely knew Jim French and thought he, too, was in farming. He'd met Richard Young once, and he'd never met any of the others. Those stories that Dudley Connell and Paul Taylor told about meeting him in a Fort Lauderdale motel room and taking home a pound of cocaine were lies, as was Jud the Dud Myers's account of working as pilot of Jimmy's command boat. He couldn't explain government exhibits demonstrating hundreds of telephone calls from his home in Fort Lauderdale to the homes of the other conspirators—maybe someone had used his telephone. As for the thirty-four separate billings from his phone to the Republic of Colombia, Chagra told the jury that he had a number of "adopted children" living there. No, he couldn't remember any of their names, or explain why he usually called them in the middle of the night.

But he remembered something else. He remembered that during the time Wallace was in Colombia (doing what, he didn't know), Wallace's wife, Betty, stayed at the Fort Lauderdale Hilton. "She came to my house every day . . . she used my phone because she said they were broke," Jimmy said, leaving the jury to speculate how a woman with no money could live for two and a half months in a Florida resort hotel.

Chagra failed to realize that the government already had passport, hotel, and airline records proving that Betty Wallace had stayed in Florida exactly three days before flying to Colombia to meet her husband. Or that Betty herself was ready to testify that she barely knew Jimmy Chagra and had never set foot in his house.

Despite Judge Sessions's gag order at the beginning of the trial, Jimmy talked freely with reporters during breaks, usually about his family—his wife, Liz, was expecting a baby any day. Late in the trial, however, he revealed a startling account of how he had accidentally run into Henry Wallace a few nights earlier at a hotel bar. Wallace was with Richard Young and two hookers, and was obviously tanked, having just downed fifteen shots of vodka. Jimmy was surprised to see the government's star witness out on the town: he had assumed Wallace was in custody or at least under constant government protection. There was a moment of tense silence, then Wallace threw his arms around his old friend and began to sob. Jimmy told Steven Peters, a reporter for the El Paso *Times*, that he felt sorry for Wallace and gave him $300.

"That doesn't make sense," Peters had said. "Why would you give money to a man who is trying to put you in jail?"

"It makes sense if you know me," Jimmy replied, winking mysteriously. "I'm always going around giving away money. I might give a hundred to a shoeshine boy if he was broke and had a wife and kid like Wallace."

The remaining pieces of this strange story came to light a short time later on the witness stand. Apparently Chagra *had* accidentally run across Wallace in the hotel bar: what followed was an attempt at extortion, or bribery, depending on which story you believed. According to Chagra, Wallace offered to change his testimony—and get Richard Young to change his—for $300,000. Wallace gave him no choice, Jimmy told the jury. If he refused, Wallace would carry through a DEA plot that would frame Jimmy for the murder of John Wood.

(This was one of the few times Wood's name was mentioned in the jury's presence.) Recalled to the stand, Wallace confirmed the meeting but said the bribery attempt was Chagra's idea. He denied the part about the DEA plot but admitted taking $1,000, which he turned over to the prosecution.

The jury took less than two hours to find Chagra guilty of continuing criminal enterprise and everything else in the indictment. Sessions released Chagra on $400,000 bond and set September 5 as the date for sentencing. But Chagra had no intention of being sentenced. A week after the trial he jumped bond and disappeared. There were rumors that Jimmy and Liz had slipped into Mexico and possibly made their way to Colombia, where they were being protected by drug traffickers. It was assumed that Jimmy had blown most of his money, though certainly not all, in the Las Vegas spree; otherwise he could have made the $1 million bond that Judge Wood had ordered the previous spring. The current $400,000 bond had been underwritten by bail bondsman Vic Apodaca, after Jimmy put up $1 million in diamonds as collateral.

By January, the FBI had Jimmy's face on a most-wanted poster, describing him as armed and dangerous. Though the poster didn't announce a reward, FBI and DEA agents spread word among informers, particularly in Las Vegas, that information leading to Chagra's capture would be worth a lot of money. Some, though not all, of the agents believed that sooner or later Jimmy would turn toward Las Vegas, which is exactly what he did. In late February, Jimmy, Liz, and their two children, who had been traveling across the country in a Winnebago, slipped into Las Vegas and took a room at a cheap motel on the Strip. Jimmy contacted a casino waiter whom he had once befriended and sent him out to buy some wigs, but instead the waiter tipped off Joseph Capale, acting agent in charge of the DEA office in Las Vegas. Capale and another agent, back by Las Vegas police, staked out the motel, and shortly afterward Jimmy came out and climbed into a white Chevrolet that had been spotted a few days earlier in front of his residence in Paradise Valley. Chagra had put on weight and grown a beard, flecked with gray by now, but the agents recognized him immediately. "When Chagra walked out of the motel," Capale said later, "I flew six feet up in the air." When the agents curbed the Chevrolet, Jimmy came out with his hands in the air, shouting that he was not armed. In a box of disposable diapers on the front seat, they found $187,000 in cash. Why had Chagra returned to Las Vegas? No one could say for certain, but it was speculated that he came to town to have plastic surgery done by a doctor known for changing the identity of underworld characters. Only at the last minute, he changed his mind. Jimmy's own story was that he came back to surrender.

Judge Sessions sentenced Chagra to thirty years without parole. In April 1980, at age thirty-five, he entered the U.S. Penitentiary at Leavenworth.

29

It was a year of presidential elections, and nobody was more keenly aware of it than Jamie Boyd. Like certain animals that detect subtle vibrations in the atmosphere or imperceptible shifts in the earth before a natural disaster, the U.S. attorney had the jitters. It seemed certain that the Republicans would nominate Ronald Reagan, and even if they didn't, Boyd's own party appeared doomed to take the pipe with Jimmy Carter. Boyd needed only a couple more years of government service to retire with full pension, but if his sense of the political climate was correct, he could be out of a job in January.

Eighteen months had passed since the attempt on James Kerr, and a full year since the murder of Judge Wood, and the term of Jamie's grand jury was about to expire with hardly anything to show for its investigation. It had looked promising for a while the previous fall. FBI director William Webster had made a symbolic trip to San Antonio to observe the six-month anniversary of Wood's death and had reminded the media: "It is slow and meticulous. It's a very difficult case for an investigator to work, because tangible results aren't produced quickly. It takes a patient investigation to work cases of this sort." Though the grand jury had interviewed a number of characters with shady reputations, including Boston crime figure Salvatore Michael Caruana, and convicted hitman Charles Harrelson (along with his wife, Jo Ann), none of them could really be described as suspects. Seven witnesses swore that Harrelson was in Dallas on the day of the murder. Caruana had never been much of a suspect: computers at the El Paso Intelligence Center (EPIC) supplied information that the Patriarca crime family was involved in smuggling weapons into Mexico, South America, and Lebanon in return for narcotics, and that the crime family controlled drug trafficking in Fort Lauderdale, where

Jimmy Chagra had run his big scam. It seemed likely that Chagra had financed some of Caruana's transactions through connections in Juárez, but this hardly implicated him in the assassination. Boyd was convinced that the same person or group "willed" the shootings of Wood and Kerr, and he was absolutely sure the Chagra family was involved; but he didn't have a fiber of evidence. Boyd had also subpoenaed Jimmy's friend Peter Krutschewski, but he was in custody in Michigan at the time and unable to appear before the grand jury. There had been tips, of course, hundreds of them; they were all worthless. "I haven't talked to a motor mouth yet who was reliable," Boyd said. "You wouldn't believe the stack of letters I've received from prisoners who claim they know something about the assassination. Of course, they all want to get out of jail first." Typical was a Fort Worth con named Robert "Cowboy" Parrish, who told the grand jury he overheard some Bandidos talking about "hitting" several judges. Parrish had been held on state murder charges since three months before Wood was killed.

Though things were supposed to be coordinated, the FBI was in fact conducting a separate investigation, one that Jamie Boyd believed was designed to undermine and discredit him. He believed the FBI was jealous, and this made him even more determined. It was claimed that the FBI had fed more than 150,000 bits and pieces of information on the Wood and Kerr cases into the National Crime Information Center computers, but Boyd knew they hadn't collected a single piece of physical evidence. From fragments recovered in Wood's body, they had identified the murder weapon as a .243-caliber rifle, a high-velocity weapon popular among deer hunters; but the ID wasn't positive: there were at least three other rifles with the same configuration. The FBI had also produced six conceptual drawings of men reported in the area when Wood was murdered, and there were reports of two cars, a red compact and a gold sedan, seen in the vicinity. All this really said was the trail was cold. At one time the FBI was said to have fifty agents working full-time on the Wood and Kerr cases, but the figure you heard now was twelve, with assistance, of course, from Washington and forty field offices. Washington had recently dispatched FBI veteran Jack Lawn, who had once worked the organized-crime beat in Kansas City and before that assisted in investigations in the murders of Martin Luther King and John Kennedy, to head the San Antonio office. Though Boyd saw Jack Lawn as a positive sign, his basic mistrust of the FBI at times reached the point of loathing, even hatred. If the Wood and Kerr cases were ever going to be brought to a successful conclusion, Jamie Boyd believed it was up to him, and time was definitely a factor.

There was one other factor that any politician needed to consider: cost. The media had repeatedly described this as one of the most intensive investigations since the assassination of President Kennedy, and it was now certain to be the most costly. There were regular updates, most recently an interview with Chief U.S. marshal Rudy Garza, who reported that the government had already spent $3 million just providing round-the-clock protection for the judges and prosecutors in the Western District. Jamie and his wife, Suzy, tried to joke about the security: they enjoyed telling about the evening that James Kerr dragged his entourage of marshals to a Mozart concert, and about their own drive across the desert from San Antonio to El Paso when they tried to convince a young marshal from Kentucky that this was hostile Indian country. "There was a chuckwagon group observing some kind of anniversary out near Sierra Blanca," Jamie remembered. "About that time these two black guys in U.S. Cavalry uniforms galloped by. I told the young marshal that the Indians couldn't be far behind." According to the chief marshal, this protection would continue "indefinitely." Nobody liked the sound of that, least of all Jamie Boyd.

In late May 1980, a few weeks before the grand jury term expired, Boyd received permission from Washington to empanel a special grand jury with extralegal powers under the organized-crime laws. The special grand jury would have a term of thirty-six rather than the usual eighteen months, and would be authorized to grant immunity to witnesses and jail them for the term of the grand jury if they still failed to testify. Almost immediately the new grand jury captured headlines by subpoenaing Joseph Marcello, brother of reputed New Orleans organized crime king Carlos Marcello, who had been indicted in the Brilab bribery case (an offshoot of Abscam) a few days earlier. Though Joseph Marcello's testimony was secret, word leaked out later that the grand jury had listened to one of the Brilab tapes in which Marcello had discussed what he called "a third-hand rumor" that some Lebanese brothers from El Paso "had something to do with killing that judge in El Paso." The fact that Marcello didn't even know Wood had died in San Antonio should have been indicative of just how little he did know about the killing, but his appearance pushed the investigation back to the top of page one. Later that summer, the grand jury also heard from two Boston men who had sold the Winnebago that Jimmy and Liz used while he was a fugitive, and from Earl McClennan, Chagra's security man from Florida, who was later convicted for aiding the fugitive.

In August, Joe Chagra traveled to San Antonio with a client, Leon "Red" Nichols, Liz Chagra's father. The grand jury wanted to question Nichols about any contact he might have had with his daughter and son-in-law while Jimmy was on the run. Jamie Boyd took this opportunity to haul Joe Chagra before the grand jury, which infuriated Joe Chagra to the point that he lashed out at the investigation, both inside and outside the grand jury room.

In a press conference in the shadow of what was now named the John H. Wood, Jr., Federal Courts Building, the youngest Chagra brother told reporters: "A million people hated Wood and that's why they'll never catch the killer."

He could have stopped there, but he didn't. He continued: "I'm tired of sitting back and seeing my brother framed and then framed again. It's like the grand jury already decided Jimmy killed Wood, so let's go out and find the evidence. I told them, 'You guys are supposed to be a fact-finding body. You're supposed to look at the evidence first and then decide who committed the crime.' I'd like to see one shred of evidence linking Jimmy to the killing. Every day I pick up the paper and all I see is 'Wood, Chagra, Wood, Chagra, Wood, Chagra!' Jamie Boyd told me, 'We don't release that kind of information to the press.' Then who does? They seem to get wind of it somewhere."

Joe admitted to reporters that he had taken the Fifth Amendment to many of the questions, especially ones that might involve attorney-client privilege. "A lot of things are not covered by that privilege," he said. "Like if they ask me if I had any conversations with Jimmy when he was a fugitive. I'm not sure that any conversations I had, if I had any, would be covered."

Jamie Boyd, who usually declined comment on grand jury matters, made an exception when he learned of Joe Chagra's remarks.

Boyd told the media: "I'm shocked at the vicious, irresponsible attack upon a departed, martyred member of the bench by a member of the bar. Such vitriolic and hate-filled language is something you'd expect for an underworld mentality. . . . " He suggested that the state bar association consider disciplinary action.

That same day Jamie Boyd decided to play his ace.

30

It was like watching time-lapse photography, the way Joe Chagra had aged. Two years ago he had looked like a kid auditioning for *West Side Story*, heavy on bluff and uncertainty, charged with supermachismo as he bobbed behind his mirrored sunglasses, a cigarette dangling from his lips—and yet so obviously fresh and clean he squeaked. Now that Lee was dead and Jimmy faced the prospect of dying in prison, Joe was the *patrón* of the family, like it or not. His hair was longer, and carefully styled. His face showed signs of weathering: he was using cocaine and other drugs again, but there was also an unmistakable element of maturity more substantial than mere false courage or a sense of well-being. For the first time in his life, Joe Chagra was able to make his own decisions. He had no choice now. He had learned to express himself, to drop the act and come down hard: you couldn't look at Joe Chagra without thinking of Al Pacino in *The Godfather*.

Until now, Joe's life had been mostly unencumbered by choice; the stream of events that was the Chagra family legacy seemed to flow down and deposit its silt at his feet. He had wanted to be a doctor, not a lawyer. He had tried working his way through undergraduate school, and he worked so hard that his grades suffered. When he realized that he wouldn't be admitted to medical school, he took Lee's advice and applied to the law school at the University of Houston, which accepted him partly because of some strings pulled by some of Lee's old friends. Lee pulled more strings to keep Joe from being drafted into the Army, arranging first for a phony arrest on a gun charge, then arranging to have the charge dropped. By the time Joe completed law school, Lee already had the conditions of their partnership worked out. Lee made all the decisions, and Joe did what he was told.

Left to his own devices, it seems unlikely that Joe Chagra would

have specialized in defending clients charged with cold-blooded murder and major drug trafficking, but for the first few years of their
partnership, that's about all the lawyers did. The case involving Bandido founder Don "Mutha" Chambers and two of his lieutenants,
Crazy Ray Vincente and Jesse Deal, was the most sensational, though
in many ways typical of the class of client Lee seemed to prefer. "They
were rotten human beings," Joe recalled. "Just unbelievable! They
had absolutely no moral values. They sold speed, bullied people, killed
for hire and for pleasure, and forced their old ladies in prostitution.
They treated their old ladies like shit." Oddly enough, the girlfriends
didn't seem to mind. Patty and the other secretaries recalled that one
of them proudly demonstrated her tattoo—it read *D.F.C.* "When we
asked what that stood for," Patty said, "she told us. Dirty Fucking
Cunt." The murder victims were two brothers from Houston, Marley
Leon Tarver, twenty-two, and Preston LeRay Tarver, seventeen, who
had made the terrible mistake of selling the Bandidos baking soda instead of methamphetamine. First, the Bandidos and their old ladies
tortured the brothers a few days, burning them with cigarettes and
taunting them with unspeakable sexual implications, then they hauled
them to an isolated spot in the desert and had them dig a common
grave. They let Marley Leon watch while they blew his younger brother
away with a sawed-off shotgun. God knows what went through Marley
Leon's mind in the few seconds he had left. "Marley Leon," Mutha
Chambers said, "Jesus is waiting!" There was another blast from the
shotgun and Marley Leon's body toppled into the grave on top of
Preston LeRay's. There wasn't the slightest doubt that it happened just that way—one of the witnesses, a motorcycle-club pledge,
was an FBI informant. The only possible defense was that the FBI
had used a questionable search warrant, and it didn't go anywhere—
all three Bandidos went away for life. Joe was relieved to be rid of
the scum, but Lee took the defeat hard: he even wrote a letter to the
court confessing that he had been negligent in preparing the defense,
hoping that the ploy would influence the court to grant a new trial.
There was a rumor around town that the Bandidos put a gun to Lee's
head and forced him to write the letter, but whoever circulated that
rumor didn't understand Lee Chagra. Joe had never really expected
to be paid for their work, but for months afterward small checks and
money orders from Bandido chapters all over the country trickled
into the law office, thanking them for the work and reminding them

of the club motto: *We are the people our parents warned us about!*

Lee always gave Joe the short end, and Joe took it because that's how it was in the family. There was a pecking order. Just as Patsy was the sister—Patsy had to serve the boys before sitting down to enjoy her own meal—Joe was the little brother. It was a protocol that had been preserved in their culture for centuries. The business, the gambling, the women, all things had to do with the family and all things were the way Lee said they were. Joe had never forgotten (though he had forgiven) the way Lee reacted when Joe confessed that he was in love for the first time: not only did Lee take Joe's girlfriend to bed, he told Joe about it at his first opportunity, as though testing him with the ultimate show of family loyalty. Lee had even made a move on Joe's fiancée, Patty—he lured her into the bedroom and took off all his clothes. Patty's natural instinct for passive resistance cooled his ardor, but Lee promised he would try again. He didn't, probably because Joe and Patty married a short time later, but Patty always had the feeling that the move was something Lee did mainly to prove that he could, that it was his *right*.

Up until Lee's death, Joe was always in his shadow. Now he was in Jimmy's shadow, doomed to follow another trail he had never intended.

It was all so unfair, and so fraught with potential for disaster. Life had not really prepared Joe Chagra for the things that were happening. Lou Esper, the man really responsible for Lee's murder, was doing a measly fifteen years: he'd be out at least twenty-five years before Jimmy could even *apply* for parole. Hardly a week passed that Joe didn't get a letter or phone call from some con offering to "kill the guy who killed your brother." Lately, he was receiving vague offers to kill Henry Wallace. It seemed to go with the territory. Now that Jimmy was a target in the Wood investigation, Joe had to screen offers from shadowy people claiming to have information about that crime. When Jamie Boyd unexpectedly called Joe before the grand jury, Joe's frustrations and feelings of helplessness came gushing out. He knew that he shouldn't have said all those things to the media, though he had no regrets speaking his mind to the grand jury. His experiences with the grand jury convinced him of what he already suspected— the government was showing signs of panic.

Several months before his grand jury appearance, Joe had had a totally unexpected experience, one that in subtle ways was working in the deepest recesses of his being. A longtime family friend, Billy

Cabrera, had telephoned and asked Joe to stop by his house. There was a man he wanted Joe to meet. When Joe arrived at Cabrera's house, he was introduced to Charles Harrelson. Joe recognized the name as one of the people who had testified before the grand jury the previous fall. Though Harrelson had apparently been cleared in the Wood murder, he came on to Joe like public enemy number one, or at least the number-one suspect. "I knew when I first heard that Wood had been killed that I'd have to fade the heat," Harrelson said. "I've been convicted of murder, and I wasn't in prison at the time." Everyone on the street knew there was a price on Wood's head, Harrelson said. He told Joe that he had never met Lee, though he had once talked to him on the phone, but that he had been introduced to Jimmy just a few weeks before the killing. That's why he knew he was a suspect, even though the grand jury had excused him. Of course, he had an alibi—seven people, including his wife and stepdaughter, had told the grand jury he was in Dallas on the morning Wood was wasted. Joe got the impression that Harrelson wasn't entirely displeased with his notoriety. He made a couple of oblique references to the killer—"that guy must have balls that drag the ground"—and his hard blue eyes went flat and cold when he talked about killing. At one point it occurred to Joe that Harrelson had come to El Paso to blackmail the Chagra family, but as it turned out Harrelson had something else in mind. He had been arrested in Houston two months earlier on drug and gun charges and wanted Joe to represent him. Harrelson knew Lee's reputation as an attorney, and assumed those qualifications had been passed along to the younger brother. The thing about Harrelson that most interested Joe Chagra at the moment was Harrelson's cocaine stash; he had an enormous supply. Joe was spending $100 a day, sometimes more, on his own habit. Joe agreed to act as Harrelson's attorney.

The search warrant used to obtain the evidence when Harrelson's Lincoln Continental was stopped back in February was questionable. Cops and agents with the U.S. Bureau of Alcohol, Tobacco and Firearms had seized two .357 magnum pistols, a .38 Colt revolver, a 12-gauge pump shotgun, and a .300 Weatherby magnum rifle with a telescopic sight—along with some cocaine and gambling paraphernalia. Though Harrelson was living at the time with his wife, Jo Ann, in the luxury Preston Towers condominiums in Dallas, he was making regular trips to gamble in Houston, and running with his old pal Hampton

Robinson III, a wealthy heroin addict who enjoyed fast company. It appeared that Hamp Robinson had set him up. Harrelson had left his Lincoln Continental with Robinson while he flew home to Dallas, and shortly after his return to Houston he was stopped and his car was searched. The agents apparently knew the guns were hidden in the car—they even had the serial number of one weapon. Robinson had experienced numerous brushes with the law—in addition to his heroin habit, he had served a prison term for the shooting death of a fellow rancher in Huntsville—but there was another motive for his turning on Harrelson: as Harrelson acknowledged, he had been carrying on with Robinson's wife, Jo Ann. In fact, he was using her name as his current alias: he carried a credit card issued to Jo Robinson. As a convicted felon, Harrelson's troubles in Houston were serious, but they were not insurmountable.

In the weeks that followed that first meeting at Billy Cabrera's, Joe Chagra and Charles Harrelson saw each other a number of times. Harrelson was hired as a bodyguard by Virginia Farah, a friend of Patty Chagra's and widow of the co-founder of Farah Manufacturing. Joe drew up the contract of employment. This was a traumatic time in Virginia Farah's life: Her son, daughter, and granddaughter had been killed in an auto accident on Memorial Day, and she was also embroiled in a bitter lawsuit with her former brother-in-law, Willie Farah. Harrelson, or Jo Robinson, as she knew him, was obviously a man who could handle himself. He was handsome, in a rugged way, and enormously self-sufficient, an old-fashioned charmer who still opened doors for women and was quick to light their cigarettes. He was patient and attentive to Virginia, and seldom used profanity around her or any other woman. He dressed well and in expensive clothes, was almost obsessively neat, even meticulous, drank expensive Scotch and fine wine, and read a variety of books. Several times during the summer of 1980, Harrelson invited Joe and Patty Chagra and their two children to the Farah home—he thought Virginia needed to be around children —and he entertained them with a dazzling array of card tricks he had mastered while spending months in solitary.

Throughout the summer, Harrelson told Joe Chagra bits and pieces about his life and his current problems. He had separated from his wife after Wood was murdered and the government began snooping around. Within two weeks of the murder, he said, a van from a meatpacking company began parking outside his Preston Towers condo; he was certain it was an FBI surveillance vehicle. He also knew that his Lincoln and his apartment were bugged: he had hired a security company to do a sweep of the apartment and found a bugging device on the telephone. Agents had talked to all their neighbors; they had even interviewed Harrelson's ex-wife, who had divorced him almost twenty years before, and Jo Ann's former husband, whom she hadn't seen in ten years. He hated all federal agents with a passion—he referred to them generically as "those shit-eating dogs"—and had evolved a theory that the DEA had supervised the assassination of Judge Wood to cover up its own crimes. Since this wasn't too different from the theories espoused by both Lee and Jimmy, and more recently by Joe himself, Joe Chagra listened and even agreed with Harrelson's frequent harangues, especially when Harrelson furnished the cocaine. Though his own habit was bad, Joe recognized that Harrelson's was much worse—he was mainlining the stuff. He saw phantoms in the trees and behind the garage, and was almost always armed to the teeth. Harrelson was quickly losing touch with reality, and so was Joe Chagra. One night Harrelson told Joe that he was willing to take the rap for Wood's murder, if it would save Jimmy. Joe had started this relationship on the premise that Harrelson knew nothing of the assassination, but lately he thought different: Harrelson had never really come right out and said that he hadn't killed Wood. Joe wasn't sure what to believe. The thought that Harrelson was trying to blackmail the family still lingered in the back of Joe's mind; the thought was somehow comforting, considering the alternatives.

Several times that summer Joe visited Jimmy at Leavenworth. By this time Joe was so spaced on drugs that he had almost put Charles Harrelson out of his mind, but he realized in late July that Harrelson had failed to show up for his trial in Houston—so had Joe Chagra, of course. Now Harrelson was officially a fugitive. As the attorney for both Jimmy and Harrelson, Joe had placed himself in the middle of what could turn out to be one of the bloodiest legal battles in history. It occurred to Joe that he might become a target of the investigation too. He couldn't help that. A time could come when the conspirators would be forced to cut their losses and make some kind of deal with the government. Joe's loyalties, of course, were to his brother. In his drug-addled mind, he saw no choice but to play for time and hope that the status quo continued to bless both clients, and their attorney as well. He knew that the chances of that happening were slim to none. In the meantime, he had to do what he could to protect Jimmy.

In late August, Harrelson telephoned Joe Chagra, half off the wall because he had seen DEA agents perched in the trees outside Virginia Farah's home. Harrelson disappeared for a few days, then telephoned again from Houston with more wild stories about helicopters that were chasing him and little men who had bored holes through the bathroom wall of his motel. Harrelson insisted that Joe tape-record a rambling, nearly incoherent, but pointedly self-serving monologue in which he denied that he and Jimmy Chagra had conspired to kill Wood or anyone else. Joe had no way of knowing it at the time, but Harrelson had also scribbled his last will and testament on a desk calendar in the motel room. He asked to be cremated and that his ashes be strewn over the John H. Wood, Jr., Federal Courts Building in San Antonio. "What a travesty!" Harrelson wrote. He wrote about his love for Virginia Farah, and for other women, and came as close as he could to an apology: "I'm sorry, not for myself, but for the pain I've caused others, both those who loved me and those who loved the people I've killed. But I've never killed a person who was undeserving of it."

A few nights after the telephone call from Houston, Harrelson called Joe again, this time from a motel on the east side of El Paso. By coincidence, Joe had received another call from the same motel earlier that night, from one of Lee's former clients, William Mallow. Mallow had just escaped from federal prison in Colorado. He had warned Joe that he might, but Mallow had less than two years to serve and at the time Joe had dismissed the warning. Ninety percent of the convicted clients of any criminal lawyer were talking about escape; Lee had believed it was a healthy way to sublimate more harmful tendencies. But here he was in El Paso, a fugitive, staying at the same motel where another fugitive client, Charles Harrelson, was holed up. Later that night Joe introduced them—Mallow was interested in some cocaine.

When Joe Chagra picked up the paper the following morning, he almost had cardiac arrest. Mallow had been involved in a shootout with El Paso cops and was critically wounded, in the hospital. When the feds discovered that Mallow and Harrelson had been registered at the same motel—and they surely would—and that Joe Chagra had seen and talked to both, they would, of course, perceive it to be another piece of the big puzzle, though in fact it was only a bizarre coincidence along the trail littered with phony clues, innuendo, and mistaken motives. What happened a fortnight later was a clue, however, or at least a signal, that the mystery of Wood's killing was finally starting to unravel.

After his narrow escape from the scene of the shootout at the east side motel, Harrelson made his way back to Virginia Farah's house. He borrowed her Corvette, with some vague notion of heading for California, but a short time later he was zooming down I-10 in the opposite direction, shooting cocaine and seeing agents' faces twisting in the later-afternoon shadows. Somewhere east of Van Horn, he stopped for gas. The kid who filled the tank forgot to replace the gas cap, probably because he was distracted by the sight of the driver sitting next to a .44 magnum and a high-powered rifle, shooting cocaine into his forearm. A few miles down the highway, Harrelson began to smell the leaking gas and hear the muffler rattling. He stopped to inspect the muffler, which he determined was beyond repair. He decided to shoot it off with his .44 magnum but missed and shot out a rear tire on the Corvette instead. Motorists reported a crazed hitchhiker wearing cut-off blue jeans, no shirt, several gold chains around his neck, sandals, and a baseball hat—leaning against a white Corvette and pointing a gun at his head. When the police arrived a short time later, they discovered the hitchhicker to be the fugitive Charles Harrelson. He held them off for six hours, pressing the muzzle of the .44 against the side of his nose as he babbled and ranted. Finally, Virginia Farah was called to the scene. She talked to Harrelson and persuaded him to surrender. Before police hauled him off to the jail in Van Horn, Charles Harrelson confessed to the murder of John Wood. He also confessed to killing John F. Kennedy.

31

Jamie Boyd's ace in the hole was a seedy little informant named Robert "Comanche" Riojas, who was facing two long prison sentences—a twenty-year state charge for murder and heroin peddling, to be followed by a twenty-five-year federal conviction for hiring five Bexar County jail inmates to kill another prisoner. Riojas had been feeding bits and pieces of information to a certain FBI agent since a few days after the Wood murder. With the exception of this one agent, hardly anyone in the FBI believed anything Riojas said. It seemed apparent that Riojas was only interested in getting himself transferred from state prison to a more comfortable federal one. Even Riojas's lawyer, Alan Brown of San Antonio, had warned that his client was something less than creditable. "Riojas is a bad joke," Brown said. "He was always stopping by my office, asking the secretary if she wanted anyone murdered. One day he'd have a story about murdering five Mafia figures in New York, and the next day he'd be talking about a shipment of machine guns. Nobody in his right mind believed Riojas."

But little by little, Jamie Boyd was beginning to believe. Riojas knew the names of a lot of people who were already on the U.S. attorney's list of suspects, or people associated with suspects—gamblers and hitmen connected to what Jamie called the Dixie Mafia.

Boyd decided to place Riojas under the federal witness-protection program. He began to feel empathy with the little snitch, much as he had with Henry Wallace: Jamie's wife, Suzy, even baked a batch of cookies for Riojas. The snitch was making heavy demands. He wanted $350,000, and he wanted the government to arrange for him to have plastic surgery that would alter his identity. A $125,000 reward had been offered by a group of citizens for the conviction of

Wood's murderer, and the government could no doubt come up with a sizable offer of its own. Without naming Riojas, a government investigator told the Dallas *Morning News*: "What he [the witness] has said has proven out straight down the line. It also says something when he doesn't ask for the money until there's a conviction." In the beginning, Riojas had seemed reluctant to supply specifics, but now that the government seemed agreeable to his demands, he started dropping names. He mentioned Jack Strauss, who had gambled many times with Jimmy Chagra, and also Little Larry Culbreath, a San Antonio tough who used to run with the infamous Overton gang of Austin, until he was convicted of the contract killing of Timmie Overton. On the same day that Joe Chagra testified before the grand jury, Riojas told the panel that a San Antonio boxer named Bobby Thomas had driven the getaway car the day of Wood's murder. Thomas, also known as Kid Death, appeared before the grand jury a few weeks later, denying the whole story. Outside the federal courthouse, Kid Death told reporters: "Riojas is an idiot. Everybody knows that. I told them [the grand jury] he was a lunatic."

Far and away the most intriguing of Riojas's stories was the tale of two clandestine meetings, one shortly before the attempt on Kerr, and the other shortly after. At the first meeting, Riojas was told that the group planned to kill "someone big," a federal official: Riojas claimed that he was offered $100,000 and a cocaine connection in Colombia if he would supply murder weapons and dispose of them after the killing. He, of course, refused. Pressed for details about the offered cocaine connection, Riojas said that all he knew was that the same people who wanted the killing also had the connection. At the second meeting, after the attempt on Kerr, Riojas recalled a lot of laughter and talk about how they had sure "scared the little bastard," and how Kerr would think twice before he got in anyone else's hair. The two men who actually fired the volleys, Riojas added, had used a professional makeup artist to disguise their appearances. During this meeting the group discussed another hit "bigger than the Kerr deal." Later, at a party at his home, Riojas recalled one of the group telling him: "You know that big hit that's going down? It's gonna be a federal judge." Riojas even supplied the FBI with pictures taken at the party, pictures that identified some of the suspects he had been discussing. Jamie Boyd realized that any casual reader of headlines could have concocted this story, but then Riojas supplied another detail that eventually led to the first pieces of what Jamie Boyd considered hard evidence—registration records from the Sea Gun resort motel, located just across Copano Bay from Wood's own resort home at Key Allegro.

The records established that Little Larry Culbreath and some other gamblers and gunmen had checked into the resort in January 1979, and had left in a big hurry just before deputies from the Aransas County Sheriff's Department could raid the room. One of the men looked a lot like Charles Harrelson, according to a motel employee who examined some FBI photographs. During their stay, the men rented a boat to take them across the bay to Key Allegro, rented it three days in a row. The boat captain described the men as "big spenders." While they were registered at the Sea Gun, the men made nearly a hundred long-distance calls, many to casinos in Las Vegas. When they realized they were about to be raided, the men split with only the clothing on their backs. In addition to articles of clothing, they left behind a TV set, airline tickets, cassette tape recordings, gambling paraphernalia, a taxicab receipt, a sexual-aid device, even a sack of dog food. The fact that all this took place four months before Wood was killed reinforced the U.S. attorney's belief that the killers had stalked Wood for months.

Jack Lawn, the recently appointed agent-in-charge of the San Antonio FBI office, was not enthralled with Riojas's stories. The fact that some gamblers and thugs had used a Gulf Coast motel for a high-stakes game hardly implicated them in the Wood assassination. High rollers used resorts like the Sea Gun all the time, as Riojas must have known. Riojas clearly was desperate to get out of prison, and when a public defender who happened to be visiting the state prison on the day Wood was murdered casually mentioned the killing to Riojas, the snitch jumped at the bait. In the eighteen months since Riojas had started jabbering, considerable damage had been done, not only to the Wood investigation, but to a number of innocent and respectable people. One Riojas story had caused the resignation of a high-ranking San Antonio police officer, and another had delayed the confirmation of a federal judge. The suspect who most interested Jack Lawn at the moment was Charles Harrelson, who had just been arrested following his wild spree near Van Horn, and was now facing enough state charges to put him away for years.

The FBI file on Charles Voyde Harrelson went back twenty years.

It traced a path from the mean, unyielding farm and lumber towns of southeastern Texas, where Harrelson grew up, to the upper levels of middle-class luxury in Houston, Dallas, Los Angeles, and Las Vegas. Charles was the sixth and final child born to Voyde Harrelson and his wife. Though Voyde Harrelson owned an eighty-two-acre farm, he supplemented the family income by working on construction projects at the State Department of Corrections main prison unit at Huntsville. Charles's uncle was a warden at the prison, and two older brothers were law-enforcement officers. One later became an FBI agent, and the other an expert polygraph examiner. When Charles was eight years old, his mother and father divorced, and he was raised by an older sister, Sybil.

Most of his boyhood years were spent in the tiny crossroads town of Lovelady—it was a café, a general store, a feed mill, a stop light, and a sign pointing to the Eastham Unit of the state prison. It was a fundamentalist town, not so much conservative as reactionary, a town that dared and begged young people to escape. Charles dreamed of little else. He was a bright, restless kid, and if he had a single passion it was his burning desire to get rich. By high school he was shuttling back and forth between Huntsville and Lovelady, playing football, singing in the a capella choir and running with a tough crowd, which included his friend Pete Kay. Pete also had an uncle who was a warden at the Texas Deparement of Corrections, and his father was Harrelson's father's boss on the TDC construction project. Kay remembered that for entertainment they learned to cheat at cards: they used to stand for hours in front of a mirror, practicing.

Midway through his junior year at Huntsville High School, Charles dropped out and joined the Navy. A few years later, while on leave in Houston, he met and married a secretary named Diane. When he was discharged, they moved to Los Angeles and Harrelson took one of the few straight jobs he ever had, selling encyclopedias from door to door. He was a great success at selling, and talked about enrolling in technical school, but then his wife left him and his plans got sidetracked. The following year, 1960, Harrelson was arrested for the first time, for theft in Orange County, California. He confessed to a string of crimes that he hadn't actually committed. "He was just a punk then, just bragging," recalls famed Texas criminal attorney Percy Foreman, who became Harrelson's lawyer a few years later when his troubles got considerably more serious. The fact that he

221

would brag to police about crimes he never committed said something about Charles Harrelson's deep resentments and needs, both of which he equated with money: where money was concerned, Charles seemed in no way inhibited by conscience. As a kid who grew up in the shadows of prison, he knew the code against snitches, knew the sense of honor in being considered a "standup guy," but when he was charged again in California, he purchased his freedom by informing on another police character, who was later sentenced to death. By the mid-1960s, Harrelson was back in Texas, making his living as a card-player and free-lance debt collector. He drove big cars and wore expensive clothes and a lot of jewelry; he was a compulsive buyer who liked to spend money without counting it, and who went out of his way to give the appearance that he had never in his life worked up a sweat doing honest work. "Money is the easiest thing in the world to make," he said once. "You could drop me broke and buck naked in the middle of downtown Houston, and in six months I'd be wearing custom-made suits and driving a Cadillac."

In the fall of 1968, Charles Harrelson was a fugitive on the run: he had been indicted in Kansas City for possessing an unregistered shotgun, and faced two separate charges of murder for hire in Texas. A key government witness in both murder cases was his former lover, Sandra Sue Attaway. Harrelson was finally arrested in Atlanta, where he was living under the name of Terry Southern, and returned to Angleton, Texas, a town near the Gulf Coast where he had been indicted for the killing of a wealthy playboy gambler, Alan Berg.

According to the indictment, Berg was killed on May 28, 1968. The date was uncertain, because Berg had been missing for some time when Sandra Sue Attaway's new boyfriend, Bernard Weadock, responding to a $10,000 reward posted by the missing playboy's father, led police to Berg's skeleton in a clump of cedars near the beach at Freeport. A rope was tied around the skeleton's neck, and there were two bullet holes in the skull. Sandra Sue told police that Berg, who had part interest in a carpet company, owed $7,000 to the owner of a decorating company, who paid Harrelson $1,500 to settle things for good.

In his own investigation, Percy Foreman learned that Berg had probably been killed at the orders of big-time gamblers: the playboy had apparently spread a rumor that the UCLA–University of Houston playoff basketball game was fixed in Houston's favor, and when

UCLA won handily, some big money went down the hole. Whatever the motive, Sandra Sue Attaway told a convincing story about how she lured Alan Berg out of the Brass Jug Club in Houston and into a red Cadillac, where Harrelson was waiting. They drove Berg to an isolated island near Freeport, where Harrelson first tried to strangle him with a rope, then fired two .25-caliber bullets into Berg's head. Sandra Sue remembered the date as May 28, the same day Berg was reported missing.

Percy Foreman had counted on this. The famed attorney had taken the case partly because he knew Harrelson's family (and partly because he wanted the deed to the eighty-two-acre family farm, which Harrelson had agreed to sign over to Foreman as the lawyer's fee), and now was prepared to do his courtroom magic. After first telling the jury that any of eleven men could have killed Alan Berg, he produced two surprise alibi witnesses—J. V. and Leon Price, members of the most powerful political family in Trinity County. The brothers testified that on May 28, Charles Harrelson was one hundred miles from the scene of the murder, negotiating the sale of a quarter horse.

Though acquitted in the Berg killing, Harrelson wasn't free: he was transferred to another jail in Edinburgh, in the Rio Grande Valley at the extreme southern tip of Texas, charged with the hired murder of grain dealer, Sam Degelia, Jr., whose body had been found in an abandoned pumphouse a month after the Berg murder. Again, Sandra Sue Attaway was a key witness—she claimed that Harrelson told her he was hired by Degelia's business partner, Pete Scamardo. The motive for this murder was supposed to have been a $50,000 insurance policy, allegedly payable to Scamardo. This time Harrelson's fee was $2,000. The prosecution produced an eyewitness, Jerry O'Brien Watkins, a gun runner who once posed as a CIA agent and tried to buy weapons for anti-Castro Cuban exiles in Miami, a scam that also involved Charles Harrelson. Watkins testified that he was with Harrelson when they picked up Degelia at a Holiday Inn in McAllen and drove him to the abandoned pumphouse. Watkins waited in the car while Harrelson, a .25-caliber pistol in hand, marched Degelia into the pumphouse and fired several shots. When Harrelson reappeared, the gun still in his hand, he told Watkins: "This is not the first son of a bitch I had to ring the bell on and won't be the last. Now move!"

Once again, Percy Foreman did his magic. First, he cast doubt on the alleged motive, establishing that the insurance money didn't go to Scamardo, as the state contended, but to the bank. Then, in a dramatic and startling demonstration, he fired a .25-caliber blank at the courtroom ceiling, using a .44-caliber pistol, thus proving that Degelia wasn't *necessarily* killed with Harrelson's gun. But again Foreman saved the biggest surprise for last. He produced another alibi witness, a nightclub singer named Louise Scott Gannon, who testified that she was having dinner with Harrelson at the time of the murder. The trial ended in a hung jury. When Harrelson was tried again two years later, Miss Gannon had moved to the Bahamas and was not available to testify. The state had gone into the case demanding the death penalty, but was happy when the jury gave Harrelson fifteen years. By the time Charles Harrelson was finally transferred to Leavenworth on the old Kansas City gun charge, he had done more than three years in various county jails (a state record for unconvicted inmates) and four years in the state prison at Huntsville. Though Harrelson sometimes made it sound as though he had spent half his life in Leavenworth, he was actually there only two years and one month before being released on parole.

When Charles Harrelson walked out of Leavenworth in September 1978, there was a rented limousine waiting for him, a token from a young woman he had never met, but who had seen him once during the Berg trial. Harrelson was acutely aware that many young women, and many older ones, too, found him irresistibly attractive, and he made the most of this asset. After he had returned to Texas and looked up his old pal Pete Kay, then met and married Kay's former lover, Jo Ann Starr, Harrelson had a secret affair with Jo Ann's daughter, Teresa Starr Jasper, and another affair with his friend Hampton Robinson's wife, whose name was also Jo Ann. At the time he was arrested near Van Horn, he claimed to be wildly in love with Virginia Farah, but then, as he FBI file revealed, he claimed a lot of things. His claim to having murdered John Wood would have been a lot stronger if he hadn't also claimed to have assassinated President Kennedy.

Not long after the arrest in Van Horn, when FBI agent-in-charge Jack Lawn decided to take another look at Charles Harrelson, one of the Houston attorneys who was representing Harrelson approached Jamie Boyd with a deal. Harrelson would plead guilty to killing Wood, provided the government met certain conditions. First,

Harrelson wanted assurances that he would be the prisoner of federal rather than state authorities: the state had a death penalty for murder. Also, he wanted it understood that he would not testify against anyone else, that he would take the full rap, quiet and clean. He wanted the government to promise him less than a life sentence, and he wanted to serve his time in Leavenworth. Percy Foreman had observed that the happiest time in Harrelson's life was when he was doing his stretch at Leavenworth. "He probably had more respect in Leavenworth than anywhere else he'd been," Foreman said. "The hired killer has a certain aura about him. I'm sure he was happy in an environment where he was the upper crust of the establishment."

Even if the Justice Department had been willing to strike a deal with the man who had pulled the trigger on a federal judge, Jamie Boyd believed that he saw through the halfhearted offer. For one thing, the Houston lawyer who made the offer on Harrelson's behalf wanted something for himself—a pardon from a gun rap that presently barred him from practicing in federal court. Harrelson's self-interest was apparent: he faced a possible life sentence on state charges in Houston and Van Horn, and state prisons were hard and cruel, all the things Harrelson had been trying to escape all his life. Under it all, Jamie Boyd didn't really believe Harrelson had anything to do with Wood's murder, though he might know who did. Jamie was still following the twisted trail laid out by Robert "Comanche" Riojas.

When Harrelson learned that his offer had been rejected, he sent word to the U.S. attorney that he knew something only the killer could know: that one of the tires on Wood's station wagon was punctured just before the assassination. The newspapers had reported that the station wagon had a flat tire, but only the investigators, and presumably the killer, knew the tire had been *punctured*.

Jack Lawn wasn't even sure the killer was responsible for the flat. It didn't make sense. If the killer had been stalking Wood, he surely knew that Wood always drove his Chevrolet sedan to the office. The sedan had the judge's official parking sticker. Nobody except Wood and his wife knew that on the morning of the murder the station wagon was due to be taken to the garage for repairs, or that Wood planned to follow his wife and then drive her downtown.

From his review of the file, Jack Lawn knew one thing for sure:

Charles Harrelson was a killer. Not a mad-dog killer, not a whacko who got off on the act itself, but a man who would do anything, absolutely anything, for money. Not a lot of money—$1,000, maybe $2,000, that had been his price ten years ago. By the fall of 1980, Jack Lawn had information that a pregnant woman had delivered a bag of cash to a young woman from Texas, probably one of Harrelson's lovers, maybe even his stepdaughter, Teresa Starr Jaspar. The FBI didn't know where the money was delivered—they had heard Corpus Christi, and also Brownsville—but they believed that the amount was $250,000. Though a trifling sum by Jimmy Chagra's standards, it was more than enough by Charles Harrelson's. A Harris County (Houston) assistant district attorney, Charles A. Rosenthal, Jr., said everything that needed to be said: "Someday when my kids study the real bad Texas outlaws, they're gonna find Charles Harrelson's name right up there with John Wesley Hardin."

32

Patty Chagra knew that things were desperate, even if Joe didn't. Joe hardly talked to Patty or anyone else anymore, unless he was scaled up on cocaine, and then he rattled on like a broken record. In recent weeks, he snorted coke all night and slept all day, and even when his brain emerged from the shadows he seemed to be preoccupied, inarticulate, and lost. His law practice was almost nonexistent, except for Harrelson and Jimmy. Patty had threatened to leave him.

"You're more alone living with someone doing coke than if he's not around at all," she said. Worse than the coke was its symptom—the easy money that had filtered down from Jimmy's smuggling operation. Even before Lee's murder, Joe used to stay up all night counting money and snorting cocaine. She'd seen the effects of the money on the entire family. The jewelry, the expensive cars, the airs and pretense. The Chagras used to be simple, decent people, a trifle eccentric, to be sure, but true to their code and ancestral traditions. Now they were acting like the Lebanese Hillbillies.

The money was more of a narcotic than the cocaine, as Patty began to realize. Many of the toys that Jimmy collected before he went to prison had come into Joe's possession, and now Joe couldn't live without them. Joe had bought his 1978 Mercedes-Benz with Jimmy's money—it was supposed to be his "fee." But it wasn't the car that he needed—what he really needed was the symbol, the show, the demonstration that he, too, was a Chagra, able to support the appearance of new affluence. Patty drove a more modest Mercedes-Benz; but except for their home and the two cars, about the only thing they really owned independent of Jimmy was a kennel in the Upper Valley. Patty had borrowed money from her parents to make a down payment on the kennel, and she took a special pride in grooming and training animals and making the kennel, which she called the Spa for Paws, the best of its kind in El Paso. Lately, Jimmy had been looking for fresh funds and talking about selling off all the gifts he had lavished on members of the family—apparently Jimmy was encountering large gambling debts, even in prison. The kennel was one thing he couldn't touch.

Patty thought, too, about her own small children, Joseph and Samantha. What did they have to look forward to, growing up in El Paso? What did anyone named Chagra have to look forward to in El Paso? Lee's son, Leader, though still in high school, was already gambling for sums that most people couldn't make in a year: they heard he'd had $20,000 riding on last year's Super Bowl. The nightmare seemed endless. Jimmy and Jack Stricklin and others had been indicted in May, just two months before the statute of limitations expired, for the 1975 marijuana shipment to Gloucester, Massachusetts, and Jimmy was almost sure to have time added to the thirty years he was already serving. Now Joe was involving himself in the Wood investigation.

By the fall of 1980, Patty was beginning to piece together the events of that summer, the visits to Virginia Farah's home, the whispers and secret conversations between her husband and the mysterious Charles Harrelson, the cocaine that appeared so frequently. "It was a weird situation," she said. "Charles was so charming you wouldn't believe it. You'd see him playing with the kids or mowing the grass and realize that here was a man who bragged about killing people." Harrelson had never told Patty that he had anything to do with Wood's murder, but it was clear from his attitude that he believed killing had improved the judge. Harrelson advocated a number of novel theories about his favorite topic, the American system. The *system* had brainwashed the public, Charlie believed; television shows such as "The Mod Squad" and "Mission Impossible" were designed to influence people to snitch on their friends and neighbors. Harrelson talked in terms of Ks and Gs and "big ones," and about cold-decking people with marked cards, and yet considered himself a member of the "public" locked in deadly combat with the "system."

Jimmy telephoned his brother from Leavenworth almost every day, sometimes several times in the same day, getting updates on the grand jury investigation, passing along prison rumors, and checking the betting line on football games. Jimmy had a running, big-stakes gin game with another inmate named Travis Erwin, who had once run with the Timmie Overton gang in Austin. Jimmy didn't know that Travis Erwin was being backed by a high roller in Las Vegas, who paid him a percentage to keep the scam on Chagra alive, even behind the walls. Jimmy owed tens of thousands of dollars to the old con, and was making plans to win it back when Travis Erwin was found dead in his cell in October, an apparent heart-attack victim, though in Leavenworth you could never be certain: heart attacks could be arranged.

On October 11, Jimmy telephoned Joe to tell him about Travis Erwin and get an update:

"So how are you doing, bro? Are you gonna get me out?"

"Oh, brother, you're getting out, man," Joe assured him. "You're getting out. There's no doubt in my mind."

"I gotta get out, brother."

"What happened to Travis?"

"He died, man. He died on me. Hey, get me out of this fucking jail, will you?"

In the six months since Jimmy had started doing his stretch at Leavenworth, almost every conversation had been the same. Jimmy kept saying he couldn't do the time, and Joe kept assuring him that his release was imminent, though, of course, Joe knew this wasn't true. A few days later, Jimmy telephoned Liz and instructed her to meet the wife of an inmate friend who would be arriving at El Paso International that night, to have cash ready. "Give her four-three-five," he said, meaning $43,500. "That's Travis's debt." Liz understood the code. "May he rest in peace," she told Jimmy. She wasn't happy about her husband's continuing gambling, though, like Joe, she believed it was her duty, at least during the early months of his incarceration, to appease Jimmy and make his ordeal as painless as possible. Liz had put herself on a budget, but she couldn't put Jimmy on one. "You've already spent more than half of what I planned to live on for the next year," she reminded him, as gently as possible. Jimmy told her he had a deal on a new mink cape, if she was interested: his new prison buddy and protector, Jerry Ray James, could arrange it. It was James's wife, in fact, who was arriving that night to collect Travis Erwin's money.

Jerry Ray James, an infamous desperado considered by lawmen in the Southwest to be the modern equivalent of Dillinger or Machine

Gun Kelly, had been transferred to Leavenworth in June, following the bloody rioting that virtually destroyed the New Mexico State Penitentiary at Santa Fe. James had been doing the equivalent of two life sentences in Santa Fe; he was supposed to have led the riot. While the New Mexico prison was being repaired, its inmates were housed at various federal institutions. James went to Leavenworth—where he had already done three stretches.

Within days of his arrival at Leavenworth, Jerry Ray James managed to meet and become fast friends with Jimmy Chagra. Travis Erwin introduced them. James seemed to know every police officer in Texas—Erwin, Little Larry Culbreath, Timmie Overton, Charlie Overton. News reports claimed he once ran with the Overton gang, but according to an FBI bulletin, the Overtons ran with "the James gang." The bulletin, published in 1967 when James was on the FBI's Ten Most Wanted List, noted that James "fancies himself as a modern-day Al Capone. . . . he reportedly told associates he will not be taken alive by law enforcement officers." Of course he *had* been taken alive, repeatedly; most recently in 1977 in Roswell, New Mexico, where he was later given two life sentences for robbery and for being a habitual criminal. He was preceded at Leavenworth by his king-size reputation as a hardnosed, stir-wise con with a well-known hatred for snitches, the kind of inmate who automatically takes charge anywhere he is sent. James appeared to have immediately taken Jimmy Chagra under his wing, and had even applied to transfer to Chagra's cellblock. He told Jimmy details of the Santa Fe prison riots, how he had broken into the comptroller's safe and removed the prison's master list of informants, and how he had personally killed nine snitches. The riot leaders hadn't merely killed snitches and guards, they had ritualistically butchered them—there were stories of decapitations, of cutting off genitals, of ramming ax handles up rectums, and welding body parts together with blowtorches. If there was such a thing as a Dixie Mafia, Jerry Ray James was surely its godfather.

Jimmy had been waiting for weeks for a visit from his family, and when they arrived at Leavenworth in the late part of October, he was jumpy and irritable. He couldn't stop talking about all the money they were spending, *his* money. "How can you spend five thousand dollars a month!" he asked Liz. He called his sister Patsy "a bitch" and noted that she "spends more money than Carter's got pills," and he reminded Mom Chagra that he was the one who had bought her $20,000 Cadillac, not Lee, as Mom had told reporters.

"Listen, Jimmy, let me tell you something," Mom Chagra said. "Don't judge people!"

"When I get out of here, I'm gonna be broke," Jimmy wailed.

Liz said: "Don't you just want to get out, though?"

"And have to go back to work?"

"No. Well, that's what's gonna happen. You won't be broke."

"I've already blown a million since I've been here," Jimmy reminded her.

"That's because you trusted your brother with the money," Liz said. "That's your fault."

Speaking in the native tongue of Lebanon, which Jimmy alone among her children understood, Mom Chagra said something about the *Massadi*, telling Jimmy that he should not be bitter about it. Jimmy told his mother in Arabic, "They're gonna kill him this week." Mom said: "May God curse them!" Then he turned again to Liz and said sarcastically: "You believe money comes out of raindrops, don't you?" It must have struck members of his family as peculiar, this obsession with money at a time when he was facing thirty years and a possibility of being charged with the murder of a federal judge, but, as usual, Jimmy had a way of looking on the bright side. They didn't know, of course, that he was at that moment planning a jailbreak. He was counting on Jerry Ray James and another inmate named Calvin Wright to help him. James was transferring to Chagra's cellblock that same day, and Wright, a shadowy figure who had worked as a mercenary for Air America (CIA), was scheduled for release in a few years. When Wright got his freedom, so would Jimmy Chagra—or that's what Jimmy made himself believe.

Later that day, when he was transferred to the new cellblock, Jerry Ray James got Chagra into a long conversation about Charles Harrelson. James wasn't sure if he remembered Harrelson from the old days at Leavenworth, but he seemed fascinated about the details of the Wood investigation, Harrelson's arrest in Van Horn, Jimmy's troubles, a whole range of events that Jimmy enjoyed recalling to his new friend.

"But he didn't say he killed Judge Wood?"

"Yes, he did," Jimmy said.

James said that Calvin Wright told him that Harrelson left a

231

note confessing the Wood murder, a revelation that Jimmy hadn't heard, and that Harrelson had also mentioned that Little Larry Culbreath killed Wood, another piece of news to Jimmy. What worried him, James said, was that Harrelson might flip. All the government needed was "corroboration."

"No, he's all right," Jimmy said. "Charlie's all right, man. He was just flipped out for a couple of days. . . . "

"But Jimmy, if they indict this son of a bitch, they're gonna put so much pressure on him. Well, Travis says he's a hell of a guy."

"Hell of a guy," Jimmy agreed. Jimmy tried to change the subject to the betting line of the weekend's football games, but Jerry Ray James couldn't get off the subject of Harrelson and the Wood murder. He had a surprising store of information on the subject, though Jimmy perhaps didn't notice this.

"Where will he be indicted? In what city?"

Jimmy said that his lawyers had affidavits claiming that Harrelson was in Houston the day Wood was killed. James corrected him: "It was Dallas or somewhere." Jimmy said that his brother, Joe, told him that the government snitch, Riojas, was talking about Jack Strauss and Little Larry Culbreath. James said that Travis had told him that Little Larry was bragging at a poker game that he knew who had killed Wood. This was yet another piece of news to Jimmy, who didn't know Culbreath at all. "Oh, yeah," James said. "Travis said that Larry was questioned a day after the murder. He was driving Charlie's car, too."

"Gee," said Jimmy Chagra. "I didn't know that."

"I don't know if it's true or not," James told him. Jimmy observed how nice it was, now that James had been transferred to his cellblock: Now they could talk without twenty people interfering.

"Goddam, I hope that's not true about Charlie getting indicted," Jerry Ray James said.

The family was worried about Liz. She was falling apart. A few days after their visit to Leavenworth, she collapsed and had to be hospitalized. When Jimmy phoned home that night, Joe told him: "She had a seizure of some sort. Her eyes kind of got real weird and she passed out." Joe didn't mention that Jimmy's wife was again using drugs heavily, but then Jimmy already knew that. He also didn't mention that when she passed out, she was with a certain jewelry salesman that she was seeing on the side. Jimmy was fairly certain

Liz was having an affair—she loved to drop hints, to feel his displeasure and his helplessness—but he had no idea of her lover's identity. This would have been particularly painful, as Jimmy and Liz had agreed to sell some of her jewelry and she was necessarily seeing a great deal of the jewelry salesman. Before hanging up, Joe told his brother that he had received a letter from "this Harrelson guy," who had been transferred from Van Horn to the Harris County Jail in Houston. "He wants to talk to me," Joe said.

"I wonder what he wants?"

"I don't know."

"Fucking idiot."

"That's what I'm gonna go find out."

Jimmy telephoned Joe again about fifteen minutes after this conversation to tell him that FBI agents were at Leavenworth interviewing his friend Calvin. It had something to do with Harrelson. The more Jimmy thought about it, the more he was sure Joe ought to represent Harrelson. That way they could keep an eye on him. "He needs help in this thing," Jimmy said. "They're making insinuations that I had something to do with it."

When he left the Harris County Jail and started walking back to his hotel in downtown Houston, Joe Chagra realized he was shaking so violently he was about to pass out. He hadn't known what to expect from his visit with Charles Harrelson, but he certainly hadn't expected *this*. Now there was no doubt that Harrelson had killed the judge. Harrelson had told Joe as much the first day they met, but until now Joe had never been certain. Harrelson had left out many of the details of the assassination, but one detail he did provide kept ricocheting around Joe's brain: "*I saw him quiver, then twist and drop in his tracks. I knew it had been a perfect shot.*" Today, Harrelson had supplied more details. He told Joe about the murder weapon: he had buried it just east of Dallas, near Lake Ray Hubbard. The only other person who knew where the gun was buried was his wife, Jo Ann, and Harrelson hinted darkly that he would see that she didn't live to tell. He drew a map, showing Joe the location. The map lacked detail—it showed a Stuckey's near an exit on I-20, then a large area that included Lake Ray Hubbard. If there really was a gun out there, a person would have to dig up a hundred square miles to find it. As soon as Joe returned to El Paso, he ran the map through the shredder in his office, but later he drew it again from memory and locked it in his safe at home. He learned later that Harrelson had apparently told at least one other person about the gun. A man Joe had met before told him that he had actually found the gun but had been too frightened to touch it. He asked Joe to contribute money to Harrelson's defense, even though Joe was already contributing his time as an attorney. Joe told Patty about this, and they agreed it sounded like a setup to trick him into looking for the gun, to trick him into implicating himself in the murder. A few months after that, someone broke into Joe's office: he believed it was the FBI looking for the map.

Less than twenty-four hours after his shocking conversation with Harrelson, Joe was in the visiting room at Leavenworth, discussing it with Jimmy. The really peculiar part of his talk with Harrelson, Joe said, was that Harrelson didn't even remember writing a letter asking Joe to visit him: luckily, Joe had brought the letter with him. He didn't believe a word Harrelson told him, and yet he was afraid not to believe: Harrelson was playing some game Joe couldn't comprehend.

"They're gonna indict me," Jimmy said sullenly.

"No, they're not."

"Why not?"

"They ain't got enough to indict you."

"Is he standing up?"

"He says he is. I'll tell you what I'd like to do. You know I told you he told me where the gun was? I'd really like to go get it. That would be the only thing that could—"

"Where'd he tell you it was?"

"He drew me a map. I'd really like to go and see. That's the only thing that can back up his story. And if they can trace anything—"

"That's what I'm saying," Jimmy interrupted. "What did Charlie sound like? Crazy?"

"He's nuts. He's full of shit."

"Well, did he sound like he's—"

"He's just fine. As far as standing up and all that, he's fine."

"Are you sure?"

"Yeah."

"You're sure!"

"I'm as sure as I can be," Joe told his brother. "He's going to

234

trial [in Houston] on December 1. If he gets convicted and he gets life, then I'll worry about the cocksucker, 'cause then he'll try to make a deal."

"Well, shit, they're already offering him deals, Joe."

"No, they haven't offered him any deals."

"You mean you're worried. Well, he's gonna get life."

"He thinks he might beat this case."

"If he beats it," Jimmy said, "I'm worried."

"I'm not. It might have been a bad search or something like that."

"They were here questioning Calvin. They know Harrelson did it."

"They think he did it."

"Who's Riojas saying did it?"

"He said some people from San Antonio did it, and Jack Strauss was with 'em. He's full of shit. He's looking at thirty-five years or something. He's trying to get out of it."

"Yeah, but . . . is Riojas saying I did it?"

"No, fuck no!"

"He's saying Little Larry did it?"

"Little Larry's got something to do with it. It was a waste of time, going to see Harrelson," Joe said. "I don't like Charlie."

"The guy's gonna talk. He's talking already."

"I don't think so. I think that's his ace in the hole."

"Maybe you better go get that thing, man."

"I've been trying to think of some reason to fly to Dallas," Joe said. "It's right outside of Dallas. You have to fly into Dallas, and then rent a car, or else I can drive it."

"I'd drive from El Paso if I were you."

"I've got to have a story, though. A reason to be going there. I'm thinking of going to Dallas, legitimately, and talking to this lawyer that represented Harrelson in front of the grand jury, looking at his affidavits. He says it's right outside of Dallas, forty-five minutes. He says it's buried. . . . I'll need a metal detector."

"It's a perfect setup to get you."

"That's what bothers me."

"Has Virginia Farah talked to him?"

"Yeah, she won't talk to him anymore. They're really on her ass. They want her to take a lie-detector test."

"She told them you were up there visiting him?"

"Yeah, that I'd been there with Patty and the kids, which I had."

"I told you not to do that, you know. I told you not to do that from the start. And you think you're so—"

"Well, we did it!" Joe said flatly.

"Sure you did it. What good is it to me if you're in jail, too?"

"I'm not going to jail!"

"Boy, you sure underestimate 'em, don't you?"

"I don't underestimate anybody. I haven't done anything. What have I done? What am I going to jail for?"

"I don't know, but they're gonna try to put that on you. You don't have to do anything to go to jail, you know. There's fucking thirty thousand people in here that ain't done nothing."

"They've done something. They've all done something to be sitting here."

"You've done something, too, Joe."

"What have I done?"

"You know Harrelson knocked off the judge."

"I don't know that," Joe said, then laughed despite himself. Jimmy had that needling way of making Joe feel guilty, of making Joe share a blame that rightfully couldn't be shared by anyone. Jimmy was willful and domineering, a bully and a braggart with nearly everyone he knew, but he was an absolute tyrant with his younger brother. Joe's inclination had always been to placate Jimmy, to laugh it off and promise to support whatever ridiculous plan Jimmy might consider. If Jimmy had suggested blowing up the Pentagon, Joe would probably have agreed.

Joe laughed again, and Jimmy smiled at him and said: "Yeah, you don't know that. Shit!"

"I don't know if he did it or not. Maybe he did. Maybe Little Larry did it."

"Look, the FBI knows I hired him to do this. They know that. Do they or not?"

"No, they don't know. They don't know. They can't prove it."

"They'll get someone so say—"

Joe interrupted, putting the answer in the form of a question: "They'll take the word of the worst guy in the world?"

"They don't have to prove it, Joe. Can I tell you something? They'll get liars to get up there and say it."

"Say what?"

"Anything they want them to say, anything!"

236

"This isn't a marijuana case, Jimmy. It's the murder of a federal judge. They're not going to indict someone unless they've got a strong case against him. What are they gonna do, offer Harrelson immunity to get *you*?

"Yeah! Of course."

"The guy that did it? I'd like to see that."

"Do you want to bet that they'd do that?"

"Well, I'd like to see it."

"Well, I'm willing to bet a lifetime that they would do that, Joe. They'll let Charlie Harrelson walk, if they can get me for hiring—"

"I can't believe that. . . . I can't believe that the jury would go for it."

"What do you mean? They're gonna have their own jury . . . their own jury. They don't have to buy a jury, all they have to do is pick the right ones."

"So what can we do? What do you want?"

Jimmy watched while a young girl studied the vending machine and made her selection. They could hear the murmurs and laughter, and sometimes catch words and phrases, as other convicts visited with their families or lawyers. Jimmy moved his chair closer to the table and whispered: "Off Harrelson! Off him, if we can get away with it. Which jail is—"

"Harris County Jail," Joe said dryly.

"Is he in solitary confinement or anything?"

"By himself."

"He's in solitary?"

"You're solving one problem and creating another."

"Here, let me ask you, if that's the case, let me ask you—"

"You think James is so solid, man. Why is he any more solid than Harrelson?"

"Because," Jimmy said, "James is a completely different type of person, completely. Are you kidding me, man? A solid sonuvabitch!"

"Well, you know, I don't like your judge of character. You liked Henry Wallace."

"I never liked Henry Wallace," Jimmy said defensively.

"Oh, you did, too!"

"I never did like him."

"You loved him!"

"Are you crazy?"

237

It was no use, Joe realized. They had argued about Jerry Ray James before, almost from the time James arrived at Leavenworth four months earlier. Joe had received a letter from an inmate at La Tuna, where James had spent a few weeks before being transferred to Leavenworth, stating flatly that James was a snitch who had already carved out a deal to nail Jimmy Chagra. Knowing Jerry Ray James's reputation, it hadn't made a lot of sense, but the more Joe thought about those two life sentences and the reward money and the other benefits, the more he distrusted James.

Jimmy had talked to Jerry Ray James and the other inmates about his plan to escape Leavenworth, and also about his plan to put out a contract on the snitch that put him there in the first place, Henry Wallace. He'd heard Wallace was living in Texarkana. One evening as Chagra, James, and some others were enjoying a picnic in the recreation area of the cellblock, James brought up the subject of "that witness in Texarkana" again.

"You still want that done?" he asked Jimmy.

"Yeah."

James, a heavyset, portly man who moved and talked with great deliberation, opened a soft drink and took a slice of onion for his hot dog. In his glory days, James had had dark, curly hair, but most of it was gone now, and what remained was almost snow-white. He looked a little like Burl Ives. "We might be able to get that on now," he said in a low voice. "Try some of this tomato. Let me borrow your salt."

"Okay," Jimmy said. "Send him by." Jimmy talked about how Wallace should just "disappear" as he placed the tomato in his hot-dog bun.

"Them bodies will show," James reminded him. "That's when the . . . goddam it, this son of a bitch is so ripe it's unbelievable! Yeah, as long as they don't ever find the body, they can't do shit."

Jimmy changed the subject to pinochle—Jerry Ray James had taken seven packs of cigarettes off him playing pinochle. He had taken a lot more than that off Chagra playing poker and gin: James had pretty much replaced Travis Erwin in Jimmy's life, for which Jimmy was extremely grateful. He was the only con in the cellblock who could laugh at Jimmy and get away with it.

James urged Jimmy to try some more tomatoes, and said he was a little worried that his friend, the hit man, might "buck when he finds out . . . what goddam heat you fellows have been in. He's a real careful guy."

Jimmy said: "They're liable to think that Wallace bucked too because he's that kinda sleaze, you know?"

As he had many times in the past few weeks, the old con reminded his younger friend that the murder weapon was the single most damning piece of evidence in the conspiracy. If there was one thing Jerry Ray James knew about, it was killing, and getting away with it. It took a special kind of man to kill. And a special kind to get away with it. "You ought to try to get that motherfucker back, Jimmy."

"Are you crazy?" Jimmy asked. "I'm not even sure there is a gun. I'm not even sure the fucker even did it. I think your other friend—"

"Little Larry?" James said, smiling. "Larry ain't got the nuts, man."

Jerry Ray James crumpled the empty soft-drink can in his fist and lobbed it into the litter basket, shaking his head at the sad conditions of modern society. In his day, he told Chagra, kids were taught from early childhood to be standup dudes. These days they were taught to be snitches. It was the system that was to blame.

"Now in school, teachers start telling you . . . all it is is just a reflection on society . . . the things they're doing now."

"Boy, there's some rotten motherfuckers in here," Jimmy Chagra agreed.

33

On Sunday, November 16, 1980, Jimmy telephoned Joe in panic. The FBI had just spent two more days with Calvin. They had played some tapes of a man—Calvin was sure it was Harrelson—talking to two women. Jerry Ray James now had Jimmy convinced that Harrelson had probably taped every conversation he'd ever had: James claimed that a friend of his, who worked in the U.S. attorney's office in Austin, told him the FBI had seized three boxes of tapes when they searched Virginia Farah's home. The thought of all those tapes had unhinged Jimmy.

Joe reassured his brother. Joe had been there when the FBI searched Virginia's house. They had gone through Harrelson's clothes, and they had tried to alarm Virginia by saying things like "Here's the shirt he wore" and "This is the belt buckle that guy described," but Joe knew it was a bluff—they hadn't even seized the clothes, much less any incriminating tapes. Nevertheless, Jimmy wanted Joe to come immediately to Leavenworth, to leave that night, and to take statements from Calvin Wright, from James, from the FBI, from anyone at Leavenworth who was talking about the Wood murder.

"I'm tired of getting railroaded around here," Jimmy said. "The problem now is, they're trying to implicate you."

Joe knew that, but he couldn't leave town for at least several days: he had two federal cases set for trial the following morning. "I'll get up there as soon as I can," he told Jimmy. "That's all I can do, man."

"You're living in some kind of dream world!" Jimmy said.

Some dream world: nightmare was more like it. Since he had last seen Jimmy, Joe had been questioned to the point of harassment by FBI agents, asked vague and ridiculous questions about his visits

240

to Charles Harrelson, about his client Bill Mallow (who was now charged with attempted capital murder), about phone calls he had made. One agent had even hinted that they knew the *real* reason Joe had made a "secret" trip to Boston: visiting the ol' mob, eh? Had the FBI forgotten that Joe went to Boston to defend his brother in yet another smuggling trial? Joe didn't look forward to his trip to Leavenworth: his depression and paranoia intensified every time he got in the same room with Jimmy. Once when he was supposed to be visiting Jimmy, Patty called his motel in Kansas City and found him so loaded on drugs he could barely talk. The whole family was pressuring Joe—Mom Chagra; his sister, Patsy; Jimmy's wife, Liz. They didn't seem to understand what was happening to Joe, but they demanded to know why he couldn't get Jimmy out of prison. Joe could no more cope with their questions than he could with Jimmy's demands. During one conversation, Jimmy raved on and on about some money that Jack Stricklin owed him, something like $140,000. "Okay, here's what I want you to go tell Jack," Jimmy had told Joe. "Just tell him it's coming from me. If you don't get that fucking money up within two weeks, I'm gonna off him. You tell him I said that. Now I'm not playing . . . I'll have him fucking bumped off. I'm telling you." What could Joe say to a tirade like that? Jimmy had also demanded that Joe personally try to bribe a member of the federal parole commission to have Jimmy transferred closer to El Paso, and had talked to him a number of times about a new drug scam that he wanted Joe to supervise as his surrogate kingpin. There weren't enough drugs in the world to obliterate this nightmare.

Joe forgot almost all of his promises to Jimmy as soon as possible, but the drug-scam talk kept his attention, partly because it demanded that Joe take some action immediately. Jimmy had run across his Colombia supplier, Theodoro, in prison, and the two of them had hatched a plan for Jimmy to arrange to off-load a shipment of marijuana that was waiting off the coast of the Carolinas. Naturally, Jimmy needed Joe's help. Though Joe smelled another trap, he promised to telephone Theodoro's contact man. Instead, he telephoned a friend and asked him to make the contact. Joe was mainly interested in checking out Theodoro, in confirming his suspicions that it was a government trap, but the next thing he knew his friend called from Colombia, and said the deal was apparently genuine and he was following through on it. Joe told him to forget it, but couldn't bring himself to tell Jimmy the same thing. Soon Joe's talks with Jimmy escalated from one shipload of marijuana into many, and then into a separate deal to smuggle millions of dollars worth of cocaine through Mexico. Joe knew that when he next visited Leavenworth, Jimmy would immediately demand to know why nothing was happening. At one point during their last talk, Joe had thrown up his hands and said: "Ah, fuck, I don't know what I'm doing, man. I'll be honest with you."

By the time Liz arrived at the Leavenworth visiting room on Tuesday, November 18, Jimmy had calmed down a little. He was still certain that the FBI had seized three boxes of tapes from Virginia Farah's house, and that they implicated Harrelson and everyone else; but as he reconstructed things in his memory he wasn't all that sure they had *him* on tape. Unless, of course, Harrelson was an FBI informant from the very start, unless Harrelson was wearing a body recorder the first time they met, which didn't seem likely.

Liz told him that Joe didn't believe Harrelson was copping out.

"*He* doesn't think that," Jimmy said. "I know for a fact now that he is. They're trying to corroborate it."

"They're trying to implicate Joe after the fact," Liz said. "Joe says that's the best thing that could ever happen, for them to try to implicate him."

"Why?"

"Because, you know, he's not guilty of that."

Jimmy whispered: "Charlie's copping out!"

"Don't say that, Jimmy."

"He is."

"Well, I don't want to know that then, okay?"

"Okay. Here, I need to know a couple of things. When you went and paid the money? Who got it?"

"It was a young . . . a very young girl."

"Did she know you as my wife?"

"Yeah."

"How did she know that?"

"She asked me. She says, 'When's the baby due?' "

"That don't mean nothing."

"Well, wouldn't that look funny if I was your hooker and eight months pregnant?"

"But I'm saying, that don't mean anything. You didn't know what you were going to pay. They know you took money and—"

"I'll never forgive you if I go to jail, Jimmy. *I'll never forgive you!*"

"You're not going to jail."

Jimmy whispered that his pal Jerry Ray James had friends in the U.S. attorney's office who told him that the FBI had three boxes of tapes, but he added that he didn't think any of the tapes contained his own conversations with Harrelson. Liz lifted her sunglasses and mopped the perspiration from her eyes and cheeks. She didn't trust Jerry Ray James. "Right now I have no choice but to believe Joe. I can't believe you'd believe somebody who's in here. I just don't believe it. Don't you see what they're doing?"

Jimmy walked to the vending machine, thinking, opening a fresh package of cigarettes, looking over the visiting room. Being the middle of the week, it wasn't as crowded as usual. He lit a fresh cigarette and sat down again, facing his wife. He motioned for her to move closer, and he spoke in a whisper: "I got an escape plan, I told you."

Liz sat straight up, blood draining from her face: "No, you didn't tell me, and I don't want to know. I don't want to know anything anymore."

"How would you like to [go to] the Orient?"

"Huh? I'd love to. I'd love to! That's what I was—"

"But I'm serious this time."

"Serious . . . oh, you're serious this time. For how long, a day or two?"

"No. Forever."

He outlined the plan for her. It would take less than two minutes for Calvin to land a helicopter, pick up Jimmy, and vanish over the walls. In another seven minutes they would rendezvous with a light plane that would fly them to Mexico. They wouldn't need passports in Mexico, only birth certificates. When the heat died a little, they would buy a boat and head for the Orient. Jimmy figured they would need $1 million to pay for the escape and buy the boat, and another $1 million to get started.

"Get started doing what?" Liz asked.

"I'm gonna deal heroin or coke or something."

Liz launched a mild protest about how she couldn't cross the street without a team of FBI agents following her, much less handle three kids and all their belongings, but Jimmy was already yapping about ways to raise the money. Jimmy had already reminded Joe that the kennel in the Upper Valley was rightfully *his*, and Joe hadn't protested too strongly. When you got down to it, everything belonged to Jimmy. Joe just said he was "sick" of hearing about it. "Jim, I never asked you for nothing," Joe had said. "I wish you'd never given it to me."

If Joe was trying to make his brother feel bad, it hadn't worked. Liz was already making an attempt to sell her own jewelry, using her friend from Albuquerque. Just off the top of his head, he could remember the platinum diamond dinner ring set with a fifteen-carat emerald-cut diamond, worth nearly $500,000 . . . and another platinum dinner ring, set with a six-carat marquise-cut diamond, and a platinum diamond bracelet, with sixteen emerald-cut diamonds and thirty square-cut baguettes, totaling twenty-five carats, worth easily $300,000. They could raise a couple of million, probably more.

"I'll make Joe sell his jewelry," Liz said.

"We need to," Jimmy agreed.

"I'll make Mom sell her jewelry."

"We need to."

"I'll make everybody sell their cars."

"Uh huh."

"You've gotta pay for everything. Everything."

"I know," Jimmy said.

When Liz visited Leavenworth again the following morning, she was the one who was in a state of panic. She had hardly slept, thinking of the things Jimmy had said. Jimmy kept using the term "corroborate"—she guessed that he'd learned it from Jerry Ray James. Jimmy was talking about corroboration for the Harrelson tapes, if they even existed, but Liz was thinking about something else. She put the question squarely to Jimmy the next morning.

"What happens if they get his daughter to corroborate? I'm in trouble."

"You deny everything," Jimmy whispered.

"Well, you do, too. That doesn't mean shit."

"Yeah, I know, but . . . how would they know what you were doing? Okay, say she said you brought her the money. But she didn't say this is for killing Wood."

"She didn't say what?" Liz appeared shocked that Jimmy would even use that name in here.

"This is for killing Wood. You're making the payoff for Wood's murder."

"No."

"Okay. Well, it could be a gambling debt. Could be anything. You know, you don't know," Jimmy told her. He could see his wife's hands trembling as she dropped them to her lap. "What are you nervous about?"

"Nothing. Why?"

"What are you shaking about?"

"I shake all the time."

"Quit your shaking."

"I can't help it, Jimmy."

When Joe arrived at Leavenworth two days later, Jimmy immediately told him he was talking too much, especially to Charlie Harrelson. If the government had three boxes of tapes, all they needed to indict both brothers was "corroboration." Jimmy was still upset that Joe hadn't dropped everything and hurried up to Leavenworth the previous Sunday, as Jimmy had told him to.

Joe didn't doubt that the FBI had played some tapes for Calvin, or that the tapes were Harrelson's voice, but he didn't believe the tapes were evidence against Jimmy: the FBI men were not above tampering with tapes, if they thought this would flush out new evidence, but they weren't about to introduce phony tapes in the courtroom.

"Why did you even fuck with Charlie Harrelson, man?" Jimmy whined. "I just can't believe that you're not smarter than that, man. I kept telling you . . . "

"Well, you know what, Jim? I did it . . . I did it trying to help you out. Stupid as that sounds."

"*How could that help me out, Joe?*" Jimmy said, as though he were addressing a very small child and wanted each word clearly enunciated.

"Okay," Joe said softly. "I don't know."

Once Jimmy had his temper under control, they talked about a possible defense in case one or both were indicted, about Jimmy's bizarre escape plan, and about the new dope scam that Jimmy was counting on to supply the money for an escape. As always when the talk concerned deals, Jimmy was the chairman of the board:

"I'm getting fifty a pound from you, right?"

"Fifty a pound," Joe assured him.

"Okay. I want thirty a pound and you get twenty. Now that's not a gift. You're earning that."

"Uh huh."

"I can sell it for four hundred a pound. Today. All of it in a day."

"But how?"

"I'll tell him where to take it," Jimmy said.

"I'm not touching it," Joe said. "I'm not getting anywhere near it."

But Joe assured his brother that two weeks after the first load arrived, there would be another, then another, then another. He could get cocaine, too, or Quaaludes, as many as Jimmy wanted, 1,000 even. Jimmy said the figure he had in mind was 10,000—at a time!

Joe had almost forgotten the bad news: according to the newspapers, the FBI had found a witness who could put Charlie Harrelson in San Antonio the day of the murder.

"In San Antonio? Or at [Wood's] apartment?"

"San Antonio," Joe said. "Not at the scene. I don't know where he saw him. But he'll come up and say he saw him somewhere."

"Did anyone see him [at the apartment] I wonder? Huh?"

"Shit, I don't know."

"Boy, we shouldn't have done that, huh, Joe?"

"Yeah."

"Huh?"

"Yeah."

"Yeah what?" Jimmy was needling him, and Joe couldn't sidestep it.

"Shouldn't have done it," Joe told his brother.

"I'd have a better shot, huh?"

"Uh huh."

"You're the one said do it, do it, do it. You're the one was all hot to do it."

Joe didn't bother denying that he had never told Jimmy to kill Wood, or, for that matter, to do or not to do anything else in his entire life. Instead, he said: "I always thought you was talking about it. I never thought you'd get someone like this guy to do it."

"Why?"

"I always thought someone like the Face, someone in the Mafia."

"I had a few thoughts like that," Jimmy admitted. "What difference does it make?"

"Well, this guy's an asshole," Joe said. "That's what difference."

"They're all assholes," Jimmy reminded him.

34

The grand jury had been in recess since October, but as Jamie Boyd prepared to reconvene it, numerous newspaper leaks reported that the FBI had turned up witnesses who had seen Charles Harrelson in the judge's townhouse complex on the morning of the murder; and an Associated Press story out of Houston speculated that "authorities may be close to a solution" in the seventeen-month-old investigation. As usual the U.S. attorney refused to comment on this speculation, but one aspect of the investigation was apparent—Jamie Boyd's tenure as its ramrod was about to end. Ronald Reagan had been elected president, and in two months a Republican administration would take power.

One day before Thanksgiving, Boyd orchestrated the most-publicized "secret" police lineup anyone in Houston could remember. Shortly after noon, Charlie Harrelson was clamped in handcuffs and leg irons and hustled out of Harris County jail by a squadron of cops with automatic rifles and shotguns. A police van, escorted by motorcycle officers with sirens blaring, delivered Harrelson to the door of the Houston police department booking room, and then to a room on the third floor where witnesses would attempt to identify the suspect. The lineup room was located about twenty-five feet from the press room. Reporters knew *something* was happening—on orders from U.S. marshals, police had cordoned off the press room and instructed photographers to take no pictures of those emerging from the room where the lineup was being held. Just to make sure there was lots of publicity, police even arrested a woman reporter from the Houston *Post*.

Famed Texas trial lawyer Percy Foreman, who happened to be visiting the Houston police station that day, guessed that the whole dog-and-pony show was a crude attempt to create speculation and perhaps get the suspects to talking: Foreman said that in his fifty-three years as a criminal attorney, he'd never seen anything like it.

"You don't move a prisoner across town from the county jail to the police department for a show-up," Foreman told Steve Peters of the El Paso *Times*. "They have facilities for a show-up in the sheriff's department, in the jail where he's confined. And there wouldn't be any publicity—there's no press room in the jail. They've probably got a lot of court-ordered wiretaps and want to start them talking. That's probably the strategic explanation. . . . Good police work would call for quietness if they weren't trying to create talk—stimulate conversation—so they could record it and hopefully make an Abscam sort of thing out of it."

The same week, the week that both Liz and Joe Chagra visited Jimmy at Leavenworth, there were also media leaks hinting that Harrelson was implicated in the August 25 shootout at the El Paso motel where Bill Mallow was critically wounded, and that the grand jury would be interviewing Pete Kay, as well as Harrelson's alibi witnesses. James Kerr, who had been in hiding for almost two years, was also scheduled to appear before the grand jury. A reporter for one of the El Paso newspapers had also been tipped off by government sources that an arrest months earlier at Philadelphia International Airport was probably connected to the Wood killing. Among the three men arrested in what police thought was a routine drug bust was one of Jimmy Chagra's bodyguards in Las Vegas—the cops didn't find any drugs, but they did find semiautomatic weapons, sophisticated coding equipment, a number of counterfeit Kentucky driver's licenses, and $22,800 in cash. "It's a red-hot lead and there are some very close connections to Jimmy Chagra," a source told El Paso *Herald Post* reporter Peter Brock.

On Friday, December 5, giant headlines in the San Antonio *Express* announced: ARRESTS EXPECTED IN WOOD SLAYING. This story had originated in Washington, D.C., where FBI director William Webster had told reporters that organized-crime figures had definitely been tied to Wood's killing and the unsuccessful attack on James Kerr. Webster went on to explain, however, that he did not mean the Mafia or La Cosa Nostra. "Organized crime is involved, but not one of the twenty-six Mafia families," the FBI director said. He defined organized crime as "any continuous criminal conspiracy involving some sort of structure motivated by profit," a near-perfect paraphrase of the kingpin statute. While Webster was making his announcement, another Washington "source" assured reporters that arrests in the Wood killing were "imminent."

That same night Jamie Boyd and his wife Suzy entertained an out-of-town guest at their apartment in San Antonio. It was a significant night to the Boyds, not so much because of Webster's press conference, but because it was the first night in two years that they had not been under twenty-four-hour protection from U.S. marshals. The visitor was surprised at the degree of paranoia that permeated the apartment. Jamie repeated his conviction that the entire Chagra family was mixed up in the assassination, and Suzy said, only half joking, that she hoped all of them weren't murdered in their sleep that night. Jamie's obsessive hatred of Lee and Jimmy Chagra wasn't news, but the main target of his wrath this particular night was the younger brother, Joe. The visitor had never heard him say much about Joe, pro or con, but now his rage seemed peculiarly directed toward the younger brother, as though Joe had been the brains, the mastermind, behind the entire conspiracy. Though the next day was Saturday, Jamie woke early and drove to his office for a secret meeting with a high official from the Department of Justice. When he returned to the apartment that afternoon, he was obviously upset, but he wouldn't talk about what had happened. "In a lot of ways," he said mysteriously, "I'm relieved."

Five days later, Charles Harrelson received a surprise visit from his stepdaughter, Teresa Starr Jasper. The FBI had told his wife, Jo Ann, about their love affair, which didn't surprise Harrelson. "That's how the bastards operate," he said. They'd even told Hamp Robinson III that the baby his new wife was carrying was Harrelson's. "It is?" Teresa asked. Charlie changed the subject and commented on her new suit. "I'd like to eat it off you . . . lick it off of you," he said. "Mmm, you pretty blond thing. . . . " Teresa professed her great love for the man facing her through the visiting-area cage. He told her that he expected to be out of jail in another month, but in the meantime to talk to no one, especially not Hamp Robinson. "He's working for the man," Harrelson said. There were a lot of rumors going around the jail, but Harrelson believed this one. He'd even heard a rumor there was a contract on his life, and Teresa said the FBI had warned her, too, that a killer was in town. She laughed when she said this to Harrelson. "Oh, goddam," Harrelson said, and you could hear the raw sex dripping from his voice. "There's a lot I'd like to tell you. I love you. . . . " A moment later, Harrelson ran his fingers beneath the countertop of the visiting cage and discovered a small microphone taped there. Then Teresa discovered one on her own side of the cage. The government's secret was out.

A few days later a spokesman at the Justice Department in Washington announced what only Jamie Boyd and a few close associates already knew—that Jamie had been fired from the Wood investigation. Jamie knew that he had become a lame duck when Reagan was elected, but he figured he'd serve at least until the new administration took office. But the people who fired him were lame ducks too: they had their own careers to consider.

Like the good and faithful bureaucrat that he was, Jamie refused public comment. He let the newspaper speculate what it would. One source speculated that the lame ducks at Justice "smelled blood and Washington wants the credit for wrapping this thing up."

Jamie told friends that Washington had taken him off the case because of a disagreement over the methods being used in the investigation. Philip Heymann, the assistant attorney general who had dreamed up Abscam, wanted to use the same tactics to trap the Chagras and Harrelson. And Jamie didn't. He thought the method was too risky. The use of government informants to trick suspects into confessions had been a valid tool of law enforcement as far back as the Jimmy Hoffa case, but bugging private conversations in which *none* of the parties was aware of or had given consent to surveillance was virgin territory, uncharted in the law. Worse yet, Boyd feared that a court might rule that the government had tampered with the concept of attorney-client privilege: a few hours before Harrelson and his stepdaughter discovered the hidden recorders, the prisoner had also received a visit from Joe Chagra, who represented him in the Van Horn case and possibly in other areas. This was the kind of thing the feds had done in the heyday of Joe McCarthy and J. Edgar Hoover, but this was the 1980s. Jamie feared the long, costly investigation would fall victim to the domino theory: one wrong move and the whole case would tumble.

Jamie Boyd knew something else, and this no doubt explained the excessive paranoia the visitor had noticed that night in his apartment—not only had the FBI men been conducting court-ordered electronic surveillance on Charles Harrelson, they had been bugging the entire Chagra family. The wiretaps had been in operation since early October, in the Chagras' telephones at home and in the pay phone in Jimmy's cellblock at Leavenworth, in the prison visiting room, even in the cells where Jimmy and his pals talked. As for Jerry Ray James, the man who hated snitches, he had become a walking bug for the FBI. Jimmy Chagra had not said a thing that hadn't been recorded, not since October.

But there was yet another reason that Washington was disenchanted with Jamie Boyd. The star of Jamie's grand jury, Robert Riojas, had been completely discredited. The government had spent millions running down rabbit trails, and all there was to show for it was a tainted grand jury. Now it would be necessary to impanel an entirely new grand jury, to hear an entirely new government theory. Once its options were clear, Washington took no chances. Jamie was permitted to finish some business with the old racket-busting grand jury in El Paso—he was able to indict bail bondsman and longtime Chagra friend Vic Apodaca, Jr., for income tax fraud, but Boyd's expectations that Sib Abraham would be indicted on the same charges did not prove fruitful. After that, Boyd was given his old job as U.S. magistrate, which would allow him to retire with full benefits, while assuring that he remained quiet about his problems with the FBI. All aspects of the Wood investigation were taken over by the FBI. Even the prosecutors who would work with the new grand jury were moved from the courthouse to the FBI office—from prosecution to enforcement.

PART THREE

The Fall of the House of Chagra

35

It was the strangest of alliances, this marriage of convenience between the Justice Department and Jerry Ray James. It would be difficult to think of a more dangerous or unrepentant criminal than James, as the FBI itself admitted. In his affidavit seeking permission for electronic surveillance from the United States District Court in Kansas, special agent Gary Hart described the government's key witness as "a career criminal who has been arrested on over thirty occasions for robbery, assault, burglary, larceny, narcotics, gambling, obstruction, weapon and escape offenses . . . has been convicted on at least six occasions and since approximately 1977 has been serving a prison term for conspiring to commit armed robbery as well as a life sentence as a habitual criminal." Yet the government was ready to give Jerry Ray James his freedom in return for his help in nailing Jimmy Chagra and solving the Wood murder. A deal had already been arranged with the governor of New Mexico, Bruce King, guaranteeing James's parole and clearing him of culpability in the Santa Fe prison riots—authorities were now claiming that James had helped contain the riots. Whatever James had done in his long criminal career, and whatever he might do in the future, was viewed by the federal government as less heinous than the murder of a federal judge. According to Hart's affidavit, James was motivated to help the government by his desire to "save his marriage by establishing some degree of respectable life." Hart didn't mention it in his affidavit, but James was also motivated by several hundred thousand dollars in reward money, which the government had promised would be his if Chagra was convicted.

According to Hart, James first approached the FBI on August 20, several months after his transfer to Leavenworth, claiming that

Jimmy Chagra had told him that he paid Charles Harrelson $200,000 to kill the judge. In the days that followed, James passed along what appeared to be carefully chosen pieces of information implicating Chagra not only in Wood's murder, but in conspiracies to put out a contract on Henry Wallace, to escape from prison, and to resume his role as drug kingpin. Money was no obstacle for Chagra, James claimed: Chagra had told him he had $40 million stashed away. James convinced the feds that Chagra trusted and respected him because of his "reputation for getting things done" and because Jimmy believed—apparently wrongly—that James had once been a friend and associate of Lee Chagra's. After several meetings with James, and several more with Justice Department attorney Michael deFeo, Hart started preparing his application for wiretaps.

Hart's affidavit pretty much laid out the government's case, as of September 1980:

• An unnamed government snitch who was incarcerated at La Tuna in 1977 claimed to have overheard Jack Stricklin telling Travis Erwin that "Lee Chagra wants Wood and Kerr wiped out" and "anything you need, any amount you want, Lee will get it for you or take care of it for you." Travis Erwin was supposed to have replied: "I'm going to pick up that bit of change when I get out." Erwin, it was noted, was in prison at the time Wood was killed. The original wiretap application had also asked permission to bug Travis Erwin's cell, but after he died on October 7, this request was deleted.

• Another former La Tuna inmate told the FBI that in 1977 Jack Stricklin offered him $100,000 to kill Judge Wood.

• A third source told the FBI that Stricklin and the Chagra brothers maintained criminal association with various members of the Bandido motorcycle gang, and that the Chagra brothers used gang members for "protection and/or to commit acts of violence in connection with their illegal activities, including illegal drug transactions." The repeated use of such terms as "the Chagra brothers" made it clear that from the beginning the FBI considered Joe Chagra a suspect in the judge's murder rather than merely Jimmy's attorney. This was a necessary subterfuge—the FBI realized that because of the attorney-client privilege, it was on shaky ground unless it considered Joe a co-conspirator.

• Not long after his own attempted assassination, prosecutor James Kerr viewed a lineup of suspects and identified Steven Barbour as the driver of the van. Hair samples found in the van were found to be identical to those of Michael Jones, a member of the Bandidos.

• A few weeks before Wood's murder, a friend of the Chagra family, William Robert Janick, asked Jimmy Chagra what he intended to do about his upcoming trial in Wood's court. Chagra told Janick: "The judge wants to send me away for a long time. . . . The situation in hand is going to be taken care of soon."

• Ronaldo Disecco, one of Jimmy Chagra's bodyguards in Las Vegas, told agents that on the morning of May 29, 1979, he drove Jimmy to his regularly scheduled Tuesday meeting with his federal probation officer, and then drove Chagra home. Records indicated that the meeting at the probation office took place between 9:30 and 10:30 A.M. Disecco had just returned home when he got a call from an upset and emotionally distraught Chagra, telling him that "somebody must have forgotten my trial date was changed, somebody killed the judge . . . they're going to blame it on me now." Disecco hurried back to Chagra's home, where he found him "crying and physically sick, including throwing up."

• Six months after Disecco's interview with the FBI, an interview with a Las Vegas woman, Cheryl Davis, gave a conflicting report on Chagra's activities the morning of the murder. According to Cheryl Davis, she, Chagra, and Disecco gambled at various casinos until the early-morning hours of May 29. At approximately 6:00 A.M., Davis, her roommate, Katy Noruk, Chagra, and Disecco had breakfast, then drove to the women's apartment, where Davis and Chagra were left alone. Somewhere between 7:00 and 8:00 A.M., Chagra called home and learned from his wife that Wood was dead. Davis overheard him saying: "Oh no . . . yeah . . . I know they'll try to pin it on me." Davis told FBI agents that Chagra told her that the murder was the "worst thing that could have happened" to him and that somebody who didn't realize his trial date had been changed must be trying to set him up.

• Subsequent to Wood's murder, Jack Stricklin took a polygraph test conducted by an FBI examiner, and results indicated he was being deceptive when he denied knowing who killed the judge.

• Several witnesses saw Jimmy Chagra and Charles Harrelson together at Binion's Horseshoe Casino in early May 1979. According to Disecco, Jimmy Chagra did not trust Harrelson, and asked Disecco to find out exactly who Harrelson was and why he was trying to get close to Chagra. Jimmy gave Harrelson several thousand dollars just to get rid of him. Disecco was certain that Chagra and Harrelson never met privately and never had any personal conversations.

• Ronald Collier, another of Chagra's associates in Las Vegas, told FBI agents that during the poker tournament at Binion's Horseshoe, "lots of persons approached Jimmy Chagra . . . offering their condolences concerning the death of his brother" and many of these offered to "kill the guy who killed your brother." Chagra treated these people with contempt, Collier said, and frequently gave them $1,000 to $2,000 "just to get rid of them." Collier claimed that Charles Harrelson was among this group, and that Jimmy asked Collier, "That guy is passing himself off as a killer, what do you think?"

• Records showed that between April 27 and May 8, Charles Harrelson and Hampton Robinson III were registered at Binion's Horseshoe Casino.

• On May 8, the same day Harrelson was believed to have left town, a telephone call was placed from Jimmy Chagra's room in Las Vegas to the home of Pete Kay in Huntsville, Texas.

• On May 10, at 2:20 P.M., a call was placed from Harrelson's apartment in Dallas to Pete Kay's residence in Huntsville. About four hours later, another call was placed from a main telephone at Binion's Horseshoe Casino to Harrelson's residence in Dallas.

• On May 11, a call was placed from Harrelson's apartment to a main telephone at Binion's Horseshoe Casino. Later that day, another call was placed from a pay phone at Preston Towers (a pay telephone known to be used by Harrelson) to a telephone at Binion's.

• On May 12, a number of calls were placed between Harrelson's Dallas number and the home numbers of Hamp Robinson in Houston and Pete Kay in Huntsville.

• In her testimony to the grand jury, Jo Ann Stafford (later Jo Ann Robinson) said that on either May 13 or May 20, Harrelson asked Hamp Robinson to meet him in Austin. Records showed that at 2:33 P.M. on May 13, a call was placed from Robinson's residence to the switchboard telephone of the Ramada Inn North in Austin. That same day, at 2:50 P.M., a call was placed from Howard Johnson's Motel in Austin to Harrelson's apartment in Dallas. The room was registered to "Gordon Stone," who gave an nonexistent address.

The man claimed to be driving an Oldsmobile Cutlass, similar to one owned by Jo Ann Harrelson. As of May 13, the trial of Jimmy Chagra was still scheduled to be held in Austin, beginning on May 29.

• On May 19, a call was made from Harrelson's apartment to the home of Earl Wright in Cottage Grove, Minnesota. Earl Wright was the father of Calvin Wright, who was at the time assigned to a halfway house in Minneapolis. The following day, May 20, Calvin Wright called Harrelson, collect. According to his own testimony before the grand jury, Calvin Wright had known Harrelson when they were both incarcerated at Leavenworth—Harrelson probably knew that Calvin Wright was an accomplished helicopter and fixed-wing-aircraft pilot. Wright said that Harrelson was attempting to "feel him out" to determine his willingness to take part in some sort of criminal activity. Wright, recalling the warning of other inmates that Harrelson had a reputation as a contract killer, declined.

• On May 24 and 25, records reflected calls to Hamp Robinson's residence from (1) a coin telephone at San Antonio International Airport and (2) the Swiss Chalet Restaurant in San Antonio, located approximately one and three quarters miles from the residence of Judge John Wood. Robinson and his girlfriend, Jo Ann Stafford, told the grand jury they couldn't remember these calls.

• Records showed that on May 27, Harrelson and Pete Kay visited an inmate at the Texas Department of Corrections in Huntsville.

• The FBI collected information that indicated the judge was being stalked by his killer on the evening of May 28. Wood had used his wife's car that evening, and by the next morning that car was disabled. Witnesses who lived nearby claimed to have seen a white male parked near Wood's apartment, using a walkie-talkie, the evening before the murder.

• Although Harrelson claimed to have been in Dallas on May 28 and May 29, efforts to corroborate his statements had failed. Harrelson had refused to be interviewed by FBI agents or to take a polygraph examination concerning Wood's murder. Harrelson denied any involvement in the murder, "but stated he dreams of how he assassinated Judge Wood."

• It was technically possible for Harrelson to kill Wood in San Antonio at 8:40 A.M. and still be in Dallas shortly after 10 A.M. Wood's apartment was a five-minute drive from San Antonio International. On May 29, a Southwest Airlines flight left San Antonio at 9:08 A.M. and arrived at Dallas Love Field at 10:02 A.M. Love Field is approximately twenty minutes from the place of Harrelson's alibi. Also, the affidavit continued, numerous private aircraft were available at San Antonio International Airport, though the FBI obviously had no specific information indicating that Harrelson used a private airplane, or even that he had booked passage on the Southwest flight.

The weakest part of agent Hart's application for wiretap was its lack of direct information linking Joe Chagra to the Wood murder. Hart built his case by pointing out that Joe had done Jimmy's dirty work in the past (notably during Jimmy's drug trial in Austin, when Joe had—according to Henry Wallace—tried to bribe Wallace to change his testimony) and by emphasizing the fact that Joe Chagra had met Charles Harrelson the previous summer. "Maids employed by Virginia Farah advised a Special Agent of the FBI that Joseph Chagra visited Harrelson at Farah's residence at times when Farah was away. . . . " The affidavit included a long narrative about how Joe had introduced Harrelson to William Mallow shortly before Mallow's shootout with El Paso police, and about the time that Joe tape-recorded Harrelson's incoherent babble while the fugitive was hiding in a Houston motel. The FBI had not yet discovered the will that Harrelson scribbled on the motel calendar: Hamp Robinson had recovered the incriminating calendar, but hadn't yet told agents. However, police had discovered a similar will written by Harrelson during his six-hour standoff in the desert near Van Horn, asking that he be cremated and that his ashes be spread over the John H. Wood, Jr., Federal Courts Building in San Antonio. Later, as police were transporting Harrelson from Van Horn to Houston, Harrelson had observed that because of the harshness of the sentences he meted out, Wood had actually committed suicide. What was interesting about this, Agent Hart noted, was its similarity to something Joe Chagra had told reporters: "Judge Wood wasn't murdered, he began committing suicide years ago."

The part of Hart's affidavit that most damaged Joe Chagra— and this was perhaps the main reason that the application for wiretap was approved—was a long section that implied that since Jimmy's incarceration, Joe Chagra was masterminding the family drug business. An unnamed source claimed that shortly before the Boston trial, he overheard Jack Stricklin and John Milliorn discussing future narcotics transactions in which one of them said that when the trial was over, everyone connected with the Chagra group was "going to get well." The source claimed that "Joseph Chagra is handling these deals for Jimmy Chagra pursuant to Jimmy's instructions, and that equipment and vehicles to transport the drugs are being purchased and stockpiled." Since neither Stricklin nor Milliorn could afford to finance a major narcotics transaction (according to the FBI, anyway), they would require "the assistance of a person of wealth such as Jimmy or Joseph Chagra." Stricklin would supervise the new operations, Milliorn would be responsible for transportation, and Joe Chagra would relay Jimmy's instructions "as well as the financing from funds previously accumulated by the Chagra brothers."

However spurious, the repeated use of terms such as "the Chagra group" or the "Chagra brothers" appeared designed to stay just within the bounds of authorized wiretaps. Gary Hart knew that Joe Chagra was an attorney of record for his brother, and that in addition to the litigation in Boston, Joe was working on an appeal of Jimmy's conviction in Austin. Though Hart could cite no specific connection between Joe and the Wood murder, the implications of an ongoing drug conspiracy gave the agents a certain latitude in their request for electronic surveillance. Hart was careful to instruct his monitoring agents to "minimize" conversations that obviously fell under attorney-client privilege—"minimize" was the government euphemism for "turn off the recording machines"—but the government had a perfect right to record conversations that were evidence of past, ongoing, or future crimes. According to Hart, a "unique" procedure was utilized in this case: in his more than one hundred experiences with wiretaps, Hart claimed, he had never "sanitized" as much material as was done here. Because of the limited physical facilities at Leavenworth, the monitoring agents occupied a room outside the prison. Working in teams of four or five to a shift, the agents were able to hear most conversations through their earphones, but taped only those in which the suspects were actually discussing criminal activity. At the end of each shift, monitoring agents turned over their tapes and logs to the team leader, who turned them over to Agent Hart, who listened to the tapes to make certain they contained no privileged material. Hart also consulted regularly with the Justice Department's top electronics surveillance lawyer, Michael deFeo, who was the final arbitrator on what material was to be excised and what was to become part of the transcript.

The wiretaps began on October 10. On November 5, when the monitors taped the conversation in which Joe told his brother about the map that Harrelson had drawn, the FBI put a new interpretation on the meaning of the attorney-client privilege. The feds took the position that Joe had never been Harrelson's attorney, not in the Wood matter at least. As for Joe's conversations with Jimmy, both men surrendered their privilege when they started talking about recovering the murder weapon. Of course, there was still the problem of getting this theory to hold up in court. Michael deFeo acknowledged that some might feel the FBI was playing close to the edge of both the attorney-client and the husband-wife privileges (in the case of conversations between Jimmy and Liz) but said that in such a "unique" criminal investigation "public policy" demanded it. DeFeo told prosecutors that he felt sure that "some court somewhere" would uphold these actions.

In a series of five court orders signed by a Kansas federal district judge, twelve members of the Chagra family, including Jimmy Chagra's three infant children, were authorized to be recorded. By February 5, 1981, when the wiretaps were lifted, more than 1,000 hours of tape was on file with the FBI.

36

Joe Chagra was outraged, defiant, and perhaps a little relieved when he heard about the bugging devices that Harrelson and his step-daughter had discovered in the visiting area of the Harris County Jail. He was certain that the recording devices were intended for him—Joe had been scheduled to meet with Harrelson that same morn-ing, but had been forced to cancel because of a conflicting case in El Paso. But Joe knew the wiretap laws: if he was the intended target, someone had to go before a federal judge and swear in an affidavit that Joe Chagra was involved in some illegal activity. "If they did," Joe told reporters, "they're liars, and you can underline 'liars.' If they did, they're perjurers. I don't care if it's a U.S. attorney, an FBI agent, who it was. If they swore to something that gave a judge probable cause to tape me they're liars and perjurers. It's getting to the point we don't know who the good guys are and who the bad guys are!"

The sudden and unexpected dismissal of Jamie Boyd from the Wood investigation had to be connected to the wiretaps, Joe be-lieved: it was possible that in his zeal to nail the Chagras, Boyd had fouled his own nest, and possibly even ruined the government's case against Charles Harrelson. It was a situation that called for a clear head, something Joe hadn't been able to manage in months. He had to get a copy of that affidavit filed with the request for wiretaps and learn for sure what evidence the government was claiming. He real-ized the situation was extremely dangerous. If Joe's head had been a little clearer, he might have realized something else, something that even now hadn't occurred to any of the Chagras—the government wiretaps weren't just limited to Charlie Harrelson.

Jimmy, meanwhile, was almost irrational with fear that Liz might cut her own deal with the FBI. Jimmy had always been insanely jealous of Liz, and now that he was helpless behind bars it was almost too much. Fortunately, Jimmy didn't know about his wife's affair with the jewelry salesman, or the situation would have been unmanageable. Anything could set Jimmy off: he'd once accused Liz and Patty of having a lesbian affair, because Patty loaned Liz a pair of panty hose. Another time in Las Vegas, he'd severely beaten Liz, then forced her to admit that she and Joe were lovers. It wasn't true, but he made Liz telephone the hotel room where Joe and Patty were staying and confess that she'd "told Jimmy the truth" about their affair.

On the morning of January 7, 1981, guards at Leavenworth notified the FBI that Liz Chagra was visiting her husband. The monitoring agents turned on their machines as the couple began to talk about the Wood investigation:

JIMMY: Well, you already thinking of copping or what?

LIZ: No, but you told me at one time to just tell 'em that . . .

JIMMY: Well, maybe, we might later . . . but, honey, you deny everything first.

LIZ: You know, there's a good chance I could go to jail.

JIMMY: Possibly, honey, but just for ten or fifteen years.

LIZ: For life. [Unintelligible] with that judge's murder.

JIMMY: Well, you didn't know anything about that. No, they're gonna use you to try to scare you and tell you you're going to jail and away from your kids, never see your kids again . . . so you just have to sacrifice me to get out of jail. And you like that idea, don't you? You *like* your ace in the hole, don't you?

LIZ: No . . . no. No, but I'm not gonna go to jail. I won't. I refuse to go to jail.

JIMMY: So you'll tell on me?

LIZ: No.

JIMMY: Why not?

LIZ: I [unintelligible] talk to [unintelligible] self. [Laughs]

JIMMY: [Laughs] Goddam. Well, what kind of broad are you really?

LIZ: You know. I'm playing.

JIMMY: You wouldn't go to jail for me?

LIZ: No, Jimmy, uh-uh. [Laughs] No way. Honey, how could I leave the kids? If we were single . . .

JIMMY: Honey, see now, that's what the FBI is gonna tell you. "How could you leave your kids? Why don't you just 'fess up?"

LIZ: How could I leave my kids? I'm not gonna confess to anything, Jimmy. You don't have to worry, but I'm not gonna go to jail. [Laughs]

JIMMY: So what are you gonna do if that's what it comes down to, jail or talking?

LIZ: I don't know.

JIMMY: Come on, don't make me worry about you. I mean, what do you mean?

LIZ: Do you think I'm gonna tell 'em? Do you really? What's to tell?

JIMMY: Would you?

LIZ: No, I wouldn't tell 'em.

JIMMY: Even if you have to go to jail?

LIZ: I don't think I'll have to.

JIMMY: I know, but even if you had to?

Jimmy asked if his wife wanted a divorce, and Liz laughed again and asked what good a divorce would do. Their spirits seemed to lift a bit as they discussed Harrelson, his stepdaughter, and the tape recorder. Liz realized that Jimmy hadn't heard all the gossip.

LIZ: Did Joe tell you what they were saying on the tape recorder?

JIMMY: No.

LIZ: He was, you know . . . he's been neaking her. That's his stepdaughter.

JIMMY: Oh, he's been neaking [unintelligible]?

LIZ: He's been neaking her for a long time, since she was real young.

JIMMY: So what happened?

LIZ: He was telling her, "I wanna [unintelligible] your pussy," and he went like this to grab the thing and that's when he found the tape recordings of him saying that. And so they had it on tape.

JIMMY: They had that on tape? Honey, I'm worried about you now.

LIZ: Honey, don't worry about me.

JIMMY: You might give me up, honey.

LIZ: I won't give you up, Jimmy!

The monitoring agents picked this moment to begin "minimizing" the recordings. When they picked up the conversation again, the couple were talking about one night in their bedroom when Jimmy apparently discussed the Wood murder with Liz.

JIMMY: [Unintelligible] I had to.

LIZ: Jimmy, tell me the truth.

JIMMY: [Unintelligible]

LIZ: [Unintelligible] Why didn't you tell me that?

JIMMY: You wanted the truth. See, you always want to know and then you're gonna cop later. See, you insisted on knowing about the . . . the Wood thing.

LIZ: I did not!

JIMMY: Yes, you did. You kept . . .

LIZ: *You told me.*

JIMMY: No, you kept . . . honey, don't you remember, we were laying . . . I remember it explicitly.

LIZ: Jimmy, I didn't [unintelligible]. Okay, what?

JIMMY: "Come on, tell me. You never tell me nothing anymore. Don't you want me to know anything. I feel so left out . . . da da da da da da da da da."

LIZ: Jimmy, you don't . . . remember when you came and told me you met this guy . . . you didn't know him? Should you do it or shouldn't you do it?

JIMMY: And what did you say?

LIZ: I said, "Yeah," but it didn't make any difference.

JIMMY: [Laughs] So see, when it comes to court, I'm telling 'em you are the dead punch.

LIZ: You would too. [Unintelligible]

JIMMY: Honey, I'll never talk to 'em about nothing. They can offer me freedom, reward. You understand that?

A few days after Liz Chagra's visit to Leavenworth, the San Antonio *Express* reported that charges in both the Wood murder and the attempted murder of Kerr would be forthcoming within two months. A separate news item revealed that Benny Binion, the seventy-six-year-old owner of the Horseshoe Casino, had been subpoenaed by the grand jury and ordered to produce records involving Jimmy Chagra's gambling activities. Joe Chagra speculated that the government believed the records would show a cash transaction from Chagra to Charles Harrelson, though he was sure that no such record existed.

Something more important happened that same week that created new speculation about electronic surveillance. At a state court hearing in Houston, called at the request of the attorneys representing Harrelson, the court was about to get into the subject of the wiretap when a woman representing the U.S. attorney's office suddenly asked permission to talk privately to the judge: she wanted to show him a copy of "a federal court order." Joe guessed, this time correctly, that the order authorized authorities to tape not only Harrelson's conversations, but those of the Chagras as well. It still hadn't occurred to him that the order had been in effect for *three months*.

When Joe visited Jimmy a few days later, he told his brother that Harrelson's discovery of the bug was "the best thing that could have happened." Joe didn't believe there was any way the government could justify the wiretaps.

JOE: He can't do that, man. Taping a lawyer room.

JIMMY: Someone has to have said that you were involved? Who would have known?

JOE: I don't know. We'll get to the bottom of it. The only thing they could get is the after-the-fact thing.

JIMMY: That's your fault.

JOE: Yeah, well, okay. It's done!

Jimmy slipped into one of his self-righteous harangues, about how he *told* Joe to stay away from Harrelson, told him a hundred times, how Joe just couldn't seem to take his advice. What about the murder weapon? What if the FBI had *that* conversation on tape? What if the FBI had already located the weapon? Jo Ann Harrelson might have led them to it. The weapon would just about cinch the government's case. Joe told his brother that the last time he had talked to Harrelson, Charlie had said forget the gun. He'd also said he wanted his wife dead, maybe his stepdaughter, too. And he'd asked Joe to smuggle a pistol into the Harris County Jail, a proposition that Joe wouldn't even consider. Something else had occurred to Joe— what if Harrelson wasn't alone when he killed the judge? What if there was another witness, someone they had never even considered?

JOE: Let me tell you something. They know. You know what's sad now?

JIMMY: What?

JOE: Regardless of what happened, they know what happened now. I don't know how the fuck or how they found out, but they know what happened.

JIMMY: They know what?

JOE: That you [unintelligible] and he killed Wood. Cause that fucking Tarrant [Harrelson's Houston attorney, Bob Tarrant] told 'em. They know, man.

JIMMY: Of course they know. I'll never get out.

When Jimmy telephoned Liz three days later, she was so upset she could barely talk. That's just what the government wanted: he had warned Liz about it before, and now he warned her again. "They'd love to see us fighting and mad and yelling," he said. "And you sick and worrying all the time about who they're harassing. To hell with them, honey. We haven't done nothing wrong. . . . "

As soon as Jimmy hung up from talking to Liz, he placed a call to Joe's law office. Joe told him that the publicity was getting to Liz, that and FBI harassment. Her father, Red Nichols, was so concerned about his daughter's well-being that he hadn't even told her about his visit from the FBI; and now Liz thought her father was also turning against her. "Is Liz taking pills again or something, man?" Jimmy asked. Joe said he didn't know, he just knew Liz was terribly upset. Joe had advised her to take another trip to Leavenworth. Maybe Jimmy could calm her down.

On January 26, 1981, a day before Liz was scheduled for another visit, Jimmy heard a rumor from the prison chaplain that the visiting room was bugged. He telephoned Joe, warning him and telling him to warn Liz. From now on, they would have to communicate with handwritten notes, which they would destroy as soon as the communication was complete. Joe told his brother: "Anything you say, man, just presume it's being heard."

When Liz arrived for what would turn out to be her final visit to Leavenworth, she brought along their young daughter, Jackie, who was not yet three, and a small notebook, which she concealed in the child's purse. Though Jimmy and Liz had every reason now to believe their conversation was being recorded, they couldn't always contain themselves.

JIMMY: Doesn't look like you're feeling well.

LIZ: Oh, I feel fine. I'm just very upset, very, very mad at you. Very mad at you. . . . You know why I'm mad?

JIMMY: What are you mad at me about?

LIZ: Because that . . . that morning on the payoff [unintelligible] it was at the house. It was one hundred and nine degrees, and Cindy was there, and you were shooting golf in the front yard and you came inside and you said, "Liz, I want you to go [unintelligible]" . . . said "I don't want to, Jimmy, I don't want to." Remember?

JIMMY: Wait a minute now.

LIZ: No, yes.

JIMMY: No, okay, wait a minute.

LIZ: No. Okay.

JIMMY: [Whisper] We went into the living . . . we went into the bedroom. And I asked you, I said, "Who can I get to take this money [unintelligible]," and you offered to [unintelligible].

LIZ: No, uh, I didn't want to.

JIMMY: *You didn't?*

LIZ: No, Jimmy, you know I didn't. You said, "Liz, you're the only one I can trust." I didn't want to [unintelligible]. But that is not what pisses me off. It pisses me off . . . because the FBI has been, the FBI has been to see my . . .

JACKIE CHAGRA: Mommy.

LIZ: What, honey? The FBI had been to see my . . . my, my [unintelligible] in Oklahoma. Someone's talking, okay? Someone's talking. And the thing that you . . .

JACKIE CHAGRA: Daddy! Mommy!

JIMMY: Let me tell you something. Can I tell you something? Someone is talking . . .

JACKIE CHAGRA: Mommy, mommy, mommy.

LIZ: What, darling? All I know is . . . I kept telling you I didn't want to. I didn't want to [unintelligible] . . .

JIMMY: Okay, honey, I'm not gonna argue. That's not the way it went down, but I'm not gonna argue with you. It's possible that that's what you said. Okay.

LIZ: I remember that's what I said. I was . . . 'cause I was afraid to death.

JIMMY: No, no, you told me . . . you . . .

LIZ: I was afraid when I did it, Jimmy.

JIMMY: You know this place is tapped. I found out yesterday the place is tapped. Can't we write? That's what I brought this for, honey. . . . Okay, come here, listen. . . .

LIZ: It's just that there's somebody, somebody that you love so much, put me in this position . . .

JIMMY: Honey, quit trying to fucking turn things around and talk that way to me.

JACKIE CHAGRA: Momma!

JIMMY: What position did I ever put you into, honey? The place is tapped, honey. Can you understand that?

LIZ: Oh, you want me to write down [unintelligible]. What do you want me to write down, okay?

JIMMY: Okay. Standup and talk. Did you come to fight with me?

LIZ: No, I didn't come to fight with you.

JIMMY: Well, what'd you want to do? I mean you've come to fight with me, telling me that I caused this problem for you.

LIZ: Yeah.

JIMMY: I talked to you . . . from the start, I didn't want to tell you anything and you insisted on knowing everything. Am I right or wrong?

LIZ: Okay, yeah.

JIMMY: So what are you getting all upset?

LIZ: I'm not upset at you. I'm upset with myself for being so stupid, that's all.

JIMMY: I know, but honey [unintelligible]. You're so pretty.

JACKIE CHAGRA: I love you.

JIMMY: I love you.

JACKIE CHAGRA: Telephone. [Pause] Mommy, the telephone.

LIZ: Yes, I know, but it's the man who's gonna answer. Here, you want to color with your colors, Jackie? . . .

JACKIE CHAGRA: Daddy, want to color in my color . . .

JIMMY: Yeah, you want to color? This book's too little, let me give you a big piece of paper. Okay? Well, don't cry.

JACKIE CHAGRA: Yeah! Here, Daddy . . . here, Daddy, here, Daddy, here . . .

JIMMY: [unintelligible] bull [unintelligible].

LIZ: What, darling? Oh, look how neat you color, darling.

JIMMY: So what was the fucking charges?

LIZ: I don't know.

JIMMY: Joe is [whisper] aiding and abetting.

JACKIE CHAGRA: Mommy, will you make a house?

LIZ: Well, let me tell you something, Jimmy. They're too damn close to the truth. Why isn't it clear?

At this point, Jimmy suggested that they take a walk. Much of the conversation after that was unintelligible as they whispered and wrote notes back and forth, the argument apparently continuing. Several times Liz appeared ready to storm out of the visiting area, but Jimmy kept calling her back. He assured her that the FBI couldn't take away her children, and Liz assured him that they could and probably would. From time to time, the monitoring agents picked up the sound of little Jackie, saying things like: "I love you guys . . . love you guys!" At one point, Liz said that what really pissed her off was that when she *was* arrested and they took pictures, "My hair is gonna look like shit. I won't be able to wash, put on makeup . . ."

"*That's* what you're worried about?"

"Yeah. My nails will all go to hell."

"That's what you're worried about, honey?"

Liz said she was sick of all the bullshit, and Jimmy told her what she really needed was a good rest in jail: "A good rest in jail, you don't think of nothing. They tell you when to eat, when to sleep, and you'll work and you'll relax, the kids won't be crying, nagging you. Look at the good rest you'll have."

After minimizing another section of conversation, the agents heard more talk about the Wood murder and again activated the machines:

LIZ: . . . we were laying in bed and you told me [unintelligible] . . . met a guy, he could do this and you ran all the details down. . . .

JIMMY: [Unintelligible] we were discussing [unintelligible] doing . . .

LIZ: Oh! And you said, "I'll leave it up to you."

JIMMY: And what did you suggest?

LIZ: And I said, "Yeah, do it."

JIMMY: [Laughs] Hey, man, as it stands now, you killed Wood.

As Liz was preparing to leave, Jimmy reminded her to destroy the notes they had been passing. Liz said she would flush them or burn them on her way home, then she paused, looked back at Jimmy, and said she still didn't trust his friend Jerry Ray James.

As Liz led Jackie out of the visiting area, she saw two FBI agents crossing in her direction. She hurried for the women's restroom, her heart beating wildly. She tore the notes into many pieces, but when she attempted to flush them, she discovered that someone had turned off the water. The agents recovered ninety-two soggy pieces from her purse and fitted them back together. Among other things, Liz had written: "Joe says the FBI knows I took some money to Teresa." By now, this was hardly news to the FBI, but of course Liz had no way of knowing that agents had been listening to her conversations with Jimmy for months. All she knew was that the FBI now had solid evidence, in her own handwriting.

On her trip back to El Paso that night, Liz Chagra was fighting for control. Two more FBI agents detained her in Denver, while she was changing planes, and two more agents were waiting to question her at El Paso International Airport. The agents had obviously decided it was time to apply the big squeeze. By the time Liz made it to her house on Santa Anita Street, next door to Joe and Patty, she was almost hysterical. She told Joe and Patty that agents had offered her a deal: $500,000 in cash and a new identity. If she didn't cooperate, they would take away her children and put her in prison for life. "They told her she had forty-eight hours to make up her mind," Patty recalled. Liz told the agents she would "think about it."

In reality, there was nothing to think about. The FBI had no intention of working a deal: they believed they had their case. It was contained in many hours of tapes, supported by testimony from Jerry Ray James and others.

A few nights after Liz Chagra returned from her final visit to Leavenworth, guards awakened Jimmy in the dead of night and told him to pack his things—he was leaving Leavenworth. In total secrecy, surrounded by elaborate security, they drove all night. Shortly after dawn, Jimmy saw the place where he would spend most of the remaining years of his life: the maximum-security prison at Marion, Illinois, 125 miles southeast of St. Louis. Marion was a small complex of gray concrete buildings located in a federal wildlife preserve. It was the toughest penal institution in America, the new Alcatraz, a warehouse for men considered too vicious, incorrigible, or criminally sophisticated for other state or federal prisons. Marion warden Harold Miller once observed: "Judges sentence criminals to prison to protect society. Wardens send prisoners to Marion often to protect other inmates." For several days neither Chagra's lawyers nor members of his family knew his whereabouts. It was several weeks before Joe Chagra or anyone else was permitted to visit or even talk to Jimmy.

Soon after Jimmy's transfer, the FBI took Jerry Ray James out of Leavenworth and hid him in an undisclosed location. A few months later, New Mexico governor Bruce King made the astonishing announcement that James had been pardoned. The news that Jerry Ray James had "flipped" sent shock waves through every jailhouse, pool hall, and police precinct from Albuquerque to Corpus Christi. Here was a criminal who had occupied a position on the FBI's Ten Most Wanted List, who, according to the FBI, was "extremely dangerous" and fancied himself "a modern-day Al Capone." The Justice Department claimed that James's release was "in the interest of justice," but the Justice Department was just about alone in believing it. The police chief in Tatum, New Mexico, who had helped send James to prison for what everyone had hoped was the last time, called the pardon "a travesty of justice," and the prosecutor who had argued for James's life sentences said: "He's as mean as they come; there are none meaner." It was reported that James's aging parents in West Texas were so embarrassed that their once-famous son had turned out to be a common snitch that they refused to go out in public. Odessa, Texas, attorney Warren Burnett, who had defended James in the New Mexico trial that resulted in the life sentences, said: "I don't know what's going through his mind. I only know that it's a lot easier to escape from wherever the government is hiding him than it is from Leavenworth."

Within days of James's departure from Leavenworth, the FBI applied to Judge Sessions for permission to search the homes of Joe, Liz, Patsy, and Mom Chagra, and of Red Nichols, Liz Chagra's father.

On February 27, 1981, seventy agents from the FBI, the DEA, and the IRS blocked off a section of Santa Anita Street, pulled their vans in place, and raided the Chagra homes. The raid was supposed to be secret, but every media outlet in El Paso knew about it in minutes. The search took fourteen hours. It turned up the map and the tape Joe had made of Harrelson's incoherent phone call from Houston. It also turned up two ounces of cocaine and five pounds of marijuana. Agents seized family assets, including several million dollars' worth of jewelry and silver coins and thousands in cash. They confiscated five of Mom Chagra's family scrapbooks and took Joe's wedding ring. They took the watch off Liz Chagra's wrist. They even took a ring that Patty Chagra's parents had given her when she was in high school. In theory, all these assets were seized as a lien against the $600,000 Jimmy owed the IRS, even though the IRS had already collected $450,000 from the sale of the house in Las Vegas and another $180,000 cash that Jimmy was carrying when he was arrested, plus a car and a $35,000 Winnebago.

While El Paso police blocked all traffic from entering the 4000 block of Santa Anita, agents carrying briefcases, cameras, and electronic equipment shuttled among the four houses. They took photographs of the trunk of a car parked in front of Liz Chagra's house and used a metal detector to scan the backyard. Other agents carted packing boxes of jewelry, money, and documents from the home to the vans. Red Nichols complained that the agents looked through every envelope, every piece of paper, even a sack of potatoes. An agent told a reporter: "If we find what we're looking for, it should lead to indictments. We're getting closer, and after today, we may be there."

The agents were as courteous and polite as they were thorough, inventorying each item as it was seized. When the intercom system at Joe Chagra's home was damaged, the agents instructed him to send the repair bill to the local FBI office. When Joe protested that some of the items were privileged, particularly the map and the microcassette with the initials C.V.H., the agents were careful to include this in their report. The report even noted that the Chagras treated agents to pizza. Various exchanges of conversation were also noted in the reports: when field tests made of the powdery white substance revealed it to be cocaine of "poor quality," Joe Chagra cracked, "That's typical!"

The agents were extremely careful to distinguish between casual conversation and what they called "interviews." According to the report, there were two interviews with Joe Chagra during the search. The first took place in the master bedroom, near the closet, and was witnessed by an attorney and friend, Richard Esper, who happened to be there at the time:

"Mr. Chagra was asked if he wished to clarify his own particular role or knowledge regarding the murder of Judge Wood. . . . He stated that, as was obvious from the search . . . the FBI incorrectly was considering him a prime suspect in the Wood murder investigation. He added that, even though the search warrant seemed primarily aimed at determining and seizing assets of Jimmy Chagra, he felt the under-lying thrust . . . was to find evidence which would be helpful in the Wood murder. Mr. Chagra was told that he was a target in the Wood murder investigation. . . ."

Several times Joe assured agents that he had no prior knowledge or involvement in planning the murder, that he in no way participated in the crime itself. Moreover, he was willing to undergo any type of questioning, including a polygraph examination, regarding his knowl-edge or involvement prior to the murder. What he couldn't talk about, he told the agents, were conversations he had with Charles Harrelson or with his brother since the murder: these fell into the area of at-torney-client relations. The agents were careful not to mention what evidence supported their theory, but they told Joe that the govern-ment took a different position on the attorney-client question.

The second interview was conducted forty-five minutes later, in one of the children's bedrooms at the back of the house. An agent asked Joe's position on the question of the whereabouts of the murder weapon—had Harrelson told him where he hid it?

More than slightly flustered, Joe told the agent that he could only answer that hypothetically.

"I'm making no acknowledgment or admission regarding that ques-tion," he said, "but hypothetically, if Harrelson had told me the whereabouts of a murder weapon, I would refuse to discuss the matter because, in my opinion, it is covered by the attorney-client privilege."

"The government takes a different position on that issue," one of the agents said. "At the time such a conversation would have taken place, you did not represent Charles Harrelson. Also, if you contend that such a conversation was privileged in that it impacts on your possible defense of your brother, an obvious conflict exists. The priv-ilege, if any, between yourself and Jimmy does not extend to any in-criminating conversations between you and Mr. Harrelson."

"Let me give you another hypothetical case," Joe said. "Say a man telephones me and tells me that he stabbed his wife, then tells me where he hid the murder weapon. As an attorney, I would not be in a position to discuss that admission with you."

"In your hypothetical situation," one of the agents pointed out, "the privilege would only extend, if at all, if the perpetrator who tele-phoned was doing so after or in the course of seeking counsel."

"I might argue that interpretation," Joe told the agent.

"Let me ask you this," the agent said. "Would the privilege exist if this person told you he shot his wife, identified the location of the murder weapon, and asked you to go get the weapon and dispose of it? And you agreed to do it?"

"No, I guess not," Joe admitted.

The agent posed another hypothetical question: "If the murderer had an accomplice and you attempted to assist the accomplice by hiding or disposing of the murder weapon, would you have stepped outside the attorney-client privilege?"

Joe realized he was getting in deeper and deeper. The FBI men knew a great deal more than he had given them credit for: the really crucial question was whether Harrelson had talked to Joe as an attorney, or because he was Jimmy Chagra's brother. Joe himself didn't know the answer to that one.

"I can understand how the government might have mistaken my role in this matter," he said.

"The evidence clearly suggests that Harrelson contacted you as Jimmy Chagra's brother and not as an attorney."

"It's a close question," Joe admitted.

One of the agents asked if Joe and Jimmy, or maybe Joe, Jimmy, and Lee, had ever discussed killing Judge Wood, and if they had, if he would consider it attorney-client privilege. Joe laughed and said that there might have been all kinds of talk about what a rotten guy Wood was, but talking about a crime was hardly the same as committing one. "All I can tell you," he said, "is I had no prior knowledge that Wood was going to be murdered. But more and more, I feel boxed in. I know things look bad for me, but I promise you I'm innocent of any crime. I won't go to jail for something I had nothing to do with."

Before the agents left, they told Joe they would be talking to him again. Maybe next time they could get "more specific about the evidence." One agent asked if Joe had hired an attorney.

"I don't think I need one," Joe said. "But I might ask for one if you want to talk to me again."

Joe followed the agent to the front door. It was dark by now and he could see a few stars over the rim of the mountains. "Do you have a brother?" he asked. "If you do, then you know how I'm caught in the middle of this thing."

37

Two weeks after the massive search and seizure, Joe Chagra flew to California to take a lie-detector test that he hoped would clear him of any complicity in the murder of Judge Wood.

The test was Oscar Goodman's idea. At this point there wasn't much that Joe Chagra could do to stop his indictment, except perhaps convince the grand jury that the government's theory was shot full of holes. The FBI used lie detectors itself, but only when they suited its purposes. For this reason, Goodman selected a highly accredited polygraph examiner named Ted Ponticelli, who had once taught at the Department of Defense polygraph school and had instructed a number of examiners who worked for the Justice Department, including the FBI's own director of polygraph experts.

Ponticelli, who was now in private practice in Santa Ana, California, asked four questions of Joe Chagra:

1. Did you have any advance knowledge that Judge Wood was going to be shot and killed?
2. Did you yourself arrange the shooting of Judge Wood?
3. Did you plan with anyone to kill Judge Wood?
4. Did you yourself shoot Judge Wood?

Joe Chagra's response to each of the questions was "no." Ponticelli mailed a copy of the charts of the examination to the FBI office in San Antonio, along with his interpretation: "Mr. Chagra was in no way involved in the shooting of the judge, he didn't arrange it, he wasn't involved and didn't have any prior knowledge. I have no doubt the man is innocent of any complicity."

Though the FBI refused comment on the test results, it was apparent that the bureau was prepared to ignore them. That same week FBI director William Webster told members of the Washington press corps that the murder of Judge Wood was essentially solved. "We already know the players," he said. "The question now is adequacy of proof."

A number of excellent attorneys from places as far away as Boston and Miami knew about the case and had offered to act as Joe Chagra's defense lawyer, but most of them wanted large fees, and Joe Chagra was virtually broke. "After the FBI left my house that night," Joe said, "I had exactly two dollars in my pocket." One respected attorney willing to represent Joe without a guarantee of future payment was Billy Ravkind of Dallas, who had represented Jim French and a number of other well-known smugglers in Texas and New Mexico. An imaginative and fast-talking attorney, Ravkind had known Lee Chagra from their days of defending the Columbus Air Force, and had helped draft the motion for speedy trial when Lee was indicted in Nashville in 1973. Though Billy and Lee had once been fairly close, Ravkind hadn't seen Lee much in the final years of his life. "He changed a lot since we first met," Ravkind recalled. "He became a hater. It was us and them. I always felt *them* meant criminals. *We* were the lawyers. Lee was having trouble making that distinction. He took the problems he was having with Wood and Kerr personally." In Ravkind's lexicon, clients were often referred to as "punks," "grease balls," or "scum bags," terms that served to endear the lawyer to certain members of the law-enforcement community. Billy prided himself on his close connections with cops, particularly federal agents, who could be frustratingly autonomous and noncooperative with most defense attorneys. The ploy had well served a number of his clients: Ravkind had a reputation for winning difficult cases. At the moment, Joe Chagra appeared to fit that category.

Ravkind recalled: "When I first talked to Joe right after the search, I wasn't even thinking about the Wood murder. I'd read about the dope they found in his safe. I assumed that was his problem." Ravkind learned different a few days later when two friends who were investigative reporters for the Dallas *Morning News* telephoned. The reporters, Howard Swindle and Allen Pusey, had been talking to an FBI agent in the East Texas town of Tyler and had learned that Joe Chagra's problems were more serious than he believed. In his own conversations with Joe Chagra, Ravkind had been assured that his client had nothing to do with the Wood murder, and he still believed that; but the FBI had *some* reason to believe otherwise.

Ravkind was curious. He arranged a meeting with the FBI agent who had been working with a team of agents attempting to recover the murder weapon from the area around Lake Ray Hubbard. This was the first time Ravkind realized the agents had seized a map from Chagra's safe. The agent didn't tell Ravkind about the one thousand hours of tape now in the government's possession, but he gave the attorney a rough idea of the FBI's theory of the murder—that Joe Chagra had encouraged his brother to hire Charles Harrelson.

"The agent assured me Joe was a prime target in the investigation," Ravkind recalled. "The theory sounded incredible, but I realized they had something, some sort of evidence. I suggested another meeting with Joe present and with other FBI agents. If they showed us their evidence, maybe we could explain it. I called Joe in El Paso and again he assured me the government had nothing that would implicate him in the murder. What they did have was two ounces of cocaine and five pounds of marijuana. That was twenty years in prison, just for openers. If they also had evidence linking him to the murder, it was gonna be a tough case to beat."

Joe Chagra agreed with Ravkind's estimation that by talking to the FBI they had very little to lose, and maybe much to gain. Ravkind wanted to head off the indictment before it was too late. On Friday, March 20, Ravkind and Chagra flew to San Antonio for a meeting with FBI officials, and during the course of a five-hour interview they learned of the existence of at least one piece of electronic evidence. An agent asked Joe if he'd ever admitted to anyone any part in Wood's murder, and Joe replied emphatically that he had not. The agent raised an eyebrow, then played a short burst of tape. Joe sat stunned as he heard his own voice during this exchange with his brother:

JIMMY: Boy, we shouldn't have done that, huh, Joe?
JOE: Yeah.
JIMMY: Huh?
JOE: Yeah.
JIMMY: Yeah, what?
JOE: Shouldn't have done it.

At this point the agent switched off the tape machine. Joe could feel the cold, sickening swirl of cocaine in his head; he looked to Ravkind for guidance. Ravkind told the agents he wanted to talk to his client outside the interview room. "Joe vaguely remembered the conversation," Ravkind said. "Jimmy was always making crazy remarks. Joe told me he got in the habit of just blowing him off, of saying anything that would get Jimmy off his back." Joe had warned the agents before the meeting that he wouldn't discuss his brother, so it was agreed that from this point forward, Ravkind would do the talking. Back inside, Ravkind told the agents: "He remembers now. Jimmy was always making crazy remarks. Joe tells me he was horrified that his brother would even *joke* about such things." The agents smiled: it was time to spring the trap. They played another burst of tape:

JIMMY: I'd have a better shot, huh?

JOE: Uh huh.

JIMMY: You're the one said do it, do it, do it. You're the one was all hot to do it.

JOE: I always thought you was talking about it. I never thought you'd get someone like this guy to do it.

JIMMY: Why?

JOE: I always thought someone like the Face, someone in the Mafia.

JIMMY: I had a few thoughts like that. What difference does it make?

JOE: Well, this guy's an asshole. That's what difference.

On their way back to the airport, the two attorneys, one of whom was now a client about to be charged with an extremely serious crime, realized that talking to the agents had been a mistake. The FBI had played only a tiny section of one reel: chances were good they had additional reels, some possibly more incriminating than the one they had just heard. They had both known that the interview was a calculated risk—anytime a client and attorney confront the evidence in advance, they risk getting themselves stuck with a story that may or may not hold. "Jimmy was always making crazy remarks"—maybe a jury would buy it, but the FBI hadn't.

"We were both in a state of shock," Ravkind recalled. "I'd assumed that everything Joe told me was one hundred percent true, but now I knew at least one thing he hadn't told me. I knew now they had some tapes that were going to require some explaining." And the FBI had assured both attorney and client that there were many more tapes in evidence. They had told Joe: "It's time to level with us. The tapes are full of talk about dope deals, and there are many other references to Judge Wood and other criminal matters. You can help yourself by helping us." Ravkind was certain of one thing: Joe wasn't about to help the FBI, not if it also meant hurting Jimmy. Dealing with Harrelson was another matter, however. Joe obviously believed that he was acting as Harrelson's attorney, but Ravkind didn't buy this, and neither did the FBI. Ravkind was already thinking about a defense, not only for the drug charges, but for the much more serious charge of conspiring to murder a federal judge. He was seeing himself as a hero.

A few days after the trip to San Antonio, Ravkind decided to take some more calculated risks. First, he leaked word to some newspaper friends about the map the FBI had seized in the search: though there had been rumors of a map, no one connected with the media knew that the map came from Charles Harrelson, or that it claimed to show the location of the weapon used to murder Judge Wood. Joe Chagra couldn't reveal his attorney-client conversations with Harrelson, but Billy Ravkind could and did.

No sooner had this sensational revelation made headlines across Texas than Ravkind leaked another choice morsel—he told reporters about the five-hour meeting with the FBI, including the playing of the incriminating tape, the contents of which he recited, to the best of his memory. Ravkind also related to reporters his theory about the substance of the electronic evidence—that Joe was easily bullied by his older brother and habitually agreed with any absurdity Jimmy might invent, not for the purpose of committing any crime but just to placate Jimmy. "It's clear that Joe is not a conspirator," Ravkind said. "Anyone with an IQ of eighty should realize that. The FBI selected the worst part of the tape, and took it out of context. No one in their right mind would call the Mafia up and ask them to kill a federal judge. It's absurd and the FBI knows it."

Ravkind had a good deal of experience with cases in which the government's evidence was chiefly recorded conversations. He believed that the best defense was to "defuse" the tapes as quickly as possible, which usually required leaking their contents, as well as explaining the more subtle meanings, to the media. "I wanted the government to be aware that we weren't pushovers, that we were prepared to fight the tapes," he said privately. "If they believed that we might even use the tapes to our own advantage, they might not indict." Ravkind learned that the FBI, rather than prosecutors from the U.S. attorney's office, was calling the shots in this investigation; and that the FBI was broken into two factions—one group that didn't want to indict Joe Chagra for conspiracy to murder, and a second, more influential group that thought the government had no choice. The government's case against Harrelson and Jimmy Chagra was absolutely dependent on the tapes, and on the material seized in the search, and unless Joe was indicted as a part of the conspiracy, every scrap of evidence might be useless in court. Ravkind knew that the prosecution already had more than enough to indict Joe. The grand jury would do whatever the prosecution instructed. If Joe was indicted, the court would no doubt set bond at some outrageous figure that couldn't be posted, and Joe would go straight to jail, for weeks, maybe months. Ravkind felt certain that Judge Sessions would insist on trying the case himself, in San Antonio where the Chagra name was anathema, in a courthouse named for the victim of the murder. "The case would be over before it started," Ravkind said. "You could walk into that courtroom with the Virgin Mary and find it hard to walk out. The jury would think that Adolf Hitler was on trial."

One week after the meeting with the FBI, Billy Ravkind staged a media event in his office in downtown Dallas, arranging for Joe to undergo a second polygraph examination and inviting members of the media to be present for the results. Ravkind described it as a "gamble," but it was nothing of the sort. To no one's surprise, Joe passed. Former Dallas police department polygraph examiner Donald E. McElroy told members of the media: "He was questioned about the death of Wood and about the planning and his responses were not deceptive —he didn't do it." As in the case of the first test in California, the results would be forwarded to the FBI in San Antonio, in the hopes that this would persuade the grand jury to not indict. "We didn't know the outcome beforehand," Ravkind reminded those present. "We had no Plan B, other than to jump off my office balcony if he hadn't passed." Ravkind talked more about the now famous map—the fact that Joe had had the map for months and had not tried to recover the murder weapon proved his innocence. Billy assumed that the FBI hadn't recovered the murder weapon either; otherwise they wouldn't still be beating the bushes for clues.

That same week a fresh panel of grand jurors, replacing the tainted panel that had vanished along with Jamie Boyd, resumed the Wood investigation in San Antonio. This new panel was so ultrasecret that even the newly appointed U.S. attorney, Reagan nominee Edward

Prado, wasn't told when and where it would meet. An entirely new group of prosecutors, headed by assistant U.S. attorney Ray Jahn and his wife, LeRoy Jahn, two of the best legal minds in the San Antonio office, were put in charge of the day-to-day running of the grand jury, but all important decisions were made in Washington. Many of the same witnesses who had appeared before the old grand jury were called again, including Harrelson's lifelong friend Pete Kay, and Harrelson's stepdaughter, Teresa Starr (now divorced, she had resumed using her family name). El Paso socialite Virginia Farah was also subpoenaed, as was Earl McClendon, who would soon be sentenced to a year in prison for helping Jimmy Chagra during his flight from justice. The government knew by now that Teresa Starr had collected the blood money from Liz Chagra, but they didn't know when or where—the FBI still believed that Liz had delivered the payoff to either Corpus Christi or Brownsville, rather than to the Jockey Club in Las Vegas.

On March 27, the second day of the new grand jury's eighteen-month term, Teresa Starr refused to answer ten questions put to her by the grand jury, including the kicker—"Do you know if Charles V. Harrelson killed Judge Wood?" Because she was testifying under a grant of immunity, Teresa had no right to remain silent. U.S. district judge Adrian Spears, John Wood's longtime friend, declared that the twenty-three-year-old was in contempt of court and ordered her confined to the city jail in Uvalde, Texas, eighty miles southwest of San Antonio, for the remainder of the grand jury term, or until she decided to cooperate. Teresa told Judge Spears that while she didn't look forward to spending time in jail, "I don't want anybody I love to go to jail, either—like my mother." Or like Charles Harrelson. It was now obvious that the government would jail anyone who refused to talk to the grand jury, and that definitely included Teresa's mother, Jo Ann Harrelson. The government knew that Harrelson wouldn't crack, but they were more than willing to test the degree of loyalty of his various lovers.

Meanwhile, the FBI was having trouble breaking Harrelson's alibi. At least two of his alibi witnesses were standing by their stories. Dallas hairdresser Ralph Mitchell was certain that he saw Harrelson in his shop on the morning of the murder, though he couldn't pinpoint the exact time. Sheryl Mendoza, a teller at the Greenville Avenue Bank & Trust in Dallas, was also uncertain of the time, but she remembered vividly waiting on a man who identified himself as Charles Harrelson, sometime before 11:30 A.M. on May 29, 1979. She recalled that he cashed several checks, using an Oregon driver's license for identification, but what she remembered most strongly was discovering a short time later that one of the checks was drawn on an account that had been closed. She had to telephone Harrelson and ask him to return the money. "I was so impressed," she said, "because he came right back that afternoon and repaid the money."

38

After an embarrassing number of statements about "imminent" indictments had been followed by inaction, the second anniversary of Judge Wood's assassination was allowed to pass without a murmur from official circles. Despite the use of unlimited federal resources, including 174,970 man-hours and more than $7 million; despite the unprecedented use of hidden microphones; despite the accumulation of mountains of documents; and despite grants of immunity for some witnesses, contempt of court citations for others, and a pardon for double-lifer Jerry Ray James, the government was not yet prepared to announce a solution to the crime of the century.

There was no pressure from Washington, or so Jack Lawn claimed. The agent-in-charge of the FBI office in San Antonio said: "Oh, we're aware it's the second anniversary. This is still the second or third most important case in the FBI's history. This case will be examined and we have to make sure all the t's are crossed and the i's dotted. . . ." Lawn had recently approved a statement by the Committee for Justice announcing that "one or more persons" had qualified for the $100,000 reward the group had offered for information leading to a conviction, and that no one else need apply. It went without saying that Jerry Ray James was among the "one or more persons."

The anniversary was noted in some quarters. A school in San Antonio was dedicated in the assassinated judge's honor. In Washington, Henry B. Gonzalez delivered another of his "King Crime" speeches on the floor of the House of Representatives. The congressman pointed out the abysmal lack of cooperation among federal agencies, and predicted that unless the Wood murder got the highest priority it would "go into the dust bin of history and oblivion as did the Jimmy Hoffa case."

285

A number of witnesses who appeared before the grand jury in the summer of 1981 who were friends, relatives, or former employees of Liz Chagra were invariably questioned about any knowledge they might have of a trip that Liz made to either Corpus Christi or Browns- ville in the month following the assassination. If the investigators had examined the Leavenworth tapes more closely they would have heard Jimmy Chagra tell his brother that Liz hadn't been out of Las Vegas that month. The only person who could shed any light on the payoff, other than Cindy Cote, who had accompanied Liz to the Jockey Club in Las Vegas but hadn't gone inside the room, was Teresa Starr; and she was still in jail, refusing to talk. The government had also man- aged to jail Earl McClendon and Pete Kay for contempt of court, despite Kay's apparently legitimate belief (an FBI agent had re- layed the message) that Harrelson would have him killed if he talked to the grand jury.

The government had focused its investigation on two critical areas —the payoff and the murder weapon. On three, actually, if you counted the question of "privilege," which the government pretended not to count.

Despite a massive search of the Lake Ray Hubbard area, not far from the Stuckey's turnoff of I-20 that was noted on the map taken from Joe Chagra's safe, no weapon had been located. In April, agents using metal detectors had combed an area east of Dallas, along the East Fork of the Trinity River. Later, a task force of twenty agents returned to an area closer to the lake. They trucked in loads of sand and constructed a three-foot dam across Buffalo Creek, near a bridge abutment spanning one of the back roads around the lake. They had used two backhoes, shovels, and finally their hands to rake through the mud, but again found nothing. Conversations from the tapes indicated that Jo Ann Harrelson knew the location of the gun, and she had been called before the grand jury four or five times by now; though she steadfastly refused to answer questions, the government wasn't yet prepared to offer her immunity and threaten her with jail. In early August, while Charles Harrelson was creating his own headlines by staging a hunger strike in the Harris County Jail, Jo Ann Harrelson was again hauled before the grand jury, and this time prosecutors asked Judge Sessions to hold her in contempt. The judge surprised almost everyone by refusing: possibly *he* was concerned that forcing her to talk would violate her right not to testify against her husband;

either that, or he knew something the prosecutors didn't know, that the FBI believed it had a major break in the case, one that would make Jo Ann Harrelson's silence irrelevant.

The "break," although it didn't immediately look like one, came in the early part of the summer when Harrelson's rich buddy Hampton Robinson III was arrested and charged with the murder of a drug dealer whose body had been found at an abandoned motorcycle track near Houston. (The charges were later dropped.) In the two years since Wood's assassination, several of Harrelson's running mates had been arrested on an assortment of unrelated state charges, and though all of them claimed to be "stand-up dudes" who would rather face a firing squad than rat on a friend, the feds never stopped trying to bring pressure on them. With Hamp Robinson, the pressure worked.

In piecing together its theory of how Harrelson stalked the judge, the FBI had accounted for most of the days leading up to the morning that Wood was killed, the Tuesday following the Memorial Day weekend of 1979. They knew, for example, that on Sunday, May 27, Harrelson and Pete Kay had visited a friend in the state prison at Huntsville. The Thursday before May 24, they had reason to believe that Harrelson had telephoned Hamp Robinson's house in Houston from a pay phone at the San Antonio airport. Harrelson had apparently called again the following day, this time from a restaurant less than two miles from the judge's townhouse. Until Robinson began talking, they couldn't account for Harrelson's whereabouts on Saturday, May 26. But now they learned that while the judge and his wife were enjoying the weekend at their resort at Key Allegro, Harrelson and his friends were celebrating at Hamp Robinson's ranch in Dodge, Texas, on the edge of the Sam Houston National Forest. It was Robinson's pre-wedding celebration. He was marrying Pete Kay's cousin, Jo Ann Stafford, and Charles Harrelson was his best man.

By weaving together various accounts, the FBI constructed a bizarre tapestry of the underworld at play. Most of the guests were armed, and there were enough drugs on hand to paralyze the audience at a Stones concert. Pete Kay arrived late Friday afternoon, with a live alligator in the back of his pickup truck. The alligator had wandered out of a swamp as Kay was driving to the party, and he decided it would be a perfect wedding present. Kay, a rotund fellow whom Harrelson had nicknamed Peterpotamus, borrowed a bottle of red nail polish and painted the words HAPPY WEDDING on the reptile's belly before presenting it to Robinson and his intended. Everyone had a good laugh, then they shot the unfortunate creature.

Later that evening, another longtime friend of Harrelson's, Greg Goodrum, whose family had helped raise Harrelson after his mother left home, arrived with a headful of drugs and a 6mm rifle, with which he managed to shoot himself in the foot. A man from California named Eric Brogan, who had arrived with Harrelson, apparently knew something about gunshot wounds and sewed up the hole with a household needle and thread. Brogan was killed six days later in a car wreck. By Saturday night, a number of guests were zonked on various refreshments, and while they were engaging in competitive shooting, some fights broke out. Pete Kay had gone home by this time, but over the next hour or so he received several hysterical phone calls. First, a friend named Dan Stone called and said he had just shot Hamp Robinson's business partner, Pat Williamson, in the chest. A few minutes later, Williamson himself called, saying he had been shot in the heart, and asking Kay what he should do. "Hell, go to the hospital," Kay said. He hung up, but seconds later Williamson's wife called, screaming that her husband was dying and begging Kay to do something. Kay tried to telephone Hamp Robinson, but couldn't locate the host. That's because Robinson was in a near-coma from having sampled some cocaine tainted with poison. He couldn't remember anything about the weekend of his wedding party.

Robinson and all his guests survived, but over the next two years a number of them started to talk to federal agents.

Hamp Robinson, who had supplied the information that led to Harrelson's arrest on gun charges in Houston back in the winter of 1980, came forward now with a new piece of information. He told the FBI that somewhere around May 13, just two weeks before Wood was killed, Harrelson asked him to buy a rifle and bring it to Austin. "Bring me something that's good up to four hundred yards" had been Harrelson's instructions.

Greg Goodrum, who faced state charges for grand theft and firearms possession (later dismissed), remembered that ten days after the party, Harrelson showed him a high-powered rifle hidden in the trunk of his blue Lincoln. Harrelson said it was his favorite gun, and described it as "the deluxe Cadillac of guns," a frequent characterization of the .240-caliber Weatherby Mark V. Although the FBI had been working for nearly two years on the supposition that Judge

Wood was murdered with a .243-caliber rifle, the .240-caliber Weatherby fires the same size bullet. It was possible that the government had spent two years looking for the wrong rifle.

Federal agents had already began to suspect this. They had traced nearly every .243-caliber sold in a three-state region for several years before the assassination; they had even called a Houston cop before the grand jury, simply because records showed that he had a fondness for the .243 and had bought a number of the rifles. The murder weapon was probably the single key piece of evidence. If there was such a weapon, and if Jo Ann Harrelson knew where it was buried, there was hardly any chance she would tell. From her jailhouse conversations with her husband, the feds realized that she was prepared to go to prison rather than testify: although the government had removed the wiretaps on the Chagras back in January, they continued to tape Harrelson's cell (and had a snitch planted in the adjoining cell) until the end of May. Harrelson had promised that as soon as this trouble was over, which he believed would be soon, he would take her on a world cruise, and had reminded her of what he called "those four little words"—"Even this shall pass."

Not long after the FBI's second massive search of the Lake Ray Hubbard area, two brothers who made their living collecting aluminum cans found a soggy rifle stock near Buffalo Creek. The stock was badly weathered and discolored, but agents were able to trace it to a manufacturer in South Gate, California. The company's chief engineer examined the stock and told agents that it could have come from four or five rifles manufactured at the plant, including the .240-caliber Weatherby Mark V. The company supplied the agents with names of dealers in Nevada, Oklahoma, and Texas, the three states requested, who sold the Weatherby Mark V. In all, there were 250 dealers. It was going to be a long, tedious process, because the FBI hadn't located the rifle barrel, which would have contained the weapon's serial number.

While teams of agents examined records of dealers and traced the purchaser of each rifle sold in the three years before the murder, five divers from the Navy Explosive Ordnance Disposal diving unit of Panama City, Florida, worked the muddy waters of Lake Ray Hubbard east of Dallas. The divers recovered a stolen motorcycle, a stolen Jeep, a safe, a truck cab, and three rifles from the mud and silt, but not the missing barrel of the Weatherby.

The search ended in late August when agents inspecting the records of a sporting-goods store in the Dallas Quadrangle shopping center discovered that the purchaser of a .240 Weatherby Mark V had given a nonexistent phone number and an address where there was no house. The Weatherby, along with a scope and a box of ammunition, was purchased on May 17, 1979, twelve days before the murder of John Wood, by a woman who gave her name as Faye L. King. *Faking*! Fingerprints lifted from the Bureau of Alcohol, Tobacco and Firearms registration form filled out by the purchaser were those of Jo Ann Harrelson. And handwriting samples from the form matched those taken from Mrs. Harrelson several weeks earlier.

On September 1, Jo Ann Harrelson was arrested in Houston and charged with using a false name to buy a weapon, a federal crime worth up to five years in prison. The FBI never did find more than the stock of the gun they believed killed Judge Wood, but now, after twenty-seven months of investigation, they had established that Jo Ann Harrelson bought a gun that *could* have been used. It was their best piece of physical evidence.

39

Calvin Wright was a practical man. Jimmy Chagra was counting on his help in escaping from Leavenworth, but when the former Air America mercenary appeared before the grand jury on September 2, he told his lawyer: "When the elephants fight, the ants get stomped. I don't want to get stomped." FBI agents now acknowledged that the tapes they had played for Calvin at Leavenworth, the tapes of Harrelson's voice that had greatly upset Jimmy Chagra, were fakes. The tapes were bait, to see what Calvin would do. What he did was call Joe Chagra. As it turned out, Calvin Wright knew nothing at all about Wood's murder. He didn't even know about Jimmy's escape plan.

Several "mystery" witnesses appeared before the grand jury in the late summer. On these occasions, the jury was secretly transferred from the federal courthouse to a room on the fifth floor of the downtown post office building. While FBI agents with walkie-talkies patrolled the premises, the witnesses, usually with their heads covered by coats, were delivered by way of an underground parking garage. One such mystery witness was Cindy Cote, the secretary who had accompanied Liz Chagra to the Jockey Club in Las Vegas a month after the murder. Ms. Cote told the jury that Liz carried a beige briefcase and was very nervous. That was all she knew. Another mystery witness matched the description of Jerry Ray James—heavyset, balding, graying, a tattoo of a panther on his right arm. Judging from the time he spent in the grand jury room, James knew a great deal.

On the morning of October 3, the mystery witness was a pretty blonde. After seven months in jail, Jo Ann Harrelson's daughter, Teresa Starr, had decided to talk.

Soft-spoken and almost painfully diffident, the twenty-five-year-old spent most of the day unburdening herself to the grand jury. She had refused to talk earlier because she was frightened for her mother, and for herself. Prosecutors had already heard that Jo Ann Harrelson had made two suicide attempts since the assassination, and now Teresa told them that for at least one of the attempts she had help: Harrelson had tried to kill his wife because he thought she was better off dead than being subjected to the hassle of the Wood murder investigation. Certainly Charles Harrelson was better off if she was dead. Teresa said that another time while Charles and Jo Ann were "eating uppers [amphetamines] in their condominium in Dallas, Charles tied her to a chair and left her to die." Prosecutors didn't take this opportunity to press the witness for recollections of her own love affair with her stepfather, except to establish that such an affair existed. Teresa had kept about twenty love letters written by the suspected killer. One letter reminded Teresa: "This will pass. Then we will share our love, just the two of us, forever and ever." Like all the letters, it was signed "Pappy."

Teresa said that her involvement in the Judge Wood affair had begun in June, a few weeks after the killing. She was living with her real father in Aransas Pass, near Corpus Christi, awaiting a divorce from her husband, Michael Jasper. Her mother called and asked Teresa to meet her and Charles Harrelson at a beachfront hotel on Padre Island. At the hotel, Harrelson asked if Teresa was interested in making some money—it would require traveling out of town to pick up a package. "You'll make a few thousand dollars if you do it," he said. Teresa agreed, and Harrelson gave her detailed instructions. She was to fly to Las Vegas, check into the Jockey Club, and await a call at a pay phone in any of three casinos she would preselect. The payoff call came on June 24, while she was waiting at the Fremont Casino. Harrelson instructed her to return to her room at the Jockey Club and prepare to leave. Teresa had just finished packing when there was a knock on the door. It was a pregnant woman with long brown hair. The woman walked into the room, placed a briefcase on the sofa, wiped away fingerprints with a piece of tissue, and left without speaking.

"Was the woman Elizabeth Chagra?" asked the prosecutor, Ray Jahn.

"I don't know," Teresa replied.

When the woman left, Teresa said, she opened the briefcase and found a box wrapped in brown paper. She didn't open the box, but she held it to her ear and shook it. "I was curious," she said. The following day she delivered it to Charles and Jo Ann Harrelson, who met her at the Corpus Christi airport. "Everyone was real happy," she said. "I took the briefcase out of my luggage and handed it over the car seat. My mother opened it as we drove out of the airport. There were several bundles of hundred-dollar bills in it. Either my mother or Charles said, 'There must be more than a quarter of a million in here.' They were pleased." Harrelson gave Teresa $5,000.

When Teresa returned home later that day, her father told her the FBI had been there looking for her. Federal agents returned the following day, but Teresa refused to talk to them. When the agents had left, she called Charles and Jo Ann. They didn't appear concerned. But later, Harrelson told her never to discuss the incident with anyone, to "take this information with you to your grave." Teresa couldn't really explain why she had allowed herself to become involved in the first place, except it was the first time in her memory that her mother had ever asked her to do anything. "I wanted to please her," Teresa said.

Two weeks after Teresa's secret testimony to the grand jury— and fourteen months after Charles Harrelson's arrest on the desert highway near Van Horn—Harrelson at last stood trial on the guns charge in Houston. Amid unusual security measures, reporters and spectators jammed the Harris County Courthouse to look at the man suspected of killing Judge Wood, and to ogle his wife and stepdaughter, who were there to demonstrate support. A Dallas jury had by now convicted Jo Ann Harrelson of the federal crime of using a fake name to purchase a rifle, and she had been sentenced to serve three years in prison. The Dallas trial wasn't the end of Jo Ann's troubles, however: she had been called again before the Wood grand jury. The government had decided to grant her "use immunity," meaning that the government couldn't use her testimony to indict her in the Wood murder, but could still indict her for obstructing justice. She was warned that if she lied in answering any of the carefully selected questions put to her in the grand jury room, she would be indicted for perjury. The government considered perjury among the most serious of crimes: each lie could add five years to her prison time. (The substance of her grand jury testimony remained secret, but the government was obviously displeased: she was eventually indicted and convicted of five counts of perjury.)

Jo Ann, who was free on bail while her Dallas conviction was being appealed, had become a minor celebrity and appeared to enjoy the role. Television cameras surrounded her as soon as she arrived at the Harris County Courthouse, and she talked freely. She complained that she hadn't been allowed to visit her husband for weeks, and that she believed that all of her conversations were being recorded. "When I communicate with my lawyers, I write it out on one of those erasable magic slates I bought for eighty-nine cents," she said. She also mentioned that a Hollywood producer had approached her about filming her life story, but the FBI had scared him off. If Jo Ann knew what her daughter Teresa had told the grand jury, she didn't show any anger about it: mother and daughter seemed to be on friendly terms, and both seemed as loyal as ever to Charles Harrelson. In the thirty-three months that Jo Ann had been married to Charles, fourteen of them had been spent visiting him in the Harris County Jail. Despite that, and despite the fact Jo Ann knew about Harrelson's affair with Teresa, she was fiercely supportive.

Something else had happened recently that gave the otherwise routine trial in Houston a special aura. Reporters had just learned that shortly after Harrelson's arrest in Van Horn, his Houston attorney, Bob Tarrant, had gone to Jamie Boyd with an offer to plead his client in the Wood murder. The offer had been rejected by the Justice Department, partly because the deal included a presidential pardon for Bob Tarrant, who had been convicted in 1971 of possessing illegal weapons—including some machine guns—and was thereafter prohibited from practicing in federal court.

Bob Tarrant's defense of Harrelson on the gun charge—it is illegal for a convicted felon to possess guns, and five of them had been found in Harrelson's car after Hamp Robinson tipped off authorities—began on an odd and acrimonious note. Tarrant delivered a seemingly endless procession of statements, opinions, and awkwardly worded motions and objections, complaining that Harrelson was the victim of a conspiracy and that the Houston trial was illegal, since authorities had bugged Harrelson's cell. Judge Putnam K. Reiter, a man of vast patience, reminded Tarrant that the Texas Court of Criminal Appeals had already ruled that the bugging was legal. What was more, Tarrant's motions and objections were not made in accordance with the rules of evidence. There were some muffled chuckles in the courtroom when Tarrant said he didn't know the rules of evidence. "I was terrible in law school and I don't know the names of all those objections," Harrelson's lawyer admitted.

As the judge offered to lend Tarrant his copy of the book on evidence, Charles Harrelson looked at the ceiling, shaking his head in apparent disgust. Prosecutors smiled, leaning back in their chairs.

Harrelson's own testimony was a fiasco. Asked why he had failed to appear when his trial was originally scheduled in July 1980, Harrelson told the jury he had overslept that day. When he had waked up, why hadn't he notified authorities? Harrelson said he had heard on the radio that Houston cops had orders to shoot him on sight. During recess, Harrelson talked and joked with reporters, and with his wife and stepdaughter. He admitted it looked bad, but he wanted reporters to understand that all cops were liars. "I'd rather be a quadriplegic than a policeman," he said.

Although maximum penalty on conviction was ten years and a fine of $5,000, the prosecution had enhanced the charge because of Harrelson's prior weapons conviction in Kansas City in 1968. The enhancement enabled the jury to double the sentence to twenty years and $10,000, which they did.

This wasn't the end of Charles Harrelson's troubles in Harris County. He still faced charges of possessing gambling equipment (loaded dice) and narcotics (cocaine), and of jumping bail. Prosecutors indicated they would pursue these charges in time. "Who is more deserving of another trial than Charles Harrelson?" asked one prosecutor. Then, too, there were still the cocaine and gun charges in Van Horn.

On December 9, 1981, Harrelson was back in Van Horn, where the Wood murder case had first begun to unravel fifteen months earlier. He pleaded no contest to multiple charges and was sentenced to another forty years in prison.

40

Nearly a year after **FBI** agents spent fourteen hours searching his house, Joe Chagra scarcely believed the nightmare was his. It was like something out of a parallel universe, something that had happened to someone who happened to have the same name. He could still see the army of agents moving with the precision of robots, unscrewing light bulbs, leafing through cookbooks, peering into the baby's diaper bag. He could hear the voice of the man with his name, protesting that this was some kind of tragic mistake, that he wasn't a criminal, he was a *criminal attorney*. Couldn't they see the distinction? It was the same argument Lee had made, the argument that had trailed him to the grave.

Joe thought a good deal about Lee these days, and about Jimmy, too. He felt Lee's ghost more than ever in the house on Santa Anita Street, the house where Lee had lived. It was a different house in many ways—the mirrored gymnasium that Joe had ordered built, the pool table, the pinball machine, the telescope, the trampoline, the pool, the his-and-hers Mercedes-Benz automobiles in the garage—and yet Lee's ghost was pervasive and relentless. Jimmy lived just next door, only he wasn't home now—he wouldn't be back until the year 2010. Mom still lived down the street, in the apartment behind Patsy's house, the house where Mom had lived when Abdou was still alive. Mom was working on a new scrapbook—it was volume thirty in a series with no end. Patsy had divorced Rick de la Torre, and he was off doing his prison time, one of the last victims of Judge Wood's wrath. Joe didn't spend much time at his law office downtown any more, and when he did there wasn't much to do except sit behind the big desk staring at the framed photographs of Abdou and Lee on the wall opposite him. Joe didn't have a photograph of Jimmy at his office. He sometimes joked that all the good pictures of Jimmy had numbers across the bottom.

Sometimes when Joe was in the backyard exercising on the trampoline, he would see Jimmy's three kids next door. Jimmy had never seen his youngest. When Joe thought of his own kids, tears welled into his eyes. One day while they were in the supermarket, four-year-old Joseph Jr. had lost sight of his father and had run up and down aisles, crying and calling, "Daddy, Daddy!" He had yelled when he saw Joe, "I was scared. I thought the government had got you!"

Whenever Joe and Patty saw Jimmy's wife, Liz, which wasn't often these days, she was either whacked on drugs or in a foul mood because she wasn't. Liz had apparently turned Jimmy against his family. She blamed Joe because the money Jimmy had counted on to make his escape—something like $500,000—had disappeared. The truth was, Joe and Patty had never seen this money. At the time of Jimmy's arrest in Las Vegas, Liz's father carried the cash back to El Paso, and in the months that followed the money vanished. Joe and Patty guessed that Liz had squandered it, or perhaps just mislaid it. She had bought an extravagant amount of new furniture, and might have given some to the bail bondsman to reclaim the jewelry he was holding as security. In his conversations with Jimmy, Joe had tried to cover for Liz, to at least hold his tongue when Jimmy raged about the missing cash. And now Jimmy—and maybe the FBI, too—believed that Joe had lost the money, or hidden it for later use. In fact, Joe was broke and had been for months. He was even trying to sell the $60,000 Mercedes that Jimmy had given him in partial payment of attorney fees.

A casual remark about his need to sell the Mercedes, a remark made in front of several federal prosecutors and FBI agents in the hallway of the courthouse at Van Horn on the day that Charlie Harrelson made his no-contest plea, reinforced Joe Chagra's feeling that he was only a cipher in an Orwellian equation, something to be used or discarded at the pleasure of the government. The casual remark ended up in an FBI report, and a few days later agents of the DEA appeared at the Spa for Paws Kennel, where Patty was working, and confiscated the car, which they claimed had been used in a drug transaction involving a former kennel employee named Tom Prout.

Prout, a Vietnam veteran who suffered strange moods of depression that he attributed to his contact with Agent Orange, trained attack dogs for an El Paso security consultant, and had gone to work as a trainer for the kennel the previous March, shortly after the FBI searched Joe's house. Though Prout said he had no experience with drug dealings, he appeared fascinated by the subject and mentioned to Joe that it sounded like an easy way to make money. Patty didn't trust Prout—she accused him of mismanaging kennel funds—and he resigned in June, but Joe continued to employ him as a weapons expert during the trial of Bill Mallow, and talk of drug dealings continued. Prout claimed to have some friends in Florida who would front cocaine for the amazingly low price of $10,000 a pound. As many times as Joe Chagra had heard this sort of rhapsodic come-on, he should have known it was another government trap; and, in fact, Joe told his friend Judge Clark Hughes that he believed Prout was a DEA plant trying to make a drug case against him. Hughes reminded Joe what had happened to Lee in the Nashville case back in 1973 and advised him to "make a record" of any drug conversations with Prout. "It might be wise to go to the authorities and tell them," Hughes said. "Or at least tell some creditable people what's going on." At the conclusion of the Mallow trial, Prout took a job in Dallas, but he continued to telephone Joe, suggesting drug deals. Joe had no way of knowing that Prout's phone calls were being routed through the El Paso DEA office, but he became positive that the affair was a setup when a secretary in Prout's office in Dallas came on the line and asked, "Is this Mr. Pool?" Tom Pool was a local DEA agent who had been instrumental in busting Jimmy.

By this time, Joe had told several friends about the suspected frame-up, and all of them cautioned him to stay away from Prout. Instead, Joe took the advice of another friend, a former DEA agent who lived in New Mexico, who suggested turning the tables on the government with what he called "a double bust"—when the DEA moved in to bust the conspiracy, a second team of friendly agents would expose the entrapment. On September 5, Prout telephoned Joe and said he had "that dog we talked about." This was a code meaning he was bringing a sample of cocaine—one of Prout's wilder ideas was to use dogs as smugglers by implanting drugs in their chest cavities. Joe picked up Prout at the airport, and they drove in his Mercedes to some isolated warehouses, where Joe inspected the half-ounce sample —the DEA later acknowledged that it had supplied the cocaine. That was as far as the deal ever went. Joe took the sample to his

friend in New Mexico for chemical evaluation, but after that he refused to take any more calls from Prout. Apparently realizing they
didn't have enough to make a case, the DEA didn't pursue the trap
until three months later, when one of its agents read the FBI report
that Joe was attempting to sell his car. That's when the agency decided to seize it.

In a hearing before U.S. district judge Lucius D. Bunton in El
Paso in January 1982, DEA agents admitted the attempted setup,
including wiretaps and supplying the drug sample. But the government took the position that "criminal intent was not relevant" to the
seizure of the Mercedes, that the mere fact the car had been used to
transport cocaine was sufficient grounds for the government action.
Joe Chagra's attorney, Bill Ravkind, argued that "the government
can't create its own crime for the purpose of forfeiture of property,"
but the prosecution told the court that the fact that Chagra had
possessed the cocaine, regardless of circumstances, gave the government power to seize the Mercedes. The prosecution even objected to
the court's hearing evidence regarding Joe's allegations of entrapment, but Judge Bunton said he wanted to hear the whole story.

As it turned out, the government's position was upheld by statute.
Judge Bunton, who had filled the vacancy left by Wood's death, ruled
that the government could keep the Mercedes. He took an opportunity
to rebuke the DEA, however, writing: "Nothing in this opinion is to
be construed as approval of the government's tactics in the Chagra
setup. It smacks of harassment from the beginning to the end . . . if
this were a proceeding in equity and the court were not statutorily
bound, the government's unclean hands would prevent the forfeiture."

By now Joe was absolutely certain that the government would
indict him in the Wood murder, regardless of the facts. At this point
no one except a few officials in the federal government knew of the
extent of the wiretaps at Leavenworth. All Joe had heard was that
one piece of tape where Jimmy told him, "You're the one that said do
it, do it," and Joe in his slapdash manner replied that he had thought
Jimmy would hire the "Mafia" to commit the murder. The only additional evidence, as far as Joe knew, was the testimony of Jerry Ray
James. But he believed that a jury would understand Jimmy's pro-
pensity for playing the big shot, that Jimmy would probably have
bragged that he had killed Abe Lincoln if he thought Jerry Ray James
would believe him. Billy Ravkind had tried to impress on Joe the

seriousness of his potential drug charges. "Forget the murder," Ravkind had said repeatedly. "What about the drugs they found at your
house? Who was the cocaine for? Who's supposed to do the fifteen
years for that?" Joe knew the penalty for cocaine possession, but he
couldn't bring himself to feel particularly guilty—it was obvious to
Joe, and he felt it would be obvious to a jury, that the drugs grabbed
during the search were nothing more than crumbs from the Wood
investigation.

There were times when Joe must have realized the government had
him boxed in, times when he remembered the childlike pleadings of
Jimmy's voice, times when Joe understood what only a brother might
understand—times when he knew that no matter what happened, no
matter what agony he might be forced to endure, he could never testify
against his brother or his brother's wife. But that's what it was coming to.

In particular, Joe could recall one conversation in which Jimmy
had been close to tears as he talked about wanting to escape. He'd
said: "After I work out this escape plot, I get on a boat to go to the
Orient . . . on a boat I can jump around. And then on searches they
can't follow me so good, you understand what I mean? They won't
know I'm on this boat. The minimum boat to make the cruise is about
an eighty-footer . . . that's at least four or five hundred thousand
dollars. Okay, I need another hundred and forty for the helicopter
and airplane to get me out of here . . . that's almost six hundred right
there. Then I need to live wherever I go . . . to the Orient or wherever.
Shit, I need a minimum of a million or more. And then that leaves
nothing for my family to live on, or my kids to grow up the rest of
their lives. Your kids have you, Joe. My kids don't have me. I'm
fucking in jail. And I know there are twenty million prisoners yelling
at their lawyers to come and see them, but I'm not twenty million
prisoners. I'm your brother! I can say, well, he can go sell his fucking
rings and Joe can sell the cars and come up with this money overnight.
It can't be done. That's what I had that money in your possession for.
You told me you wouldn't touch it. And all of a sudden you come up
and, well, I have four-seventy, then the next week I have two-twenty.
I mean, I don't know what happened to it. It's not fair, Joe, not fair
to me. You're free. I'm not free. And you think I like to tell you these
things now? I'm not gonna spend twenty years in jail, Joe, while you
try to beat my fucking appeals and they indict me on this other thing.

And now I'm trying to fucking cover your ass. There's one thing you oughta know, I'll never let you go to jail. If it comes down to it, I'll just tell them that . . ."

Tell them what? That Joe wasn't involved in the Wood murder? They already knew that; if they had half a brain, they knew that. What was obvious to anyone was that Jimmy could save his brother and his wife, too, if he would just tell the truth about what really happened. But Jimmy wasn't going to do that. That wasn't Jimmy's style. Joe would have to live with that fact, and so would the FBI.

In his own confusion, fear, and depression, Joe wanted someone to understand *his* situation. In an interview with Ann Reifenberg of the Fort Worth *Star-Telegram* Joe came as close as he knew how to baring his soul:

"One thing I just can't get anybody to understand is that there are certain principles that every human being has to live by. I have certain principles I have tried to live by and live with, and I just cannot compromise my integrity and my beliefs to accommodate the federal government or anybody else. You know, I have to live with myself when this is all over, regardless of what happens. It's not fun, and I regret it, what I've put my wife and my family through. But I don't feel sorry or embarrassed or ashamed of anything I've ever done."

Around the second week of March 1982, attorney Billy Ravkind met FBI agent Mick McCormick, in San Antonio, and the two of them had dinner with the government's husband-and-wife prosecutorial team, Ray and LeRoy Jahn. Ravkind had established a good rapport with McCormick as well as with the Jahns, so good in fact that other lawyers close to the case believed that Billy was, as one of them phrased it, "in bed with the government." Ravkind believed he was doing what any good lawyer should—he was attempting to save his client. Ravkind had convinced the FBI to give Joe yet another polygraph test, this time by an examiner who actually worked for the FBI. The results supported Joe's claim of innocence in the Wood murder, but failed to support his claim of attorney-client relationship with Charles Harrelson. Despite their pretenses, Ravkind knew that the government was worried that the claim of attorney-client privilege might be upheld in court. Earlier, the government had hoped to provoke a chain of plea bargaining that conceivably could resolve the protracted investigation without a single trial, but that hope had vanished. Joe was the government's only chance, short of a full-blown trial. Ravkind knew that his client wouldn't testify against his brother, but if he would agree to give up Charles Harrelson, a deal might be made. Ravkind knew by now that Harrelson had admitted killing Wood in his talks with Joe. The question was *when*. Ravkind didn't know the answer himself, but he allowed the prosecutors to believe he did. If Harrelson had admitted the murder on his very meeting with Joe, before there was any talk of an attorney-client relationship, then Joe could divulge what he knew, and Ravkind could make a deal.

After dinner, at a meeting in the den of the Jahns' home in San Antonio, Ravkind again approached the subject of plea bargaining. Ray Jahn, a large, portly man with a disarming teddy-bearish demeanor, reminded the attorney that the final decision would have to be made in Washington, but he was prepared to recommend that the government drop the drug and murder charges if Joe would plead guilty to one count of obstructing justice. Maximum sentence was five years: with good time—and Jahn was willing to help with the parole board—Joe could be free in about eighteen months. Jahn would even entertain the suggestion of helping Joe regain his license to practice law. "I need an answer right away," Jahn reminded Ravkind. "We're ready to indict. After the indictments come down, there's nothing I can do."

The following day, Ravkind flew to El Paso and ran down the offer for his client. Joe protested that he was innocent. "How can I plead to obstructing justice, when I know I didn't do it?" Joe asked his lawyer.

"Joe, they're not even talking about murder," Ravkind said. "They've got you on the drug count, if they want to go that way. What they're offering is a good deal."

Joe said he would talk it over with Patty and let Ravkind know the answer.

A few days later, Joe and Patty flew to Dallas for a meeting in Ravkind's office with the Jahns and with FBI agent Mick McCormick. Ray Jahn laid out the same offer to Joe that he'd laid out at the meeting in San Antonio—one count of obstructing justice. But what Jahn wondered was what Joe could do for the government. "He wants to hear your proffer," Ravkind told his client. "Otherwise, the government would be buying a pig in a poke." While Ravkind and Patty were out jogging, Joe Chagra told the prosecutors what they wanted to hear.

Joe flew back to El Paso without accepting the government's offer: he needed more time to think about it. Patty recalled: "Billy Ravkind and Mick McCormick came out a few days later. McCormick said this was absolutely Joe's last chance. But Joe just couldn't do it. He didn't think he should—he didn't think they had him. He knew they had some tapes, but he didn't know how many, and he didn't know how bad they were. He really had no idea what kind of case the government had against him." Before leaving, McCormick told Joe the cold hard facts: in a few weeks the government would indict Jimmy, Liz, Joe, and Charles Harrelson on charges of killing Judge Wood, and Jo Ann Harrelson on charges of obstructing justice. The government planned to recommend bonds in excess of $1 million dollars each, which meant that Joe wouldn't get out of jail for months, and probably years.

McCormick had not exaggerated. On April 15, 1982, almost three years after the assassination of Judge John Wood, the grand jury indicted all five. Jimmy Chagra and Charles Harrelson were charged with murder, which carried an automatic life sentence on conviction. Joe Chagra and Liz Chagra were charged with conspiracy to commit murder and obstruction of justice; the conspiracy charge carried a life sentence. Jimmy and Joe were also indicted on drug charges. In a separate indictment, all three Chagras, along with Liz Chagra's father, Leon "Red" Nichols, were charged with trying to defraud the federal government of income taxes for 1979.

The defendants who were not already doing prison terms were arrested and jailed that some day. Bond for Jo Ann Harrelson was set at $250,000. Liz Chagra's bond was $1.1 million, and Joe Chagra's was $1.6 million.

41

By the time pretrial hearings began the first week in August, a formidable array of legal talent had assembled on behalf of the five defendants. Liz Chagra had retained famed Texas trial lawyer Warren Burnett more than a year earlier, about the time of the search, and Burnett had already formulated the essence of what appeared to be a solid defense—that Liz didn't realize that the money she had delivered to the Jockey Club was a payoff for Wood's murder, and that despite the implications of the tapes, she had no real knowledge that her husband was involved in the crime. Charles Harrelson, Jo Ann Harrelson, and Jimmy Chagra pleaded poverty and requested that the court appoint their attorneys. Harrelson wanted Tom Sharpe, who had assisted the retired attorney Percy Foreman in his murder-for-hire cases years earlier. Jimmy asked for his longtime Las Vegas attorney, Oscar Goodman. Although prosecutors objected that both Burnett and Goodman should be disqualified for conflicts of interest—Burnett had once defended the government's star witness, Jerry Ray James, and Goodman had defended another potential government witness, former Chagra bodyguard Brad Bryant—Judge William Sessions overruled the objections and allowed the defendants the lawyers of their choice. Sessions wasn't prepared to risk being overturned by a higher court in such a big case, particularly on such an elementary issue: he realized that rulings of far greater significance, including a motion that he disqualify himself from hearing the case, waited just ahead.

Since Jo Ann Harrelson had not requested a particular lawyer, Sessions appointed a respected San Antonio attorney, Charles Campion, to represent her. In addition to her indictment for obstructing justice in the murder case, Jo Ann faced five additional charges of lying to the grand jury. The perjury charges would be tried separately, as would the charges of tax fraud against the three Chagras.

Billy Ravkind was still lead counsel for Joe Chagra, and a number of other lawyers had agreed to assist or advise, including Sib Abraham and his new partner in El Paso, Charles Roberts, and Ed Mallet and Sam Guiberson, both of Houston. Gerald Goldstein of San Antonio, one of the best constitutional lawyers in Texas, was available to advise Joe Chagra's defense team—or any of the defense teams, for that matter. Goldstein, Mallet, and Guiberson were added to the defense team primarily to advise in the relatively virgin area of electronic surveillance: Guiberson, in fact, was one of the few lawyers anywhere who specialized in tape-recorded evidence.

In the three and a half months between the indictments and the pretrial hearings, Guiberson reviewed all 914 reels—more than 1,000 hours—of government tape. Using linguistic experts and computers, he made his own transcripts, which differed significantly from the government version. The equipment and techniques used by Guiberson were considerably more sophisticated than those used by the Justice Department, and the results showed. Sometimes the differences were small variations of punctuation or emphasis. And sometimes they were enormous. In one place where government technicians had transcribed Joe Chagra saying, "Kill him, kill him," he had actually said, "Get them, get them." Warren Burnett, a lawyer who was seldom impressed by the work of a colleague, was euphoric when he spoke of Guiberson. "What he's doing is unique," Burnett said. "No one else in the country is even close. The prosecution is still in the horse-and-buggy era compared to the defense's tapes."

Not that the defense was unified in a common strategy—each defendant faced unique problems. Charles Campion, for example, would find it necessary to continually remind the jury that Jo Ann Harrelson was not charged with being a party to the murder, but of obstructing its investigation. The key to the government's case was establishing that a conspiracy existed between Jimmy Chagra and Charles Harrelson—Liz and Joe were merely bit players, without whom the government would be hard pressed to establish the central conspiracy. The interests of the lawyers defending Jimmy Chagra and Charles Harrelson therefore were not necessarily the interests of the lawyers defending Liz and Joe.

If there was a weak link in the chain of common cause, several of the lawyers believed it was Billy Ravkind. "It would be impossible to overstate his closeness to the FBI and the prosecutors," Warren Burnett observed. In the aftermath of the search of the Chagra homes, at a time when Joe Chagra was still convinced he owed privilege to Jimmy, Liz, and Charles Harrelson, Ravkind's first impulse was to deliver Joe to the FBI. "As far as I can tell," Burnett said, "Ravkind convinced his client to give up everything he knew right from the start." Almost all of the defense attorneys were critical of Ravkind's frequent leaks to the media. The defense attorneys were united in their desire to have the trial moved out of San Antonio, and especially out of the courthouse named for the murder victim, arguing that the massive publicity had undermined any chance to pick an unbiased jury, and yet Ravkind took every opportunity to talk to reporters.

Long before the public should have even been aware of the existence of the government tapes—much less their content—Ravkind allowed a reporter for KDFW-TV in Dallas to inspect the transcripts. What followed was a dramatic three-part series in which a narrator read some of the most damning passages. Among other things, viewers in the Dallas–Fort Worth area (and, soon readers all over Texas) learned of conversations in which Jimmy and Joe discussed killing Harrelson, Joe told Jimmy that Harrelson wanted to kill his wife and stepdaughter, Jimmy discussed his bizarre escape plan with Liz and then with Joe, and Jimmy blamed both Joe and Liz for masterminding the murder. In one passage broadcast by KDFW-TV, the Chagra brothers talked about the attempted murder of James Kerr:

JIMMY: I don't know who did it. Pick handled that. I don't know who or why or what.

JOE: I wished I knew where Pick was.

JIMMY: He says he hired some guys from Boston. What a botched job that was.

Reporters who had closely followed the saga of Jimmy Chagra knew that Pick was the nickname of Robert Piccolo, who was supposed to have been one of Jimmy's underlings when the Fort Lauderdale dope operation was in full swing. At the time of Jimmy's drug trial in Austin, both the prosecution and the defense were attempting to locate the elusive Pick.

Billy Ravkind had a way of annoying the judge as well as the other defense lawyers. While **FBI** special agent Gary Hart, who supervised the electronic surveillance at Leavenworth, detailed his methods and offered statistical analysis, Ravkind slouched in his chair and made paper airplanes. At one point, Ravkind astonished and dismayed the other defense attorneys by offering to accept without additional testimony the documents that Hart was offering. Judge Sessions said curtly: "Well, *I* want to hear more." At another point in the pretrial, the judge's immaculate demeanor crumbled completely. During a conference at the bench, when Sessions was asking Ravkind about his advice to his client regarding attorney-client conversations with Charles Harrelson, spectators heard the judge bellow, "You told him to tell the FBI *what?*" Sessions then bolted out of his chair and into the privacy of his chambers, court still technically in session. When the judge reappeared a few minutes later, fairly well composed by now, he explained that he was merely checking to make sure Billy Ravkind was authorized to practice in the Western District of Texas.

By the finish of the first week of pretrial, lawyers and reporters were referring to the hearings as "the zoo." Charles Harrelson mugged for reporters and took one opportunity to complain that the feds had planted perfume and women's clothing in his cell for his wife to find. While Jimmy and Liz traded dirty looks, Charles and Jo Ann whispered and touched so frequently that the bailiff had to order them to move to opposite ends of the defense table. Harrelson had supposedly been on another hunger strike (his second or third in less than a year), but he looked lean and mean and ready. Before he started the hunger strike and got himself transferred to the prison hospital, Charlie had been chopping cotton at the Easthem Unit just outside of his old hometown of Lovelady.

Joe Chagra had lost weight, too. He'd been confined most of the summer in a tiny, non-air-conditioned cell in the town of Seguin, northeast of San Antonio, where the daily fare consisted of a sweet roll in the morning and TV dinners for lunch and supper. Normally, he would have been incarcerated in the spacious and modern federal lockup in Bastrop, but the government had decided to transfer Jimmy from the maximum-security prison at Marion to Bastrop and didn't want the two brothers housed in the same prison. Both of the women were jailed in the Bexar County lockup in San Antonio. Jo Ann looked fresh and pretty in a pink dress, but Liz looked like a

troop of Girl Scouts in a sleeping bag. Slender and svelte as a fashion
model at the time of her arrest four months ago, she had gained
forty pounds in jail. Though a sex scandal was brewing in the Bexar
County Jail—women were reportedly swapping sex for drugs—it
didn't appear to have fazed her appetite. Relatives who had visited
them reported that both Jimmy and Liz had undergone religious
conversions in recent weeks. Liz claimed to have been reborn. Jimmy
made no such claim, but Patty Chagra reported that he was reading and quoting the Bible. He told Patty that a few years back he
had "traded his soul to the devil" in exchange for wealth—he meant
it literally, a classic Faustian swap—but now saw the error of his
ways. Patty asked him bluntly: "Does that mean you're going to tell
the truth and get Joe and Liz out of this?" But Jimmy told her that
wasn't his style.

Everyone in the Chagra family was wondering how Jimmy would
react now that the mother of his children faced a long term in prison.
"What is Jimmy gonna do?" a friend asked his sister, Patsy, and
Patsy turned it around and asked: "What would *you* do?" Jimmy
was probably doomed to spend the remainder of his life in prison,
regardless of what happened in this trial. It seemed to be a fairly
simple matter for him to step forward to take the blame, but in
Jimmy's convoluted code of ethics, nothing was simple. Until Joe
began to read the voluminous transcripts of the tapes, realizing for the
first time the force of the government's case, he assumed, as did almost everyone else, that Jimmy's motive for wanting Wood dead was
purely selfish. But there was a short section of tape, a section that
no jury would hear, that shed a softer light on the character of
Jimmy Chagra. Jimmy and Jerry Ray James were smoking grass
and mellowing out one evening when Jimmy confessed that the real
reason he had had the judge hit was to avenge Lee's murder. "I did
it for Lee," he said, and you could almost read the tears in his voice.
It sounded crazy, but in Jimmy's mind those two events merged—
Wood's harassment of Lee, and Lee's death. Joe had never even considered this possibility until now, but if he read Jimmy right, the
terrible act of retribution was also an act of love.

Despite the tapes, there were still holes in the government's case.
The government didn't have a murder weapon, merely the stock of
one of the ten thousand Weatherby Mark V rifles sold in this country
in recent years. Several people, under hypnosis, remembered seeing

Charles Harrelson at the Dijon townhouses on the morning of the murder; but the government didn't have an eyewitness to the actual shooting. Teresa Starr couldn't even make a positive identification of the pregnant woman who delivered the money. And most of all, the government really didn't have proof that a conspiracy existed between Jimmy Chagra and Charles Harrelson—Joe was the missing link. As for the matter of privilege, that still had to be argued before Judge Sessions, and even if he ruled for the government, which seemed likely, the feds realized that the ruling could still be shot down by a higher court. Oscar Goodman had presented a good argument that if the government was permitted to violate the marital and attorney-client privileges "it would do away with the Fourth Amendment."

At this point the government came up with its most Machiavellian device yet—it presented documents suggesting that both Liz Chagra and Charles Harrelson were bigamists, hence the marriage vows under which they sought shelter were not valid. In Harrelson's case, the evidence was his own words—years ago when he was being tried for killing Alan Berg, Harrelson had claimed that the prosecution's star witness, Sandra Sue Attaway, was his common-law wife. Therefore, he could not be married to Jo Ann. The judge in state court had not accepted the claim, but Judge Sessions might. Efforts to dissolve the marriage of Liz Chagra had proved more complicated. It had been twenty years since the teenage Liz had run off to California with a fifty-three-year-old actor and meatpacking-company heir (and cocaine salesman) named Charles Chauvet. The government had gone to considerable trouble locating Chauvet, who hadn't reported to his parole officer in four years, but finally located him in the Central American country of Belize. Chauvet was promptly arrested—he described it as "kidnapped"—and flown to Miami, where agents were waiting to arrest him for parole violation. Now Chauvet was in San Antonio, prepared to testify that Liz was his common-law wife. The prosecution had presented an interesting dilemma to Judge Sessions, asking him in effect to grant summary divorces to four of the five defendants. Fortunately for the Judge, Warren Burnett was able to produce his own document showing that Charles Chauvet had entered into another common-law marriage in 1978.

Sessions backed the defense in the bigamy contentions, but that was just about the only defense victory in the pretrial. Sessions denied the motion that he disqualify himself from hearing the case, despite the testimony of a psychiatrist that a judge who had delivered a eulogy for the murder victim, and had himself worn a flak jacket as protection against an assassin's bullet, could not possibly function in a judicial manner; and despite Billy Ravkind's threat to call Sessions as a defense witness if the government got into the matter of the attempted bribe of Henry Wallace. The defense presented a powerful argument to back up its motion for change of venue. Ed Mallet argued that "the crime of the century" ought to be tried in some city where it was in no danger of encountering the "Jack Ruby syndrome." "A juror might get the impression that the reputation and honor of the community was at stake," Mallet reminded the court, especially when that juror was seated in the John H. Wood, Jr., Federal Courthouse. To absolutely no one's surprise, Sessions denied the change of venue motion, too. At one point, Billy Ravkind figured that Sessions had overruled one hundred straight motions by the defense attorneys.

Joe Chagra was starting to panic. A few days before the deadline for plea bargaining, he asked his attorneys to make another run at the government. Ravkind guessed that the government would jump at the offer, but when he told Ray Jahn that his client wanted to make a deal, the chief prosecutor said dryly, "Does he now?" Jahn said he would call Washington. A few days later, Jahn reported back that Washington was willing to allow Joe Chagra to plead guilty to conspiracy of murder and let him off with a mere thirty years in prison.

When Patty Chagra heard the government's latest offer, she began to panic, too. She telephoned another lawyer, a friend of Sib Abraham's named Abraham "Chick" Kazen III, who practiced in Austin. Kazen was from an influential South Texas family of judges and politicians, and he was a personal friend of Ray and LeRoy Jahn's. Since Kazen had been monitoring the case anyway as a favor to Sib Abraham, he was a de facto member of the defense team. He called Billy Ravkind, who had already talked to his FBI friend Mick McCormick, about the government offer. Apparently the Justice Department had made the offer without consulting the FBI, which had serious doubts about the government's case: without Joe Chagra's testimony, it was going to be almost impossible to prove a conspiracy. To make the case, Joe would have to admit being a part of the conspiracy, of course, but he would have to do more than that. He would have to come up with a proffer that would support the government's theory and evidence. McCormick told Ravkind that if the defense could arrive at a suitable proffer, he thought they could make a deal in which Joe Chagra would only have to serve ten years. Ravkind ran the offer by several other lawyers, including Jimmy's attorney, Oscar Goodman. All agreed that ten years was fair, under the present circumstances. Goodman had a selfish reason, of course, for hoping that Joe would cop a plea—it meant that Jimmy's trial would be severed from the trial of the other accused conspirators, since Joe had made it clear that he wouldn't testify against his brother. It also meant the government's case against Jimmy was mostly dependent on the testimony of Jerry Ray James.

On Monday, September 13, attorneys Ed Mallet and Chick Kazen were given a room in the old federal courthouse and a full day to try to talk some sense into their client, Joe Chagra. In that way that lawyers have of protecting their own backsides, they had calculated that Billy Ravkind, who would make the actual proffer to the government, shouldn't be present as they discussed various scenarios with the client. The story that Joe had already told the FBI, about how Harrelson admitted the murder at their first meeting, before there was an attorney-client relationship, solved part of the problem, but there was still the problem of the tapes. Since the government had to live with the tapes, so did their witness. Maybe Joe had forgotten something. What about the hearing in Judge Wood's court in Midland, the hearing a few months before the murder when Wood had refused to disqualify himself? Maybe there had been some fighting words spoken at the defense table? During a recess, maybe? You could almost see a light bulb appear above Joe's head—his eyes glazed over, like a man under the spell of hypnosis. "I do remember something. . . . " he said tentatively. It was during a recess. Everyone had left the courtroom except Jimmy and Joe. "Jimmy told me he was never gonna get a fair trial and if I thought he should try and have Judge Wood killed." Yes, yes, and Joe said? "I told him he should," Joe replied feebly. Over the next several hours the lawyers prompted the client to recall yet another incident in which Jimmy ruminated on the possibility of having Wood killed and Joe encouraged him. The second time was about ten days after the hearing in Midland, while Jimmy and Joe walked in the garden of Jimmy's

Las Vegas home. Jimmy asked Joe if he still thought he should have the judge killed, and Joe replied that he did. It was the perfect proffer. It explained the part of the tapes where Jimmy told his brother that he was the one who kept saying "do it, do it, do it." It would stand up against the tapes; it would stand up against cross-examination; and it would conform to the government's theory and proof. Best of all, no one could ever contradict it—the only evidence was from the witness's own mouth.

The next day, just hours before deadline, Ravkind took the proffer to the government and the deal was made. Joe Chagra would be the star witness of the government's case against Charles Harrelson. Jimmy's trial would be separate: the star witness against Jimmy would be his old Leavenworth pal Jerry Ray James. Judge Sessions agreed with the recommendations of the prosecution that Joe's prison sentence not exceed ten years. Under the current guidelines, Joe would be eligible for parole after fifty-four months.

When Warren Burnett learned that Joe had made a deal, he realized that defending Liz would become more difficult. Though the agreement apparently stipulated that Joe would not testify directly against his sister-in-law, Joe's testimony would make it indisputable that a conspiracy existed between Jimmy and Harrelson: the mere fact that Liz was being tried in San Antonio, in the same courtroom with Charles and Jo Ann Harrelson, was a major obstacle to the defense. But Burnett had won tougher cases—he still believed he could convince the jury that his client lacked full knowledge of the purpose of the money she delivered to Teresa Starr. Something more transcendental than adequacy of proof worried the attorney, however: he was troubled by his twenty-eight-year-old client's newly born zealotry for the Christian faith. People who had known Liz Chagra before her arrest found it difficult to believe that this was the same woman, and what might appear to be a blessing to a casual observer was a potential curse to the practical mind of an attorney. It wasn't the forty pounds she had gained, or the way she had put aside the vanity of manicured nails and styled hair: the beatific smile that had replaced Liz Chagra's familiar flinty scowl had the edge of guilt. Liz had told members of her family that she thanked God for sending her to jail "because if I had never come I would never have found Christ." In principle, Burnett did not approve of the practice of allowing a local religious ministry group to work with inmates awaiting trial. "Those people do not have your best interest at heart," the attorney advised the client, adding, "All that praying, whooping, and hollering is silly behavior."

A few weeks before the start of the trial, the chief prosecutor, Ray Jahn, telephoned Burnett with a piece of news that stunned the attorney. Jahn had just visited Kathryn Wood, the judge's widow, and read the contents of a letter that Liz Chagra had written to Mrs. Wood, admitting that she had delivered the payoff and asking the widow to forgive her. Mrs. Wood had, of course, given the letter to the FBI. No one seemed to know for sure how the letter had been sent, except that it had been smuggled out of the Bexar County Jail and hand delivered.

The letter said, in part:

Dr. Mrs. Wood,
I am a newly born Christian and after making peace with God, I decided to try and make peace with mankind and especially you. My name is Elizabeth Nichols Chagra. . . .

I will write a true scenario about what happened. Remember that I'm writing about the old "Liz" because the new "Liz" has the strength and courage and respect for you to explain my involvement in this case.

One day in March three years [ago], I was in the kitchen cooking fried chicken, when my husband came home and said, "I'm going to kill Judge Wood." I had heard my husband on many occasions use this phrase. And never before had anything happen to this people. I said, "Ok, honey." Then went about cooking dinner, never giving it any more thought.

I was not involved in a plot or plan for I never sat down and conspired to have your husband murdered. God knows that I am guilt free of that crime.

I was visiting my mother when I first heard the news and that is when shock really set in. I flew home to Las Vegas and confronted my husband. He denied any involvement to me at that time. I guess I more or less figured it out but choosed to close my eyes and believed him in my heart. Nothing more was mentioned and on several occasions I heard him deny any knowledge about your husbands murder.

Two months had passed and one day my husband received a rather strange phone call. He took me aside and asked me to deliver some money (which, by the way, I did deliver money for Jimmy's gambling debts on many, many occasions.) Anyway I protested because we had several guests at our house and I was seven months pregnant and mostly because it was 110 degrees outside. I asked him to send his bodyguard. That is when he took me aside and spoke sternly to me. He said that this was for the payoff for your husband's murder and he could only trust me, his wife. At that point I can honestly say I was shaking and told him I wouldn't do it. But

Jimmy persisted and I weaken and ended up involving myself in this crime. . . .

I thank God every day for sending me to jail because if I had never come I would never have found Christ. And it is with Christ strength that I write you this letter. . . .

42

Tom Sharpe, a large, impressive, silver-haired attorney, who practiced in Brownsville at the southern tip of Texas, where the Rio Grande emptied into the Gulf of Mexico, had known Charles Harrelson for more than ten years, but couldn't really swear he knew him. Harrelson was a complex blend of forces and counterforces, and he changed appearance before your eyes. Even before their first meeting in the county jail at Angleton in 1969, Sharpe had seen pictures of the man accused of the savage, cold-blooded murder of playboy Alan Berg: the pictures seemed to show a slender, raw-boned, wild-eyed punk, his crewcut grown long and slicked back, a punk who might kill for a fee so small it wouldn't even make a down payment on his Cadillac; but Sharpe learned that there was nothing simple about Charles Harrelson.

"There was an aura of hardness about him," Sharpe said. "It's as though his skin was on too tight. It took us a year to get him to relax so that he didn't look like he was being prosecuted every day of his life. Once he learned to relax, I found out he loved to play chess—he was very good at it—and read. He read anything and everything." The fact that he faced now a mandatory life sentence on conviction did not seem to bother Charles Harrelson as much as his deep-seated fear that he wouldn't appear properly dressed or uphold his image as a man who glided rather than struggled through life. Harrelson had more or less dedicated his life to escaping his original punk image, and now he appeared almost debonair in his three-piece suit, gold-rimmed glasses, and a gold pinky ring that Sharpe had loaned him for the occasion.

Even with the testimony of Joe Chagra, the case against Harrelson was mostly circumstantial. The government had structured an

315

elaborate theory of how Harrelson had "stalked" the judge almost from the time of his meeting in Las Vegas with Jimmy Chagra, how he had tried to get Hamp Robinson to buy the murder weapon and then prevailed on his wife to buy it, how he had used the alias Gordon Stone at motels in Austin, San Antonio and Midland. There had been rumors for months that the FBI was on the trial of a gold Oldsmobile Cutlass reportedly seen at the Chateaux Dijon townhouses on the morning of the murder, and as the trial started Tom Sharpe learned that the government had not only located the car, which had been owned by Jo Ann Harrelson until Harrelson sold it after the murder, but had information that would place it in the parking lot of San Antonio International Airport about the time Wood was gunned down. The government also had a cab driver who claimed to have driven Harrelson from the airport to the judge's townhouse the night before the murder, and several witnesses who, under the influence of hypnosis, remembered seeing him just before Wood was shot.

It was difficult for any of the attorneys to get a fix on the jury, except that nine of the twelve were women; three were Hispanics, and two were blacks. Judge Sessions had not allowed the lawyers to question the jurors individually; instead, the judge had trimmed the original panel of 174 to 107, then to 46, before giving each side its strikes. It was logical to assume, however, that anyone who lived near San Antonio had heard of the case and knew the names of those on trial.

Both sides made use of the fact that the FBI had called Wood's murder "the crime of the century" and that the long investigation had cost the taxpayers perhaps $10 million. By the time testimony began on October 11, the government had prepared elaborate charts, maps, calendars, even a scale model of the Chateaux Dijon. In his opening remarks, prosecutor Ray Jahn told the jury: "The story is a simple one. It is a story of fear. It is a story of greed and a story of murder. Jimmy Chagra was fearful of Judge Wood because of his sentencing procedures."

It was Tom Sharpe, however, who introduced the first real intrigue to the trial, promising that the defense not only would prove that Charles Harrelson was innocent of the murder of Judge Wood, but would reveal the identity of the real killer. Sharpe had developed his own scenario, using the government's evidence and witnesses—he told the jury that Harrelson and Chagra *did* conspire to commit a crime, but the crime had to do with narcotics, not murder. What's more,

Harrelson and his fellow conspirators, Pete Kay and Hamp Robinson, had no intention of working a narcotics deal; they merely wanted to swindle Jimmy Chagra. The lawyer claimed that the payoff in Las Vegas—he told the jury it was $150,000, not the $250,000 claimed by the government—was the result of the swindle. "They intended to take the money and run, and that's what they did," Sharpe said. "It had nothing to do with killing Judge Wood."

Charles Campion, Jo Ann Harrelson's court-appointed attorney, told the jury that his client was nothing more than "a concerned mother and devoted wife" and had in no way obstructed justice.

In his opening remarks, Warren Burnett described Liz Chagra in much the same way—as a young woman (she was only twenty-five at the time Wood was killed) who was bullied by her forceful husband. "This accused citizen didn't even know who Charles Harrelson was until many, many months after the death of Judge Wood," Burnett said. "She never even saw him until she was arrested." The Chagra marriage, he told the jury, was stormy and turbulent—Jimmy was a domineering husband given to "braggadocio, extravagant claims about involvement in criminal matters shown by later events to be false. It was not uncommon for Jimmy Chagra to threaten to take the lives of people—many people—not only Judge Wood." In support of this theory, Burnett said, he would introduce into evidence a letter that Liz Chagra wrote the widow of the slain judge. Since he couldn't stop introduction of the letter by the government, Burnett calculated that the next best thing was to make it sound as if it were his idea. "At that point," he admitted later, "our only strategy was to act in as winning a way as possible."

The prosecution's first order of business was to establish Charles Harrelson's presence in San Antonio, then at the Chateaux Dijon, at the time of the murder. A cabdriver named Wesley Coddington identified Harrelson as the man he picked up at the airport and drove to the Dijon complex in the early evening of May 28, the evening before the shooting. A second man wearing a fatigue jacket and "a cruddy-looking blond Afro haircut" was waiting for Harrelson in the townhouse parking lot, the cabdriver said. Harrelson was carrying a thin black case—"the kind you would carry a telescope in"—inside a brown paper sack. Coddington's testimony was weakened somewhat by the fact that he had waited eighteen months before telling his story to the FBI. Coddington was one of the witnesses hypnotized at the

FBI's request. Another witness, whose memory was enhanced by hypnosis, told of seeing a man near the townhouse the following morning, but couldn't positively identify him as Harrelson. The government never identified or explained the second man in the fatigue jacket and blond Afro.

The government's most effective witness in the opening week of the trial was Chrys Lambros, a twenty-eight-year-old attorney, who told of literally bumping into Harrelson in the townhouse parking lot less than an hour before the murder. Miss Lambros was positive of her identification. "I will never forget Mr. Harrelson's eyes," she told the jury. "I have never forgotten that face."

Two weeks after the murder, Chrys Lambros agreed to undergo hypnosis to enhance her memory. In a videotape of the hypnosis session, the jury heard Dr. Richard Gabler, an Air Force psychiatrist and specialist in hypnotherapy, tell Miss Lambros that hypnosis is like "a structured daydream to enhance your memory, a sort of memory walk through the events of May 29, 1979." Her voice slower and softer as she submitted to the effects of hypnosis, the attorney remembered leaving her own apartment at the townhouse. "I got to the bottom of the stairway," she said on the videotape. "The air was cool and fresh. It was a very lovely day. Yes, I see him clearly. He has flaxen hair, is wearing sunglasses, dark blue pants, loafers and a white tattersall shirt. It's like a Polaroid film developing before me. I see my car and a light blue Toyota near it. And I see a green station wagon. It's Mrs. Wood's car. The man is walking toward me, between me and the Toyota. The man is clean-shaven and his hair is long and shaggy. He walks into me on purpose, I think: Why is he standing in the parking area? I don't feel any fear. I am curious about him. He walks past me. I dropped my keys when he bumped into me and I stoop and pick them up. I get into my car and as I pull into the main driveway, I see the man walk back into the parking area toward a car. I can only see the roof. It's a rust-colored car. . . ."

In the packed courtroom of the John H. Wood, Jr., Federal Courts Building more than three years after the videotaped hypnosis session, prosecutor Ray Jahn asked the witness to point to the man she saw that morning. Chrys Lambros pointed without hesitation at Charles Harrelson, who stood and smiled.

The courtroom was again packed two days later as Kathryn Wood, a dark-haired woman with a kindly face and voice choked by tears, told of cradling her husband's head as he lay dying, and asking: "Who shot you, John H.?" The judge's eyes were open, she said, but he never answered. Asked about the letter from Elizabeth Chagra, the letter admitting not only the payoff but prior knowledge of the murder, Mrs. Wood said that she could never forgive the young woman. "I felt she found Christ too late," Kathryn Wood said bitterly.

Though Tom Sharpe never delivered on his promise to produce the real killer, he made a number of points with his cross-examination of a string of Harrelson's running mates that the government called to bolster its own theory. Hampton Robinson III told the jury that Harrelson had bragged that "killing people and getting away with it is my long suit" and had once told him that Wood "committed suicide by the way he sentenced people." (Judge Sessions ordered the jury to disregard the statement about Wood.) Sharpe was able to enhance his own theory of the murder, however, by prodding Robinson to acknowledge his own unsavory reputation—that he was a former cocaine and heroin addict, who had been indicted for murder on two separate occasions, and had been admitted to hospitals three times in the past three years for psychological and narcotics problems.

Sharpe also drew from another government witness, Pete Kay, the opinion that Hamp Robinson was "flaky," "a baby running around in a man's outfit." In direct examination, Kay told the jury that Harrelson had once told him "a person's head is just a watermelon with hair on it," but later, with Harrelson staring at him from the defense table, Kay admitted he wasn't sure who actually made the statement. "I can't say Charles made the statement in all truthfulness," Kay said. "It could have been me who made it." Pete Kay denied the defense's claim that he and Harrelson had attempted to fleece money out of Jimmy Chagra with a phony drug deal, but under cross-examination admitted that he had once tried a shakedown of Chagra. Kay said that after he heard about Wood's murder, he telephoned Chagra in Las Vegas and tried to convince him he knew something that would implicate Chagra. He hoped that Chagra would give him either money or marijuana, but the attempt failed. "He wouldn't come with nothing," Kay admitted.

Another of Harrelson's lifelong friends, Greg Goodrum, whose family had helped raise Harrelson after his mother left home, told the jury that shortly after Wood's murder Harrelson told him that he had used his wife's gold Cutlass "on a job" and needed to sell it quickly. Two previous witnesses told the jury they saw a gold Cutlass in the townhouse parking lot on the morning Wood was murdered, and the government produced records proving that the car was parked at the San Antonio airport for seven days in the two-week period before the assassination. For the most part Harrelson seemed content with the way his lawyer was handling the cross-examination of his old friends, but at one point when Tom Sharpe was eliciting some unflattering remarks from Goodrum about Harrelson's mother, he could feel his client go tense. "I could feel the hatred running through Charles," Sharpe said later. "You'd think he would be bitter about his mother, but he couldn't sit there and listen to someone else knock her down." In his long relationship with Harrelson, Sharpe had never once seen his client demonstrate a shade of physical violence: even the prosecution had acknowledged that Harrelson wasn't "a mad dog killer," just a man who would kill for money. But Charles Harrelson had his own code of ethics, and it included the provocation of hatred when someone slandered his mother. Sharpe had already decided it would be necessary to put Harrelson on the witness stand, but he knew the peril involved: no matter how carefully Sharpe planned his questions, he wouldn't be able to contol his client's answers.

Though the government's evidence was largely circumstantial, the accumulation had its effect. Over the next several days, the prosecution introduced the rifle stock, and two documents in Harrelson's handwriting, both implicating him in Wood's murder. The jury may or may not have believed the weathered rifle stock came from the murder weapon. The clerk who sold the gun to Jo Ann Harrelson had no independent recollection of the sale, though he identified the sales receipt and weapons transaction form made out in the name of Faye L. King. He couldn't even say for certain that the stock belonged to a gun sold in his store. "There could be ten thousand stocks like this one," the clerk told the jury. Tom Sharpe had already reduced the impact of the rifle purchase, claiming that Jo Ann Harrelson bought the weapon for her former lover, Pete Kay.

Considerably less easy to explain were the two documents—a "will" that Harrelson had written in his Monthly Minder diary while holding off police in the desert outside of Van Horn, and a note written on the back of a postcard that Harrelson had torn up and scattered beside the road that same night. Prosecutors read to the jury excerpts from the diary, dated August 30, 1980:

"I'm sorry—not for me but for the pain I've caused others, both those who've loved me and who've loved the people I've killed—but I've never killed a person who was undeserving of it. I wish to be cremated with absolutely no religious services. My ashes should be spread over the John H. Wood, Jr. courthouse in San Antonio."

Another entry in the diary said: "Please excuse my handwriting but I am high on cocaine (as usual). I, Charles V. Harrelson, killed John H. Wood, Jr. acting solely on my own."

The writing on the back of the torn postcard, which the government had pieced together and identified with Harrelson, said: "Since death is certain, I should only be credited with speeding up a natural process. My marker should read, 'He did his part for Z.P.G.—Zero Population Growth.' " Tom Sharpe tried to convince the jury that Harrelson was making a little joke about a recent vasectomy, but none of the jurors were grinning.

There were some minor disruptions in the courtroom as Teresa Starr took the witness stand. Spectators moved to get a closer look at the pretty twenty-five-year old, and at the three defendants whose lives were about to be affected by her testimony. Most spectators knew by now about Teresa's strange love affair with her stepfather, and they wanted to see firsthand the reactions when she told the sordid details. But first, prosecutors directed the witness through a step-by-step account of how she picked up the payoff.

Avoiding eye contact with the three defendants, Teresa told the jury that at the time of her trip to Las Vegas, she believed her job was to pick up a package of drugs—payment for a gambling debt. A day before the trip, she and her mother went shopping for a new dress and a carry-on piece of luggage. Jo Ann Harrelson made sure the luggage had a lock and key. On June 23, Jo Ann drove her daughter to the airport in Corpus Christi and made her flight arrangements under the name of Terri Tower. Teresa was given a little less than $1,000 for travel expenses and told to pay for her hotel room at the Jockey Club "a few days in advance because we didn't know how long it was going to take." She checked into the Jockey Club Hotel using the same alias, Terri Tower. Harrelson had instructed her to find three pay telephones, all in a row, at three separate casinos, and told her to always use pay phones. After checking into the Jockey Club, Teresa walked along the Strip, from casino to casino. She located telephones at the Dunes, the Aladdin, and the Barbary Coast. Then she telephoned Harrelson at the Padre Island Hotel and gave him the numbers. They agreed on the times she would wait by each particular phone. "I was told to be close to a slot machine," Teresa told the jury. "So I could hear the phone ringing. I was told to keep myself occupied and not dress too flashy because I might be mistaken for a hooker. I was told not to talk to anyone."

When she failed to receive any calls on June 23, Teresa returned to the Jockey Club and waited. Soon Harrelson telephoned her. "He said I had missed the call. He said it would happen tomorrow night. I then talked to my mother and she said it was okay. I guess she was trying to console me because I was upset and very nervous." At noon the next day, she took a cab from the Jockey Club to downtown Las Vegas "because the casinos were a lot closer to each other there and I was told not to use the same phone twice." On Fremont Street in the heart of Glitter Gulch, she located phones that she would use later that afternoon—at the Four Queens, the Golden Nugget, and the Fremont Casino. "I phoned my numbers to Charles and I went to my phone and started waiting," she said. She received the call she'd been waiting for at the Fremont: Harrelson instructed her to return to the Jockey Club and wait for the package to be delivered.

"There was a knock on my door," she told the jury. "A woman was at the door. She had long, dark brown hair and was pregnant. She was dressed casual but nice. We didn't have a conversation. She sat the briefcase on the sofa, took a Kleenex out, wiped off her fingerprints, and left. It took only about three minutes."

Prosecutor Ray Jahn asked Teresa to identify the beige briefcase, which had already been admitted into evidence, but didn't ask her to point out the woman who had delivered it to the Jockey Club —Teresa had repeatedly failed to identify Liz Chagra. The briefcase had been identified earlier by Cindy Cote, Liz Chagra's social secretary, who had driven with her to the Jockey Club, but hadn't gone inside and apparently didn't know of the payoff. At one point in the investigation, the FBI had got Cindy Cote to telephone Liz and try to implicate her in the murder, but the call, which had also been taped, had produced nothing except idle talk.

The prosecutor asked the witness if she had ever been intimate with her stepfather. Teresa hesitated, glancing first at her mother, who was wearing the trace of a smile. Then she looked at Harrelson, who was grinning widely, and said: "Yes, in December 1979. The affair lasted until February 1980. My mother discovered we had an affair and, of course, it caused problems between us." Teresa said she first refused to testify before the grand jury because she wanted to protect her mother. "I was asked all kinds of questions. I wrote the questions down later and turned them over to my attorney. Later, my mother said the government was only guessing. She said the government was trying to pin it on Charles, that it was all made up—their involvement with Judge Wood's murder." As Teresa read parts of the love letters Harrelson wrote while she was jailed for refusing to testify before the grand jury, Jo Ann Harrelson chewed her lips and stared down at the defense table.

Lawyers for all three defendants subjected Teresa to long cross-examinations, but the most grueling, and the most dramatic, was the cross-examination by Jo Ann Harrelson's attorney, Charles Campion, who revealed to the jury that the FBI had persuaded Teresa's estranged husband to make secret recordings of their conversations. The jury learned that shortly after her affair with Harrelson, Teresa returned to Dallas to live with her husband. "I had nowhere else to go," she admitted. She knew that Michael Jasper had been contacted by the FBI, but she didn't know that the FBI was paying rent on their apartment, or that recorders had been hidden under the bed, in the kitchen, in the living room, and in the car. "I just found out about the recorders a couple of weeks ago," she said. "But I knew I hadn't said anything to him. I didn't trust my husband or anybody else."

As Campion questioned the witness about whether her mother had applied any pressure to keep her from testifying, Teresa's voice became louder and edged with anger. "My mother and I always had conflicting personalities," she replied. "I left home when I was thirteen. I was raised to keep my mouth shut."

The government was coming to the heart of its case—Joe Chagra's testimony. But first there was a poignant moment in which the jury got a glimpse of the tedium, frustration, and bad timing that had dogged this long and costly investigation. Two FBI agents who worked out of Corpus Christi told of following Charles Harrelson's blue Lincoln shortly after Harrelson and his wife picked up Teresa

Starr at the Corpus Christi airport and drove her to her father's home in Port Aransas. The agents trailed the Lincoln for nearly two hundred miles as it traveled northeast along the coast, paralleling Matagorda Island, through the small town of Rockport, near Judge Wood's retreat, along the flat coastal plains to the small town of Sargent. "They had been aware we were behind them," said FBI special agent Bruce Stepp. "They looked at us and they waved at us as they drove by." Near the town of Sargent, Harrelson stopped at the side of the road and walked back to the agent's car. He shook hands with the agents and said: "I realize the problems we're in with the FBI." They talked for a few minutes, then they went separate ways. The agents didn't learn until much later that a briefcase containing the payoff money for Wood's murder was in the blue Lincoln.

43

Before the government's key witness was allowed to testify, defense attorneys took one last shot at the two issues they had been contesting since the beginning—the issue of privilege, and the introduction into evidence of the FBI's tapes. Following Joe's plea-bargaining deal, the government had edited the 914 reels into ten composite tapes: more than 1,000 hours of conversation had been reduced to about five. Warren Burnett, who led the defenses' common challenge of the tapes, argued that the government had edited out important information that would explain the statements. With the jury out of the courtroom, Burnett read off a long list of conversations that he believed were taken out of context in the abridged version that the government wanted the jury to hear.

"For example," Burnett told the court, "one of the tapes begins with a statement by Jimmy Chagra in which he says, 'Boy, I wish I hadn't done that.' It sounds like a confession to Wood's murder when in fact Chagra was talking about all the money he had spent."

Among the many conversations missing from the edited version was the one in which Jimmy insisted that Joe urged him to "do it, do it, do it. You're the one that was all hot to do it."

Prosecutor Ray Jahn replied: "We would have loved to include that, but we could not see that it furthered the conspiracy charge. It was brothers heaping guilt on each other."

Burnett, who had a booming evangelical voice and a marvelous command of the language, repeatedly referred to the tape-recorded evidence as "eavesdropping," especially when the jury was present; he argued forcefully that when the government was allowed to narrow hundreds of hours of conversation down to less than five, it was almost impossible to determine what had been cut from the original. Burnett no doubt realized that Judge Sessions was not about to overrule the government's position on attorney-client or marital privilege or on the tapes—the attorney was arguing for the sake of the record—but he had another more imediate motion that the court would be hard pressed to refuse: Burnett wanted the judge to block the government from introducing the ninety-two pieces of torn notepaper agents had seized from Liz Chagra's purse after her final visit to Leavenworth, the pieces Liz had tried to flush down the toilet. Although the FBI did obtain a search warrant from a magistrate in Kansas City, it was necessary to detain Liz and her three-year-old daughter, Jackie, for four hours while the warrant was secured. Prosecutors argued that the agents believed they had "probable cause" to detain Liz Chagra, since they had overheard Liz and Jimmy talking about other "criminal matters" in the visiting room. Since this was said in front of the jury, Burnett immediately moved for a mistrial. "I know of no instructions [to the jury] that can cure this type of misbehavior," the attorney told the court. Judge Sessions denied the motion for mistrial, but Burnett won his point: the judge ruled that the ninety-two pieces of notepaper would not be admitted as evidence.

As Joe Chagra had anticipated, Harrelson's lawyer, Tom Sharpe, took a long time grilling him on the subject of attorney-client relationship. Joe had talked to both Sharpe and Charles Harrelson about this subject during the pretrial, before Joe decided to make his deal with the government. Even if Joe decided to testify, the government still had a serious problem with privilege—the issue was *Harrelson's* privilege, not Joe's. Joe had researched the question: he was positive that a higher court would overturn Harrelson's conviction, if it was based on what Harrelson believed to be attorney-client conversations. The trouble was Harrelson himself—he was determined to take the stand in his own defense. Harrelson had conjured up his own story about how he had arranged that first meeting for the purpose of conning Joe out of some money, about how he had never even thought of Joe as an attorney, merely a pigeon to be plucked. Back during the pretrial, Joe had strongly considered the outcome of a trial in which *none* of the defendants took the stand: challenge the government to make its case, not just to the jury, but to the appeals courts. It was Joe's opinion then, and it was his opinion now, on the eve of his own testimony, that the government would lose the argument of privilege. "On the other hand," he said later, "if I refused to testify on the grounds of privilege, and Harrelson got up there and said he'd never even thought of me as his attorney, I'd be caught in the middle." Harrelson's determination to testify had been one of the main reasons that Joe Chagra decided to make his agreement with the government.

With the jury out of the courtroom now, Sharpe repeatedly asked Joe Chagra about discussions of the Wood murder with Harrelson.

"I was talking to him continually about the investigation from the day I met him," Chagra said. Joe didn't remember the exact date he had met Harrelson at Billy Cabrera's house; it was sometime in March 1980, but he had considered himself Harrelson's attorney starting on March 25. His first private discussions with Harrelson centered on the Houston firearms and drug violations, Joe recalled, "and we also talked about the case of Wood's death. He had already testified before the grand jury. We talked about my brother being investigated. I continued to talk to Mr. Harrelson about the grand jury investigation."

"When did you stop representing Charles Harrelson?" Sharpe asked.

"I don't know how to answer that question," Joe said. "After Mr. Harrelson's arrest [in Van Horn], I was told by an FBI agent that I was also a target in the Wood investigation, and that I would not be accepted as an attorney for anyone connected to the same investigation. It was always a problem. I backed off. I intended to represent my brother."

"Do you believe that information between an attorney and his client is confidential?"

"That's what I used to believe," Chagra replied.

As expected, Judge Sessions ruled that no attorney-client relationship existed and ordered that the jury be returned to the courtroom to hear Joe Chagra's testimony. After hours of legalistic wrangling, Joe appeared tense and haggard. Charles Harrelson rocked gently in his chair, his cold, flat eyes trained on the witness. Joe sighed and bowed his head, took a deep breath, and told his story:

"I received a call from Billy Cabrera asking me to come over to his place at the King's Hill Apartment in El Paso. He wanted to tell me something. Cabrera was standing in the parking lot next to a car. He introduced me to Mr. Harrelson. We shook hands and embraced each other. Mr. Harrelson told me he knew my brother Lee, that he had respect for him, and that he had met Jimmy once in Las

Vegas, and now he wanted to meet the youngest brother. He then asked Billy if he would excuse us so we could talk in private.

"We talked some about his problems with the firearms charge in Houston, then he changed the conversation to Wood's murder. I asked him if he was the man who killed Wood. He said he was. I asked him how was it he was cleared by the grand jury? He said there had been six witnesses who testified that he was in Dallas on the day Judge Wood was killed. That they were his alibi witnesses. He said they were perfect strangers and had no reason to lie. He mentioned a person who parked his car at a valet parking lot. He said he did something so the individual would remember him that day.

"He then began to tell me specifics about the crime. He said he had shot Judge Wood with a high-powered rifle, that Judge Wood was standing by his car and as he reached into his car with his briefcase, he shot him in the back. He said it was a clean shot. He said nobody had seen him and anyway that if someone had seen him no one would recognize him because he was disguised.

"He said he had walked past Judge Wood earlier that morning wearing the disguise. After he shot Judge Wood he drove from San Antonio to Dallas. I asked him how did you get through the roadblock? I remember reading in the paper about roadblocks being set up at the city limits. He said there were no roadblocks.

"I asked him why did you shoot him that day? He told me that was the day Jimmy was going to trial. But then I told him the date on Jimmy's trial had been changed and he said he didn't know about it. He said he had tried once before to kill Judge Wood in Midland, but there were too many people around the judge and he couldn't do it. . . ."

Joe Chagra's testimony fit precisely the government's theory that Harrelson had stalked Wood throughout the Western District. The government even presented a motel telephone billing to show that Harrelson, using the alias Gordon Stone, had telephoned the federal courthouse in Midland on May 14, apparently to check on Wood's whereabouts. FBI agents were still trying to nail down solid evidence that Harrelson was in Midland the following day. Agents had recently established that Harrelson registered in the Townhouse Motel in San Antonio the night before the murder. Using the alias Bill Bannister, Harrelson paid cash in advance. The motel was about a four-minute drive from Wood's residence.

With prosecutor Ray Jahn drawing forth one incriminating detail after another, Joe Chagra told the jury that his brother first suggested killing Wood while the two of them sat in the nearly deserted courtroom in Midland during a recess. Judge Wood had just finished denying more than twenty defense motions, including a motion asking him to step down from Jimmy's case. "Jimmy told me that he was never going to get a fair trial and asked if I thought he should try and have the judge killed," Joe testified. "I told him he should." A few weeks later, he continued, Jimmy again mentioned killing Wood, this time as the brothers walked alone in the garden of Jimmy's Las Vegas mansion. "He asked if I still thought he should do it. I asked, 'Do you know anybody who would do it?' and he said he did. I said, 'Do it.' He told me he didn't want to tell me anything else about it because he didn't want me involved."

"But you became involved?" Jahn asked.

"Yes," Joe replied. "About two months after the murder, I was going over a list of persons who had been subpoenaed before the grand jury and Jimmy pointed to Mr. Harrelson's name and said he was the person he hired to kill Judge Wood."

With the jury, the defendants, the lawyers, and the judge wearing headphones, following the conversations with transcripts, the government began playing sections of the tape. For the first time the jury heard discussions of Jimmy's escape plan, talk about the map and the murder weapon, and several references to "offing" people, including Harrelson, Henry Wallace, and, later, former U.S. attorney Jamie Boyd. "What does that mean—to off him?" Jahn asked. "To kill him," Joe replied flatly. Joe said that Harrelson told him of sending his wife, Jo Ann, to purchase the murder weapon—as a joke, she used the name Faye King, which translated as *faking*. Several reporters, who until that moment hadn't caught the double meaning of the alias, laughed, and an FBI agent, who perhaps hadn't understood either, looked chagrined.

To Joe Chagra's great surprise, none of the defense attorneys subjected him to serious cross-examination about the two recollections in which he allegedly encouraged his brother to kill Wood. "I thought they would at least press me for details about the talk in the garden—who else was at the house, what else we talked about, that sort of thing," Joe said later. Equally curious was the conversation in the courtroom at Midland. Oscar Goodman and others who had been there at the time couldn't recall a single moment when the two brothers were alone at the defense table, though this wasn't brought out at the trial in San Antonio.

Before the start of cross-examination, the prosecution played a section of the November 21 tape in which the brothers talked about Harrelson and corroboration for the government's case:

JIMMY: His daughter received the money from Liz.

JOE: Well, that's not corroboration.

JIMMY: No. She had a lot of my gambling debts. She didn't even know who it was going to or anything.

At this point, Ray Jahn got Joe Chagra to acknowledge that Jimmy's use of the term "gambling debt" was merely code for payoff money. Defense attorney Warren Burnett returned to this point later as he attempted to show how Jimmy Chagra maneuvered his wife and his brother into numerous false admissions, how he "tricked" them into saying whatever suited his purposes. Burnett played part of the November 5 tape in which Jimmy attempted to get Joe to admit he knew that Harrelson had killed the judge:

JIMMY: There's fucking thirty thousand people in here that ain't done nothing.

JOE: They've done something. They've all done something to be sitting here.

JIMMY: You've done something, too, Joe.

JOE: What have I done?

JIMMY: You know Harrelson knocked off the judge.

JOE: [Laughs] I don't know that.

"Is that true, Joe?" Burnett asked softly, firmly. "That's what I said," Joe admitted, dropping his eyes. Burnett continued reading from the transcript:

JIMMY: You know that's a . . .

JOE: No, I don't know that. I don't know if he [Harrelson] did it or not. Maybe he did. Maybe Little Larry Culbreath did it.

JIMMY: Look, the FBI knows I hired him to do this.

JOE: No, they don't know. They can't prove it.

The defense attorney zeroed in on Chagra's earlier testimony that Jimmy had pointed out Harrelson's name from a list of grand jury witnesses and confessed that this was the man who killed Wood: Burnett was having trouble believing that Joe Chagra was telling the truth. "And you asked how Jimmy knew?" Burnett said to the witness. There was a long pause, then the attorney answered his own question: "And he said, 'I hired him'?"

"That's correct," Joe said softly, his head bowed as though in prayer.

In his first four days on the witness stand Joe Chagra said little to implicate his sister-in-law. For the most part he agreed with defense attorney Burnett's evaluation that Jimmy was "a braggart and bombastic liar" constantly shooting off his mouth and putting a price on the heads of his enemies. On the fifth day, however, Burnett was surprised at Joe's reply to a key question. Burnett asked: "Was there ever a time when your brother Jimmy, either before or after his arrest, ever suggested to you that his wife had any prior knowledge of the death of John H. Wood?" Joe glanced at Liz, who had been following the cross-examination intently, paused, then replied: "Yes, he did. In the holding cell here in this courthouse. He said, 'We [Jimmy and Liz] had an agreement concerning the transcripts.' Liz was screaming and telling him she had not told him to do anything, and he said that he thought she did."

The following day when prosecutors played the January 26, 1981, tape, in which three-year-old Jackie Chagra could be heard laughing and saying, "I love you guys," Liz cried openly. Several women jurors also appeared near tears. Liz had seen her three children only once since her arrest six months earlier—through a glass window in the jail visiting area.

By now the trial was in its fifth week of testimony. The government had bombarded the jury with more than one hundred exhibits and the testimony of more than eighty witnesses. Among the final witnesses for the government were the owner of a Midland, Texas, motel, and the supervisor of the Midland airport parking lot, who established that Charles Harrelson, using the alias Bart Bannister and driving the gold Cutlass, spent the night of May 15 in the West Texas oil town where Judge Wood was trying cases—less than twenty-four hours earlier, records showed, Harrelson had telephoned the courthouse in Midland from a motel in Austin. Although the FBI had known for weeks that Harrelson had stalked Wood in Midland, they hadn't located the actual evidence until a few days before the jury heard it.

The government probably should have wrapped up its case at that point, but there was one more witness for the jury to consider—

John Lee Spinelli, who had occupied a cell next to Harrelson in the Harris County Jail; for fifty-six days, during the spring of 1981, Spinelli allowed himself to be what defense attorneys called "a walking bug" for the FBI. An admitted rapist, bank robber, and kidnapper, with more than twenty felony convictions on his record, Spinelli met Harrelson briefly in September 1980, before Spinelli was transferred to the maximum-security unit of the Texas Department of Corrections near Huntsville. But Spinelli convinced the feds to turn him into a walking bug and transfer him back to Houston to help nail Harrelson—the court-ordered wiretap had expired, and since Spinelli was a "consensual" party to the new wiretaps, no additional court authority was required. In return for this favor, the government had agreed to remove Spinelli from the state "snake pit" in Huntsville and, once his services were no longer needed, allow him to serve his time in a federal institution.

In the fifty-six days that he was in the adjoining cell, Spinelli made seven tapes—most of them conversations between himself and Harrelson, or conversations between Harrelson and his visitors. All of Harrelson's visitors were women—his wife, Jo Ann; his stepdaughter, Teresa Starr; his former employer, Virginia Farah; and his best friend's wife, Jo Ann Robinson. The jury heard Harrelson swear his undying love to each woman, each of whom would later be a witness (or, in Jo Ann Harrelson's case, a defendant) at the trial. Harrelson used Spinelli's visiting privileges to stagger his visits from his lovers.

Perhaps the government looked on John Lee Spinelli as comic relief. The snitch told how he played chess with Harrelson, and how Harrelson helped him with his grammar and vocabulary, which obviously needed help. Harrelson once corrected him when Spinelli recounted an argument with a waiter who charged him for a gratuity. "I told him I don't need no gratuity. I just had a pizza." Spinelli described Harrelson, as well as the other suspects in the Wood murder, as "cult figures" among prison inmates.

The tapes that Spinelli narrated for the jury were considerably more titillating than incriminating. In one tape Harrelson warned his wife that Teresa might have access to "Sidney and Cecil and all those other people" while she was in jail. Sidney was prison slang for speed; Cecil meant cocaine. In another tape, he told his wife he would "cop out for two new Rolls-Royces painted attitude pink," and promised her: "Baby, when we get out we're going on a world cruise. They'll pay me to go. Them suckers will be lined up just to get to meet us."

The only two remarks that really incriminated Harrelson were not even on tape. Spinelli claimed to have overheard Harrelson tell his wife to "tell Teresa to keep her mouth shut" but, unfortunately, he failed to capture it on tape. He also failed to record a remark that Harrelson allegedly made while watching the evening television news alone in his cell. Spinelli had just returned from taking a shower when he overheard Harrelson say to himself, "If she talks, they'll burn me for ringing Wood's bell." Spinelli's credibility was additionally damaged when the defense made known to the jury how the witness had once mailed a sample of marijuana to federal prosecutor John Emerson, an apparent attempt to make Emerson believe the snitch had uncovered a drug-smuggling operation inside prison walls. Spinelli's true character came in focus when one of the lawyers asked if the witness found prison a pleasant environment. "Yes and no," Spinelli said. "I got along good in prison. My only problems are when I get out on the street."

The jury, and most of the spectators, missed the real high comedy of Spinelli's testimony. It came during the pretrial when Harrelson was testifying about how any inmate who would allow the FBI to wire him would probably kill little children and use their bones for toothpicks. Unexpectedly, assistant prosecutor John Emerson said to the witness: "I don't guess you'd ever allow that to happen to you, would you, Mr. Harrelson?" Harrelson went pale and his eyes began to flutter—Emerson obviously knew about the incident in 1962 when Harrelson had allowed himself to be wired and had sent a fellow prisoner to the gas chamber in California.

In a holding cell later, Jimmy Chagra began to needle Harrelson about his days as a government snitch. "You're really a scum bag, you know that? You're nothing but a punk," Jimmy told the man who had killed the judge. Joe Chagra recalled: "Harrelson really lost it right there. He started stammering about how it wasn't a wire, it was a *bug*, and anyway, this guy had shot some little girl's arms off, and besides that, he was young at the time. Jimmy just looked at him. He just cut Harrelson apart with that little half-smile of his. Harrelson knew the truth. We all did. Harrelson was just a cheap punk."

44

The gaggle of twelve-year-old Catholic school girls looked disappointed, even angry, when a television camera man outside the drum-shaped John H. Wood, Jr., Federal Courts Building told them that Charles Harrelson wouldn't be testifying that day. They had made a special trip across town to hear him. Spectators who watched the early parts of the trial expecting to see the soap-opera drama portrayed by the media had been mostly benumbed by legal wrangling and witnesses who testified about motel registrations and telephone records, but now that the defense was ready to present its side, citizens of the old Alamo City were in a dither.

It was difficult to watch television or listen to the radio without learning something about the trial. Even the smallest radio stations broadcast regular bulletins from the courthouse. It was impossible to walk the streets of downtown San Antonio and avoid the screaming banners overlaid on newsstands—"Stepdaughter Bares Love Affair with 'Pappy.'" A popular columnist noted that Charles Harrelson was making eyes at an attractive San Antonio television reporter, and his newspaper teased the column beneath a front-page banner proclaiming, "Convicted killer ogles TV newscaster." In mid-November, shortly before Harrelson was scheduled to testify, the Bexar County district attorney announced that if the federal trials ended in convictions, his office would try the defendants again on state charges and ask for the death penalty—the tactic was apparently legal under the concept of dual sovereignty, though many attorneys doubted that the FBI tapes would be admissible under Texas rules of evidence. On the afternoon of the local DA's announcement, at about the same time the jurors were headed to lunch, a headline screamed: DEATH TO WOOD'S KILLERS!

At this point, attorneys for the defense asked Judge Sessions to declare a mistrial, or at least have the jurors sequestered for the remainder of the proceedings. Sessions refused both requests. The judge continued to remind members of the jury to avoid exposure to the media, as though that were possible in a city conditioned to the exploitation of violence. At the same time, Sessions ran his courtroom with the iron will and severe demeanor of a puritan missionary among pagans. More than once, the judge halted proceedings and delivered stern lectures to spectators caught "registering emotions." Five burly U.S. marshals prowled the courtroom, wagging fingers at would-be offenders. At the start of each day's proceedings, one marshal lectured everyone present: "All right, for those of you new in the courtroom, the judge don't want no whispering, no laughing, no passing notes, no gum chewing, and no candy while the court is in session."

Before calling Charles Harrelson, defense attorney Tom Sharpe laid the groundwork that he hoped would establish that Jimmy Chagra had no motive to kill Judge Wood. Former assistant U.S. attorney Ron Guyer, one of the men who had prosecuted Chagra on the kingpin charge, acknowledged that the government had offered to allow the kingpin to plead guilty to a single fifteen-year cocaine count. Jimmy's lawyers had countered with an offer to plead to two five-year marijuana counts. "You don't kill a judge over a five-year difference of opinion," Tom Sharpe reminded the jury.

Sharpe also reminded the jurors of something he had promised in his opening statement—that he would produce witnesses to prove that within an hour of Wood's murder, Harrelson was 270 miles from the scene, conducting business near his home in Dallas. The government's only explanation of how Harrelson got from San Antonio to Dallas was Joe Chagra's testimony. Sharpe intended to prove that his client could not possibly have driven that distance in such a short time. Earlier in the trial, the government had taken some of the bloom off the promise of an alibi—Billy Dyer, a Dallas gambler and nightclub owner, admitted that shortly after Wood's murder he signed a false affidavit claiming he saw Harrelson in Dallas on the morning of the assassination. Dyer told the jury that he lied, at Harrelson's request, because "I didn't think the man was guilty." He changed his mind when he realized he could be tried for perjury.

But Sharpe had four more alibi witnesses who appeared solid. Sheryl Mendoza, a teller at the Greenville Avenue Bank and Trust in

Dallas at the time, repeated the story she told the FBI, about selling Harrelson a $600 cashier's check before 11:30 A.M. on the morning of May 29, 1979. It stuck in her mind that Harrelson paid with several checks, one of which turned out to be drawn on an account that was closed. She telephoned Harrelson, who promptly returned to the bank before lunch and repaid the amount.

A. B. Piper, Sr., chief valet at the Preston Towers condominiums, remembered Charles Harrelson well—he always tipped Piper from $3 to $5. He recalled parking Harrelson's Lincoln sometime before 11:00 A.M. on the morning in question. Hair stylist Ralph Mitchell, a gambling partner who admitted recruiting "marks" for Charles Harrelson, remembered that the suspect came by his salon between 9:15 A.M. and 10:15 A.M. to pay a gambling debt. Mitchell was positive of the time— he recalled that it was unusually early for Harrelson to be up and about.

The fourth alibi witness, Dick Cronk, who ran a security services company in Dallas, told the jury that he conducted a survey of Harrelson's apartment on the morning of either May 29 or May 30— hypnosis under FBI direction failed to improve his recall. While prosecutors found some minor holes in the testimony of all four alibi witnesses, they could not shake their basic stories.

Judge Sessions overruled Sharpe's attempts to question FBI agents concerning their investigations of commercial and private flights out of San Antonio on the morning of the murder; but it was apparent that the government had no evidence Harrelson had traveled by plane. Sharpe also demonstrated that the police lineup in Houston on November 20, 1980, in which three residents of the Chateaux Dijon complex attempted to identify Wood's killer, was unfairly stacked in the government's favor. An FBI agent admitted that the would-be witnesses were shown photographs of Harrelson about a week before the lineup. Even then, the only one of the three who picked out Harrelson was Chrys Lambros, the San Antonio attorney who had told the jury earlier of literally bumping into Harrelson in the townhouse parking lot. Sharpe tried to introduce testimony that might impugn Lambros's credibility, but the government objected, and Sessions agreed.

Sharpe was able to account for the mysterious man in the "fatigue jacket and cruddy Afro haircut" that the taxi driver claimed to have seen speaking to Harrelson at the townhouse complex the night before the murder. Charles Foster, who worked for a San Antonio service station at the time, told the jury that he went to the complex that night to collect on a bad check and stopped to ask directions from two men standing near a parked yellow cab. Foster couldn't identify Harrelson as one of the men, but speculated that the man the taxi driver saw might have been Foster himself. "I was wearing a fatigue jacket and a watch cap about five sizes too big," he explained.

For the first time since the start of testimony more than six weeks earlier, Tom Sharpe seemed to be making serious dents in the government's case. Then, on the Monday before the Thanksgiving break, he called Charles Harrelson to the witness stand.

A small band of TV cameramen and women spectators shivered in the predawn chill as U.S. marshals delivered the chained and manacled defendant to the courthouse. By the time Harrelson was sworn in, the courtroom was jammed. Harrelson had promised to "dazzle" the jury, and for three days that's what he did, regaling all present with accounts of his abilities as a gambler and con artist, his hatred of law-enforcement agencies, and his sexual conquests. With an almost boyish pride, Harrelson talked of his skill at cheating at cards and his robust use of cocaine. The jury had already heard of his numerous love affairs, and now Harrelson told them of a one-night stand in Midland—that's why he had been in Midland that night in mid-May. He also admitted being in San Antonio the night before Wood was murdered. He claimed that he used a phony name checking into the Townhouse Motel because he was having an affair with the wife of a CIA agent. He had no idea that the motel was close to Judge Wood's townhouse: Harrelson told the jury he had never been to the Chateaux Dijon in his life.

The most dazzling part of Harrelson's story concerned his relationship with the Chagras. The whole thing started, Harrelson told the jury, when his pal Pete Kay dreamed up a plan to make Jimmy Chagra believe they were going to deliver some drugs. Harrelson didn't bother explaining why a kingpin drug trafficker would waste time with two small-time Texas hustlers, but according to Harrelson the scam worked like magic—Jimmy Chagra paid the pair $200,000 in three payments, the final $150,000 in the package Teresa Starr picked up in Las Vegas. The jury might well imagine Harrelson's surprise when he realized months later that the payment was actually blood money for Wood's murder.

Harrelson told the jury that his ultimate revelation of the sordid affair came about in this manner:

Pete Kay met Joe Chagra in El Paso in either November or December 1979, while Jimmy was still a fugitive, and Joe offered Kay and his friend Harrelson a contract to kill Henry Wallace. (As the jury no doubt recalled, this was the period when the FBI recorded conversations mentioning a contract on Wallace.) When Kay relayed Joe Chagra's offer, Harrelson confessed his confusion: "I didn't even know why Joe Chagra would be making such a request." That's when Pete Kay told him: "I don't know how to tell you this, but the so-called drug scam for which we collected the money from Jimmy wasn't a drug scam. When I got to Las Vegas shortly after Wood was killed, Jimmy was looking to find out who did it. And I saw a chance to get into his pocket. I told him, Charlie, it was you who killed Judge Wood."

Harrelson admitted to the jury that he spent time with Joe Chagra during the summer of 1980. In fact, he recalled that Joe gave him some cocaine and some guns, and offered him $40,000 to kill U.S. attorney Jamie Boyd. "Joe hated Jamie Boyd with a passion," Harrelson said. "He was always after me to kill Boyd." Naturally, Harrelson refused. He made Joe Chagra a counteroffer, however. "I had an agreement with Joe Chagra that if I was captured I would confess to killing Wood, with the proviso that all the FBI harassment of my family and friends would stop. In return, Joe Chagra would pay $100,000 to each of my three sons in Lebanon, Ohio. In addition, he would pay Jo Ann some money to take care of her in perpetuity."

After his arrest in the desert near Van Horn, Harrelson told the jury, he kept his part of the bargain. "But Joe Chagra never did," he said, shaking his head in apparent despair. Not long after the arrest, Harrelson spotted another chance to profit from the Chagras. During a visit to the Harris County Jail in Houston, Joe Chagra brought up the subject of the murder weapon, and this gave Harrelson an idea. He remembered giving Pete Kay a .240-caliber rifle on May 18—Kay needed it as a gift to a Mexican government official. "This was the gun I told Joe Chagra I disposed of," Harrelson said.

"I told him this in an effort to extract more money from him. I told him I had thrown a gun away and Jo Ann had been with me and because of that I was afraid of her because she might get it and run to the police with it or the FBI."

That's when he gave Joe Chagra a rough map of an area east of Dallas, an area that Harrelson and others had used as a drug transfer point. "I knew he would never find it because there never was a gun there." Harrelson was extremely careful to avoid saying that Jo Ann bought the rifle he gave to Pete Kay. Harrelson said that he "found" the rifle, along with the sales slip, dated May 17, 1979, in the trunk of his Lincoln. But he added, "I don't know where it came from." The jury already knew, of course, that Jo Ann Harrelson had been found guilty of purchasing such a rifle on May 17, 1979. Perhaps Harrelson wanted the jury to perceive that he was not the kind of guy who would rat on his wife.

When Tom Sharpe handed his client the weathered stock of a rifle the government contended was used in Wood's murder, Harrelson looked it over and declared it similar to the one he had given Pete Kay. Then he shouldered the stock and pointed it at the prosecutors' table a few feet away. Smiling, he said: "The last time I saw that rifle, it was in the trunk of Pete Kay's car."

Before surrendering the witness to cross-examination, Tom Sharpe asked Harrelson if he had any theories about who had really killed Judge Wood.

"It is my belief," Harrelson said, "that rogue elements of the Drug Enforcement Administration or some other agency perpetrated the killing and were perpetuating the cover-up. I still believe that."

Sharpe asked about Harrelson's old friend Pete Kay.

"It is my belief," Harrelson said, "that Pete Kay is an officer of the U.S. government and the Drug Enforcement Administration and has been for many years."

Finally, Sharpe handed his client some FBI composite drawings of people seen in the area the day Wood was murdered. None resembled Pete Kay, but Harrelson thought he recognized two of the men in the drawings. He thought they resembled two other acquaintances, Warren Routen and Ronnie Weeden. Weeden's name had been mentioned earlier in the trial, when Pete Kay was testifying that he feared for his life. Weeden was one of the men who was supposed to have a contract on Pete Kay's life; at least that's what an FBI agent told Kay. Kay heard later that Weeden was dead, but speculated that Harrelson had probably given the contract to someone else.

Chief prosecutor Ray Jahn had listened patiently, objecting infrequently, as the defense attorney guided Harrelson through seventeen hours of friendly interrogation. A Justice Department staff prosecutor handpicked for the Wood case, Jahn was a skilled interrogator himself, though he didn't look the part. He was overweight and wore thick glasses, and his voice had a flat, slightly nasal quality that made his speech sound strained. If you had to guess, you would have guessed that his hobby was playing solos on the tuba. Several of the defense attorneys had heard that Jahn was quietly ambitious, that he was angling for a promotion to the big staff in Washington, and would probably get it if he won the Wood case. But hardly anyone regarded Jahn as a brilliant adversary. Compared to the other attorneys—and especially compared to the witness, Charles Harrelson—Ray Jahn appeared almost comically ineffectual, chubby and soft as a pet hamster.

Jahn shuffled papers as he approached the witness, who was smiling placidly. Moments later, after Jahn depicted Harrelson as an acknowledged killer and card cheat, the smile curdled. "You can call it cheating if you wish, sir," Harrelson replied. "But the people I play with are like me. We cheat each other. I just cheat better."

Jahn directed the defendant's memory back to the meeting with Jimmy Chagra in Las Vegas a few weeks before the murder. Harrelson had said that his initial idea was to lure Chagra into a poker game: he had calculated that he could make maybe $2 million cheating Chagra at poker. The second idea was a drug scam. "If the idea involved murder," Jahn said, fixing his eyes on Harrelson, "that was your idea, wasn't it?"

"The idea did not involve murder," Harrelson replied, and for the first time in the trial he looked upset. "That was not *my* idea. I don't have to kill anyone to make a living. I can do very well with these ten fingers and a deck of cards. I can play God!"

The prosecutor shuffled papers again, turning his back on the witness as though he had heard nothing. For several minutes Jahn asked questions that seemed designed to bait the witness, to encourage him to ramble and sneer and condescend. When Jahn suggested for the second time that Harrelson would do anything for money, including murder, Harrelson's sneer tightened into rage and he shook his finger at the prosecutor and shouted: "I don't have to kill people and you know it. You know that standing right there that I didn't kill that judge. You know it . . . you know it! You have to get someone because you've got Washington D.C. climbing all over your body and soul. And it's easy to convict me because I've already been convicted for murder. Isn't it?"

Jahn led the witness back through sections of his previous testimony, how he had claimed that the meeting with Jimmy Chagra in Las Vegas was almost accidental, how the two of them had never even had a private conversation. Harrelson had recalled that at one point Chagra telephoned Pete Kay in Huntsville. Was there a private conversation with Harrelson after that?

"Our only private conversation consisted of exactly six words," Harrelson said. "Jimmy Chagra handed me an envelope full of cash [$40,000], and said, 'This is for you and Pete.' "

"Those six words he said," Jahn asked, glancing quickly at the jury, "could those six words have been 'This is to kill the judge'?"

Harrelson's face turned red and his eyes got wild. The finger that he had been shaking under the prosecutor's nose became a fist and he snarled: "Did your mother dress you funny as a child?"

At this point, Judge Sessions warned the witness, "Just respond to the question, Mr. Harrelson," but Harrelson again shook his fist at the prosecutor, then turned toward the judge with that same angry snarl and said: "I don't know anything about Judge Wood or the murder. He knows it, and I know it, and you know it, too, judge!"

Throughout the remainder of the day, Ray Jahn maintained his calm and composure, allowing Harrelson his numerous tirades. Several times the judge warned the witness against continued outbursts. Only once did Ray Jahn flinch—a bat of the eye, really—and that was when Harrelson told the prosecutor in dead earnest: "I wouldn't tell you the time of day if you were dying. I despise you people."

Harrelson apparently got a grip on his temper during the Thanksgiving break, because when the trial resumed on November 29, 1982, the defendant sat through Jahn's cross-examination with little more than an insolent sneer. Harrelson did accuse the prosecutor of having "a severe case of tunnel vision" for not accepting his theory of what happened, but there were no more violent outbursts. Harrelson did clash with the judge, however. When the witness insisted on telling the jury, despite earlier warnings from Sessions, that he wasn't given enough time to listen to all the government tapes, Sessions sent the jury out of the courtroom and threatened Harrelson with contempt. Reminding the defendant that the tapes were turned over to the defense nearly seven months ago, the judge said stiffly: "Discovery procedures have been followed fully and completely, Mr. Harrelson. This court will not allow you to suggest to this jury that procedures were or were not followed."

After that Harrelson shut up and Tom Sharpe hurried to rest his case.

Charles Campion rested his defense of Jo Ann Harrelson after less than an hour. He called only three witnesses. Campion had decided against putting his client on the stand.

From the time during pretrial when he learned of Liz Chagra's letter to Wood's widow Warren Burnett had realized it would be necessary for Liz to testify in her own defense. The government took the position that Liz had joined the conspiracy that day when Jimmy walked into the kitchen of their home in Las Vegas and told her he was planning to kill the judge, and Liz replied, "Okay, honey," then went back to frying chicken. Calm and confident in her black suit and white blouse, Liz Chagra listened carefully to her lawyer's questions and answered them slowly and deliberately. Tears came to her eyes once, when she talked about her children, and most courtroom spectators believed that the jury was on her side as she spoke of her turbulent life with Jimmy Chagra. "He was always threatening to have someone killed," she said. "His friends, his business associates, his brothers, even me. He was a very kind and big-hearted man, but he had a violent temper. He beat me a number of times, so badly I needed medical attention. But I never believed he killed Judge Wood. He was my husband, the father of my children."

Liz acknowledged that when her husband first mentioned having Wood killed that day in the kitchen, she probably did reply, "Okay, honey." But now she told the jury: "It was a way to pass him through the kitchen. He was just mouthing off. It was his way of letting off steam. He would usually calm down after that and get back to normal. I usually took it with a grain of salt. Actually, I was more concerned that the chicken I was frying was not yet cooked."

Burnett asked his client to describe the day that her husband asked her to deliver money to the Jockey Club.

Liz told the jury: "We were just sitting around the den. Jimmy and his bodyguard and other friends were there. Jimmy took the money there in the den. He asked to speak to me and we went in the office right off the den. He seemed very upset and nervous."

"What happened next?" Burnett asked.

"That's when he told me he needed me to take some money to the Jockey Club. The money was in two envelopes. They were already in the bag."

"And you became upset?"

"Yes, sir. When he said he needed me to take some money I was upset. First, because there were guests in the house and because I wasn't feeling very well. I was seven months pregnant at the time and it was very hot that day. I asked him if his bodyguard couldn't take the money instead. He whispered through clenched teeth that it was the money for the judge's death. That's all he said. He was pretty mad. I was pretty much in a panic. I didn't want to go. But he took me in his arms and said, 'Now, you know I was only playing with you. This is just another gambling debt.' "

"What else, if anything, did he say?" Burnett asked.

"He told me if I took the money I wouldn't have to cook that evening. That I could pick up some chicken on the way home. So Cindy and I drove to the Jockey Club and pulled up right in front. There was construction going on. I asked Cindy to wait in the car. I got in the elevator and went up to the room."

"When you got to the room did you meet a young woman?"

"Yes, sir. I remember her being very young. I remember her wearing a bathing suit. I can't tell you [if] it was Teresa."

"Did you at any time try to disguise or hide what you were doing?"

"No, sir. I really didn't think it was anything that was serious. Jimmy had convinced me it was just another debt."

On cross-examination, Ray Jahn pressed the witness to reveal exactly when she learned the truth about Wood's murder. Liz replied that she learned the truth around September 1, 1980, after Charles Harrelson's arrest near Van Horn. Her brother-in-law, Joe Chagra, told her.

"He was asking me specific questions," she said. "I asked him to tell me what he was getting at. That's when he told me . . . told me Charles Harrelson was the man Jimmy had hired to kill Judge Wood. That's what Harrelson had told Joe."

Shortly after that, Liz continued, she went to Leavenworth to confront Jimmy. "Joe was telling me one thing. Jimmy was telling me something else. Jimmy never told me the truth about anything." Liz couldn't recall the exact date, but agreed with the prosecutor that it may have been November 18, the visit in which Jimmy first discussed his plans to escape and meet Liz in the Orient.

"Where in the November 18 tape did you confront him?" Jahn asked pointedly.

"This [tape] is only a small part of the whole conversation," Liz said. "I visited Jimmy five to six hours per day, six to eight days per month."

Liz was about to recite a particular part of the conversation when Jahn interrupted with an objection. "The matters that she wants to refer to are not in evidence," the prosecutor told the court. "If she believed additional tapes should have been played, she should have had her attorney introduce them. They were provided with all the tapes and all the transcripts." Judge Sessions agreed with the government.

Liz spent her final day on the witness stand sobbing and listening as Ray Jahn replayed the tapes of her final visit to Leavenworth, on January 26, 1981.

JIMMY: Okay, honey, I'm not gonna argue. That's not the way it went down, but I'm not gonna argue with you. It's possible that that's what you said. Okay.

LIZ: I remember that's what I said. I was . . . 'cause I was afraid to death.

JIMMY: No, no, you told me . . . you . . .

LIZ: I was afraid when I did it, Jimmy.

JIMMY: You know this place is tapped. I found out yesterday the place is tapped. Can't we write? That's what I brought this for, honey. . . . Okay, come here, listen. . . .

LIZ: It's just that there's somebody, somebody that you love so much, put me in this position . . .

JIMMY: Honey, quit trying to fucking turn things around and talk that way to me.

JACKIE CHAGRA: Momma!

At the conclusion of the replaying of the tape, Liz tried her best to hold in her emotions, but her voice broke and trembled as she told the prosecutor: "You are wrong. I am not a participant in this crime. I am not guilty in this."

After the final defendant had rested, the government called several rebuttal witnesses, including Joe Chagra, who told the jury that Harrelson had lied about almost everything, particularly about Joe's giving him guns and cocaine and offering money to kill Jamie Boyd, and in his claim that Joe offered money if Harrelson would take the rap. By now it was the second week in December. Judge Sessions ordered members of the jury to report back with their suitcases: it was time for them to hear final arguments and deliberate their verdict.

Leading the government's summation, assistant prosecutor John Emerson told the jury that Charles Harrelson was "an amoral, cold-blooded killer" who would continue killing "as long as he can get away with it. The murder of Judge Wood was the greatest act of terrorism he could [commit] against the system he despised." As for Harrelson's four alibi witnesses, Emerson described them as either friends or people who were honestly mistaken about the time they saw Harrelson in Dallas. "Most of what Harrelson says about what happened is based almost solely on his own testimony," Emerson said. "If you come to the conclusion that the alibi is fabricated, you should consider that strong evidence of guilt."

Of the three defense attorneys, Tom Sharpe made the most impassioned plea for his client, a man who, because of his prior murder conviction, was "the perfect candidate to be named, blamed, pushed, shoved, bashed, whatever you want to call it—plug him into this case." Sharpe called the government's case one of "sand bagging, overkill and magnification." The attorney must have suspected that members of the jury found his arguments unconvincing. Nevertheless Sharpe decided to read aloud a poem that he had written on his legal pad the previous night:

> Death, of death, it comes to all,
> No matter be they big or small ...
> When death comes early, we are quick to blame
> We look for persons who may have caused the death
>   of him we thought a shame.

The final arguments of Charles Campion and Warren Burnett were less passionate and more to the point. Campion told the jury that the government had produced "no tangible evidence" that Jo Ann Harrelson had obstructed the investigation. Burnett reminded the jurors of what he had established earlier in the trial—that Liz Chagra was a young and confused woman dominated by a man who bullied and coerced everyone around him.

During the final two hours of arguments, chief prosecutor Ray Jahn hacked away at the various arguments and theories suggested by the defense attorneys. All three defendants, he reminded the jury, had powerful reasons to lie, most of all Charles Harrelson, who had claimed that his "long suit is killing people and getting away with it. Well, the government has proved that Charles Harrelson killed Judge Wood. And he has spent the last three and a half years trying to get away with it. Charles Harrelson will lie no matter how cold and hard the facts are. If there had been a videotape of him shooting Wood, he would have said, 'That was my long-lost brother Cecil who, as a baby, was floated down the Trinity River in a wicker basket.' "

Possibly sensing that defense attorney Warren Burnett had succeeded in soliciting considerable jury sympathy for his client, Jahn reserved his most vitriolic remarks for Liz Chagra. Though her attorney pictured her as a stupid, abused "little mouse," Jahn said, it was clear to him from that section of the tapes where she calls Jimmy a "dummy" and tells him to stop panicking that her husband did not totally dominate their relationship. Jahn also reminded jurors of another part of the tapes, where Liz said: "Yeah, do it." Jahn turned away from the jury and looked straight at the defendant as he said: "The accuser against Elizabeth Chagra is herself. No matter how much you lie, no matter how much you cry, you can't get rid of it."

In a parting shot aimed partly at Liz Chagra's much-publicized religious conversion, but also directed at the jury's sense of duty and civic responsibility, the prosecutor noted that in her letter to Wood's widow, she had referred to a new Liz and an old Liz. Jahn said: "She must take responsibility for what the old Liz did. If she knows that Jesus loves her, she knows Jesus loved Judge Wood, Jesus loved Mrs. Wood, and Jesus loves this community."

On Saturday, December 10, after ten weeks of complicated, emotional, and often tedious testimony and legal bickering, jurors began their deliberation. At 9:50 A.M. the following Tuesday, word reached the courtroom that they had reached a verdict. The courtroom was deathly silent as the jurors, some of them obviously on the verge of tears, filed to their seats for the last time. Judge Sessions sat ramrod-straight as his clerk read the verdicts:

Charles Voyde Harrelson . . . guilty.

Jo Ann Harrelson . . . guilty.

Elizabeth Chagra . . . a fraction of a second before the clerk pronounced the word "guilty" there was a loud sob, almost a wail, from the jury box. Stunned courtroom spectators and attorneys looked on with amazement as one of the jurors, Patricia Schulz-Ormond, wept openly. So did Mary Kathleen Mills, the jury foreman. Within seconds all nine women and one man were crying. None of the attorneys or case-hardened members of the media could recall anything like this display of emotion. Warren Burnett, who had defended and, early in his career, prosecuted—even sent to the electric chair—some of the most violent and notorious criminals in the Southwest, said later: "There is nothing in my experience that could have prepared me for the reaction of the jury." Charles Harrelson wore his customary smirk, but tears welled in the eyes of his wife, Jo Ann. Liz Chagra forced a smile as she looked at the weeping jurors and mouthed the words: "That's all right." ("She doesn't have a full grasp of what has happened to her," Burnett said.) As Judge Sessions polled the jury, asking each in turn to affirm each of the verdicts, Patricia Schulz-Ormond and several others continued to weep. Jury foreman Mary Kathleen Mills was still crying, too, but when her turn came to affirm her decisions, she held her head high, turned to each defendant, then answered "Yes, your honor" to each question.

Ray Jahn, looking more haggard and spent than victorious, refused comment, pointing out that the government still had to try Jimmy Chagra. For reasons that were not explained, Judge Sessions had decided to move Jimmy's trial not only out of San Antonio, but out of Texas. It was scheduled to begin in January, in Jacksonville, Florida. Sessions announced that he would postpone sentencing until March 1983, after the completion of Jimmy's trial.

Back in El Paso, members of the Chagra family were in seclusion. The only family member who spoke with reporters was Mom Chagra, who was in her small apartment behind Patsy's house when a reporter knocked on the door. Mom's face was swollen from crying, and the tears started again when she saw the reporter. It was almost Christmas and the middle-class brick and frame houses on Santa Anita Street were decked with holly and Christmas angels and nativity scenes that obscured the normal decor of station wagons and boats.

After a few seconds the reporter realized that Mom was not necessarily crying over the verdict in San Antonio. It had been almost exactly four years since the death of her oldest son, Lee Abdou Chagra. "It's been four years of hell," she said.

45

Hardly anyone in official circles used the term "crime of the century" any longer, though it was more appropriate than ever. Wood's murder had certainly produced the *investigation* of the century—the most extensive and most costly in history, finally eclipsing the probe into the assassination of President Kennedy. After the verdict in San Antonio, there was jubilation among high officials at the Justice Department in Washington. San Antonio made it all seem worthwhile.

Prosecutor Ray Jahn, who had worked in Washington until the department transferred him to San Antonio in 1972, wondered if the celebration wasn't premature. There was still the matter of convicting the man that the government maintained was responsible for the whole affair. Even as the government was trucking more than a ton of files, charts, graphs, scale models, tape-recording consoles, and speakers across the country to the federal courthouse in Jacksonville, Florida —to the very courtroom, in fact, used by John Wood when he was a visiting judge there two months before his murder—Jahn and his staff worked fifteen hours a day preparing for the most important trial of all, the one that could finally bring Jimmy Chagra to justice.

The Wood case was a make-or-break situation in the career of Ray Jahn, and, to a lesser extent, the career of his wife, LeRoy. The husband-and-wife team had built a reputation with their painstaking research and their knowledge of the intricacies of federal law, but nowhere in their background—nowhere in *any* prosecutor's background—was there a case in which the government put its prestige more flatly on the line. LeRoy, who had met her husband when they were both attending law school at the University of Texas, was the legal tactician and the expert in appellate matters. Ray was the classical trial lawyer, the government's go-getter. The Wood case could be the making of a great career, a promotion to the staff in Washington, or even the ultimate reward for most lawyers, a federal judgeship. That was one side of the situation. The other side was the official reaction if he lost. "If he loses," one attorney explained, "he'll be in line for a transfer to Duluth, Minnesota—in the dead of winter."

The trial in Jacksonville would be a shortened version of the trial in San Antonio, a replay but with one major exception—instead of Joe Chagra, the government's star witness would be Jerry Ray James. Jahn no doubt recognized that without Joe Chagra, the verdict in San Antonio could have been much different. Joe's testimony and, more than the testimony, his clean-cut good looks, his forthrightness, and his honest and painfully contrite bearing were indispensable weapons for the government. Jerry Ray James made the prosecutor nervous. If there was a man on earth meaner and more disreputable than Charles Harrelson, it was the government's star witness in Jacksonville.

On the other hand, Oscar Goodman, attorney for the defense, felt very good about Jerry Ray James, who had been his client's best friend for a while in Leavenworth. The discovery that James had been an informer had jolted Jimmy Chagra. Jimmy was genuinely frightened, maybe for the first time in his life. His religious conversion, while not as pronounced as the one that gripped Liz, wasn't just an act. It was as real as anything else in Jimmy's system of dreams and values. Jimmy was older and considerably more subdued than the defendant who had insisted on taking the witness stand three and a half years ago in Austin. Maybe he wasn't a "new" Jimmy, but he wasn't the cocky old Jimmy, either—he was content, even eager, to let his attorney call the shots.

It had been weeks since Jimmy had talked to Joe, or even heard from him, except for an occasional message of hope and love passed along by their sister, Patsy. Jimmy had always maintained that he wouldn't allow his wife or brother to serve time in prison, but as things turned out, Jimmy didn't have much choice. As Oscar Goodman understood better than anyone, there was never any chance that Jimmy would help the government. In the beginning, Jimmy resented Joe's plea-bargaining deal. He had warned Joe what they did to "snitches" in prison. But when Oscar Goodman explained that it was the best thing that could have happened to Jimmy—it forced the government to sever his case from Harrelson's—Jimmy had understood and forgiven.

Joe had appeared genuinely contrite as he stood before the bench for sentencing, knowing that the judge had considerable latitude. (While Sessions had postponed sentencing the others until after Jimmy's trial, he decided to sentence Joe Chagra separately, before Jimmy's trial.)

"I know it probably sounds shallow and inadequate to say I'm sorry, but I'm sorry," Joe told Sessions. "I don't know if there is anything I can say now that will change anything that is going to happen here today. But I made a commitment to my wife, and my life is going to change." Prosecutor Ray Jahn had done his part, assuring the judge that Joe had "cooperated fully" as a government witness. (In private conversations, Jahn had called the testimony "Joe Chagra's finest hour" and had spoken of "the Greek tragedy" of the whole affair between the Chagras and Judge Wood.) Before passing sentence, Judge Sessions told Joe: "I do respect what you have done in your plea bargain. It was absolutely right and had to be done. If you sense that you've done that, you've already started the restoration process." To the surprise of some, the judge then gave Joe Chagra the maximum sentence allowed by the terms of the government's deal—ten years. Several weeks before the start of Jimmy's trial, Joe was already doing time at the minimum-security facility at Pleasanton, California, near San Francisco Bay.

In Oscar Goodman's estimation, the government had a good case against Jimmy: the trial in San Antonio proved that. A good case but not a great case. Jacksonville wasn't San Antonio. With the exception of a few judges and lawyers who had met Wood when he served as a visiting judge in March 1979, few in Jacksonville remembered John Wood, except as the judge from Texas who loved seafood and chocolate candy and played a mean game of tennis. Most potential jurors had never heard the nickname Maximum John or seen the adjective "beloved" in front of Wood's name. There was no John H. Wood, Jr., Federal Courts Building in Florida.

Oscar Goodman liked to tell a story about his strongest impression of San Antonio:

"When I was leaving San Antonio one day during the pretrial," Goodman recalled, "this cab driver asked me what I did. I told him

I was a lawyer. He asked if I was on the Chagra case, and before I could answer he started in about how he hoped they hung those sorry bastards and what a wonderful man Wood was and how he stopped drugs in San Antonio. Finally he said, 'Who do you represent?' I told him I represented the government."

It was Goodman's firm belief that the jury in San Antonio convicted the defendants not on the strength of the evidence but because they believed it was their *duty* to convict. "How could they face their family and friends if they failed to convict the people that the government said were responsible for Judge Wood's death?" the attorney said. On the other hand, the people of Jacksonville seemed to be actually rooting for the defendant. "I don't know why," Goodman said, "but I get a strong feeling from talking to people around my hotel that they're on our side. The government is going to have to prove its case."

Goodman had noticed during pretrial that the prosecutors seemed supremely confident. One tipoff was the government's unexpected concession that any potential juror who had even *heard* about Liz Chagra's conviction, or Joe Chagra's guilty plea, be excluded from jury duty. "They argued about it at first," Goodman said, "but they were so confident of victory they didn't pursue it." It was rumored that before leaving San Antonio one of the FBI agents purchased a Mexican *piñata*—a clay jar painted and decorated with colorful paper streamers and filled with goodies: at Christmas, kids in Mexico blindfold each other and take turns trying to bust the jar with a stick. This particular *piñata* was in the form of a devil. Someone had painted the letters C.H. across the chest. At the conclusion of the trial in Jacksonville, FBI agents and prosecutors apparently intended to break out the champagne and celebrate victory by busting the old *piñata*.

The most difficult problem for the defense, Goodman believed, was not overcoming the testimony of Jerry Ray James, or even the tapes, but the basic job of attacking the four-count indictment. "Indicting the case the way they did was a brilliant maneuver," Goodman said. "It's a textbook indictment, joining the obstruction to the marijuana to the conspiracy to the murder—joining those four elements. It makes the case almost impossible to defend. Because of the tapes, a lawyer has to virtually concede the drugs and obstruction charges.

But you have to fight the murder and conspiracy to murder. If you argue that the government has no evidence of drugs or obstruction, you lose your credibility. See, that was the problem Joe Chagra faced."

Oscar Goodman began his attack in the opening seconds of the trial, objecting to FBI agents' being seated at the prosecution table. In his opening remarks to the jury, he virtually conceded that his client was guilty of obstructing justice and of marijuana conspiracy, but warned the jurors they faced an "almost inhuman task" of sorting through the massive amounts of testimony and evidence that would be presented. Goodman wanted the jury to understand the "lawless . . . deplorable . . . reprehensible" situation that existed in West Texas back in 1979. He told them of the bitter feelings that existed between Judge Wood and the Chagra family, of Judge Wood's highly questionable "professionalism" that so inflamed the situation that Lee Chagra was preparing a lawsuit against the judge, of Lee's murder and the attempted murder of James Kerr. Situations such as this have a way of taking on their own momentum, he said, until every agent of the federal government believed it was his solemn duty to bring the entire Chagra family to justice.

Goodman described the plea-bargaining negotiations that took place before Jimmy Chagra's trial in Austin, and posed the logical question: "Is someone going to hire someone to kill a federal judge over a five-year differential?" The defense attorney didn't deny the government's claim that Jimmy Chagra delivered money to Charles Harrelson. It wasn't blood money, however, but simple extortion money paid after Harrelson confronted the defendant and said, "Chagra, I killed the judge. I want to get paid for it."

"We will not attempt to disprove that Charles Harrelson shot Judge Wood in the back on May 29, 1979," Goodman told the jury. "Jimmy Chagra does not know if Charles Harrelson killed Judge Wood."

Finally, on the subject of the tapes, the defense lawyer said that Jimmy Chagra talked like a tough guy "in order to survive in prison." But he reminded the jurors that each of them had promised to keep an open mind, and he said: "When you keep your mind open, look for motive. And when you listen to the conversations, ask yourself if these are *real* things that are being discussed."

353

Ray Jahn brushed off the old "story of fear and greed" talk that he had made to the jury in San Antonio, rewriting sections to fit the new situation. The story started, he said, in Las Vegas when Charles Harrelson "offered his services" to kill Lee Chagra's murderers. "But Jimmy Chagra wasn't concerned for his brother, but for his own case." He knew that in a few weeks he would stand trial before a judge they called Maximum John.

Jahn told the jury: "Jimmy Chagra was afraid of this. Jimmy Chagra tried every legal means to remove Judge Wood. Jimmy Chagra decided to have him murdered. It was the only recourse, the only salvation for Jimmy Chagra. Fate intervened and Charles Harrelson offered his services. There will be no evidence presented that Jimmy Chagra pulled the trigger."

The government's leadoff witness was Chrys Lambros, the San Antonio lawyer who remembered bumping into the strange man with the unforgettable eyes. "There was a look about him that was very different," she said. "He didn't look as though he belonged in the neighborhood. He struck me as someone who came out of a West Coast bar. I said, 'Good morning' and he just grunted. . . ."

Following Kathryn Wood's testimony of how she cradled the head of the dying judge in her arms, the government called the medical examiner, who described in grisly detail the results of his three-hour autopsy. Sixteen bullet fragments were removed from the judge's body—on the X-ray the body looked like a "snowstorm." The bullet severed Wood's spinal cord, shattered and ripped apart his aorta, and did major damage to the organs in his abdomen. "The liver looked like mashed potatoes," the medical examiner recalled. (A reporter smiled at the mention of Wood's liver: the judge was a celebrated drinker.)

Grace Sampsell, who was Wood's docket clerk in El Paso and Midland, gave evidence of motivation as she described watching Jimmy Chagra on several occasions in the courtroom at Midland. At the bond hearing in February, she recalled, Chagra "was frightened. He didn't say anything. He was scared." At the pretrial hearing in April, Jimmy Chagra entered the courtroom wearing a large smile. "He was carefree," Sampsell recalled. "He was out on bond." Then the attorneys for the defense filed thirty motions, and the judge routinely denied twenty-nine of them—he did agree to move the trial out of San Antonio, to Austin seventy miles to the north. By the time Wood got around to denying the most important motion of all, the one asking that he recuse himself from hearing the case, the atmosphere of the courtroom had taken a dramatic turn. "It was explosive," Sampsell told the jury.

The government introduced two letters that John Wood wrote to Judge Sessions while Wood was still trying cases in Jacksonville. The letters were Wood's way of replying to newspaper articles in which Joe Chagra accused Wood of being overly cozy with prosecutor James Kerr. While it was true that Wood and Kerr occasionally dined "on a Dutch treat basis," Wood denied that he was overly friendly with the prosecutor. "I know of only one instance during the past almost nine years when Mr. Kerr and I have been on the same airplane," Wood wrote, then added this cavalier flourish: "I do not even fly in the same section of the aircraft as the government prosecutors." In a second letter to Sessions, dated March 9, 1979, Wood insisted that he had gone out of his way to be good to the Chagra brothers. In fact, federal agents and prosecutors had complained that Wood was "overly sympathetic" in allowing members of the Chagra family to "avail themselves of our library, coffee bar, Xerox facilities and the hospitality of our chambers generally."

The government called a number of friends and associates of Jimmy Chagra to establish Chagra's extravagant life-style—his "royal" treatment at the casinos, his luxury home with maids and private secretaries, footlockers full of cash, millions of dollars risked at the gambling tables. Gloria Stroupe, who had been Jimmy's secretary and "girl Friday" in Las Vegas, told of paying household bills with stacks of cash that Jimmy provided, and described the home that Jimmy and Liz had refurbished in North Las Vegas, dwelling on the master bedroom. She told the jury that the house had "ten or fifteen" telephones, though Jimmy believed they were tapped and usually used a pay phone a block away.

The government also called a number of Charles Harrelson's friends and associates, partly to establish his reputation as a killer but also to begin the elaboration of the government's stalking theory. A large calendar listing all the days in May 1979 was posted near the witness stand. Prosecutors had already introduced records from motels and airport parking lots in San Antonio, Austin, Midland,

and Las Vegas: it was time for the jury to hear some firsthand accounts of Harrelson's activities from people like Pete Kay and Hampton Robinson III.

The prosecution received an unexpected jolt, however, when Pete Kay testified under cross-examination that Hamp Robinson was "a deranged dope addict."

Assistant prosecutor John Emerson tried to save the day by asking Kay's definition of the word "deranged," but it just got worse.

"My understanding of the word 'deranged' is Hampton Robinson," Kay replied. "He's just a real flaky guy. He's a dope fiend."

The government had no choice except to put Hamp Robinson on the witness stand. Robinson immediately acknowledged that he had been buoyed for the occasion by a shot of methadone. Robinson told the jury how he and Charles Harrelson went to Las Vegas with the intention of cheating Jimmy Chagra in a rigged poker game. Shortly after Robinson's return to Houston, Harrelson telephoned and asked him to buy a rifle. "He said he had some business to take care of. He asked me how good I was at four hundred to five hundred yards." Robinson said that he once watched Harrelson kill a small bird 250 yards away with a single-shot rifle and a telescopic sight. Just before Memorial Day weekend, 1979, Harrelson telephoned again—he wanted Robinson and his fiancée, Jo Ann Stafford, to meet him in Austin on May 27. At Robinson's instructions, Jo Ann Stafford told Harrelson he was sick and couldn't come.

"Is there some reason you didn't want to meet him?" asked John Emerson.

"I figured something was going to happen," Robinson replied. "I didn't want to be a participant."

Jo Ann Robinson testified that Harrelson became "upset" and "said he would handle the business himself and see us in a few days." On the afternoon of May 29, Harrelson called from Dallas and said he had "taken care of his business." Later, he asked Hampton Robinson to help him dispose of his wife's gold Cutlass.

On cross-examination, Oscar Goodman produced a copy of an FBI interview with Hampton Robinson, conducted in March 1981. Robinson had recounted a bizarre episode in which Joe Chagra and two unidentified men came to his ranch and strangled his dog, at which time Robinson claimed to have killed the two men. Goodman could almost hear the sighs of resignation at the prosecutors' table as he instructed the witness to read back his own statement, then asked:

"Where were the bodies buried?"

"There weren't any," Robinson said softly.

"Why?"

"It was probably a hallucination," the witness admitted.

"Where was Joe Chagra?" Goodman asked sharply. "He wasn't there, was he?"

"No," Robinson said.

Teresa Starr was called next and asked to tell the jury of her trip to Las Vegas to pick up the bag of money. The government now was ready to introduce the tapes and Jerry Ray James. They got a break when the judge allowed the introduction into evidence of the ninety-two pieces of torn paper that FBI agents seized from Liz Chagra's purse at Leavenworth. One of the notes, enlarged on a poster for the jury, read: "If the FBI is just guessing, how did they hit it right on the head that a PG lady paid Teresa?"

Jerry Ray James avoided Jimmy Chagra's glare as he made his way to the witness stand. The forty-four-year-old habitual criminal was dressed in a three-piece brown suit, but the beer belly, the balding head, and the graying beard made him look considerably older and strikingly out of the place. Still, James had obviously been well prepared for this moment. In his gruff, singsong voice he told the jury how he had been transferred to Leavenworth after the riots that gutted the New Mexico State Prison and took the lives of thirty-three guards and inmates. A mutual friend, another inmate named Travis Erwin, had introduced him to Chagra and they became friends after an incident in which Chagra slapped around an old con who Jimmy believed had cheated him in a card game. Jimmy had lost $1,600, but refused to pay, and a short time later three members of a prison gang known as "the Mexican Mafia" and a fourth from another gang called "the Aryan Brotherhood" came to Jimmy's cell to collect. "He was scared when he saw them coming," Jerry Ray James said. "But when I stood up with him, they backed off." Not long after that, as the two inmates sat under shade trees in the recreation area, Jimmy confessed his darkest secret.

"Just out of the clear blue sky, he said, 'Jerry, I'm the one that had Judge Wood killed,'" James told the jury.

Three weeks of courtroom calm ended abruptly as Jimmy Chagra bolted to his feet and shouted: "You're a liar! Scum bag! He's lying, your honor."

Judge Sessions warned Chagra about his courtroom conduct—fortunately, the jury was out of the room and didn't see the outburst. After that, two marshals were stationed between Chagra and the witness stand.

Over the next two days, Ray Jahn questioned the witness about the numerous drug deals that Jimmy Chagra was planning to help finance his escape, and about various criminal conversations between Chagra and James. The informant told the jury that Jimmy had become particularly upset when he heard that Charles Harrelson had been arrested near Van Horn. He talked about ways to kill Harrelson, even though Harrelson was apparently secure in jail. "He talked about having someone go in and blow up the whole jail," James said. There was a long list of people that Jimmy Chagra wanted dead—including Jack Stricklin, Henry Wallace, and the three men who were responsible for the murder of his brother Lee. On one occasion, James recalled, Jimmy talked about how he had personally gunned down a man named Mark Finney. This was during Jimmy's trial in Austin. There was some kind of drug deal involving Jack Stricklin and Mark Finney, an argument erupted, and Jimmy shot and killed Finney, or so he claimed. He told James that he had buried Finney's body in some woods west of Austin.

James told the jury about an incident on November 10, 1980, when Chagra almost discovered that his conversations were being recorded. A prison lieutenant, apparently unaware that James was working with the FBI, discovered recorders and microphones in James's cell. "Jimmy and I were at work one morning when the lieutenant came into the office furious. He threw a recording device and thirty or forty feet of wire right on the desk in front of us." After that, Jimmy Chagra became excessively paranoid, though from time to time he mentioned things about Wood's murder.

"Did he ever indicate a motive?" Jahn asked.

"Jimmy said he was afraid at the time that Judge Wood would give him a life sentence," James replied.

At the beginning of his cross-examination, Oscar Goodman provided the jury with a review of James's impressive criminal history.

By the time he was twenty, James was already serving a prison sentence for burglary. By his thirtieth birthday, he had made the FBI's Ten Most Wanted List. By the time he met Jimmy Chagra, James had been charged with at least forty-one crimes and convicted of thirteen felonies, including bank robberies, assaults, and escapes. James acknowledged that he had spent so much time in prison that he referred to his cell as "my home." James also conceded that he was one of the most "respected" inmates in New Mexico at the time of the bloody Santa Fe riots.

"Are there not allegations against you for the murder of several persons in the riot?" the defense attorney asked.

"Not true," James replied.

"Are there not allegations that you forced inmates to stay in the gymnasium where five bodies were found?"

James replied that no criminal charges had been filed against him in connection with the riot. Oscar Goodman knew that James and about thirty others had been hauled before a New Mexico prison disciplinary court. James had been accused of setting fire to the warden's office, and of leading a search for the names of prison snitches, many of whom were murdered in spectacularly bloody ways. He also knew that no criminal charges had been filed against James, or against any of the suspected leaders of the riot.

The trial was now in its fourth week, and Oscar Goodman sensed that the jury was becoming restless and losing interest. Except for the playing of the tapes, the government had about finished its case. Looking back over what had happened—and what had not—Goodman was starting to rethink his own strategy. He could have stretched out the cross-examination of Jerry Ray, but Goodman decided against this. There were just a few more questions he needed answered—for the moment, anyway.

Noting James's previous testimony that Jimmy Chagra was always bragging about big-time drug deals or making grandiose plans to have someone murdered, Goodman said: "Mr. Chagra was doing an awful lot of talking to show he was important—that he was heavy into criminal activities, right?"

"Yes," James agreed, adding that he and Jimmy once plotted several Colombian smuggling deals—one of them for forty tons of marijuana, and another for twenty-two pounds of cocaine. Jimmy's

brother, Joe Chagra, was supposed to be handling the deals on the
outside.

"But nothing ever came of it?"

"That's right," James admitted.

On Friday, January 29, the government finished playing a tape
in which Jimmy Chagra told James: "He wasn't supposed to do it
until after the trial—when the appeal was coming up. That way I
could get a different judge." Then the government rested its case.

As Goodman tried to assess the damage over the weekend, he kept
thinking about the jury and contrasting it with the jury in San
Antonio. No doubt about it, the government had convinced the San
Antonio jury that it was "the conscience of America." It was the
government's strongest argument, one that hadn't worked in Jacksonville. Goodman had repeatedly reminded the jurors to keep an
open mind as he spooled out his own scenario—how Charles Harrelson
had felt the law closing in and, realizing Jimmy Chagra was a prime
suspect in the Wood murder, used his leverage to extort money. Goodman had told the jurors that he would be calling maybe a dozen prison
inmates to prove that Jimmy was always shooting off his mouth and
playing the role of big shot, and that nothing had come of the tough
talk. The attorney had led the jurors to believe that the defense would
finish with a flourish, that Jimmy Chagra himself would likely take the
witness stand. "The jury had all weekend to think about who I might
be putting on the witness stand," Goodman said later. "I began to
realize how fortunate that was, how lucky that I would be starting
my defense on Monday morning." What Goodman had in mind was a
gamble, but considering the stakes, hardly a desperate gamble.

The defense that Oscar Goodman presented for the man accused
of masterminding the crime of the century lasted twelve minutes.

First, Goodman recalled Jerry Ray James and asked him about
his earlier testimony that Jimmy had bragged about "offing" a man
named Mark Finney.

"Describe how Mr. Chagra told you he killed Mark Finney," Goodman instructed the witness.

"I think he said he shot him."

"Are you sure of that?"

"I'm sure he told me he offed him," James said, sounding slightly
annoyed by the question.

"You're as sure of that as you are that Mr. Chagra told you he murdered Judge Wood?"

"That's right," James said, glancing at the table of prosecutors, who seemed to be absorbed at the moment in their own problems.

"No more questions," Goodman said. "Call Mark Finney."

When Finney had been sworn, Goodman shuffled some papers as though trying to decide what question to ask first. Walking slowly and stopping a few feet from the witness, Goodman smiled and said: "Mr. Finney, how are you feeling?"

"Pretty good," Finney said.

"Did Jimmy Chagra ever point a gun at you and shoot you?"

"No, sir," Finney said.

"No more questions," the lawyer said. He walked back toward the defense table, where Jimmy Chagra sat grinning. Then he stopped abruptly, turned to the bench, and said: "Your honor, ladies and gentlemen of the jury, the defense rests."

In his final argument, prosecutor John Emerson told the jury that Jimmy Chagra's fear of having to serve life in prison, coupled with his fear of losing his opulent life-style, prompted him to hire Harrelson to kill the judge. "His solution to his problems was nothing more than an absolute assault on our system of justice, an act of terrorism against the system and Judge Wood," Emerson told the jury in a weary monotone. "Judge Wood unknowingly and unwittingly set his own execution date when he refused to disqualify himself from hearing the case." Emerson asked jurors to recall the tape in which Jimmy told his brother: "The FBI knows I hired him to do that."

"The most incriminating evidence of Mr. Chagra's guilt is his own admission that he hired Charles Harrelson to kill Judge Wood," Emerson said. "There is no reasonable basis to doubt the truthfulness of the conversations."

Oscar Goodman began his extraordinarily effective summation by attacking what he believed to be the heart (or at least the major flaw) of the case—the lack of motive. "I submit that this case did not take place in a vacuum," he said, reminding the jury again of the attempted assassination of James Kerr that occurred a month before the murder of Lee Chagra and six months before the murder of John Wood. "Somebody took on a certain ruthlessness, a certain callousness in the

Western District of Texas before Jimmy Chagra was even indicted on the drug charge for which he was ultimately convicted."

He reminded the jurors of the particulars of Jimmy's drug indictment and said: "Now that's important because the counts of the indictment were such that Jimmy Chagra was eligible for parole had he been found guilty on any of those counts or if he entered into a plea bargain as far as those counts were concerned. He knew that. No matter what sentence any judge was going to give him, he knew that he was eligible for parole. And it is with that state of mind that the scenario develops between any type of communication, no matter how limited it was, between Jimmy Chagra and Charles Harrelson. . . ."

Goodman reviewed the wording and intent of Jimmy Chagra's motion that Wood recuse himself—the government had been telling the jury that the motion was itself a threat, and therefore proof of motive. Goodman said that the motion contained "probably the most forward accusations against a federal judge that one could make. Jimmy Chagra said, 'You are unfair. You are unfair because of the way you treated my brother, Lee, in your courtroom. You are unfair because of the way you treated my brother, Joe, in your courtroom. I want Joe as my lawyer and he can't practice before you because of the way that you feel about him. You can't give me a fair trial because you virtually consort with James Kerr, the assistant United States attorney. And I think, judge, based on all of that, you should disqualify yourself.' No secret about that, it's in the pleadings, filed with the court. And he demands a public hearing and the judge gives it to him. . . ."

The government had maintained that the motion produced at the hearing had made sinister references to Kerr's near brush with death and hinted that a similar fate awaited Wood. "But if you read that affidavit," Goodman continued, "the immediate succeeding paragraph . . . says, 'Because I know that Judge Wood is under some type of a marshal protection service.' Nothing of a sinister connotation, straightforward. And during the hearing, and it was vigorous, as Miss Sampsell says, certainly it was an explosive environment. There was an atmosphere of electricity because it's not an everyday affair where somebody comes into a courtroom in this country and points a finger at a judge and says you can't be fair. And the last witness that Mr. Chagra attempted to call was Judge Wood himself. And Judge Wood . . . refused to testify. And there's no question that the participants on Mr. Chagra's side of the room at the conclusion of this vigorously contested hearing were disappointed. . . . It's a natural thing. This is an adversary system that we're in. . . . So there's no question that Mr. Chagra and the others left the courtroom unhappy that day. But they didn't run out and hire somebody to kill a federal judge. . . ."

After spending the better part of his allotted two hours disassembling the government's theory of murder, item by item, Goodman took a few minutes near the end to review the other charges in the indictment. The government's proof that Jimmy Chagra obstructed justice rested mostly on the fact that he wanted to escape. "I can't look at you and candidly and sincerely state to you that Mr. Chagra did not want to escape from Leavenworth, doing thirty years without parole," Goodman told the jury. But he reminded them: "The means which he chose are incredible. The means he discussed were unbelievable. . . . It was a fantasy. . . . And I'm not sure it was a conspiracy to obstruct justice. I submit that it was a sad, sad situation where a human being was looking to break loose from his cage, not to obstruct justice, but to get out."

As to the charge that Jimmy and Joe conspired to import and distribute drugs, Goodman continued, this was more fantasy. "Even though there was a conversation between the two brothers," Goodman said, "I submit that Joe Chagra was doing what Jimmy Chagra was doing with Jerry James. He was placating. I urge you to listen to . . . the conversation of November 21st. If you have ever seen Abbott and Costello in their routine about who's on first, this beats it. Joe Chagra is trying to tell Jimmy Chagra with whom he's dealing. And every other sentence he had a different name, a different mispronunciation, a different place where the person is. But what he's trying to do, he's trying to preserve his brother's hope that in fact he's doing something which is going to result in his being able to get out of the prison environment. Once again, I can't tell you that the words aren't there. But I can tell you that when you listen to the words you will see what Joe Chagra time and time again says, 'I don't know what I'm doing here. I don't know what we're talking about. I don't know what's happening.' Time and time again."

In conclusion, the defense attorney asked the jurors to use their common sense, and to not concern themselves with public opinion but "to do what you said you would do as jurors."

"Based on the evidence which has been presented to you in this case by the prosecution against Jimmy Chagra, I submit to you that the ultimate tribute that you could pay to the Honorable John H. Wood, Jr., who sat as the United States district judge, sworn to uphold the laws of the United States, the ultimate tribute you could pay to him would be to return a verdict of not guilty."

In rebuttal, Ray Jahn played more tapes, including one where the brothers talked about "fabricating" a story of Harrelson blackmailing Jimmy, and the chief prosecutor told the jurors that "an acquittal would be nothing more than a travesty." But it was clear that Oscar Goodman had won the day, if not the war.

The jury began its deliberation on Friday, February 3, 1983. By Saturday they had listened again to portions of fifteen of the recorded conversations. Late Saturday afternoon there was word that the jurors had apparently agreed on two of the four charges, but would continue deliberations. The jurors had done a curious thing, Goodman noted. They had asked the government to supply them with a burn bag that could be used to destroy their notes. "If they had reached a verdict on two of the counts," Goodman reasoned, "and if they had found the defendant guilty, why would they care about burning the notes? I had to believe they had voted for acquittal." Goodman had guessed correctly. On Monday afternoon, the jury delivered what Oscar Goodman later, in a moment of immodesty, called "the most important acquittal in the history of jury trials." It was their opinion that Jimmy Chagra had not hired the killer of Judge Wood. They did find the defendant guilty of two lesser charges—obstructing justice and conspiring to smuggle drugs—but the government had allowed the biggest fish of all to get away.

A dejected Ray Jahn complimented Goodman, pointing out that Goodman had "a national reputation and deservedly so." Jahn added: "The jury has spoken. If you believe in the system, you believe in it all the way."

Even Jimmy Chagra was momentarily silent and in awe of the system, or at least the situation. "Thank God for Oscar Goodman," he said.

(It was learned later that the government had almost lost on all four counts. By Sunday, the jury had already voted to acquit on the two most serious charges. The remainder of the deliberation was devoted to the lesser charges of which Chagra was finally found guilty.)

Nowhere was the government's defeat more celebrated—and more lamented—than in El Paso. Jimmy's sister, Patsy, was at Columbo's Restaurant when her daughter, Lori, telephoned with the news. Patsy stood up in the middle of the restaurant and shouted: "Not guilty!" People at surrounding tables began to whisper and then applaud. "Finally!" Patsy shouted again. "It's been so long since we've won!"

Patsy hurried home, where Mom Chagra and other family members were already having their own victory celebration, amid swarms of photographers and reporters. Mom said that Judge John Wood had come to her in a dream and promised to help her family. Mom was crying, but these were tears of joy. She said: "I'm crying because I'm happy. Maybe now my little Liz will get out of jail and come back to her children."

In her way, Mom Chagra had hit on the tragic irony of the Wood case. How could Liz be convicted of helping her husband plan a murder that a second jury said he had nothing to do with? How could Joe Chagra plead guilty to a crime that didn't happen? It was just one of the peculiarities of the American system. Noting that "the essential difference was that Joe Chagra did not testify in Florida," Warren Burnett delivered a special lament to the system: "Trials are nothing but stiffly run festivals to distract the people from their true problems."

Judge William Sessions set March 18 for sentencing. Before that date, Jimmy and Liz Chagra pleaded guilty to income tax evasion, and, in a separate trial, Jo Ann Harrelson was found guilty of five counts of perjury for lying to the grand jury. No one dared speculate how the verdict in Florida would affect the punishments that Sessions would inflict. The verdict had wrecked the plans of San Antonio district attorney Sam Millsap to prosecute Jimmy Chagra under the state law, seeking a death sentence. "As strange as it may seem," Millsap said, "the law may preclude further prosecution when there is a not-guilty verdict." It was also unclear how the verdict affected Jerry Ray James's financial status. James told the Jacksonville jury that the government had promised him $250,000 reward money if Chagra was convicted. Some of the money had apparently been paid, because James's wife was observed driving a new Mercedes-Benz. As for Jerry Ray James, he was now a free man, as long as he stayed out of the state of New Mexico.

On the day of sentencing, the government filed a motion seeking to recover the cost of the investigation and the trial from the defendants. The bill came to $11.4 million. Sessions ruled that the defendants would not be billed for costs unless they somehow "profited" from their long legal ordeal. Hopes for book and movie deals suddenly evaporated.

Jimmy Chagra was the first to be sentenced. Before sentencing, he told the judge: "You don't care about honesty or truth. One day you and I will stand before a higher judge. If you can live with the sentences you give me, so can I." Sessions had the power to add twenty-five years to the thirty-two that Jimmy was already serving. Instead, he gave Jimmy an additional fifteen years, plus a fine of $220,000. With good time, it was possible for Jimmy Chagra to be released by the year 2007.

Charles Harrelson also took the opportunity to address the court before sentencing. He spoke of "Gestapo tactics" and the "unspeakable evil" perpetrated by government agents. "This court should consider a charge against itself of rape and murder," Harrelson said. "You have killed the Constitution of the United States. You have had carnal knowledge of every defendant who came before this court."

Sessions gave Harrelson two life sentences, to run *consecutively*, he added, biting down on the word with what appeared to be satisfaction. Under the guidelines, Harrelson wouldn't begin serving the life sentences until he completed the seventy years he faced in state prison. Still, it was barely possible that the forty-four-year-old defendant could be back on the street by the time he was seventy-nine.

Before sentencing Liz Chagra, the judge admitted that the jury had shown "strong feelings" for the defendant, though he wasn't sure the jury was speaking up for leniency. Sessions sentenced Liz to thirty years on the conspiracy charge, and added two more five-year sentences for obstruction and income tax evasion. The two five-year sentences would run concurrently with the longer sentence. She would become eligible for parole in 1992.

Considering the charges against her, Jo Ann Harrelson faced the toughest sentences of all. The judge could give her five years for obstruction, and another twenty-five for lying. Defense attorney Charles Campion argued before sentencing that her answers to the grand jury were technically correct, though she might have omitted some things. Sessions didn't agree. He gave her a total of twenty-five years.

In some ways it was all over, and in others it was just beginning. All five of the original defendants were in prison, or on the way. The Justice Department, of course, announced no recriminations for the investigators and prosecutors who had permitted Jimmy Chagra to escape justice, but that didn't mean none were planned. A Dallas television station reported that before the Jacksonville trial, Jimmy Chagra had offered to plead to both the murder of Wood and the attempted murder of Kerr—and also to "name names" of South American smugglers—if the government would set his wife free. But Washington nixed the deal, the television station's source said, adding, "They got greedy." As it turned out, this report was incorrect. "No deal was ever discussed, period," said Oscar Goodman.

Ray Jahn had told it right. It had been a story of greed and fear. It had been a Greek tragedy. There were three brothers from El Paso. The oldest one got greedy and got killed. The second got greedier and was accused of killing a federal judge. And the third went to prison for it.

46

Alcatraz still sits on its lonely rock in San Francisco Bay, cold and forlorn and shrouded with fog. It is abandoned now, like some decaying mausoleum to crimes of another age. Fifty years ago, Alcatraz was where they sent men convicted of heinous crimes. Those were simpler times, the so-called golden age when heroes like Babe Ruth, Commander Byrd, Amelia Earhart, J. Edgar Hoover, and Bonnie and Clyde titillated the public imagination. There was a certain jungle of justice, practiced with a machine gun: Al Capone's gang celebrated St. Valentine's Day by massacring Bugs Moran's gang.

In those simpler times, the country satisfied its need to regulate morals by bringing about an experiment called Prohibition. A few bootleggers went to jail, and a few got deported, but the major effect of Prohibition, the one that is burned in our common memory, is that it raised the tariff of the outlawed product to a point where men were willing to kill over it. The lesson of that great experiment, the lesson that the ruined fortress of Alcatraz starkly symbolizes, is that morals can't be legislated. The law of demand corrupts the law of supply. If people want something, and can afford it, it will be provided. It is a phenomenon subject to a higher law called human nature. Given the panic that preceded our own generation of drug laws, and the stridency, stringency, and bias with which the laws were enforced, the affair of Judge Wood and the Chagras seems not surprising but rather preordained, a tragedy compounded by its own inevitability. What's hard to believe is that it started over an illegal weed.

At the opposite end of the bay from Alcatraz, in the Livermore Valley, in the rolling hills of the wine country east of the bay, stands the federal correctional institution of Pleasanton. When the inmates of Pleasanton joke about "real prisons," they mean places like Leavenworth and Marion, places like what Alcatraz used to be. Pleasanton looks like a small California junior college surrounded by two high fences between which runs a ten-foot no-man's-land of white pebbles and cactus. There are no guard towers, and not too many guards. The facility sits in one corner of a virtually abandoned military post, Fort Parks, backed against the hills. In another corner of the old post, behind rows of rotting barracks and the weed-choked drill fields, is an area sometimes used to temporarily contain special groups of prisoners. In the summer of 1983 it was the site of gigantic circus tents sheltering several hundred men, women, and children, antinuclear protesters charged with trespassing and being detained until the government could figure out what to do next. Daniel Ellsberg, one of the leaders, refused even to give his name, much less to plea-bargain for probation, and advised others to do the same. The government had a real dilemma but for the moment it was hidden from public view, swallowed up by the same mammoth, nearly deserted government facility that also swallowed up criminals like Joe Chagra and Sara Jane Moore—the aging crazy who tried to off Gerald Ford in San Francisco.

Two-thirds of the inmates are women. Before it went co-ed, Pleasanton was *the* maximum-security prison for women. Now it houses both sexes, small-timers and short-timers mostly, drug dealers, illegal aliens, an occasional Mafia informant: a majority of the inmates at Pleasanton are under some type of witness-protection program. Joe Chagra had imagined that he would be singled out—the man who snitched off the man who killed the judge—but after a few weeks he realized he was no one special. Just another inmate doing time.

Joe stayed mostly to himself. He had an easy, boring job as clerk typist in food services, and he shared his modern dorm room with a young illegal alien who would be gone in a month or two. Joe was lifting weights several times a week and had become a vegetarian. When he was arrested fifteen months before, he had weighed 155 pounds; now he weighed 190, all muscle. He had stopped smoking and stopped using drugs, though drugs were easily available at Pleasanton. He stayed clear of the women prisoners, too. There were strict rules concerning contact with the opposite sex. Holding hands was permitted but if a man was caught with his arm around a woman, both were given a "shot," as it was called—a shot usually meant time in the hole. If they were caught in the act of making love—they often were—both were immediately transferred to a real prison. "I don't take any chances," Joe said. "I just want to do my time and get out."

The hardest part was not knowing when that would be. Normally, an inmate is eligible for parole after doing one-third of his sentence. In Joe Chagra's case that would be forty months. At the time of his plea-bargaining agreement, parole-board guidelines for Joe's particular crime, murder, required the inmate to do at least fifty-four months. Since then the guidelines had changed. Depending on whether the parole board decided to follow the old or the new guidelines, Joe would be eligible for parole in either October 1986, or sometime in 1989. He was hoping that Ray Jahn and perhaps FBI agent Mick McCormick would write letters to the parole board, pleading his case and detailing his special situation.

If Joe had believed that he really did something wrong, maybe the time would have been easier. Joe found himself looking back a lot, which is what you do when looking ahead is blank space. Even now he didn't regret turning down the government's original offer, five years for a plea of obstruction. He had refused on principle: in his own mind, he hadn't obstructed justice. He did what he believed lawyers were supposed to do. True, the feds had found a small quantity of drugs when they searched his home, using a search warrant of questionable validity, but the drugs were hardly enough to justify sending a first offender to prison. Joe was in prison because it was the only way the government could convict Charles Harrelson. He was in prison for a crime he hadn't committed: he knew that, and so did the government.

"They did a real number on me, holding me without bond after my arrest," he said. "All those weeks and months in solitary. Over and over I kept thinking: what am I doing here, what am I trying to prove? I really believed I was fighting for a principle, for the right of a client to talk openly and freely with his attorney. People ask me how we could have been talking so freely on those tapes—I never dreamed they would dare listen to, much less record, an attorney-client conversation. I would have bet a million dollars they couldn't do that. But they did. Then they used the tapes to get a warrant to search my home. There was no real evidence to support a search warrant, except repeated references to 'the Chagras.' The Chagras did this, the Chagras did that, our source says the Chagras said . . . It was like saying, if your name is Chagra, you are guilty.

370

"I really believed there would be a great outcry from lawyers all over the country. I thought it would be a major issue. But it didn't turn out that way. Finally, I began to realize there in solitary that I would get thirty-five to forty years. A week later nobody would even remember what happened."

Sometimes Joe thought back to his meeting with Charles Harrelson. He had been charmed by Harrelson in the beginning, but Harrelson had turned out to be the lowest of low lifes. In his testimony, Joe had actually sugar-coated some of Harrelson's conversations. Harrelson had told him in great detail about killing the judge, about watching the judge quiver, then drop in his tracks. "He was laughing when he told me," Joe remembered. "He *wanted* to kill Wood. The money was secondary." Jimmy probably never intended for it to happen, though Joe realized that Jimmy had gone out of his way to leave that impression. Jimmy's mistake was shooting off his mouth in front of a punk like Harrelson. Jimmy could be hopelessly naive: he had underestimated Harrelson. The next thing he knew, Wood was dead. Tom Sharpe, Harrelson's attorney, had been reminded of the scene in *Becket* when the distraught king raved: "Will no one rid me of this meddlesome priest!" In the next scene three or four hoods are slashing Becket to ribbons.

Joe thought a lot about Jimmy: there had been a measure of revenge in Jimmy's acquittal. The brothers didn't write any longer, though their sister, Patsy, was constantly relaying messages. "I still love him and I know he loves me," Joe said. "That's all I need." He thought about his wife, Patty, too. He didn't know if they would ever get back together. "I know it can never be the same," he said.

Most of all he thought about Lee. If Lee hadn't been killed . . . what? Jimmy might not have been indicted. Or even if they had indicted and convicted Jimmy and sent him to Leavenworth, it would have been Lee there talking to Jimmy. Until Lee was killed, Jimmy had never discussed criminal matters with Joe, and Joe was happy pretending he didn't know what was happening. After Lee's murder, Joe became the surrogate. There was no way of knowing how Lee would have handled Jimmy's prison harangues. He certainly wouldn't have allowed himself to be bullied. He probably wouldn't have been so naive about the tapes. Lee knew from bitter personal experience that the government loved to cut corners; surely he would have been sufficiently astute to prevent them from cutting corners on something as sacrosanct as the attorney-client relationship. Then again, maybe not.

There were so many *ifs* it made him dizzy. If he hadn't decided to plea-bargain . . . if the government had gone ahead with its original plans to try Jimmy and Charles Harrelson in the same courtroom, at the same time. Imagine Jimmy and Harrelson in the same courtroom. Imagine the Ayatollah running across the Mad Monk of Monrovia in a phone booth. What if the San Antonio trial had been held in Jacksonville, or Omaha, or Seattle? There might have been acquittals all around. For $11.4 million, the government had given the taxpayers a royal stiffing. What if Joe had never gone to law school? What if Lee had never gone to law school? What if Jimmy *had*?

"We were a good family—that's what people forget," Joe Chagra said, leading his visitor out of the enclosed area to a patio overlooking Pleasanton's softball fields and jogging track. "Looking back, I can see where it all started coming apart. It started coming to pieces in 1975, 1976, the time of Ardmore and Colombia and all that stuff, when Lee got greedy and started siding with Jimmy. It was the money. Patty always thought the dope was my downfall. That was part of it —a convenient part, as it turned out. It gave me an excuse. But the real downfall of our family was the money. You can't know what it does until it happens to you . . . until everyone is chin-deep in millions of dollars."

It was almost dark, a signal that the visiting period was ending and it was time for all prisoners to return to their rooms. Outlined against the dim, pastel hills, the silhouettes of two joggers moved as silently as the night. "I know one thing," he said. "If Lee hadn't been killed . . . Judge Wood wouldn't have been either."

Author's Note

For the most part, the conversations reported in this book were taken from the government's original unedited transcripts of wiretaps. Though the transcripts were greatly reduced before the two trials, the discrepancies between the versions submitted by the government and the defense, where they were considered important, are noted in the text. Conversations reported in this book that were not part of the official evidence came from interviews with the participants.

Gary Cartwright was born and raised in Texas and has lived there all his life. He is the author of the best-selling *Blood Will Tell: The Murder Trials of T. Cullen Davis* and two novels: *The Hundred Yard War* and *Thin Ice*. He has for many years been a staff writer for *Texas Monthly*, and in 1982 he was named associate editor of that magazine. He has three children, and lives with his wife Phyllis in Austin.